D1726973

European Yearbook of International Economic Law

EYIEL Monographs - Studies in European and International Economic Law

Volume 25

Series Editors

Marc Bungenberg, Saarbrücken, Germany
Christoph Herrmann, Passau, Germany
Markus Krajewski, Erlangen, Germany
Jörg Philipp Terhechte, Lüneburg, Germany
Andreas R. Ziegler, Lausanne, Switzerland

EYIEL Monographs is a subseries of the European Yearbook of International Economic Law (EYIEL). It contains scholarly works in the fields of European and international economic law, in particular WTO law, international investment law, international monetary law, law of regional economic integration, external trade law of the EU and EU internal market law. The series does not include edited volumes. EYIEL Monographs are peer-reviewed by the series editors and external reviewers.

Christopher Frey

World Trade Law
and the Emergence
of International Electricity
Markets

 Springer

Christopher Frey
Berlin, Germany

ISSN 2364-8392   ISSN 2364-8406   (electronic)
European Yearbook of International Economic Law
ISSN 2524-6658   ISSN 2524-6666   (electronic)
EYIEL Monographs - Studies in European and International Economic Law
ISBN 978-3-031-04755-8   ISBN 978-3-031-04756-5   (eBook)
https://doi.org/10.1007/978-3-031-04756-5

Dissertation, Faculty of Law, University of Dresden

This Springer imprint is published by the registered company Springer Nature Switzerland AG
The registered company address is: Gewerbestrasse 11, 6330 Cham, Switzerland

Meinen Eltern, Burckhard und Renelde

Preface

This book is based on my doctoral dissertation, which I defended in September 2020 at TU Dresden. I wish to express my profound gratitude to my supervisor, Professor Dr. Thilo Rensmann, for his constant support and encouragement and his shared curiosity for the topic. I also wish to thank Professor Karsten Nowrot for his support and immediate willingness to assume the role as second examiner.

With hindsight, it is not easy to recall my initial motivation to dedicate years of my professional life and countless lonely hours behind books and articles to the law of electricity trade. I ascribe it in part to early family narratives about ancestors who had helped to electrify their home valley in Western Germany. Professor Jürgen Grunwald at the Europa-Institut of Saarland University clearly contributed as well. His master's course on European energy and environmental law was special as it transcended the world of norms and paragraphs and connected law with physics and chemistry.

We are living in times of great transitions. There is a chance that a society based on renewable energy sources can be more peaceful and equitable than the past century which was largely powered by fossil fuels and the struggle for securing them. But that is not a given. The risk of cementing existing dependencies, power disparities and resource curses is real. I am deeply convinced that multilateral institutions and a rules-based system of equal partners—yet to be established—are the way forward.

Many people in different places have contributed in their own way to this work. In addition to the ones already mentioned, I am grateful to my former colleagues at the research project Global TranSAXion in Dresden, where many fruitful research ideas were born and where first pages of this study developed. Tilman Dralle deserves specific mentioning as I am deeply thankful for his companionship during long days at the library, his good humour and bright mind. At the TU Dresden, I also benefitted greatly from numerous discussions with students from the electrical engineering and energy economics departments. Some of them, like Maria Kosse, Caroline Wever and Andreas Leibenath, turned into friends. A research period at the Faculty of Law of the University of Canterbury on the beautiful South Island of New Zealand brought not only valuable insights but resulted in lasting friendships.

Above all, I wish to thank Christian and Emma Riffel for their hospitality and kindness and Abdul Hasib Suenu for proofreading parts of this work. I greatly appreciate the support of the TU Dresden Graduate Academy which made this unique and fruitful experience possible. Over the past couple of years, I expanded my horizon working alongside my numerous talented colleagues at ENERCON and Sunfire. I am especially grateful to Aram Sander for being an intellectual sparring partner and for critically reading some chapters of this book.

Finally, I want to thank my family for their enduring support and Lena for her companionship and constant encouragement. Without you, I would not have seen this through.

Berlin, Germany   Christopher Frey
March 2022

Contents

Abbreviations

AB	Appellate Body
AC	Alternating current
ACER	Agency for the Cooperation of Energy Regulators
APEC	Asia-Pacific Economic Cooperation
ASEAN	Association of South-East Asian Nations
ATC	Available transfer capacity
B.C.	British Columbia
CETA	Comprehensive Economic and Trade Agreement between Canada and the European Union
CFE	Comisión Federal de Electricidad (Mexico)
CHP	Combined heat and power
CISG	United Nations Convention on Contracts for the International Sale of Goods
COM	European Commission
CPC	Provisional Central Product Classification of the United Nations
CPTPP	Comprehensive and Progressive Agreement for Trans-Pacific Partnership
CRIE	Comisión Regional de Interconexión Electrica (Central America)
CUSFTA	Canada–United States Free Trade Agreement
CUSMA	Canada–United States–Mexico Agreement
CWE	Central Western European Electricity Market
DAM	Day-ahead market (Southern African Power Pool)
DC	Direct current
DSU	Dispute Settlement Understanding of the WTO
ECJ	European Court of Justice
ECOWAS	Economic Community of West African States
ECT	Energy Charter Treaty
EEA	European Economic Area
EFTA	European Free Trade Association
ENTSO-E	European Network of Transmission System Operators for Electricity
EOP	Ente Operador Regional (Central America)

EPA	Economic Partnership Agreement
EPCA	Enhanced Partnership and Cooperation Agreement
EPR	Empresa Proprietaria de la Red (Central America)
ERERA	ECOWAS Regional Electricity Regulatory Authority
EU	European Union
EURATOM	European Atomic Energy Community
FTA	Free trade agreement
FIT	Feed-in tariff
GATS	General Agreement on Trade in Services
GATT	General Agreement on Tariffs and Trade
GEIDCO	Global Energy Interconnection Development and Cooperation Organization
HVDC	High-voltage direct current
Hz	Hertz
IADB	Inter-American Development Bank
IEC	International Electrotechnical Commission
ILA	Agreement on Import Licensing Procedures
IPP	Independent power producer
ISO	Independent system operator
ITA	Information Technology Agreement
ITC	Inter-transmission system compensation
kV	Kilovolt
LNG	Liquefied natural gas
MER	Mercado eléctrico regional (Central America)
MFN	Most-favoured-nation
MW	Megawatt
MWh	Megawatt hour
NAFTA	North American Free Trade Agreement
NERC	North American Electric Reliability Council
NSOG	North Sea Offshore Grid
NT	National treatment
NTC	Net transfer capacity
OECD	Organisation for Economic Co-operation and Development
OJ	Official Journal of the European Union
OPEC	Organization of the Petroleum Exporting Countries
OTC	Over the counter
OU	Ownership unbundling
PPA	Power purchase agreement
PTA	Preferential trade agreement
PSO	Public service obligation
PUHCA	Public Utility Holding Company Act
PV	Photovoltaic
RCEP	Regional Comprehensive Economic Partnership
RES	Renewable energy sources

RERA	Regional Electricity Regulators Association (Southern African Power Pool)
RTO	Regional transmission operator
SACREEE	SADC Centre for Renewable Energy and Energy Efficiency
SADC	Southern African Development Community
SADCC	Southern African Development Coordination Conference
SAPP	Southern African Power Pool
SCMA	Agreement on Subsidies and Countervailing Measures
SGCC	State Grid Corporation of China
SIEPAC	Sistema de Interconexión Eléctrica de los Países de América Central
SPS	Agreement on Sanitary and Phytosanitary Measures
STE	State trading enterprise
STEM	Short-term day ahead market (Southern African Power Pool)
TBT	Agreement on Technical Barriers to Trade
TEC	Treaty establishing the European Community
TEN-E	Trans-European energy networks
TEP	Third Energy Package
TEU	Treaty on European Union
TFEU	Treaty on the Functioning of the European Union
TPA	Third party access
TRIMS	Agreement on Trade-Related Investment Measures
TSO	Transmission system operator
TWh	Terawatt hour
TYNDP	Ten-Year Network Development Plan
UCC	Uniform Commercial Code (United States)
UCPTE	Union pour la coordination de la production et du transport de l'électricité
UCTE	Union for the Co-ordination of Transmission of Electricity
UHV	Ultra-high voltage
UN	United Nations
U.S.	United States
UNCTAD	United Nations Conference on Trade and Development
VCLT	Vienna Convention on the Law of Treaties
WAPP	West African power pool
WBGU	German Advisory Council on Global Change
WCO	World Customs Organization
WERC	Western Electricity Coordinating Council
WPDR	Working Party on Domestic Regulation
WTO	World Trade Organization
WTOA	Agreement Establishing the World Trade Organization
W/120	Services Sectoral Classification List

Part I
The Technical and Regulatory Foundations of Electricity Trade and the Emergence of International Electricity Markets

Chapter 1
General Introduction

Electricity permeates modern life. It is an invisible force on which we are now so dependent that we notice it only when it is missing. Demand for electricity has been growing rapidly and an end is not in sight.[1] At the beginning of the twenty-first century, it is difficult to imagine any production process or service sector that does not rely on electricity to deliver the goods and services the society wants.[2]

The degree of access to electricity for private households is a measure of civilizational progress and achieving universal access has been identified as a policy priority by governments around the world.[3] Yet 13% of humanity still lacks access to modern electricity.[4] This equals 840 million people, two-thirds of which are located in Sub-Saharan Africa.[5] At the same time as policy-makers and entrepreneurs are

---

[1] According to the International Energy Agency (IEA), electricity demand has increased by around 70% since the year 2000. See Bouckert and Goodson (2019).

[2] A WTO dispute settlement panel has recognized the important role of electricity in an obiter dictum by stating: 'Electricity is the lifeblood of modern society. Yet it is invisible to the naked eye and often unnoticed in the day-to-day lives of billions of people. There is little doubt, however, that reliable systems of electricity are the engines that drive economies world-wide, bringing power to a host of consumers for a myriad of uses and applications including in homes, factories, offices, farms, transportation systems and telecommunications networks. Most goods depend upon electricity for their production, as do essential services ranging from healthcare to banking. Few discoveries can boast such wide-ranging impacts on the quality of human life as electricity.' WTO, *Canada – Measures Relating to the Feed-in Tariff Program*, Report of the Panel (19 December 2012) WT/DS426/R [7.10].

[3] United Nations (2021b), Sustainable Development Goals, SDG 7 ('Ensure access to affordable, reliable, sustainable and modern energy for all'). The main indicator for the sub-target of ensuring universal access to modern energy by 2030 (SDG 7.1) is the proportion of the population with access to electricity. https://sustainabledevelopment.un.org/sdg7.

[4] United Nations (2021a), Sustainable Development Goals https://www.un.org/sustainabledevelopment/energy/.

[5] International Energy Agency, SDG7: Data and Projections (November 2019) https://www.iea.org/reports/sdg7-data-and-projections/access-to-electricity.

© The Author(s), under exclusive license to Springer Nature Switzerland AG 2022
C. Frey, *World Trade Law and the Emergence of International Electricity Markets*,
EYIEL Monographs - Studies in European and International Economic Law 25,
https://doi.org/10.1007/978-3-031-04756-5_1

seeking to tackle this vital challenge, the existing energy landscape is undergoing a fundamental transformation. Having come to accept climate change as a major threat to permanent human existence on earth, governments around the world have started to phase out the use of fossil energy sources and to engage in a transition towards relying on renewable energy. Two trends can be observed in this respect: The first is a replacement of the use of fossil energy in transport, heating, cooling and industrial processes with electricity, a development that will undoubtedly drive further growth in the demand for electricity. The second is the replacement of electricity generated using fossil fuels with electricity generated from renewable sources. In parallel with this international energy transition, a less visible development is taking place: the interconnection of formerly isolated national electricity systems and the emergence of international electricity markets. With the rapid development of technology, visions of long-distance electricity transmission are turning into reality. The United Nations (UN) has committed to promoting investment in energy infrastructure and clean energy technology within the framework of the Sustainable Development Goals.[6] Addressing the global community of states, Chinese President Xi Jinping announced in 2015 that China would seek ways to create a 'global energy internet'.[7] The first concrete steps to realize a global energy interconnection based on long-distance electricity transmission have been taken since that announcement.[8] While the technology for the transportation of electricity over thousands of kilometres continues to advance rapidly and the necessary financial means would be available, the regulatory framework of an ever-more global electricity trade has so far been largely neglected. It is often simply assumed that the general trade rules which have been developed since the end of World War II will lend themselves to application to trade in electricity. This study seeks to critically scrutinize this claim and to examine whether the issues arising from cross-border electricity trade are adequately addressed by the existing normative framework of world trade law. Along the way in this analysis, possible regulatory gaps will be identified. Moving beyond this assessment, this study then suggests ways how to further develop and possibly expand on international trade law in its present state.

---

[6] United Nations (2021a).

[7] Xi Jinping, Remarks at the UN Sustainable Development Summit (26 September 2015), https://sustainabledevelopment.un.org/content/documents/20548china.pdf.

[8] One notable measure was the establishment of the Global Energy Interconnection Development and Cooperation Organization (GEIDCO) with headquarters in Beijing and regional offices on several continents. GEIDCO regularly convenes high-level stakeholders and advances research on interconnections and high-voltage transmission technology.

1.1   The Current State of Research

The frequency of publications on the energy-trade nexus and the application of world trade rules to the energy sector have intensified in recent years. Up until very recently, electricity as a separate subject of international trade law was hardly covered at all.[9] Rather, a constantly growing body of international economic law literature treated energy in a horizontal fashion by looking at issues of relevance for several or all energy sources.[10] Reflecting the economic realities of international trade in energy at the time, the focus was mostly on oil and gas and it was sometimes simply assumed that the findings were transposable to the electricity sector. Publications treating the electricity sector in its own right are still rather exceptional in the international economic law literature, although the picture is starting to change.[11] *Gudas* has explored the framework for the interconnection of electricity networks in EU and international economic law in his published dissertation.[12] His findings mainly relate to the phase of development of cross-border electricity transmission projects and the actual impediments to trade once infrastructure is established are touched upon only in relation to access and transit obligations.

Despite the increasing academic interest regarding the law of international electricity trade, many issues remain underexplored. The applicability of trade rules of general application to the characteristic features of electricity deserves more attention. This applies specifically when interconnectors have been constructed and electricity is traded internationally on a commercial basis, i.e. when trade 'actually happens'. Few authors have engaged in a thorough and critical examination of the notion that trade in electricity can be subsumed under the rules of the General Agreement on Tariffs and Trade (GATT), the General Agreement on Trade in Services (GATS) and trade agreements concluded outside the WTO. Suggestions on how to adapt these rules to contemporary and future challenges in electricity trade are even rarer.[13] Scholars commenting on electricity in international trade law usually pay little attention to the multitude of features that distinguish electricity from the goods, services and commodities international trade lawyers are more familiar with.[14] This thesis seeks to remedy this gap by analysing world trade law

---

[9] A first in-depth engagement with the specifics of electricity trade was published in 2004 with the edited volume by Bielecki and Desta (2004). Very few journal contributions treating the subject can be found even earlier. See especially Pierros and Nüesch (2000).

[10] See, e.g., the recent book by Marhold (2021), and the contributions in the volume edited by Selivanova (2012).

[11] Two notable exceptions are a book by Gudas (2018) and a volume edited by Cottier and Espa (2017).

[12] Gudas (2018).

[13] Some authors have pointed to the need for energy-specific rules within the WTO Framework. See, e.g., Cottier et al. (2011) and Poretti and Rios-Herran (2006).

[14] One notable exception is Espa (2017).

disciplines based on a solid understanding of the technical and economic features which make electricity a 'special case' in international economic law.

1.2 The Structure of This Book

The present study consists of four main parts. Part I aims to lay the foundations by examining the relevant physical features of electricity, the main technical aspects of electricity systems and the realities of contemporary electricity markets and their regulation. It also sketches the ongoing development towards more international trade in electric energy. Part II analyses the general applicability of the rules of world trade law to the electricity sector. Part III deals with actual barriers to trade in electricity and examines the relevant disciplines in the WTO Agreements, the Energy Charter Treaty (ECT) and some preferential trade agreements that are not sector-specific (PTAs). Based on the findings in Parts I–III, Part IV proposes a way forward concerning the multilateral regulation of electricity-specific trade challenges.

References

Bielecki J, Desta M (eds) (2004) Electricity trade in Europe: review of the economic and regulatory challenges. Kluwer Law International, Alphen aan den Rijn

Bouckert S, Goodson T (2019) The mysterious case of disappearing electricity demand. IEA Commentary, 14 February 2019. https://www.iea.org/newsroom/news/2019/february/the-mysterious-case-of-disappearing-electricity-demand.html

Cottier T, Espa I (eds) (2017) International Trade in sustainable electricity: regulatory challenges in International Economic Law. Cambridge University Press, Cambridge

Cottier T, Malumfashi G, Matteotti-Berkutova S, Nartova O, De Sepibus J, Bigdeli SZ (2011) Energy in WTO law and policy. In: Cottier T, Delimatsis P (eds) The prospects of international trade regulation: from fragmentation to coherence. Cambridge University Press, Cambridge

Espa I (2017) The treatment of restrictions and financial charges on imports and exports of electricity under EU and International Law. In: Cottier T, Espa I (eds) International Trade in sustainable electricity: regulatory challenges in International Economic Law. Cambridge University Press, Cambridge

Gudas K (2018) The law and policy of international trade in electricity. Europa Law Publishing, Waterstraat

International Energy Agency (2019) SDG7: Data and Projections. https://www.iea.org/reports/sdg7-data-and-projections/access-to-electricity

Jinping X (2015) Remarks at the UN Sustainable Development Summit on 26 September 2015, https://sustainabledevelopment.un.org/content/documents/20548china.pdf

Marhold A (2021) Energy in International Trade Law. Cambridge University Press, Cambridge

Pierros P, Nüesch S (2000) Trade in electricity: spot on. J World Trade 34:95

Poretti P, Rios-Herran R (2006) A reference paper on energy services: the best way forward? Manch J Int Econ Law 3:2

Selivanova Y (ed) (2012) Regulation of energy in International Trade Law. WTO, NAFTA and Energy Charter. Kluwer Law International, Alphen aan den Rijn

United Nations (2021a) Sustainable Development Goals. https://www.un.org/sustainabledevelopment/energy/

United Nations (2021b) Sustainable Development Goals, SDG 7. https://sustainabledevelopment.un.org/sdg7

Chapter 2
Technical and Regulatory Foundations of Electricity Trade

The present chapter aims to set the stage for the subsequent legal discussions. The goal is to carve out the distinguishing features of electricity that make it special from a trade regulation perspective. Electricity possesses fundamentally distinct properties when compared with the goods and services that make up the majority of international commercial transactions and for which the rules and procedures of world trade law have been defined. These specific features of electricity have a multitude of consequences for the regulation of its production, trade, and consumption. Against this background, the present chapter aims to lay the foundations for the application of the rules of international economic law to international trade in electricity. It also introduces the terminology of trade-related electricity issues which will be used throughout this thesis.

The present part starts by explaining as briefly as possible the most important features that make electricity a unique phenomenon. In a second step, the evolution of electricity networks from the end of the nineteenth century until the present day is briefly sketched out, followed by a short overview of the state of the art of transmission technology and the electric grid. Ultimately, likely future developments of relevance for international electricity trade are discussed. The concept of an electricity system lies at the heart of this analysis. The term 'electricity system' as used here comprises the whole of the technical infrastructure within a certain regulatory area necessary to fulfil the tasks of production ('generation') of electricity, its transport ('transmission') and delivery to end-users ('distribution').[1]

---

[1] Schwab (2015), p. 30. It bears mentioning that the literature on electricity systems is as vast in volume as in disciplinary diversity, comprising such disciplines as engineering, economics, mathematics and IT, among others. The following discussion is strictly limited to what is considered relevant for the subsequent legal analysis presented herein.

2.1 Technical Aspects of Electricity Systems

2.1.1 The Physical Properties of Electricity

Electricity is a form of energy. It appears as a natural phenomenon in lightning and magnetism, but also in biological systems for the transmission of nerve impulses. For the purposes of modern economic use, electricity is always the result of a conversion process. Primary energy sources like coal or natural gas are converted to electric energy by using devices called generators. The process of conversion using primary energy sources makes electricity a secondary energy source. Once generated, electricity is a process rather than a substance. From a physical point of view, electrons in a conductor (usually a metallic wire) are situated between metallic atom cores and the generator induces a directional motion of these electrons. When the generator sets the electrons in a directional motion, nothing of mass or substance is added or 'produced' in this process. The electrons are in the wire ab initio and their number remains constant throughout the entire process.[2] A wave of electrons moving back and forth in a wire is called 'alternating current' (AC). When the electrons in a wire are moving constantly in one direction the process is called 'direct current' (DC).[3] With respect to AC, the number of pendular movements of the electrons per second is referred to as 'frequency', which is usually denoted by the term 'Hertz' (Hz). Electricity systems operate on either one of two standards, 50 or 60 Hz. In the United States (US), Canada, Japan, Taiwan, the Caribbean and some parts of South America, the prescribed frequency is 60 Hz. In all other parts of the world including Europe, the standard is 50 Hz.[4] Direct current has a zero frequency as electrons do not oscillate back and forth.

The pattern in which electricity spreads over an electric grid is determined by laws of physics referred to as Kirchhoff's laws. In an electric grid consisting of several wires, the electric current will always take the path of least resistance. The properties of the flow of electric energy over wires have been likened to water flowing through a network of interconnected pipes. When one wire is 'full', i.e., running at maximum capacity, electricity will seek the wire not yet running at maximum capacity, if available.[5] An electric signal spreads through the wires at close to the speed of light. The term 'voltage' describes the amount of electrical pressure or tension, i.e., 'the force that causes current through an electrical conductor'.[6] As a rule of thumb, higher voltages mean more electricity can be transmitted

---

[2]Ferrey (2004), p. 1910.

[3]Brown and Sedano (2004), p. 37.

[4]Massachusetts Institute of Technology (2011), p. 244; Laloux and Rivier (2013), p. 5.

[5]Brown and Sedano (2004), p. 29.

[6]Graf (1999), p. 835.

via a given conductor. Electricity networks (so-called 'grids') operate at different levels of voltage ranging from less than 1 kV to more than 1000 kV.[7]

The character of electricity as a physical phenomenon as opposed to an object or tangible property has important consequences for its generation, transmission and consumption. The terms 'order and delivery' of electricity, while sensible from a commercial point of view, can be misleading when looking at the electricity network from a technical perspective. Kirchhoff's Laws prevent a targeted flow of electrons along a precise predetermined path in the network. To safeguard the stability of the electricity system, the fundamental characteristics voltage and frequency have to be maintained at the same level with only very minor deviations tolerated. Voltage and frequency are maintained by generators feeding electricity into the network and consumers withdrawing electricity (referred to as 'load') at different points of the network. The sum of generation and load within a network must be zero. Thus, rather than 'delivering' and 'receiving' electric power in a bilateral transaction, generators and consumers on different ends of an electricity network contribute to maintaining the stability of the system.[8]

Importantly, the consumer cannot be certain of the origin of the electricity unless there is only a single line directly connecting the generator and consumer. As consumers are usually connected to a grid structure with multiple entry points for generators, it will not be possible in most cases to ascertain where the electricity consumed at a certain point in time is coming from.

The contractual arrangements between the different market participants in the electricity sector in principle say little about the physical flows of electricity.[9] As electrons cannot be steered along a certain path in the grid, the only variables that can be influenced are generation and load. Therefore, the commercial electricity trans-actions must be notified to the operator of the transmission system for balancing supply and demand. In this way, the financial and physical sides of trade in electricity are brought together.

In some regions, most notably in Europe, the assignment in accounting terms of certain electricity consumption to amounts of production is realized via so-called 'balancing groups'. In a balancing group, a number of generators and consumers are pooled together purely for accounting purposes. When imbalances occur, a designated balancing responsible party is obliged to level these imbalances, e.g., through procuring additional amounts of electricity. This procedure seeks to ensure an overall system balance of supply and demand. Countries where electricity is traded over designated exchanges are usually divided into one or more 'bidding areas' for which electricity is traded at one identical spot price.

---

[7]It is difficult to make generalized statements in this respect. Some Low-voltage local area networks for the supply of residential end-consumers operate at voltages as low as 0.4 kV.

[8]Cf. Buchmüller (2013), p. 60, who likens electricity available between generators and consumers to a lake, the water level of which always remains the same, the balance being achieved by a constant equilibrium between supply and demand.

[9]Brown and Sedano (2004), p. 33. See also Lakatos (2004), p. 123.

All electrons in the grid have the same physical properties.[10] Accordingly, electricity is not distinguishable anymore once it is fed into the grid.[11] In light of the preceding observations concerning the physical and contractual flows of electricity, it might intuitively be a surprise that electricity consumers are increasingly willing to pay a higher price for certain 'types' of electricity. Electricity suppliers have started to offer their customers special products, such as electricity marketed as 'green' (electricity from renewable sources), for which consumers are often ready to pay slightly higher tariffs. However, the decision of a consumer to enter into a contract with a supplier offering electricity from renewable sources does not instantaneously result in a delivery or 'flow' of renewable electricity to the consumer. It merely guarantees that the share of renewable electricity in the overall electricity mix rises. The consumer willing to pay more for 'green' power thus provides the supplier with additional capital to invest in more renewable generation capacity.[12] Some countries have established national or regional green certificate schemes to verify the desired quality of electricity generation labelled as renewable. Only when a given electricity system is fed entirely by renewable energy can the consumer be certain of receiving 'green' electricity. Until then, the electricity will always be a mix of different generation sources.

Another aspect that needs mentioning here is that in interconnected networks, the physical flows over transmission lines are not easily attributable to the owners of the networks. In interconnected networks, the fact that electricity does not take the shortest path over a network but the one with the least resistance can result in the unintended use of networks not owned by the network operators receiving compensation for their transmission services.[13] This phenomenon is referred to as 'loop flow' and will be discussed below in the context of import and export restrictions and transit.[14]

2.1.2 Grid Dependency and Capacity Constraints

One of the most important distinguishing features of electric energy is that its transport is only possible via immovable physical infrastructure. Once generated and fed into the grid, the electricity is transported via transmission lines operating under either DC or AC. Transmission infrastructure can be installed in the form of overhead lines or underground cables. When the connection crosses sea straits, special submarine cables are used for the transmission. At present, there is still no technically and economically viable alternative to these forms of fixed

---

[10] Hunt (2002), p. 35, refers to electricity as 'the most homogeneous product imaginable'.

[11] Lakatos (2004), p. 123.

[12] Schwab (2015), p. 37.

[13] Brown and Sedano (2004), p. 33.

[14] See below in Chap. 11, p. 170.

infrastructures. Thus, unlike primary energy sources like coal, oil or liquefied natural gas (LNG), electricity cannot be moved in larger quantities by mobile means of transport on roads or rails, through the air or on the sea.[15] This obvious fact deserves emphasis because it has several important consequences for the application of legal provisions.

Electricity lines are limited in capacity. It is not possible to increase the capacity of an existing line on short notice to respond to an increased demand at one end of the line. When the capacity limit of an existing power line is reached and the forecasted load will exceed this limit, there are in principle only two ways to further enhance the capacity: Improving the existing power line technically or building new power lines.[16] As the first option is limited by technological constraints and the second often makes no economic sense, the transmission of electricity is widely regarded as a natural monopoly. This natural monopoly character requires special procedures concerning capacity management and network access on non-discriminatory terms.[17]

Several types of constraints limit the capacity and length of transmission lines. Much like water flowing through pipes, electricity transmitted over long distances gradually loses pressure (i.e. voltage).[18] Furthermore, electricity is lost during transmission as it dissipates into the air in the form of heat.[19] These technical constraints have led commentators to characterize electricity as principally a 'local' form of energy.[20] At the same time, however, it must be noted that recent technological advances have allowed electricity transmission over ever-longer distances while reducing losses. These technological developments have also led to proposals for the interconnection of electricity networks on a global scale.[21]

The construction of new transmission lines requires large capital investments and involves planning and permitting procedures which will take several years in some jurisdictions. Rights-of-way must be established and a number of interested parties have to be consulted. While large-scale infrastructure projects regularly face public opposition, the resistance to new overhead power lines is often particularly fierce. Today, most jurisdictions also require mandatory environmental impact assessments before authorizing the construction of a power transmission line. As a result of the multitude of concerns and competing interests surrounding the construction of high-voltage transmission lines, it can take up to a decade or longer for new transmission

---

[15] It could be argued that the electricity stored in electric vehicle batteries constitutes a mobile means of transport, as the energy can be discharged from the car in a different location. It is indeed conceivable that in the not-too-distant future the sum of electric vehicle batteries will constitute an important means of flexibility for the electricity system.

[16] Massachusetts Institute of Technology (2011), p. 39.

[17] This issue is dealt with in more detail below in Sect. 2.2.2, pp. 27 et seq.

[18] Brown and Sedano (2004), p. 35.

[19] Ibid.

[20] Müller (2001), p. 27. See also Botchway (2001), p. 3, who argues that 'By necessity (...) electricity transactions primarily have to be regional.'

[21] See below in Sect. 3.2.7, pp. 74 et seq.

lines to be put into operation. In the European Union (EU), the planning and permitting stages of electricity infrastructure projects have frequently lasted for more than 10 years.[22] The European Commission has made repeated attempts to expedite this process.[23] The construction of new power lines, especially in the high-voltage range, also requires considerable capital investments. These are usually the responsibility of either the electricity generators, the transmission system operators as regulated utilities, or 'merchant' transmission companies that invest in new power lines between different price zones and generate revenue in the form of congestion rent.[24] The technical constraints described above in combination with the capital intensity and the administrative barriers limit the trading possibilities and, to a certain extent, the degree of competition on the electricity market.

2.1.3   Storage of Electricity

Considering the nature of electricity as the result of a physical process requiring the constant flow of electrons, it is not surprising that electric power as such is not storable except on a very limited scale. 'Storage' of electricity has traditionally meant the conversion of electric energy into other forms of energy, like heat or mechanical energy.[25] While the methods have increased in efficiency over time, energy is always lost in the process. The use of hydro storage is limited by geographical conditions and in addition, hydro storage facilities are controversial due to their impact on the surrounding landscape and ecosystems.[26] Batteries are advancing in capacity at an impressive pace but do not yet present an economical alternative to additional generating capacity (i.e. new power plants) in most places. The conversion of electricity to hydrogen for transportation via pipelines and mobile means of transport and reconversion of hydrogen to electricity is seen by some as a possible way forward.[27] The development and deployment of efficient storage options will be a fundamental pillar of the transition from a fossil fuel-based generation landscape to an energy supply largely made up of variable renewable sources, like wind and solar photovoltaics (PV).[28]

---

[22] European Commission, Commission Staff Working Paper: Energy Infrastructure Investment Needs and Financing Requirements, SEC (2011) 755 final, p. 5, citing the electricity interconnector between France and Spain, the commissioning of which took more than 40 years.

[23] Regulation (EU) No 347/2013 of the European Parliament and of the Council of 17 April 2013 on guidelines for trans-European energy infrastructure [2013] OJ L 115/39.

[24] Brown and Sedano (2004), p. 22. On merchant transmission investments see Gerbaulet and Weber (2014); Joskow and Tirole (2005), p. 233; Brunekreeft (2005), p. 175.

[25] Buchmüller (2013), p. 59.

[26] Gatzen (2007), p. 2.

[27] See, e.g., Meyer and Thomas (2021).

[28] Casazza and Delea (2010), p. 132; For an overview of storage options and application strategies see Gatzen (2007), p. 4. See also below in Sect. 2.1.6.3, pp. 19 et seq.

The impracticality of storing large amounts of electricity in short term makes the matching of supply and demand the most critical factor in securing electricity supply. Generation must respond immediately to substantial changes in consumption. As electricity cannot be brought to the market from warehouses, silos or tanks, the generation capacity and the transmission and distribution infrastructure always have to be oriented towards maximum load to serve consumers in peak demand times.[29] Demand-side management methods are only slowly penetrating the electricity sector. This distinguishes electricity supply from services like telecommunications, where customers can be 'put on hold' if the requested party is busy.

The lack of storage options makes electricity systems dynamic and highly complex balancing mechanisms.[30] Disturbances at one end of the system will have (almost) instantaneous effects throughout the entire system.[31] A temporary disequilibrium between supply and demand frequently leads to serious problems for the whole system. It also distinguishes electricity transmission from the transport of consumer goods. The latter can be temporarily stuck in road traffic when the medium of traffic (roads) is congested without seriously endangering the entire system. The storage problem of electricity combined with the varying demand and occasional peaks also leads to considerable variations in the wholesale price of electricity.[32]

2.1.4 The Evolution of Electricity Systems

The history of electricity systems comprises developments from lighting an incandescent lightbulb to serving billions of people and involving a multitude of actors on the stages of generation, transmission and distribution. The emergence and widespread use of electrical energy in urbanized areas is closely associated with the 'second industrial revolution' which is deemed to have taken place during the last decades of the nineteenth century in the US and parts of Europe.[33] The electrification of cities spurred industrial development and subsequently revolutionized households and improved the lives of millions of people. Many names and places are associated with the evolution of the electric system around the end of the nineteenth and early twentieth centuries.[34]

Thomas Alva Edison deserves specific mention for his inventions, which paved the way for ensuing commercial developments in the electricity industry. Initially, Edison was looking for an alternative to gas lighting, which was the prevalent source of lighting in American and European cities. His answer was the incandescent

---

[29]Cf. Müller (2001), p. 26.

[30]Laloux and Rivier (2013), p. 2.

[31]Ibid.

[32]Hunt (2002), p. 32.

[33]Hughes (1983), p. 176.

[34]On the 'early phase' of this development see Passer (1953).

lightbulb, which was powered by generators positioned in close geographical proximity to the lamps. The ultimate goal of Edison, however, was the introduction of central power stations that would supply electricity not just to their owners but to the general public.[35] Around 1880, several central stations commenced operation in the US and United Kingdom (UK). The steam-powered Holborn Viaduct Station in London and the Pearl Street Station in Chicago marked the birth of the electric utility industry. A few years later, central lighting stations were operating in many major cities, such as Milan and Berlin.[36]

The supply of energy from central stations that were located at the heart of the city centre was limited to what in modern electricity systems would be called 'distribution' because the technological constraints only allowed for the transport of electricity over short distances.[37] There was thus no such thing as a power grid in the sense of an interconnected system of power plants linked by transmission lines. The solution to the problem of transmission emerged in the form of (single-phase) AC, which allowed for the transport of electricity over longer distances much more efficiently than DC.[38]

In 1891, the first long-distance AC transmission took place between the German town of Lauffen am Neckar and the site of the International Electrotechnical Exhibition in Frankfurt am Main, spanning a distance of 175 km.[39] The Lauffen-Frankfurt connection was an example of 'point-to-point transmission', providing an uninterrupted long-distance supply. A further decisive step in the evolution of the electricity system was for point-to-point transmission to evolve into 'grids', by integrating switching stations into the system that allowed power plants to feed-in electricity and consumers to connect at various points of the grid.[40] AC power transmission allowed utilities to connect their systems and agree on the joint operation of a network. The industry structure changed accordingly and larger companies began to gradually replace the small local operators.[41] In contrast to other planned infrastructure systems like interstate highways, the early electric grids thus evolved due to the consolidation of a patchwork of formerly isolated utilities that—by merger or other forms of cooperation—began to operate jointly and connect their networks.[42] This allowed for the exploitation of economies of scale

---

[35] Hughes (1983), p. 41.

[36] Ibid, at 46.

[37] Cf. Brown and Sedano (2004), p. 2. Thomas Edison himself predicted in an interview with the New York Sun on 20 October 1878 that his central station would 'furnish light to all houses within a circle of half a mile.' See Hughes (1983), p. 32.

[38] The inventors of the AC system were Nikola Tesla and Galileo Ferraris. See also Hughes (1983), p. 106; El-Hawary (2008), p. 1.

[39] On the Lauffen-Frankfurt transmission see Elektrizitätswerk Heilbronn (ed) (1991); See also Müller (2001), p. 30.

[40] Hughes (1983), p. 364.

[41] Brown and Sedano (2004), p. 3.

[42] Kaplan (2009), p. 2.

in generation and led to the standardization of technical equipment.[43] This development also prompted regulators to extend their jurisdiction from other network industries, especially railroads, to electric companies.[44] The end of World War II heralded the start of a 'golden age' for electric utilities. The demand for electricity was rising rapidly and technological innovations and economies of scale facilitated continuous cost reductions.[45] Utilities in the electricity sector closely coordinated their operations, and networks were interconnected in order to reap the benefits of economies of scale, the reduction of fuel costs and the sharing of risks.[46] At the same time, the electricity sector in the US witnessed the establishment of regional and interregional planning organizations.[47]

The use of AC electricity transmission also allowed for the harvesting of new energy resources that were located further away from the urban centres of consumption. The high-voltage transmission of electricity generated by brown coal became more economical than the transport of the coal by railroad to coal-fired power plants near the load centres.[48] Hydroelectric power plants were, by their nature, also often located far away from load centres. In the first quarter of the twentieth century, voltages above 100.000 allowed for the transmission of electricity over hundreds of kilometres.[49] Another decisive move came with the introduction of high-voltage direct current (HVDC) lines. Because HVDC is not as limited by stability restraints, it does not have the same length limitations that apply to AC.[50] HVDC can transmit more power for a given size of the conductor and requires less space to be built.[51] While HVDC is superior to AC in long-distance point-to-point transmission, it has not been very practicable in tightly-meshed networks because it is more complicated and costly to build DC converters.[52] The world's first HVDC link, commissioned in 1954, was a 60-mile submarine cable operating at 100 kV and connecting the island of Gotland with the Swedish mainland.[53] Presently, the longest DC line connects the Xiangjiaba Dam in China with the city of Shanghai over a distance of 2070 km.[54] This 800 kV line was completed in 2010.

Because of the distinguishing features of electricity—the lack of large-scale storage options and the need for the continuous balance of production and consumption—information, coordination and standardization have been important features of

---

[43] El-Hawary (2008), p. 2.
[44] Brown and Sedano (2004), p. 3.
[45] Casazza and Delea (2010), p. 8.
[46] Ibid.
[47] Ibid.
[48] Hughes (1983), p. 314; Casazza and Delea (2010), p. 8.
[49] Hughes (1983), p. 364.
[50] Massachusetts Institute of Technology (2011), p. 41.
[51] Casazza and Delea (2010), p. 111.
[52] Massachusetts Institute of Technology (2011), pp. 41–42.
[53] Long and Nilsson (2007), p. 26.
[54] Massachusetts Institute of Technology (2011), p. 42.

electricity systems throughout their history.[55] It is mainly in the operational and informational aspects that electricity systems evolved further towards the end of the twentieth century. Starting in the 1980s, the focus shifted to market reform and regulation to allow for effective competition in the electricity sector.[56] The transition from fossil fuels to an electricity sector mainly powered by renewable energies has begun to spur innovations in the integration and transmission of electricity generated from distributed renewable energy generation. Another possible driving factor for grid innovations might come from the political support for the interconnection of electricity networks on a regional or even global scale.[57] This will require further investments and advances in grid technology.

2.1.5   Contemporary Electricity Systems

The development of electric power systems has taken a similar path in most countries and a comparable structure now exists all over the world.[58] The electricity networks are designed, in conformity with the different levels of generation capacity and the load profiles of electricity consumers, into a hierarchical structure according to voltage levels.[59] The general rule is that the higher the generation capacity of the power plants, the higher the voltage used for transmission.[60] Substations at various points in the electricity network perform the important function of stepping the voltage up or down to connect various network levels. Different categories of electricity consumers connect at different levels. Larger industrial factories like steel or aluminium plants usually connect to higher voltage levels either because the machines used in their manufacturing processes require this higher voltage, or because the companies operate substations of their own.[61]

Most advanced electricity systems today comprise three main subsystems: the transmission, sub-transmission and distribution systems. For present purposes, it suffices to focus on the transmission system. The transmission system comprises lines with voltages of 380 or 220 kV in Europe, while in North America the transmission system operates at voltage levels of up to 765 kV.[62] In some

---

[55] Hughes (1983), p. 368 calls this 'a science of information and control'.

[56] See below in Sect. 2.2.1, pp. 25 et seq.

[57] See below in Chap. 3, pp. 41 et seq.

[58] Laloux and Rivier (2013), p. 5.

[59] Schwab (2015) 33.

[60] Laloux and Rivier (2013), p. 7.

[61] Ibid.

[62] Vittal (2010), p. 5. Indeed, according to Article 2 (3) of the EU Electricity Directive, transmission means 'the transport of electricity on the extra high-voltage and high-voltage interconnected system with a view to its delivery to final customers or to distributors, but not including supply.' Directive 2009/72/EC of the European Parliament and of the Council concerning common rules for the internal market in electricity and repealing Directive 2003/54/EC (13 July 2009) OJ 2009/L 211/55.

geographically large countries like Russia and China, the transmission networks can reach voltage levels above 1000 kV.[63] Thermal and nuclear power stations and large wind farms are connected to the transmission level.[64] In most European countries, around 60% of total generation capacity is connected to the transmission level, but this is decreasing due to the emergence of small-scale renewable energy technologies that are connected to the distribution system.[65] The transmission system is operated and controlled by system operators called transmission system operators (TSOs) in Europe, most of Asia and Africa and independent system operators (ISO) in the US. The transmission system has a meshed structure and is characterized by high levels of automation and control.[66] The flows in the transmission system are generally bidirectional, but transmission lines are increasingly used in one direction (e.g. to transmit electricity from offshore wind parks in the Baltic Sea to the industrial manufacturing centres in the South of Germany).[67] The activities of market participants are focused on the transmission grid, which has therefore been referred to as the 'wholesale market facilitator'.[68] Cross-border interconnections for international electricity trade are also made up of transmission lines. In this sense, the transmission grid is the focal point of the rise of regional electricity markets.[69] It is also the network level at which international trade issues are most likely to emerge.

From a topological perspective, the grid consists of nodes (usually corresponding to substations) where generators or consumers connect to transmission lines or where different lines interconnect. Nodes represent the smallest entity of the transmission system. Several nodes are pooled into a control area which is subject to the responsibility of a system operator.[70] As grids used to be confined to national boundaries in the past, the areas of responsibility of a system operator mostly correspond to parts of a national geography or an entire country. In recent years, efforts have been initiated in some regions to better coordinate system operation across borders.[71]

---

[63] Müller (2001), p. 163.

[64] The output voltage at a power plant is usually in the range of 6–20 kV and it is immediately transformed to the voltage required for connection to the transmission system. See Laloux and Rivier (2013), p. 6.

[65] Schwab (2015), p. 34.

[66] Vittal (2010), p. 5.

[67] Schwab (2015), p. 34.

[68] Laloux and Rivier (2013), p. 21.

[69] Ibid. See also below in Sect. 3.2, pp. 45 et seq.

[70] Mäntysaari (2015), p. 40.

[71] In the EU, new rules for cross-border cooperation of system operators were adopted in 2019 in the framework of the 'Clean Energy for all Europeans' legislative package. The relevant provisions of the new Market Design Directive include a requirement for TSOs to publish biennially a regional investment plan which forms the basis for grid investment decisions. Furthermore, the Regulation delegates to TSOs the task of establishing among themselves regional coordination centres. See Articles 34-36 of Regulation 2019/943 of the European Parliament and of the Council on the Internal Market for Electricity (5 June 2019) OJ 2019/L 158/54.

2.1.6   The Electricity System of the Future

While the existing technologies for transmission and distribution are relatively mature, the current transformation of the electricity generation landscape is challenging engineers to design electrical systems that are smarter and more resilient than in the past. This includes a new approach to grid planning to manage the integration of increasing volumes of (distributed) renewable generation and the shutdown of conventional power plants; the upgrading of existing grids to smarter networks using modern telecommunication services; new storage options and increased capacities of batteries; further cross-border interconnections and the regional integration of electricity networks by, *inter alia*, planning and developing 'overlay'-grids superimposed on an existing transmission network. Depending on the political will and economic feasibility, energy sources in remote areas like solar PV from the African and central Asian deserts or wind energy from arctic regions might be tapped into and connected to existing grids.[72]

Given all of these developments and considering the political targets for the integration of new forms of electricity generation, the electricity industry is arguably facing its biggest transition since its inception almost 150 years ago.

2.1.6.1   The Impact of the Energy Transition

The principal challenge to the traditional electric power system is the transformation of the electricity generation landscape in the direction of carbon neutrality or "net zero".[73] For electricity systems, the ever-increasing share of renewable sources in the generation mix of countries is a disruptive development for two main reasons. The first is the intermittency of renewable power generation due to fluctuating wind speeds and fluctuating intensity of solar radiation. The second reason is the remote location of the most suitable sites for large-scale generation of renewable energy.

The problem of intermittency is straightforward. The patterns of wind speeds and the intensity of solar radiation are not correlated to the demand for energy and can

---

[72] See in this respect Liu (2015). See also below in Sect. 3.2.7, pp. 74 et seq.

[73] The Paris Agreement on Climate Change, which as of January 2020 has been ratified by 191 Parties to the United Nations Framework Convention on Climate Change (UNFCCC) commits Parties to '[h]olding the increase in the global average temperature to well below 2°C above pre-industrial levels and pursuing efforts to limit the temperature increase to 1.5°C above pre-industrial levels'. United Nations Framework Convention on Climate Change, Paris Agreement (2015) FCCC/CP/2015/L.9/Rev1. Available at http://unfccc.int/resource/docs/2015/cop21/eng/l0 9r01.pdf. The OECD, based on findings of the Intergovernmental Panel on Climate Change (IPCC) estimates that '[l]ow-emissions pathways consistent with the Paris Agreement require global emissions to peak as soon as possible, with a subsequent rapid fall in emissions, and net emissions approaching zero or becoming negative in the second half of the [21st] century.' OECD (2018).

fluctuate extremely in some regions. As opposed to the constant and flexible generation possible when using fossil fuels and (to a lesser extent) nuclear power plants, wind and solar energy can only react in a limited way to changes in demand. The intermittency problem underlines the need for storage options to make efficient use of excess wind or solar power capacities. Regional cooperation is one approach to mitigate the challenge of intermittency, as will be elaborated further below.[74]

The fact that most electricity systems have been designed for generation near the centres of consumption implies that in many countries long-distance transmission capacity is not yet available. Solar power, offshore wind and new hydropower generation are often located at long distances from major consumers. In the EU, the energy transition entails the development of large offshore wind farms in the North Sea and Baltic Sea. The electricity generated there must be transported to consumption centres located in the Southwest of Germany, France, the Netherlands and Belgium. In the US, the most attractive sites for onshore wind are located within a corridor roughly stretching from Texas to the Canadian border (the so-called 'wind belt').[75] For solar, the best suited locations in the US are situated in the sparsely populated desert in the Southwest of the country.[76] China has started tapping into the vast solar and wind potential of its Western provinces, but most larger cities are located thousands of kilometres away. Hence, the energy transition makes new long-distance transmission infrastructure necessary. The required infrastructure will inevitably cross sub-national and national borders, regions of responsibility of different system operators, and private as well as public (and possibly protected) areas.[77]

Different scenarios are being discussed concerning the integration of renewable energy sources (RES) into the existing electricity systems. On one hand, large single power reinforcements could be built connecting renewable energy generation sites with load centres. A more ambitious approach would be to design an overlay grid that would connect generation sites distributed throughout a large geographical area. Plans for such 'electricity highways' exist, but their costs have so far stood in the way of the realization of these projects. At the other extreme, a decentralized system of supply combined with increased storage capacities could build on the existing transmission infrastructure and make new large-scale transmission lines superfluous. This would include the rollout of smart grids and the use of domestic battery storage systems.[78] A decentralized generation scenario would involve distributed generation, where a number of small-scale generators in the high kW or low MW range are connected. Apart from small solar PV parks or onshore wind turbines, this could also comprise smaller gas turbines or hydrogen fuel cells.[79] The most likely scenario involves a combination of both decentralized generation with partly autonomous

---

[74] See below in Sect. 3.1.3, pp. 44 et seq.

[75] Massachusetts Institute of Technology (2011), p. 12.

[76] Ibid.

[77] Ibid, at 78.

[78] Ibid.

[79] Ibid, at 109.

supply on the one hand and large-scale renewable generation in the most suitable regions on the other.

2.1.6.2 Smart Grids and Microgrids

One important element of future electricity systems will be information and data management. The electricity network is in the process of becoming an increasingly automated system.[80] The term 'smart grid' is now widely used to describe a more intelligent connection between generation and load. This is achieved with the help of new communication and control systems and the coupling of telecommunication networks to the electric grid.[81] The smart grid allows consumers to play a more active and responsible role in the electricity system. Modern sensing technologies in consumer devices already allow for the optimization of electricity usage according to price signals. This enables the consumer to minimize costs by choosing the appropriate tariff and by reducing consumption during peak hours.[82] The electricity supplier, on the other hand, can offer tariffs designed to manage load imbalances. This could reduce the need for additional investments in network capacity.[83]

A concept related to the smart grid is the micro grid, which operates more or less in autarchy from centralized planning and balancing. Such a micro grid can include various forms of distributed generation like wind turbines, small-scale solar PV generation, small-scale hydropower or combined heat and power (CHP). These generating entities can be coordinated to operate as a 'virtual power plant'. A micro grid may deliver electricity to small commercial areas or residential neighbourhoods.[84] In the case of an imbalance due to supply shortages or sudden spikes in demand, the micro grid can be reconnected with the distribution grid. Otherwise, it will run in complete autarchy from the electricity network.

2.1.6.3 New Storage Options for Electricity

Due to the physical properties of electricity alluded to above, it is unlikely that short-term storage options for large volumes of electricity will emerge in the foreseeable future. Batteries are evolving in capacity and decreasing in size but will not be able to store sufficient volumes of electricity to provide a back-up for the supply of entire cities or regions in the near future. The diffusion of electric vehicles could be harnessed to provide storage services if users are incentivized to charge in times of low electricity demand and to feed electricity back into the grid in times of peak

---

[80]Vittal (2010), p. 10.

[81]Massachusetts Institute of Technology (2011), p. 20; Schuler (2010), p. 40.

[82]Schwab (2015), p. 256.

[83]Ibid.

[84]Casazza and Delea (2010), p. 146.

demand. In this way, the sum of thousands of small batteries could have a significant impact.

The conversion into other forms of energy remains an alternative to the direct storage of electricity in batteries. The conversion of electric energy into potential energy like water in pump-storage plants has been used for decades. An emerging option for medium- to long-term storage is the conversion of electricity into molecules ('power to gas' or 'power to liquid'), which can be used for heating or as fuel for transport.[85] One of the most promising applications in this respect is the use of electricity to produce hydrogen through a process called 'electrolysis'. Hydrogen could fuel larger vehicles, buses, and trains as well as provide energy and feedstock for industrial processes.

While not providing a 'storage option' in the strict sense, the international interconnection of electricity networks presents a way of mitigating the intermittency problem of renewable energies and thereby also functions as a sort of long-term storage.[86]

2.1.7 Interim Conclusions on the Technical Aspects of Electricity Systems

The preceding considerations have illustrated that any regulatory framework for electricity generation, trade and consumption must factor in the laws of physics. Electric energy exhibits similarities with other network-bound forms of energy like natural gas and with other network industries like telecommunications. However, it is important to also be aware of the fundamental differences that exist between these industries. Electricity is characterized by its homogenous quality, meaning that it always exhibits the same physical characteristics. Its safe use requires a high degree of standardization. Electricity can be transmitted instantaneously over long distances, but the transmission depends on fixed infrastructure which is expensive to install and requires long lead times for planning and permitting. Consumers are provided with electricity by the utility of their choice, but there is typically no direct physical connection between buyers and sellers of electricity. The generators sell their electricity on the market, feed it into the grid, and the rest is taken care of by the operators of the transmission and distribution networks. The transmission grid has been identified as the focus area of the development towards international electricity markets and it is thus the network level where international trade issues are most likely to emerge.

Coordination may be considered as the most important aspect of electricity trade. This involves coordinated planning of the entire system as well as real-time

---

[85] On this topic, see World Energy Council (2018); Fasihi et al. (2016), p. 243.

[86] See below in Sect. 3.1.3, pp. 44 et seq.

coordination of electricity flows. Most major blackouts in recent times were caused by a lack of coordination among system operators.[87]

Based on these special features it is worth exploring whether trade in electricity faces similar barriers compared with other goods and services when crossing national borders or whether it evokes sui generis challenges and barriers. The costs for constructing an electricity interconnector, for example, are considerable and often financed by international consortia. Once such an infrastructure is established, there would seem to be a shared interest in a seamless and uninterrupted flow of electricity between countries, similar to long-distance natural gas pipelines. And yet, the record is a mixed one with regards to the latter, as gas pipeline disputes are common and at least one has even reached the WTO dispute settlement bodies.[88]

In conclusion, the development and growth of the electric system and the electric power industry can be characterized as an interrelationship of technological innovation and regulation.[89] There is no reason to believe that this will not be the most likely path forward, especially as the complete phase-out of fossil fuels to achieve carbon neutrality will bring about technological innovations and necessitate novel regulatory approaches.

2.2 Regulatory and Commercial Aspects of the Electricity Sector

The previous chapter concluded that the physical features of electricity to a certain extent predetermine the choices for a regulatory structure. The regulation of the electricity value chain indeed involves unique arrangements found in no other industry.[90] Commercial laws applicable to most other sectors of the economy are not easily adaptable to the case of electricity.[91] In contrast, distinct rules for electricity have to be 'designed' to accommodate its special nature. While the electric systems of different countries are very similar in their physical and operational aspects, various approaches have emerged with respect to their regulation. Hence, the following considerations aim at presenting a brief summary of and insight into the regulatory approaches that have surfaced over time and are employed in countries around the world today and to introduce the most common market arrangements of contemporary electricity sectors.

---

[87] International Energy Agency (2014).

[88] See below in Sect. 5.1.2, p. 91.

[89] Massachusetts Institute of Technology (2011), p. 240.

[90] Hunt (2002), p. 34.

[91] Ibid, at 123.

2.2.1 Development of Electricity Sector Regulation

Electricity systems have evolved from simple, one-directional distribution lines mainly used for lighting streets and buildings into complex networks providing even the most remote places with reliable electricity, enabling the most energy-intensive industrial processes and involving a sophisticated infrastructure for balancing and control. The regulation of the industry has also undergone significant developments. At the start of the electricity supply industry around the end of the nineteenth century, private initiatives and competition among different technologies and utilities were prevalent.[92] A regulatory framework was not yet in place for the newly-emerging technology and regulators sought to apply frameworks used in other network industries, especially railroads.[93] The rapid, largely unregulated growth of the infant electricity industry in the early years was quickly met with strong governmental intervention at the start of the twentieth century. In the US, the Public Utility Holding Company Act (PUHCA) of 1935 created vertically integrated utilities.[94] These remained in private hands and were regulated by sector-specific agencies on the state and federal levels.[95] In the same year, the German Energy Industry Act entered into force, granting exclusive rights to several private utilities to supply electricity in a geographically defined service area and thereby creating regional cartels.[96] Similar approaches were followed in other European countries, notably in France, where a state-owned monopoly supplied electricity for the whole country.[97] Public ownership of utilities and their treatment as regulated monopolies were central elements of the prevailing regulatory philosophy of the time in Europe and Latin America.[98] Indeed, far into the second half of the twentieth century, the power sectors of most countries were characterized by large, mostly state-owned, monopolies. Vertical integration meant that these companies were responsible for generation (building and operating power plants); building, owning and administering transmission networks; coordinating supply and demand; and supplying electricity to end consumers. The final electricity prices ('tariffs') were determined by regulators to represent all of the above functions and were usually subject to cost-of-

---

[92] Batlle and Ocaña (2013), p. 132.

[93] See above in Sect. 2.1.4, p. 17. See also Brown and Sedano (2004), p. 3.

[94] Ibid.

[95] Correljé and de Vries (2008), pp. 69 et seq.

[96] Energy Industry Act of Germany (Energiewirtschaftsgesetz) (1935) RGBl. I S. 1451. The preamble of the Act mentions that the regional cartels are justified to 'prevent adverse economic effects of competition' (author's translation).

[97] On the different approaches to the regulation of the power sector in the twentieth century see von Danwitz (2006), p. 423.

[98] Batlle and Ocaña (2013), p. 132.

service regulation.[99] This early mode of strong regulatory and state intervention did not permit a market for electricity to emerge.[100]

Over the past decades, the electricity industry has evolved in a more market-oriented direction, now sharing many features with other industries producing goods or services. During the 1980s and 1990s, a wave of reforms was set into motion aiming at establishing more competitive and market-oriented structures for the electricity sector.[101] Chile is often cited as a pioneer of electricity sector reforms. Indeed, vertical and horizontal separation of the generation, transmission and distribution segments started there in 1981. Further restructuring steps in the country were introduced through the 1982 Electricity Act.[102] The example set by Chile inspired other Latin American countries like Argentina, Bolivia, Peru and Colombia. Further candidates for reform were England and Wales (1990), Norway (1991), Australia and New Zealand (1992) as well as some states of the US.[103] The early reforms continue to have a strong demonstrative effect and countries in different stages of economic development have been following the early examples.[104]

In analysing the electricity reforms mentioned above, three main elements can be identified, namely: restructuring, liberalization, and privatization.[105] These are the tools to achieve the goals of introducing competition, enhancing efficiency, and bringing down costs and prices for consumers. Restructuring underlies virtually all reforms of electricity markets previously characterized by vertical integration. The most important element of restructuring is the separation of the generation, transmission, distribution, and supply functions (the so-called 'unbundling') to introduce competition in the generation and supply stages. Liberalization entails the freedom of consumers to choose their electricity supplier and the granting of non-discriminatory access to electricity networks. Privatization of formerly state-owned electricity companies has been employed in some countries but does not seem to be a necessary precondition for the establishment of a well-working and competitive electricity market.[106] To ensure the implementation of restructuring and liberalization efforts in the electricity sector, another important element of electricity market reform is the establishment of an independent regulator. Regulatory agencies

---

[99] In cost-of-service regulation (or rate of return regulation as it is sometimes called) prices are determined based on the costs of providing the service in question, allowing for a fair rate of return for the regulated service provider. The profitability of an energy utility is thereby effectively determined by the regulator. On the concept of cost-of-service regulation see McDermott (2012).

[100] Batlle and Ocaña (2013), p. 132.

[101] Green (2005), pp. 67 et seq.

[102] General Law for Electric Services (Ley General de Servicios Eléctricos) (1982), Ley No.1 de Minería, available at https://www.cne.cl/en/normativas/electrica/sector-electrico/.

[103] Crastan (2009), p. 78.

[104] Bacon and Besant-Jones (2001), p. 331 et. seq.

[105] On this terminology see, e.g. Sioshansi and Pfaffenberger (2006), p. 41.

[106] In Norway, which is often cited as an example for a well-functioning electricity market, 90% of electricity generation capacity is in the hands of municipal, county and central authorities. OECD, Fossil Fuel Support Country Note Norway (April 2019), available at http://stats.oecd.org/.

with differing shades of competencies and degrees of oversight over the electricity sector have emerged in many countries.

In the course of the electricity market reforms, independent power producers (IPPs) emerged and now co-exist alongside traditional energy utilities (the former monopolies) in many markets.[107] IPPs generate electricity and sell the electricity to the market or a single off-taker, but do not own network assets. As an intermediate step between the 'classical' model of vertically integrated monopolies and a fully restructured and completely liberalized market, a number of countries introduced a single-buyer system. The single-buyer model allows competing generators to coexist but obliges these generators to sell their electricity to one monopoly utility. Mexico was one of many examples of the single buyer model until extensive energy market reforms were enacted in 2013.[108]

As a result of the sketched developments, four regulatory models have emerged which exist to varying degrees all over the world. These are an integrated monopoly, a single-buyer model, competition at the wholesale level and full competition including at the retail level. While the aims of reform are undisputed—reducing prices and enhancing consumer welfare—no global consensus seems to have emerged on a specific regulatory path to be followed. Some markets work well with public ownership, others do so after privatization. Furthermore, the process of market liberalization is still ongoing in most places and an example of a perfectly liberalized electricity market has not yet emerged.[109] One important consequence of the liberalization and restructuring efforts is that electric energy has emerged as a commodity which can be traded independently whereas previously it was part of a regulated service provided through an integrated structure.[110]

2.2.2 The Natural Monopoly Character of Transmission and Distribution

The special requirements of electricity make coordination of the generation, transmission and distribution functions an essential objective from the point of view of system operation. However, leaving these responsibilities all in the hands of one company militates against the objectives of real competition between generators and

---

[107] Several developing countries had to open their market to foreign owned IPPs as the state-owned utilities were unable to finance the necessary rapid expansion of domestic generating capacity. WTO, Council for Trade in Services, Energy Services—Background Note by the Secretariat (09 September 1998) S/C/W/52 [65].

[108] Padilla (2016). On the Mexican reforms see also below in Sect. 3.2.2.2, p. 54.

[109] Correljé and de Vries (2008), p. 65, state that only few electricity markets 'have actually reached a state that could be described as commensurate with the economics textbook ideal of a liberalized, competitive market. Perhaps the electricity markets in the UK, Argentina, Texas, New Zealand, Chile, and Alberta have come closest to this ideal, at least in terms of market design.'

[110] Besant-Jones (2006), p. 10.

the freedom of consumers to choose an electricity supplier.[111] It has now become generally accepted that the generation of electricity can be distinguished and treated separately from its transport and supply to final consumers.[112] This insight has been the underlying rationale of most restructuring and liberalization efforts since the 1980s.

However, the generation and transmission of electricity differ considerably with respect to their potential suitability for liberalized and competitive market structures. While the generation of electricity can easily be fitted into competitive market structures, its transmission and distribution have consistently been regarded as a natural monopoly because of the grid dependency of electricity and the prohibitively high investments necessary in new infrastructure.[113] The main insight underlying the natural monopoly concept is that competition in the transmission and distribution segments can lead to technical inefficiency and as a result total costs per unit of service will not be at their lowest.[114] One high-voltage electricity transmission line can transmit electricity from one point in the network to the other at much lower cost than several competing lines.[115] Increasing the number of parallel lines in a given electricity system is for the most part neither necessary for meeting demand nor justified on economic grounds.[116] It is therefore not considered desirable to have several competing transmission entities in one given area.[117] Of course, as with any natural monopoly, there is a real threat that the incumbent will maximize profits to the detriment of consumers. In electricity transmission, the threat of competition will hardly be sufficient to discipline the monopoly as the costs of new investment, which represent sunken costs for the monopoly, are prohibitive for new entrants.

Because of the natural monopoly character of transmission, the transmission business continues to be highly regulated as regards access to networks and network tariffs. Non-discriminatory access for third parties to existing transmission networks is essential in order to ensure competition at the generation and supply stages, as transmission networks are the 'bottleneck' of the entire electricity system. The determination of the right access tariff is one of the fundamental aspects of energy sector regulation.[118] The challenge facing the regulator lies in providing the network operators with enough incentive to invest in the maintenance and, if necessary, the extension of their networks while avoiding monopoly rents and discriminatory pricing. In principle, the regulator can choose between a cost-based and an

---

[111] Hunt (2002), p. 62.

[112] Crastan (2009), p. 105.

[113] Ibid.

[114] Dee and Findlay (2008), p. 344.

[115] Rivier et al. (2013), p. 262.

[116] Ibid.

[117] Rivier et al. (2013) concede that the line capacity could be made subject to a competitive auction, but only one company, the successful bidder and consequent owner of the line, can provide the service of transmission. See ibid, at 263.

[118] Von Danwitz (2006), p. 442.

incentive-based model of regulation. The former will reimburse the system operator for actual costs incurred, while the latter provides for either a revenue cap or a price cap, incentivizing the system operator to operate efficiently and to invest in the necessary transmission infrastructure.

Ownership of the natural monopoly differs from country to country. Many governments still maintain ownership of transmission and distribution networks.[119] In most EU Member States, the ownership and operation pertain to private TSOs (sometimes as a continuation of the old exclusive territorial concessions).[120] In the US, most assets belong to investor-owned utilities but the system operation is carried out by Independent System Operators (ISOs) and Regional Transmission Operators (RTOs). While in the EU the transmission grid is owned by 18 entities, the US grid is owned by roughly 140 entities.[121]

In sum, most electricity systems that have undergone a process of restructuring are characterized by competition at the generation and supply levels, while the services of transmission and distribution remain heavily regulated and are often carried out by monopoly undertakings. Competition in the electricity sector thus consistently refers to competition only with respect to generation and the commercial functions of wholesaling and retailing, but not the network-related functions of transmission and distribution.[122] Arguably, system operation also exhibits elements of a natural monopoly as there has to be a real-time overall supervision of the whole electric network.[123] Pricing takes place according to market signals only for those segments of the electricity network where competition has been introduced. Transmission and distribution tariffs are set by regulators, either at the national or sub-national level.

2.2.3 Electricity Supply As a Public Service

In the course of the liberalization and privatization efforts described above, governments have sought ways to ensure their continued ability to adequately supply energy services, including electricity services, in the general interest. The accessibility and affordability of these 'services of general interest'[124] became central

---

[119] Hunt (2002), p. 25.

[120] The European TSOs are mostly a product of the unbundling regime in the EU which was introduced through the so-called Third Energy Package. See Directive 2009/72/EC of the European Parliament and of the Council concerning common rules for the internal market in electricity and repealing Directive 2003/54/EC (13 July 2009) OJ 2009/L 211/55. See also Mäntysaari (2015), p. 48, and below in Sect. 3.2.1.2, pp. 49 et seq.

[121] Pierce et al. (2017), p. 236.

[122] Hunt (2002), p. 3.

[123] Ibid.

[124] Unlike public service obligations which are applied in many jurisdictions, 'services of general interest' are a concept characteristic of EU law. The European Commission defines the concept as

objectives requiring a certain degree of reregulation.[125] To achieve these aims, the supply of electricity and gas were among a group of services characterized as 'public service obligations' (PSOs).[126] The late Advocate General at the European Court of Justice *Ruiz-Jarabo Colomer* eloquently expressed the concept of PSOs in one of his opinions as follows:

> The creation of an open market is the first step of this [liberalization] policy, but once barriers have been removed there remain certain requirements which the market alone is not able to meet. Hence the origins of public intervention, in the form of 'services of general interest' and 'public service obligations', imposed by the authorities on undertakings in liberalised sectors in order to safeguard public interests which, because they are inalienable, cannot be left to market forces to take care of.[127]

He goes on to conclude that '[p]ublic service obligations constitute a method of structuring that exceptional state intervention (. . .) It is the great challenge of economic law today to define the limits of this state activity.'[128]

Hence, energy suppliers have been assigned PSOs to continue the reliable supply of energy to citizens and industry in the general interest. The supply of electricity to citizens 'at reasonable, easily and clearly comparable, transparent and non-discriminatory prices' is characterized as a universal service obligation in EU electricity law.[129] Indeed, the EU has been both a forerunner and one of the most ardent supporters of the concept of PSOs.

---

covering 'market and non-market services which the public authorities class as being of general interest and subject to specific public service obligations'. European Commission, 'Services of General Interest in Europe' (Communication) COM (2000) 580 final 37.

[125] Delimatsis (2015), p. 326.

[126] In the European context, PSOs have been defined as 'obligations which the undertaking (. . .) if it were considering its own commercial interests, would not assume or would not assume to the same extent or under the same conditions'. See Article 2 of Regulation (EEC) 1191/69 of the Council concerning the obligations inherent in the concept of a public service in transport by rail, road and inland waterway. The EU Electricity Directive states that '[h]aving full regard to the relevant provisions of the Treaty, in particular Article 86 thereof, Member States may impose on undertakings operating in the electricity sector, in the general economic interest, public service obligations which may relate to security, including security of supply, regularity, quality and price of supplies and environmental protection, including energy efficiency, energy from renewable sources and climate protection.' It goes on to state that '[s]uch obligations shall be clearly defined, transparent, non-discriminatory, verifiable and shall guarantee equality of access for electricity undertakings of the Community to national consumers.' Article 3 (2) of Directive 2009/72/EC of the European Parliament and of the Council concerning common rules for the internal market in electricity and repealing Directive 2003/54/EC (13 July 2009) OJ 2009/L 211/55.

[127] European Court of Justice, Case C-265/08 *Federutility and Others v Autorità per l'energia elettrica e il gas* [2010] ECR I-03377, Opinion of AG Ruiz-Jarabo Colomer [3].

[128] Ibid [43 ff].

[129] Article 3 (3) of Directive 2009/72/EC of the European Parliament and of the Council concerning common rules for the internal market in electricity and repealing Directive 2003/54/EC (13 July 2009) OJ 2009/L 211/55. The European Court of Justice has qualified the uninterrupted supply of electricity in sufficient quantities as a service of general economic interest in Case C-393/92 *Municipality of Almelo and Others v NV Energiebedrijf Ijsselmij* [1994] ECR I-1477 46 ff.

A delicate need for balancing exists between allowing an entity to serve as the single supplier of a 'service of general economic interest' and the need to ensure competition in the respective market. This balance is sought to be achieved through the introduction of special regulatory regimes.[130] The imposition of PSOs on a certain undertaking can also have repercussions for international trade.[131] This is especially the case if they are applied in a non-transparent manner and the exact scope and limits are not clearly delineated. Under such circumstances, PSOs can be used as a justification to protract market opening and refrain from the enforcement of competition laws.[132]

2.2.4 Regulation of Access to the Electricity Network

An important consequence of the grid dependency and the associated concept of the natural monopoly of transmission networks is that trading requests cannot always be accommodated due to capacity limits. As the infrastructure belonging to the transmission and distribution natural monopoly is the bottleneck of the entire system, the importance of access regulation cannot be overstated. Absent regulation of access to the network, the incumbent monopolist can charge disproportionate transmission fees and discriminate against new entrants or unwanted potential competitors.[133] Thus, there must be some regulatory incentive for incumbent owners of the transmission infrastructure to allow access on non-discriminatory terms. Considering the paramount importance of network access, it is not surprising that regulation of access has now emerged all over the world as one of the principal functions of energy regulators.[134] The regulatory challenge lies in finding the right balance between the legitimate property interests of the owner of the assets on the one hand and the need, on the other hand, to ensure that new entrants can make use of the infrastructure based on non-discriminatory, transparent and reasonable terms.[135]

Broadly speaking, two competing regulatory philosophies exist with respect to access regulation. One is third-party access (TPA), and the other is a single buyer system.[136] The latter entails that an entity functions as the single buyer and responsible party for the electricity supply in a certain geographical area while independent

---

[130] Krajewski (2003), p. 345; WTO, Council for Trade in Services (n 121) [70]; Deruytter (2011), pp. 65 et seq.

[131] See below in Sect. 10.1.3, p. 158.

[132] In the EU it is generally acknowledged that competition law is applicable to services of general economic interest 'only in so far as the application of those paragraphs does not obstruct the performance, in law or in fact, of the particular task assigned to them.' Cf Art. 106 (2) of the Treaty on the Functioning of the European Union.

[133] Wälde and Gunst (2004), p. 183.

[134] Ibid, at 188.

[135] Ibid, at 194.

[136] Lakatos (2004), p. 148.

suppliers can enter commercial contracts directly with customers. The single buyer is usually obliged to purchase the volumes of electricity from those bilateral contracts at a price which may include a transparent and non-discriminatory fee for the use of the transmission system.[137] While single buyer systems continue to exist, many countries have implemented a TPA requirement. The TPA can be either regulated, meaning subject to pre-established terms and conditions set by a regulatory agency, or negotiated. Negotiated TPA allows the transmission operator to bilaterally establish terms and conditions with upstream (producers) and downstream (consumers) users of the infrastructure.[138] The capital-intensive establishment of new transmission infrastructure might require the granting of exceptions with respect to TPA for this type of infrastructure. Conversely, with regards to already existing infrastructure the costs of which are depreciated, there will be less ground for tolerance vis-à-vis the incumbent owner of the transmission system.[139]

The implementation of an access regime requires several issues to be settled, among which are the technical interoperability of user's devices with the grid, the financial conditions for the use of an electricity infrastructure (tariffs), and the methods of allocating capacity in case of congestion (congestion management).[140] When lines experience congestion, access cannot be guaranteed for all trading requests. Congestion can be managed in different forms, and a broad distinction can be drawn between a *pro rata approach*, where new entrants are granted a share of the available capacity and existing commitments are consequently curtailed, and the *allocation of access rights only for free capacity* where existing commitments are left untouched. The spare capacity can then be allocated either on a first come first serve basis, according to competitive auctioning or based on source-specific priorities, e.g., by giving preference to renewable energy sources.[141]

While network access is important with respect to any electricity transmission line also in a purely national context, it becomes all the more significant with respect to international trade over the relatively few cross-border interconnectors available. Whereas dealing with domestic congestion is usually the responsibility of the network operator administering the control area in which congestion occurs, solving cross-border congestion issues can involve two or more system operators. And there is yet another important difference between domestic and cross-border congestion. Domestic congestion usually means short-term physical congestion—lines are

---

[137]The single buyer system was one option that Member States of the European Union were allowed to implement under the first EU Electricity Directive until the 'Acceleration Directive' entered into force in 2004. Cf. Article 18 of the Directive 96/92/EC of the European Parliament and of the Council concerning common rules for the internal market in electricity (19 December 1996) OJ 1997/L 27/20.

[138]Lakatos (2004), p. 148.

[139]Wälde and Gunst (2004), p. 196.

[140]Congestion occurs when elements of the electricity network cannot accommodate additional physical flows which would be necessary to carry out electricity transactions between market participants.

[141]Cf. Lakatos (2004), p. 197.

operating at their physical maximum. Cross-border congestion has a broader meaning as existing interconnectors are almost by definition insufficient to accommodate all trading requests. The procedures for cross-border congestion management and potential issues for international electricity trade will be dealt with in Part III below in the context of import and export restrictions.[142]

2.2.5   Wholesale Markets for Electricity

Just like many commodities nowadays, electricity is traded on wholesale and retail markets according to general principles of supply and demand. Retail is the sale of electricity to final customers, i.e. end users. The wholesale market is where generators and electricity suppliers meet to determine the price for a certain amount of electricity.[143] Absent other complicating factors, the wholesale electricity price is determined through the so-called merit order, the sequence in which generators sell their electricity to the market according to their marginal costs of production. There are in principle two ways to trade electricity on the wholesale market: Over the counter (OTC); or via an organized electricity exchange.[144] An electricity exchange provides a spot market with standardized products on which electricity is traded for physical settlement either on the same day (intraday trade) or the day following the trade on the spot market (day-ahead). The spot market price reflects external factors like weather conditions or any technical difficulties of certain generators.[145] Contrary to bilateral trades, exchanges create a visible market-clearing price. On the financial markets, options and futures for electricity are traded to secure against price risks. A well-functioning wholesale market can provide incentives for optimizing the construction and operating costs of new and existing capacity, respectively, and encourage innovation.[146] It should be pointed out again, however, that the commercial and physical operations do not necessarily coincide in the electricity sector. The decision of the network operator to request the service of a certain generator (the so-called 'dispatching' of generation) ultimately happens according to network signals and thus independently of contracts for delivery between market participants.[147] The main objective of long-term contracts, much like on other commodity markets, is to alleviate the problem of price volatility rather than to exchange actual physical electricity volumes.[148]

---

[142] See below in Sect. 11.2, pp. 177 et seq.

[143] The latest spot price on the European Energy Exchange (EEX) can be consulted at https://www.eex.com/en/market-data#/market-data.

[144] Mäntysaari (2015), p. 11.

[145] Ibid at p. 13.

[146] Joskow (2008), p. 11.

[147] Hogan (2002), p. 117.

[148] Ibid.

Wholesale markets for electricity generally necessitate a certain extent of liberalization and competition on the generation and supply stages to be effective. In countries with state-controlled dominant players, a wholesale market is unlikely to emerge. Many developing countries experience a lack of liquidity, i.e. an insufficient number of competing generators in the market. The more liquid a wholesale market becomes, the more reliable will be the price signal it sends out.[149] In addition to 'energy only' marketplaces, markets also exist for transmission capacity. More recently, markets for the provision of system services have begun to come into existence.[150] On these markets, generators can offer products like balancing energy to help stabilize the grid.

Wholesale markets today are still largely confined to national borders. In Europe, several regional markets are emerging through a process called 'market coupling'. Market coupling refers to a common methodology for settling supply and demand and a common approach to the allocation of capacity.[151] Market coupling will be most effective when there are sufficient interconnection capacities between the coupled markets. If this is not the case, it is unlikely that prices between the market areas will converge completely, as electricity flows will not be sufficient to offset the differences between higher and lower price areas.[152]

A frontrunner of the power exchange—and still the arrangement of choice for many electricity markets—is a power pricing pool. Such power pools have come into existence mostly due to government involvement as opposed to private initiatives.[153] By establishing power pools, governments aim to broaden the matching of supply and demand beyond a single utility and to gradually introduce competition and replace trade via long-term bilateral contracts. In a power pool, there is often a central coordinating authority managing the bids of generators for a certain time period. Power pools were introduced in Argentina, California, Chile and Spain, among others.[154] Not all experiences with power pools have been positive: The UK abandoned its system in 2001, 10 years after the start of its operation.

---

[149] Mäntysaari (2015), p. 15.

[150] System services, sometimes also called ancillary services, can be understood as the provision of certain features necessary for maintaining the overall stability of the electric grid. They can be provided by generators, transmission system operators or other market actors. Examples are balancing energy, reactive power, voltage control and load following. System services are increasingly supplied and remunerated on a market basis. The EU has established common principles for the balancing of electricity which aim to allow a larger number of actors to provide services for balancing. Cf. Commission Regulation (EU) No 2017/2195 establishing a guideline on electricity balancing (23 November 2017).

[151] For examples of market coupling in Europe see below in Sect. 3.2.1.2, p. 51.

[152] European Parliament, Briefing: Understanding Electricity Markets in the EU (November 2016) 7 http://www.europarl.europa.eu/RegData/etudes/BRIE/2016/593519/EPRS_BRI(2016)593519_EN.pdf.

[153] Roggenkamp and Boisseleau (2005), p. 20.

[154] Ibid.

Wholesale electricity markets involving more than one country are still an exception. As will be discussed in detail further below, however, cross-border integration of electricity markets is currently happening on several continents.[155]

2.2.6 Power Purchase Agreements (PPAs)

Outside of the wholesale market, bilateral electricity supply contracts have been negotiated in the electricity sector for decades. Power purchase agreements (PPAs) are agreed directly between a generator or marketer and a supplier (utility) or directly with the end consumer. Thus, no central trading platforms are needed for PPAs, unlike for OTC trades on wholesale markets. The main aim of a PPA is to offer the investor in electricity generation a secure offtake and both parties safeguards against the high volatility of wholesale market prices. PPAs can come in a variety of forms, and either as a fixed price or a discount on market prices. A further distinction can be drawn between on-site PPAs—where generation is situated in geographical proximity to the consumer (e. g. a large steel mill or chemical plant) and connected via a direct line—and off-site PPAs with connection to the public grid.[156] In the latter case, the contractual connection between the generator and consumer will have to be evidenced by a guarantee of origin certificate. While PPAs have been in existence for many years and have been a popular method to source electricity in regions like Latin America, one can notice a renewed interest in the direct sourcing of renewable electricity. The reason is that large corporations with high electricity demands are coming under increasing pressure to purchase more electricity from low-carbon sources as part of their corporate social responsibility policies.[157]

2.2.7 Interim Conclusions on Regulatory and Commercial Aspects

For almost a century, electricity sectors around the world were characterized by complete vertical integration. This structure resulted in markets being dominated by

---

[155] See below in Sect. 3.2.

[156] In India, more than 40% of electricity generated by renewable sources in 2018 was procured through direct lines from off-site generators and without using the general grid. This is mainly due to the poor reliability of the Indian grid. See The Climate Group, RE 100 Progress and Insights—Annual Report (November 2018) 9 https://www.there100.org/sites/re100/files/2020-09/RE100%20 Annual%20Report%202018.pdf.

[157] According to RE100, an industry initiative, PPAs represent 26% of renewable electricity consumed by member companies of the initiative equalling about 31 TWh. See The Climate Group, RE 100 Annual Progress and Insights Report 2020 (December 2020) https://www.there100.org/growing-renewable-power-companies-seizing-leadership-opportunities.

either a state-owned energy utility or a privately-owned, but heavily regulated monopoly undertaking. The situation began to seriously change in the 1980s when the first countries enacted reforms. While 'no two countries anywhere in the world have taken the same approach to the regulation of the power sector',[158] a rather recent overall tendency can be observed towards competitive market structures and liberalization. On the commercial side, this development has separated electricity as a tradable commodity and allowed new actors like independent power producers and electricity brokers to emerge.

Despite the breaking up of the traditional structures of integrated utilities, the characteristics of electricity supply mandate that some parts of the supply chain remain under natural monopoly conditions, while others are better suited for liberalization. Transmission, the regulated part, is put into the hands of an independent system operator in most liberalized markets while generation and supply are in the hands of other market players.

Liberalization has not meant deregulation, however. On the contrary, to function properly electricity markets need a sophisticated regulatory design.[159] Moreover, implementing a textbook model of restructuring and liberalization does not suffice. There is no guarantee that actual competition will emerge, as many examples have shown. Indeed, the high degrees of market concentration remain a concern, and the regulatory framework needs constant improvement and adjustment.[160] The natural monopoly character of the transmission segment mandates the imposition of transparent and non-discriminatory access rules. Indeed, the transmission monopoly in combination with the vital importance of a secure electricity supply frequently result in an exceptional legal status of electricity system operators. Moving beyond the imposition of penalties for certain behaviour, legislators impose obligations of conduct on transmission system operators and enforce these obligations if necessary. The system of rights and obligations imposed on transmission system operators is unparalleled in the regulation of other economic undertakings.[161]

In some jurisdictions, electricity supply continues to be regarded as a service of general interest subject to a public service obligation. In some parts of the world, wholesale markets are emerging after liberalization and the first steps have been undertaken to integrate these markets with neighbouring countries. At the same time, large consumers are increasingly contracting electricity directly from generators to hedge against price risks and to improve their environmental footprint.

---

[158] Batlle and Ocaña (2013), p. 131.

[159] Hogan (2002), p. 104 ('Power markets are made, they don't just happen'). See also Newbery (2002), p. 16 ('All of this suggests that workable electricity liberalization is very different from deregulation. If anything, the regulatory requirements to ensure security and quality of supply, not just in surplus but also tight markets, are far more demanding than for other utilities, as the speed with which system-wide problems can emerge is considerably faster').

[160] International Energy Agency (2005), p. 63.

[161] Held and Wiesner (2015).

References

Bacon R, Besant-Jones J (2001) Global electric power reform, privatization, and liberalization of the electric power industry. Ann Rev Energy Environ 26:331

Batlle C, Ocaña C (2013) Electricity regulation: principles and institutions. In: Pérez-Arriaga IJ (ed) Regulation of the power sector. Springer, Berlin

Besant-Jones J (2006) Reforming power markets in developing countries: what have we learned? Energy and mining sector board discussion Paper No. 19. https://documents1.worldbank.org/curated/en/483161468313819882/pdf/380170REPLACEMENT0Energy19.pdf

Botchway F (2001) International trade regime and energy trade. Syracuse J Int Law Commer 1:1

Brown M, Sedano R (2004) Electricity transmission: a primer. National Council on Electricity Policy, Washington

Brunekreeft G (2005) Regulatory issues in merchant transmission investment. Utilities Policy 13: 175

Buchmüller C (2013) Strom aus erneuerbaren Energien im WTO-Recht. Nomos, Glashütte

Casazza J, Delea F (2010) Understanding electric power systems: an overview of technology, the marketplace and Government regulation. Wiley, Hoboken

Correljé A, De Vries L (2008) Hybrid electricity markets: the problem of explaining different patterns of restructuring. In Fereidoon P. Sioshansi, Competitive electricity markets: design, implementation, performance. ElsevierAmsterdam.

Crastan V (2009) Elektrische Energieversorgung. Springer, Berlin

Dee P, Findlay C (2008) Trade in infrastructure services: a conceptual framework. A handbook of international trade in services. Oxford University Press, Oxford

Delimatsis P (2015) Services of general interest and the external dimension of the EU energy policy. In: Krajewski M (ed) Services of general interest beyond the single market. Springer, Berlin

Deruytter T (2011) Public service obligations in the electricity and gas markets. In: Delvaux B, Hunt M, Talus K (eds) EU energy law and policy issues, vol 3. Intersentia, Cambridge

Elektrizitätswerk Heilbronn (ed) (1991) Moderne Energie für eine neue Zeit: Die Drehstromübertragung Lauffen a. N. ZEAG, Zementwerk Lauffen - Elektrizitätswerk Heilbronn AG

El-Hawary M (2008) Introduction to electrical power systems. Wiley, Hoboken

Fasihi M, Bogdanov D, Breyer C (2016) Techno-economic assessment of power-to-liquids (PtL) fuels production and global trading based on hybrid PV-wind power plants. Energy Procedia 99: 243

Ferrey S (2004) Inverting choice of law in the wired universe: thermodynamics, mass and energy. Wm Mary Law Rev 45:1839

Gatzen C (2007) The economics of power storage: theory and empirical analysis for Central Europe. Oldenbourg Industrieverlag, Munich

Gerbaulet C, Weber A (2014) Is there still a case for merchant interconnectors? Insights from an analysis of welfare and distributional aspects of options for network expansion in the Baltic Sea Region. DIW discussion paper 1404

Graf R (1999) Modern dictionary of electronics, 7th edn. Newnes, Oxford

Green R (2005) Electricity and markets. 21 Oxford Rev Econ Policy 67.

Held C, Wiesner C (2015) Energierecht und Energiewirklichkeit. Energie Manag

Hogan W (2002) Electricity market restructuring: reforms of reforms. J Regul Econ 21:103

Hughes T (1983) Networks of power: electrification in Western Society 1880–1930. The Johns Hopkins University Press, Baltimore

Hunt S (2002) Making competition work in electricity. Wiley, Hoboken

International Energy Agency (2005) Lessons from liberalized electricity markets. https://www.iea.org/reports/lessons-from-liberalised-electricity-markets

International Energy Agency (2014) Seamless power markets. https://www.iea.org/reports/seamless-power-markets

Joskow P (2008) Lessons learned from electricity market liberalization. The Energy Journal, Special Issue – The Future of Electricity: Papers in Honor of David Newbery

Joskow P, Tirole J (2005) Merchant transmission investment. J Indus Econ 53:233

Kaplan S (2009) Electric power transmission: background and policy issues. Congressional Research Service Report for Congress

Krajewski M (2003) Public service and trade liberalization: mapping the legal framework. J Int Econ Law 6:341

Lakatos A (2004) Overview of the regulatory environment for trade in electricity. In: Bielecki J, Desta MG (eds) Electricity trade in Europe: review of the economic and regulatory challenges. Kluwer Law International, New York

Laloux D, Rivier M (2013) Technology and operation of electric power systems. In: Pérez-Arriaga IJ (ed) Regulation of the power sector. Springer, Berlin

Liu Z (2015) Global energy interconnection. Elsevier, Amsterdam

Long W, Nilsson S (2007) HVDC transmission: yesterday and today. IEEE Power Energy Magazine 5:23

Mäntysaari P (2015) EU electricity trade law: the legal tools of electricity producers in the internal electricity market. Springer, Berlin

Massachusetts Institute of Technology (2011) The future of the electric grid: an interdisciplinary MIT study

McDermott K (2012) Cost of service regulation in the investor-owned electric utility industry. Edison Electric Institute, Washington. https://www.ourenergypolicy.org/wp-content/uploads/2012/09/COSR_history_final.pdf

Meyer G, Thomas N (2021) Hydrogen: the future of electricity storage? Financial Times Online. https://www.ft.com/content/c3526a2e-cdc5-444f-940c-0b3376f38069

Müller L (2001) Handbuch der Elektrizitätswirtschaft: Technische, wirtschaftliche und rechtliche Grundlagen, 2nd edn. Springer, Berlin

Newbery D (2002) Regulatory challenges to European electricity liberalisation. Swedish Economic Policy Review 9:9

OECD (2018) Implementing the Paris agreement: remaining challenges and the role of the OECD. OECD, Paris. http://www.oecd.org/mcm-2018/documents/C-MIN-2018-12-EN.pdf

Padilla V (2016) The electricity industry in Mexico: tension between the state and the market. Problemas del Desarrollo – Revista Latinoamericana de Economía 47:33–55

Passer H (1953) Electrical manufacturers 1875–1900: a study in competition, entrepreneurship, technical change and economic growth. Harvard University Press, Cambridge

Pierce R, Trebilcock M, Thomas E (2017) Regional electricity market integration: a comparative perspective. Compet Reg Network Indus 8:215

Rivier M, Pérez-Arriaga I, Olmos L (2013) Electricity transmission. In: Pérez-Arriaga I (ed) Regulation of the power sector. Springer, Berlin

Roggenkamp M, Boisseleau F (2005) The liberalisation of the EU electricity market and the role of power exchanges. In: Roggenkamp M, Boisseleau F (eds) The regulation of power exchanges in Europe. Intersentia, Cambridge

Schuler R (2010) The smart grid. The Bridge 40:43

Schwab A (2015) Elektroenergiesysteme: Erzeugung, Transport, Übertragung und Verteilung elektrischer Energie. Springer Vieweg, Berlin

Sioshansi F, Pfaffenberger W (2006) Why restructure electricity markets? In: Sioshansi, Pfaffenberger (eds) Electricity market reform. Elsevier, Amsterdam

Vittal V (2010) The impact of renewable resources on the performance and reliability of the electricity grid. The Bridge 40:5–12

Von Danwitz T (2006) Regulation and liberalization of the European Electricity Market – A German view. Energy Law J 27:423

Wälde T, Gunst A (2004) International Energy Trade and access to networks. In: Bielecki J, Desta MG (eds) Electricity trade in Europe: review of the economic and regulatory challenges. Kluwer Law International, New York

World Energy Council Germany (2018) International aspects of a power-to-X-Roadmap. Report prepared by Frontier Economics. https://www.weltenergierat.de/wp-content/uploads/201 8/10/20181018_WEC_Germany_PTXroadmap_Full-study-englisch.pdf

Chapter 3
The Advent of International Electricity Trade

The transmission of electrical energy across national borders is not a new phenomenon. In fact, the first cross-border electricity transmission took place in 1901 between the US and Canada. However, in recent years there is an increasing trend towards the integration of electricity markets on a regional scale. The reasons for this are numerous, as will be discussed below. After briefly explaining the benefits of interconnection and cross-border electricity exchanges, the following pages of this study will take stock of the existing regional initiatives and examine how far the developments towards international electricity trade have advanced to date. The focus is on infrastructure, regulatory arrangements and institutional design. A final question to be answered below is whether electricity market integration can be expected to become a truly global trend.

3.1 The Benefits of International Electricity Trade

While cross-border trade in energy commodities like oil and gas is indispensable for many countries without sufficient domestic resources, the traditional motivation for cross-border electricity trade is to be found in mutual assistance and the better utilization of generating capacity.[1] Interconnecting national electricity networks for international cooperation has several advantages of both economic and technical nature. While many of the benefits will also materialize when it comes to domestic grid reinforcement, the effects are especially pronounced when networks are connected on a large geographical scale spanning two or more countries. The economic advantages include pooling of resources; increased competition; the optimization of generating costs; in short: economies of scale. From a technical

---

[1] Wälde and Gunst (2004), p. 180.

© The Author(s), under exclusive license to Springer Nature Switzerland AG 2022
C. Frey, *World Trade Law and the Emergence of International Electricity Markets*,
EYIEL Monographs - Studies in European and International Economic Law 25,
https://doi.org/10.1007/978-3-031-04756-5_3

point of view, interconnections also offer reliability benefits as the network conditions tend to be more stable in larger networks. For neighbouring jurisdictions with already developed and highly meshed networks, cross-border linkage may entail costs not significantly above or even below those of internal network reinforcement.[2]

3.1.1 Scale Benefits and Security of Supply

Connecting different regions to pool more electricity consumers together has clear advantages of both a technological and economic nature. More electricity consumers (more 'load') usually translate into a more efficient operation of power plants. Building large conventional power plants with a capacity of more than 1000 MW will only be viable if the load is sufficiently large.[3] Equally, some renewable energy technologies can only efficiently and economically be employed in electricity systems with a large load. Offshore wind energy, for example, has particularly high and fixed up-front costs and investments will only be made once the electricity can be supplied within a large, interconnected area. A higher load factor usually also corresponds to lower generating costs per kilowatt.[4]

As production and consumption peaks are often decorrelated across countries, a pooling of generators and consumers on a larger geographic scale can optimize the efficiency of power plants.[5] Studies have shown that costs in national autarchy cases requiring either storage or curtailment of temporal excess capacities are up to ten times higher when compared with a market integration scenario.[6] This is mainly because an integrated market spanning a larger geographic area allows for electricity exchanges between regions with different climatic conditions, slight differences in daylight hours as well as different cultural habits, which result in differences in daily load profiles.[7] Taking Europe as an example, there is a difference in electricity demand over the course of a day between Scandinavia and southern Member States of the EU like Greece, Italy, Spain and Portugal. This non-simultaneous demand can be harnessed as a flexibility option to mitigate the effects of increasing intermittency in electricity generation.[8] This effect of regional integration could be especially helpful for developing countries, where wholesale markets are often not coming into existence because there are not enough market actors.[9]

---

[2] Verneyre (2004), p. 50.

[3] Schwab (2015), p. 37.

[4] Verneyre (2004), p. 50.

[5] Ibid.

[6] Agora Energiewende (2015), p. 8.

[7] Ibid, at 6.

[8] Most notably, each region within Europe has its annual peak load at different times of the day and year. See ibid.

[9] Ferrero (2012), p. 778.

By pooling a large number of generators of different kinds, the security of supply can also be enhanced. A diverse generation portfolio allows for solidarity in emergency situations and can provide greater resilience to external shocks caused by extreme weather conditions or sudden load growth above forecast.[10] Furthermore, the pooling of generation reduces the need for a reserve margin in case one or more plants need maintenance or break down unexpectedly.[11] In the past, interconnections between systems with a large share of hydropower and those where thermal power generation dominated provided for meaningful synergies.[12]

3.1.2 Optimization of Generation Costs

As regards the costs of generation, interconnectors and cross-border trade allow for a larger portfolio of power plants from which to choose those with the lowest marginal costs.[13] This can lead to a considerable optimization of overall generating costs and a resulting reduction in end users' prices when the benefits are passed on to the final consumers. The more liquid a market is, the more cost-reflective the pricing of electricity will be. For developing countries, the main benefits of cooperation on electricity trade could be the decrease in energy prices and a greater resilience against power outages.[14] Trade in electricity between countries has been found to provide an effective substitute in the absence of real competition at the national level.[15] While there are undisputed benefits for countries with high electricity prices, critics of electricity market integration argue that the opposite effect will occur in markets where prices are already low, threatening the competitiveness of electricity-intensive industries in these markets.[16] In the EU, financial benefits of between €16–30bn per year are expected from electricity market integration, resulting from the effect of placing large-scale renewable energy generation where it can be most effectively harnessed.[17] The necessary investments in new transmission capacity are considerable, but are expected to be much lower than the investments needed for scaling up generation capacity at a national level.[18] The economic benefits will be more pronounced when the physical interconnection is followed by regulatory convergence and common commercial rules.[19]

---

[10] Hooper and Medvedev (2009), p. 25.

[11] Cain and Lesser (2007).

[12] Wälde and Gunst (2004), p. 180.

[13] Agora Energiewende (2015), p. 33.

[14] Pollitt and McKenna (2014).

[15] Hooper and Medvedev (2009), p. 25, citing Amundsen et al. (1998).

[16] Cohen (2003), p. 7.

[17] Booz & Company (2013), p. 89.

[18] Ibid, at 90.

[19] Ibid, at 3.

3.1.3 Benefits of Cross-Border Trade for the Integration of Renewable Energies

Cross-border electricity flows have a special significance for the integration of renewable energy sources (RES). As described above, one of the main challenges of integrating RES into the existing power system is intermittency, resulting in a surplus in generation when wind and sun conditions are favourable and shortages when conditions are poor. In times of surplus generation, generators will have to be taken off the grid to maintain the prescribed frequency if counter-trading is not an option and as long as sufficient storage capacity is not available. This 'waste' of available energy is somewhat of a paradox as generation shortages are a frequent problem above all in developing economies. Cross-border exchanges can have a 'smoothing effect' on the intermittency of RES generation and as such function as alternatives to energy storage.[20]

Surplus generation can be minimized by integrating markets with different load profiles. As a study has demonstrated for the EU, when renewable energy producers are aggregated over a large geographical area, peaks in generation are reduced and generation shortages also decrease.[21] Likewise, the need for balancing power is reduced significantly. The effect of integration will be especially pronounced in regions, like Europe, where the traditional electricity systems have been designed for generation close to load centres and where the transmission system does not readily connect to remote renewable generation sites.[22] The European case study illustrates the benefits of physical interconnection. The Nordic countries (Norway, Sweden, Denmark and Finland) have considerable potential for the generation of renewable energy while their demand is comparably smaller than in other European regions. The resulting generation surplus is destined for export to Central Europe.[23] On the other hand, surplus generation in Germany or the Netherlands on extremely windy or sunny days can be 'stored' in the abundant hydropower facilities of the Nordic countries, if sufficient transmission capacity is available.

While interconnection has a positive effect on the efficient usage of RES, the contribution of cross-border electricity transmission to CO_2 reduction depends on the exact generation profile of the countries trading with each other. Excess hydropower capacity in one country can, for example, replace more expensive coal-fired generation in an adjacent country.[24] Indeed, case studies carried out by the World Bank have shown that regional electricity market integration supports the

---

[20] International Electrotechnical Commission (2016), p. 18.

[21] Agora Energiewende (2015), p. 28.

[22] Booz & Company (2013), p. 13.

[23] Agora Energiewende (2015), p. 18.

[24] Hooper and Medvedev (2009), p. 26.

development of new hydropower generation while the evidence in this regard is much less clear for other renewable energy sources.[25]

3.2 The Emergence of Regional Electricity Markets

On most continents, recent decades have seen an increase in the transnational interconnection of electricity transmission networks and a parallel increase in volumes of electricity traded across borders. Global cross-border electricity trade amounted to 728 TWh in 2018, an increase of 24% from 2010 when it was 588 TWh.[26] European countries are leading the ranks as total electricity imports accounted for 9.1% of the total electricity supplied in Europe in 2018. Africa comes second with 4.5%, followed by the Middle East (2.2 %), the Americas (1.9 %) and Asia (0.6%).[27]

Aside from the economic and technological benefits of power system integration already discussed above, regional electricity markets are also emerging in the context of regional political or economic integration, as the energy sector is seen as an important pillar of such developments. Against this background, the phenomenon of cross-border electricity trade and electricity market integration merits further examination.

The focus of the following considerations will be on the physical infrastructure, regulatory design and commercial aspects of regional electricity integration initiatives. As will become clear, initiatives aimed at regional electricity market integration differ considerably with respect to the size of the concerned territory and number of consumers involved, the ambition of integration efforts (the objectives and means employed), and the available financial resources and investments in infrastructure. The regional electricity markets discussed below are at different stages of development, ranging from a single interconnection for assistance in emergency situations to liquid short-term markets with common regulatory institutions.

Several preconditions must be fulfilled for market integration to be successful. First and foremost, the transmission networks of the participating jurisdictions must be physically interconnected to allow for the exchange of electricity. A second precondition is cooperation between network operators, in order to ensure that the networks operate in synchronized mode and to balance generation and load on both sides of the border. Finally, it seems reasonable to assume that a certain degree of liberalization is necessary for international market integration to go forward.

---

[25] World Bank (2010), p. 31.

[26] International Energy Agency (2020), p. 38.

[27] Ibid.

3.2.1 The EU Internal Electricity Market

When the Single European Act established the overall objective of completing the EU internal market by 1992, this aim was meant to apply to the energy sector as well.[28] Hence, the integration of the national electricity markets of EU Member States has been a fundamental aim of EU energy policy for decades. While the elimination of virtually all barriers for intra-Union trade in a vast range of goods and services can be regarded as one of the main achievements of European integration, barriers to trade in electricity have proven harder to eliminate and are still not fully removed. Nonetheless, the EU is currently on the way to achieving a fully integrated and competitive wholesale electricity market showcasing the most sophisticated example of international electricity regulation to date.

3.2.1.1 Development and State of Interconnection

Decades before concrete steps for European political integration were undertaken and the signing of the Treaties of Rome brought the European Communities into existence, visionary electrical engineers were already advocating the construction of transboundary electricity transmission networks in Europe.[29] The actual development of cross-border infrastructure started in the early 1920s as the first single lines were constructed between France, Switzerland, and Italy to exchange electricity generated from hydropower.[30] After the end of World War II, European electricity cooperation was again taken on the agenda. Several interconnected and synchronous regional systems emerged over time in wider Europe.[31] These systems operated largely in isolation from each other and with very limited exchanges via single interconnecting DC lines.[32] To coordinate electricity exchanges and foster overall cooperation between the different systems, the Union for the Co-ordination of Transmission of Electricity (UCPTE) was founded in 1951.[33] It initially brought together the system operators of eight countries and was subsequently enlarged.[34]

---

[28] For the general goal see European Council (Rhodes, 2 and 3 December 1988), Presidency Conclusions, p. 2 http://www.europarl.europa.eu/summits/rhodes/rh1_en.pdf.

[29] For a detailed historical account see Lagendijk (2008).

[30] De Montravel (2004), p. 24.

[31] A synchronous grid comprising most of continental Europe (previously called UCTE) existed alongside a Scandinavian synchronous grid (NORDEL) comprising Finland, Norway, Sweden and some Danish territories. Moreover, the UK (UKTSOA) and Ireland (ATSOI) each operated their own synchronous grid. In Eastern Europe, the former CIS countries operated a wide area synchronous transmission grid called Integrated Power System (IPS) encompassing today's EU Member States Lithuania, Latvia and Estonia.

[32] De Montravel (2004), p. 24.

[33] Ibid, at 25.

[34] The operational tasks of UCPTE (which was renamed UCTE in 1999) were taken over by the European Network of Transmission System Operators for electricity (ENTSO-E) in 2009.

The former UCTE grid remains the most important synchronous grid on the European continent. It comprises all of the continental EU Member States with the exception of Sweden and Finland (as well as parts of Denmark) and the three Baltic Member States of the EU.[35] In more recent times, the synchronous grid of continental Europe was also synchronized with the grids of Turkey, Ukraine, Albania and three Northern African states (Morocco, Algeria and Tunisia).[36]

Despite the synchronous operation of the national continental European grids, the physical interconnections still allow only a fraction of the electricity generated in Europe to be traded across borders. Bottlenecks persist between neighbouring EU Member States, and the limited capacity does not allow for reaping the benefits of a truly integrated electricity market. The capacity of cross-border transmission lines in the EU today amounts to roughly 11% of installed generation capacity.[37] At the bottom end of the spectrum, cross-border transmission lines allow Spain to trade only 3% of its electricity generation capacity with its neighbours while Malta and Cyprus do not yet trade any electricity with other EU Member States. On the other end of the spectrum is Luxemburg, which has cross-border transmission lines in place corresponding to 245% of its generating capacity.[38] A large number of interconnectors are currently being developed, as documented by the most recent Ten-Year Network Development Plan (TYNDP) drawn up by the European Network of Transmission System Operators for Electricity (ENTSO-E).[39] Insufficient investment and tedious planning and permitting procedures are most often cited as reasons for the rather slow progress of interconnection projects.[40] The European Council in 2002 had set out the goal that by 2005 interconnections should be capable of allowing cross-border trade of 10% of installed generating capacity.[41] The Member States collectively failed to achieve this target. The European Commission has made repeated attempts to accelerate the construction of international infrastructure by proposing legislation based on the competence granted to the EU legislator

---

[35] The TSOs from Lithuania, Latvia and Estonia submitted an application in September 2018 for joining the Continental Europe Synchronous Area by 2025. The request is now being considered within ENTSO-E. ENTSO-E, Annual Work Programme 2019 (January 2019) 30 https://docstore.entsoe.eu/Documents/Publications/ENTSO-E%20general%20publications/AWP_2019.pdf.

[36] L'Abbate et al. (2014), p. 226.

[37] International Energy Agency (2014), p. 10.

[38] European Commission, 'Achieving the 10% electricity interconnection target, making Europe's electricity grid fit for 2020' (Communication), COM (2015) 82 final.

[39] ENTSO-E, Ten-Year Network Development Plan (2020) https://tyndp.entsoe.eu/.

[40] European Commission, 'Energy Infrastructure: Priorities for 2020 and Beyond – A Blueprint for an Integrated European Energy Network' (Communication), COM (2010) 0677 final, 5.

[41] European Council (Barcelona, 15 and 16 March 2002), Presidency Conclusions, 15 ('In the field of energy, the EU Council (. . .) urges the Council and the EU Parliament to adopt as early as possible in 2002 the pending proposals for the final stage of the market opening of electricity and gas, including (. . .) the target for Member states of a level of electricity interconnections equivalent to at least 10% of their installed production capacity by 2005'). See also European Commission, 'Achieving the 10% electricity interconnection target - Making Europe's electricity grid fit for 2020' (Communication) COM (2015) 82 final.

by the EU Treaties in the field of Trans-European Energy Networks (TEN-E).[42] The most recent TEN-E Regulation adopted a novel approach by laying down a coherent framework for planning and implementing certain infrastructure projects of common European interest. The projects identified qualify for EU funding through the so-called Connecting Europe Facility.[43] Infrastructure corridors of priority for the internal energy market include the North Sea Offshore Grid, north-south electricity interconnections in Western Europe, and a Baltic Energy Market Interconnection Plan.[44] The TEN-E Regulation was also subject to the first genuine energy dispute in the WTO, albeit not with respect to its provisions on electricity.[45]

3.2.1.2   The Regulatory and Institutional Framework

For much of the twentieth century, energy markets in the EU were dominated by either state-owned or, in some cases, privately owned vertically integrated monopoly utilities. The EU institutions started prescribing liberalization and the introduction of competition on certain market segments to the Member States in the late 1980s. Early examples of such market reforms had already been carried out in the UK and Norway. It has been an exclusive feature of EU electricity market integration that it developed past prescribing market access and non-discrimination obligations and that EU policymakers actively pursued energy market liberalization.

Despite the early examples of energy market liberalization in some European countries, many EU Member States for a long time were reluctant to admit that energy, and electricity specifically, is a commodity that can be traded across national borders like the other goods already benefitting from free movement within the EU internal market. The Member States regularly invoked the status of electricity supply as a service of general economic interest not falling under the disciplines of EU competition law.[46] While the European Commission shared this view at the beginning, it gradually came to accept that the electricity industry should be opened to competition at least with respect to the generation and supply segments. The European Court of Justice repeatedly ruled that electricity could be regarded as a

---

[42] Article 17 of Regulation (EU) 347/2013 of the European Parliament and of the Council on guidelines for trans-European energy infrastructure and repealing Decision No 1364/2006/EC and amending Regulations (EC) No 713/2009, (EC) No 714/2009 and (EC) No 715/2009 [2013] OJ L115/39, 58.

[43] Regulation (EU) 1316/2013 of the European Parliament and the Council establishing the Connecting Europe Facility, amending Regulation (EU) No 913/2010 and repealing Regulations (EC) No 680/2007 and (EC) No 67/2010 [2013] OJ L 348/129.

[44] Annex I of Regulation (EU) 347/2013 of the European Parliament and of the Council on guidelines for trans-European energy infrastructure and repealing Decision No 1364/2006/EC and amending Regulations (EC) No 713/2009, (EC) No 714/2009 and (EC) No 715/2009 [2013] OJ L115/39, 62.

[45] The case is discussed below in Sect. 5.1.2, p. 91.

[46] Meeus et al. (2005), p. 26.

good subject to commercial transactions, thereby rejecting the proposition that viewed electricity exclusively as a service.[47]

The early beginnings of the development of a regulatory framework for intra-Union electricity trade were marked by the Directive on the transit of electricity through transmission grids ('the Transit Directive'), which entered into force in 1990. In the Directive, transit was defined as the exchange of electricity between Member States, meaning the crossing of at least one intra-EU border.[48] The Directive introduced an obligation to allow transport of electricity originating from another Member State through national grids on a fair and non-discriminatory basis.[49]

The legislative opening and liberalization of energy markets in the EU proceeded mainly through three 'packages' of targeted legislation. The three EU energy packages mark a development from the harmonization of national legislation via market integration to a common EU-wide institutional and regulatory framework. The process started with the entering into force of the first electricity[50] and gas[51] directives in 1997. The second package including a revised electricity[52] and gas[53] directive followed in 2004 and the Third Energy Package entered into force in 2009. The third package requires, *inter alia*, full ownership unbundling of utilities in the electricity sector.[54] Besides unbundling, the introduction of a system of TPA was a fundamental pillar of the opening of electricity markets through EU legislation. As previous chapters have shown, the natural monopoly character of electricity transmission and distribution makes the regulation of access an essential factor. Through

---

[47] See below in Sect. 5.2.4, pp. 98 et seq. See also Meeus et al. (2005), pp. 26–27.

[48] Cf. Article 2 (1) c of Council Directive (EEC) on the transit of electricity through transmission grids [1990] OJ L313/30, 31 ('The Transit Directive'). As will be elaborated further below, this definition does not correspond to the general understanding of 'transit' in international economic law which requires the crossing of two borders or at least the crossing of one and the same border twice. See below in Chap. 12, pp. 197 et seq.

[49] Art. 3 of the EEC Transit Directive (n 223).

[50] Directive 96/92/EC of the European Parliament and of the Council concerning common rules for the internal market in electricity (19 December 1996) OJ 1997/L 27/20.

[51] Directive 98/30/EC of the European Parliament and of the Council concerning common rules for the internal market in natural gas (22 June 1998) OJ 1998/L 204/1.

[52] Directive 2003/54/EC of the European Parliament and of the Council concerning common rules for the internal market in electricity and repealing Directive 96/92/EC (26 June 2003) OJ 2003/L 176/37.

[53] Directive 2003/55/EC of the European Parliament and of the Council concerning common rules for the internal market in natural gas and repealing Directive 98/30/EC (26 June 2003) OJ 2003/L 176/57.

[54] Directive 2009/72/EC of the European Parliament and of the Council concerning common rules for the internal market in electricity and repealing Directive 2003/54/EC (13 July 2009) OJ 2009/L 211/55; Directive 2009/73/EC of the European Parliament and of the Council concerning common rules for the internal market in natural gas and repealing Directive 2003/55/EC (13 July 2009) OJ 2009/L 211/94. On the unbundling regime see Dralle (2018).

Directive 2003/54/EC the EU introduced one common system, namely regulated TPA.[55]

In December 2018, the EU Member States and the European Parliament agreed on a new set of rules for the EU electricity market. These new rules are embodied in yet another Market Design Regulation[56] and Directive.[57] The updated market design is specifically aimed at making the EU electricity market 'fit for' the integration of larger shares of renewable energy.[58]

The consecutive energy packages also created an institutional framework specific to the energy sector. The second Electricity Directive required Member States to designate or newly appoint a regulatory authority tasked with the approval of tariffs, the monitoring of congestion management and the settlement of disputes.[59] The Third Energy Package went a step further by establishing the Agency for the Cooperation of Energy Regulators (ACER).[60] ACER plays a central role in the development and regulation of the internal market for electricity. The Agency is tasked with supervising the cooperation of national regulatory authorities and harmonizing their activities. Arguably, ACER is slowly moving beyond its function as a forum for cooperation and evolving into a European energy regulator, as documented by its important role in drafting targeted electricity network regulations.[61]

The TSOs of 35 European countries are currently coordinating their operations through the European Network of Transmission System Operators for Electricity (ENTSO-E). The Regulation on Cross-border Electricity Exchanges, which entered into force in July 2009, requires the TSOs of all EU Member States to accede to ENTSO-E. The task and mission of ENTSO, in the words of the organization itself, is to be 'the focal point for all EU, technical, market and policy issues related to TSOs, interfacing with the power system users, EU institutions, regulators and national governments'.[62] Another central task of ENTSO-E is the drafting and publication of a Ten-Year Network Development Plan (TYNDP) for the European

---

[55] For an explanation of the TPA concept see above in Sect. 2.2.4, pp. 31 et seq. See also Meeus et al. (2005), p. 29.

[56] Regulation (EU) 2019/943 of the European Parliament and of the Council of 5 June 2019 on the internal market for electricity (5 June 2019) OJ 2019/L 158/54.

[57] Directive (EU) 2019/944 of the European Parliament and of the Council of 5 June 2019 on common rules for the internal market for electricity and amending Directive 2012/27/EU (5 June 2019) OJ 2019/L 158/125.

[58] European Commission, 'Clean Energy for All Europeans: Commission welcomes European Parliament's adoption of new electricity market design proposals' Press Release (26 March 2019).

[59] Meeus et al. (2005), p. 29.

[60] Regulation (EC) 713/2009 of the European Parliament and of the Council establishing an Agency for the Cooperation of Energy Regulators (13 July 2009) OJ 2009/L 211/1.

[61] Gottschal (2009), pp. 51 et seq. The European Commission is of a different opinion, pointing to the 'very limited decision-making rights' of ACER. European Commission, 'launching the public consultation process on a new energy market design' (Communication) COM (2015) 340 final 12.

[62] ENTSO-E Objectives https://www.entsoe.eu/about/inside-entsoe/objectives/.

Union which sets out the anticipated need for new electricity infrastructure. Both ACER and ENTSO-E also play an important role in the drafting of framework guidelines and network codes for electricity. These are specific technical regulations for issues of cross-border significance, like network security and reliability, third-party access, data exchange, or transparency.[63]

Another important piece of the emerging regulatory framework for the internal electricity market is the mechanism for inter-transmission system compensation (ITC). The ITC sets out rules for the compensation of TSOs the networks of which are being used for cross-border electricity flows. The mechanism is governed by the EU Regulations 714/2009[64] and 838/2010.[65] According to Article 13 (2) of the former, compensation is the responsibility of the operators of the national transmission systems from which the flows originate and those where the flows end.[66] The amount of the compensation payments due is determined by the European Commission (Article 13(4)) on the basis of the physical flows measured during a given period of time (Article 13(5)). The costs reflect losses and investment in new infrastructure, among others (Article 13 (6)). Guidelines have also been established with regards to capacity allocation and congestion management, two fundamental aspects of cross-border electricity trade.[67]

Several regional market integration initiatives have been successfully implemented within the EU through the mechanism of market coupling.[68] The Nordic Market was the first in 2000 and involved Norway, Sweden, Finland and Denmark. A coupling of the markets of Central West-Europe (CWE) followed in 2010, comprising Belgium, the Netherlands, Luxembourg, France and Germany. The Nordic Market and the CWE were successfully coupled in 2014, joined by Great Britain to form the North-West Europe market coupling (NWE).[69] The ultimate goal is an EU-wide integrated electricity market with converging prices.[70] Finally, it is worth mentioning that the EU energy 'aquis' is also applied by the Members of the

---

[63] See Article 8 of Regulation (EC) 714/2009 of the European Parliament and of the Council on conditions for access to the network for cross-border exchanges in electricity and repealing Regulation (EC) 1228/2003 (13 July 2009) OJ 2009/L 211/15, 20.

[64] Ibid.

[65] Commission Regulation (EU) 838/2010 on laying down guidelines relating to the inter-transmission system operator compensation mechanism and a common regulatory approach to transmission charging (23 September 2010) OJ 2010/L 250/5.

[66] Regulation (EC) 714/2009 of the European Parliament and of the Council on conditions for access to the network for cross-border exchanges in electricity and repealing Regulation (EC) 1228/2003 (13 July 2009) OJ 2009/L 211/15, 22.

[67] Commission Regulation (EU) 2015/1222 establishing a guideline on capacity allocation and congestion management (24 July 2015) OJ 2015/L 197/24.

[68] On the mechanism of market coupling in general see above in Sect. 2.2.5, p. 34.

[69] Energy Charter Secretariat (2015), p. 50.

[70] The European Commission has defined a 'target design model' for electricity markets based on the principles of 'energy only' and 'market coupling'. See also Keay (2013).

Energy Community, an international organization currently comprising nine neighbouring states of the EU.[71]

3.2.1.3 Outlook

The project of a European internal market for electricity is not yet fully completed. Nonetheless, even though differences persist between Member States with respect to market concentration, the degree of interconnection and other aspects, the former patchwork of foreclosed national electricity markets is a thing of the past.[72] The EU has come a long way from harmonizing certain singular aspects and providing for the non-discriminatory transit of electricity to a largely liberalized and almost fully unbundled electricity sector where consumers can freely choose their supplier. The existence of regulations laying down common grid codes to be implemented by market actors is another feature which reflects the considerable progress the EU has made. The liberalization process, which the EU regards as a precondition to the successful integration of electricity markets, has been implemented at the national level and the EU is currently in the process of coupling regional marketplaces. The markets already coupled can be seen as steppingstones towards a single EU-wide electricity market.

The three consecutive energy packages were developed against the background of an electricity sector initially characterized by large-scale, centralized power plants serving a limited area. As this concept is in the process of changing profoundly, new market rules are necessary. The EU legislator has responded to this challenge by adopting the 'Clean Energy for all Europeans' legislative package in 2018.[73] The new market design contained therein takes into account the increasing share of decentralized renewable energy generation and the increasingly proactive role of electricity consumers.

Cross-border transmission capacity remains the most important bottleneck to achieving further market integration in the EU.[74] Long-term visions include a European 'Supergrid' as a lay-over grid connecting large-scale renewable energy generation sites all over Europe. A 'Mediterranean ring' could also involve North Africa in the single electricity market project. South-East Europe will also be integrated into the single electricity market in the near future.[75] While the process

---

[71] Treaty Establishing the Energy Community (signed on 25 October 2005) OJ 2006/L 198/18.

[72] See also Glachant and Ruester (2014).

[73] European Commission, 'Clean Energy for all Europeans Package Completed: Good for Consumers, Good for Growth and Jobs, and Good for the Planet' Press Release (22 May 2019).

[74] ACER, 'Market Monitoring Report 2012' (01 December 2012) 69. https://www.acer.europa.eu/ Official_documents/Acts_of_the_Agency/Publication/ACER%20Market%20Monitoring%20 Report%202012.pdf.

[75] The year 2002 marked the start of the 'Athens Process' named after the place where the respective Memorandum of Understanding was signed, which foresees the creation of a regional South-East European energy market with the aim of eventual integration into the EU internal electricity market.

of creating the single electricity market has already taken almost 30 years, no comparable regional market with a similar degree of integration has yet been established anywhere in the world.[76] Even in purely national systems, many electricity markets remain more fragmented and isolated than the emerging EU single market for electricity.

3.2.2 Electricity Trade Among the US, Canada and Mexico

The energy markets of the three members of the Canada-United States-Mexico Agreement (CUSMA) are characterized by interdependencies but they are far from fully integrated.[77] The energy trade relationships remain bilateral rather than trilateral.[78] Oil and gas are traded in considerable volumes, with most flows going from Canada to the US.[79] Compared to trading volumes of fossil fuels, electricity trade among the three countries is still rather limited. The share of US-Mexico electricity trade, for example, amounts to less than 0.01% of total US electricity consumption.[80] US-Canada electricity trade is slightly more robust and continuously increasing.[81] While none of the three countries appears to generally depend on the import of electricity, the potential mutual advantages of cross-border trade have been recognized. Among these advantages are the exploitation of complementary generation and load profiles, increasing system stability, and providing emergency assistance.[82]

3.2.2.1 Development and State of Interconnection

In the US, five different frequency areas, the so-called 'interconnections', have emerged over time, with one of them stretching into Canada. These are the Western

---

The MoU was superseded by the Energy Community Treaty signed in 2005 by the European Commission and several South-East European states. See Karova (2011), pp. 80 *et seq*.

[76] Glachant and Ruester (2014), p. 222.

[77] Fickling and Schott (2011), p. 18. On 30 November 2018, the three NAFTA parties signed the text of a revised Agreement, the Canada-United States-Mexico Agreement (CUSMA). It entered into force and replaced the NAFTA on 1 July 2020 upon ratification by all three countries. See Canada-United States-Mexico Agreement (signed on 30 November 2018, entry into force 1 July 2020) text available at https://international.gc.ca/trade-commerce/trade-agreements-accords-commerciaux/agr-acc/cusma-aceum/text-texte/toc-tdm.aspx?lang=eng.

[78] Pineau et al. (2004), p. 1468.

[79] Fickling and Schott (2011), p. 18. According to the Department of Natural Resources of Canada, 93% of Canada's total energy exports were destined for the US in 2014, amounting to almost $140 billion. Natural Resources Canada (2015), p. 5.

[80] U.S. Energy Information Administration (2013).

[81] International Energy Agency (2020), p. 38.

[82] U.S. Energy Information Administration (2015).

Interconnection, the Eastern Interconnection, the Texas Interconnection, and the Quebec and Alaska Interconnections. These interconnections are made up of AC transmission lines and operate at a frequency of 60 Hz, but are not synchronized among each other. A few DC lines tie the synchronous areas together and allow for the exchange of electricity in modest volumes.[83] Most of these interconnections are subdivided into so-called 'balancing' or 'operating' regions (which do not usually correspond to state boundaries), where transmission planning and operation are the responsibility of a single entity.[84]

Electricity transmission between Canada and the US has existed since 1901, when a line was constructed over the border at a hydropower station on the Niagara Falls.[85] Today, more than 30 electricity transmission lines connect the US and Canada.[86] Alberta and Quebec are interconnected with the Western Interconnection of the US.[87] Canada exports about 10% of its electricity generated domestically to the US, which is the only Canadian electricity export destination.[88] The Canadian electricity sector is characterized by large hydropower generation facilities and an increasing penetration of other RES, mainly wind power. For the US, electricity from Canada amounts to 98% of total electricity imports, and 2% of domestic electricity consumption.[89] While Canadian imports are generally of minor or no significance for the electricity supply of most US states, some states in the vicinity of the Canadian border do rely substantially on imports from Canada.[90] New England and New York are responsible for the bulk of electricity imports from Canada, followed by Minnesota and North Dakota.[91]

The Pacific Northwest region of the US is exporting more electricity to Canada (mostly British Columbia[92]) than it is importing, especially in periods of high precipitation and corresponding high watermarks in rivers and reservoirs, due to its considerable hydropower generating capacity.[93] Although the current trade volumes are small, the transmission lines between the US and Canada constitute an important infrastructure for the Northern states of the US, not least because of the

---

[83] International Energy Agency (2014), p. 39.

[84] Ibid.

[85] U.S. Department of Energy (2015), p. 6-3.

[86] U.S. Energy Information Administration (2015).

[87] Western Electricity Coordinating Council, '2016 State of Interconnection' https://www.wecc.biz/Reliability/2016%20SOTI%20Final.pdf.

[88] Natural Resources Canada (2015), p. 5.

[89] Ibid.

[90] Fickling and Schott (2011), p. 18; see also WTO Secretariat (2010), p. 52.

[91] U.S. Energy Information Administration (2015).

[92] US exports are overall less significant to Canadian provincial electricity supply with the exception of British Columbia, which gets almost 10% of its electricity supply from US states. Fickling and Schott (2011), p. 18.

[93] U.S. Energy Information Administration (2015).

reliable and abundant hydropower facilities in Canada.[94] Some Canadian generators have prioritized exporting their electricity to consumers across the border rather than opting for domestic trade.[95] Projects currently under construction between the two CUSMA Members will further increase bilateral trade in electricity.[96]

US-Mexican electricity systems are less integrated than those of the US and Canada. The southern US states of California, New Mexico and Texas each share several small cross-border transmission lines with neighbouring Mexican states. The first cross-border lines were built in 1905 for the exchange of electricity between private utilities on both sides of the border.[97] Baja California shares a few transmission lines with the South of California on the US side (belonging to the Western Interconnection), mainly for the supply of electricity to the San Diego urban area.[98] Texas exchanges limited volumes of electricity with the Mexican states of Tamaulipas and Chihuahua via low voltage AC lines, leaving the connected systems in independent operation.[99] Exchanges occur mainly during emergency situations. A 230 kV line to connect a large wind farm on the Mexican side of the border with the California grid was recently put into operation.[100]

While the present cross-border electricity flows between Mexico and the US are small, increased amounts of power generated from wind and solar on the Mexican side of the border could potentially be exported to the consumption centres on the California coast and in Texas in the future.[101]

3.2.2.2 The Regulatory and Institutional Framework

No specific regulatory framework with respect to electricity is in place between the three NAFTA Members. Cooperation takes place mainly on a voluntary basis, and the North American Electric Reliability Council (NERC) fulfils the important role of ensuring a certain degree of cooperation of the transmission systems by developing

---

[94] Ibid.

[95] Cabrera-Colorado (2018), p. 86, citing U.S. Department of Energy (2015), p. 6-6.

[96] These include a mostly underground 330-mile HVDC line linking renewable generation sites in Quebec with the New York City Metropolitan Area (Champlain Hudson Power Express) which is scheduled for commissioning in 2025 and the 500 kV so-called 'Great Northern Transmission Line' from Manitoba to Minnesota which was energized during the final months of 2019 and has since delivered hydropower from Manitoba in Canada to consumption centres in Minnesota. Several applications recently filed for Presidential permits in the field of cross-border electricity transmission with Canada suggest a growing demand for Canadian hydropower in the U.S, partly to meet the climate-related targets of some states. U.S. Department of Energy (2015), p. 6-7.

[97] U.S. Energy Information Administration (2013).

[98] Ibid.

[99] Ibid.

[100] Mark Del Franco, 'Meet the Wind Project that Knows no Borders' *North American Wind Power* (Southbury, CT, February 2016) https://nawindpower.com.

[101] Fickling and Schott (2011), p. 18; U.S. Department of Energy (2015), p. 6-9.

and enforcing reliability standards in the electricity sector. Three regional entities of NERC provide their services across the border into Canada.[102] The Western Electricity Coordinating Council (WERC), which is an entity tasked with the creation, monitoring and enforcement of reliability standards, is comprised of 14 states of the Western US, two Canadian provinces (Alberta and British Columbia) and the northern part of Baja California.[103]

There has been some convergence in the administration and operation of the transmission systems between the US and Canada. As already mentioned, some of the synchronous interconnections of mainland US extend into Canada. A large part of the transmission system in the US is administered by a regional transmission organization (RTO) or an independent system operator (ISO), the roles and responsibilities of which are comparable to TSOs in Europe. The RTOs and ISOs operate under the jurisdiction of the Federal Energy Regulatory Commission (FERC). The ten currently existing RTOs consolidated a patchwork of 130 local service providers, each responsible for a small part of the system.[104] Some Canadian provinces have joined the ISO/RTO scheme.[105]

In the absence of meaningful sector-specific trade regulation in the region, general trade policy plays an important role in the governance of electricity trade among Canada, Mexico and the US. Before the entry into force of NAFTA in 1994, the trade relations between the three countries were governed by the GATT of 1947 and the Canada-US Free Trade Agreement (CUSFTA), which entered into force in January 1989.[106] The CUSFTA included a chapter on energy which, apart from incorporating core GATT obligations and laying down a few GATT-plus provisions, also entailed some specific provisions with respect to electricity.[107] These primarily concerned an obligation on the part of the American utility active in the border region with British Columbia to grant access to cross-border transmission networks ('interties') based on the MFN treatment principle.[108] When NAFTA entered into force in 1994, the energy provisions that were bundled in Chapter 6 of the Agreement were largely modelled on the CUSFTA. There was also an explicit clarification

---

[102] U.S. Department of Energy (2015), p. 6-6.

[103] Additional information can be found on the website of the Western Electricity Coordinating Council (WECC) at https://www.wecc.org.

[104] Hufbauer and Schott (2005), p. 399.

[105] Alberta and Ontario are both operated by separate ISOs. The transmission system of Manitoba is administered by the Midcontinent Independent System Operator, along with the transmission systems of several states in the US Midwest.

[106] Mexico became a Member of the GATT in 1986. Canada and the US were both original Members of the GATT 1947.

[107] For details see Nakagawa (2016), p. 191.

[108] Annex 905.2 (2) of the Canada-United States Free Trade Agreement (2 January 1988) 27 I.L.M. 281 (1989). ('The United States of America shall cause the Bonneville Power Administration to modify its Intertie Access Policy so as to afford British Columbia Hydro treatment no less favourable than the most favourable treatment afforded to utilities located outside the Pacific Northwest').

that energy regulatory measures were subject to the NAFTA disciplines on national treatment, import and export restrictions, and export taxes.[109] Furthermore, NAFTA's energy chapter included a clarification with respect to the application of certain exceptions of the GATT to energy export restrictions.[110] The revised version of the NAFTA Agreement, the Canada-United-States-Mexico Agreement (CUSMA), does not continue the tradition of a separate energy chapter. As opposed to the telecommunications sector, which is covered through a separate chapter in the CUSMA, the former Chapter 6 of the initial NAFTA on energy was removed by the negotiators.[111] According to a statement by the Canadian authorities, this does not fundamentally alter the obligations previously assumed under Chapter 6 of NAFTA as individual provisions of relevance can now be found across the text of CUSMA.[112] Furthermore, the relationships in the energy sector between Canada and the US will be additionally informed by a side letter on energy to the CUSMA.[113] An annex to the letter includes commitments on enhanced regulatory transparency and cooperation. These bilaterally agreed disciplines will not affect the rights and obligations of Mexico. In the side letter, Canada and the US 'recognize the importance of enhancing the integration of North American energy markets based on market principles (...)'.[114] More concretely, the Parties agree to maintain or establish independent regulatory authorities in the energy sector.[115] Finally and of great importance for electricity trade, Canada and the US subscribe to ensuring access to electric transmission facilities and pipelines 'that is neither unduly discriminatory nor unduly preferential' and that tolls, rates or charges for access to the infrastructure are just and reasonable.[116]

An important limitation on the liberalization of energy trade in the region has consistently been the special status of Mexico's state-owned energy sector and the dominant role of its vertically integrated monopolies—Pemex and Comisión Federal

---

[109] WTO Secretariat (2010), p. 180.

[110] Article 605 of the North American Free Trade Agreement (17 December 1992) 32 I.L.M. 289 (1993).

[111] Reportedly, this happened at a rather advanced stage of CUSMA negotiations upon request by the Mexican Government which assumed office in December 2018. See Weekes et al. (2019).

[112] Government of Canada, 'Canada-United States-Mexico Agreement: Energy Provisions Summary' https://www.international.gc.ca/trade-commerce/trade-agreements-accords-commerciaux/agr-acc/cusma-aceum/energy-energie.aspx?lang=eng.

[113] Government of Canada, Letter from the U.S./Letter from Canada on Energy (30 November 2018) https://www.international.gc.ca/trade-commerce/assets/pdfs/agreements-accords/cusma-aceum/letter-energy.pdf.

[114] Ibid, Article 3. This could specifically enhance coordination between the two countries in the electricity sector. See to this respect Kirkland & Ellis, Blogpost: USMCA Energy & Environmental Takeaways https://www.kirkland.com/publications/blog-post/2020/09/usmca-energy-and-environmental-takeaways.

[115] Government of Canada (n 288), Article 4 of the US-Canada Side Letter.

[116] Ibid, Article 5.

de Electricidad (CFE).[117] Mexico was able to secure several exemptions from the energy-related provisions on goods, services and investment in NAFTA. After the entry into force of NAFTA, the CFE retained its right to supply electricity as a public service.[118] Mexico allowed for independent power production (IPP) and foreign investment into IPP generating sites, but required the electricity generated to be sold to the CFE under bilaterally agreed contracts.[119] Furthermore, in cases where an IPP located in Mexico and an electric utility from another NAFTA Member wanted to engage in cross-border electricity trade, CFE would negotiate the terms and conditions, which the NAFTA Members could subject to regulatory approval.[120] In the years following the entry into force of NAFTA, the Agreement did not function as a catalyst for reform of the domestic energy sector in Mexico.[121] It was not until 2013 that a fundamental reform of the Mexican energy sector was set in motion by former President Enrique Peña Nieto. The reform amended the relevant Articles 27 and 28 of the Mexican constitution and introduced a new Electric Industry Law which became effective in August 2014.[122] The aim of the reform was to introduce competition and to allow foreign investment into the formerly foreclosed and state-owned sector dominated by CFE.[123] The reform abolishes the single buyer model and allows private electricity generators to sell to certain customers directly or via the wholesale market.[124] The Electric Industry Law also introduces the principle of open access to transmission and distribution grids.[125] Furthermore, Independent System Operators are established for managing electricity transmission.[126] Whereas the old regime did not foresee provisions for interconnection with other countries and relied on model contracts, the National Energy Control Center (CENACE) can now enter into agreements with system operators from the US.[127] Market actors are allowed to import and export electricity, subject to a permit requirement.[128]

---

[117] Hufbauer and Schott (2005), p. 418. See also Cabrera-Colorado (2018), p. 89.

[118] See Art. 602.3 para 1 c of NAFTA (n 285); see also Rios-Herran and Poretti (2012), p. 359.

[119] Annex 602.3 5 (c) of NAFTA (n 285); see also Cabrera-Colorado (2018), p. 93.

[120] Annex 602.3 5 (c) of NAFTA (n 285) ('Where an IPP located in Mexico and an electric utility of another Party consider that cross-border trade in electricity may be in their interests, each relevant Party shall permit these entities and CFE to negotiate terms and conditions of power purchase and power sale contracts. The modalities of implementing such supply contracts are left to the end users, suppliers and CFE and may take the form of individual contracts between CFE and each of the other entities. Each relevant Party shall determine whether such contracts are subject to regulatory approval.')

[121] Rios-Herran and Poretti (2012), p. 336.

[122] Ley de la Industria Electrica (11 August 2014). https://www.cenace.gob.mx/Paginas/Publicas/MercadoOperacion/Leyes.aspx.

[123] Nakagawa (2016), pp. 191 et seq.

[124] Ibid, at 191.

[125] See Article 4 of the Ley de la Industria Electrica (n 297).

[126] US Department of Energy (2015), p. 6-7.

[127] Cabrera-Colorado (2018), p. 94.

[128] Ibid, at 97.

While both the CUSFTA and the NAFTA have helped facilitate energy trade in North America, neither has brought about harmonization of energy policies nor a significant convergence of prices for energy products.[129] The provisions are far from adequate to integrate the electricity markets into a single market. NAFTA's energy chapter has not provided for the creation of common institutions. Nor did it prescribe harmonized rules on network operation, congestion management or the construction and financing of interconnectors. The important issue of access to infrastructure has only been dealt with at national level and bilaterally, but not specifically in the NAFTA/CUSMA context.[130]

3.2.2.3   Outlook

The electricity markets in North America remain dominated by national policy considerations and federal, state and provincial oversight. Physical interconnection of networks did however begin more than a hundred years ago and is still improving. The potential for renewable energy generation from hydropower and wind (Canada) and wind and solar PV (US and Mexico) correlate with the growing demand for electricity in all three countries. The Canadian and the US markets are integrated to some degree through common power pooling arrangements and the RTO/ISO structure, which has been established in both countries without much regard to national borders. Cooperation is happening through voluntary arrangements and especially through the NERC. Despite all of this, cross-border trade in electricity is still of minor significance in the North American region and prices still differ considerably between the three countries.[131]

The energy sectors of the three countries have evolved in an 'uneven nature'[132] between the pro-competitive and market-oriented policies in the US and Canada and a state-oriented monopolistic electricity sector in Mexico. The entering into force of NAFTA did not change the pre-existing state of affairs, but rather confirmed it by allowing for the almost complete opt-out of Mexico.[133] Whether the 2014 reforms of the Mexican energy sector provide a new impetus to North American electricity integration remains to be seen.

The NAFTA reforms which started in 2018 were seen by some as an opportunity to further the integration of the three electricity markets.[134] At least at first glance at the new Agreement, this hope does not seem to be fulfilled as energy has not received the attention it deserves. Mexico remains cautious to open its domestic

---

[129] Hufbauer and Schott (2005), p. 396.

[130] Rios-Herran and Poretti (2012), p. 336.

[131] The manufacturing sector in Mexico, for example, pays 75% more than their counterparts in the United States. See Lajous (2014), p. 22.

[132] Hufbauer and Schott (2005), p. 426.

[133] Ibid.

[134] Cabrera-Colorado (2018), p. 87.

electricity sector as witnessed by its reported opposition to a full-fledged energy chapter and its abstention from the additional provisions in a (now bilateral) side letter. To what degree CUSMA is a step back from NAFTA will have to be analyzed based on a closer scrutiny of the entire Agreement and the practice of the three contracting parties to the Agreement.

From a political economy perspective, all three countries stand to gain from closer regulatory cooperation and the interconnection of their networks, as well as cooperation on climate change mitigation and the roll-out of renewable energies.[135] California and other progressive states in the US have ambitious plans for emission reductions and the deployment of renewable energies, and Canada and Mexico are also called upon to act following their ratification of the Paris Agreement on Climate Change.[136]

3.2.3 The Southern African Power Pool

The Southern African Power Pool (SAPP) is based on an agreement signed in 1995 by the Member States of the Southern African Development Community (SADC). Out of the currently 16 SADC Members, 12 are participating in the SAPP.[137] The SAPP grew out of the insight that the lack of interconnections divided the Southern African region into two separate and isolated areas, a northern one characterized by hydropower generation and a southern one with generation based largely on thermal power stations.[138] Enabling the exchange of electricity between the 'northern' and 'southern' networks promised the benefits of optimizing the use of energy resources in the whole region and making emergency support possible.[139] Building interconnections to facilitate the creation of an electricity market spanning the entire region was thus one of the main motivations for setting up the SAPP. As electricity demand in Southern Africa is increasing rapidly along with the general industrialization of the region, the electricity industry is becoming not just the backbone of the local economy but also a pillar of regional political integration.[140] The rapidly growing demand is also one of the key challenges for the electricity sector in the region. At

---

[135] Fickling and Schott (2011), p. 19.

[136] In its first Nationally Determined Contribution (NDC) to the Paris Agreement Objectives, Mexico has pledged to reduce its greenhouse gas emissions by 25% in 2030 compared to business as usual. Canada pledged an economy-wide reduction of greenhouse gas emissions of 30% below 2005 levels until 2030. The current status of NDC's can be consulted at the UNFCCC NDC Registry https://www4.unfccc.int/sites/ndcstaging/Pages/Home.aspx.

[137] These are Angola, Botswana, the Democratic Republic of the Congo, Lesotho, Malawi, Mozambique, Namibia, Zambia, South Africa, Swaziland, Tanzania and Zimbabwe.

[138] Renewable Energy Policy Network for the twenty-first Century (REN 21) *SADC Renewable Energy and Energy Efficiency Status Report 2015* (REN 21 Secretariat 2015), p. 26.

[139] Ibid.

[140] Spalding-Fecher et al. (2017), pp. 403 et seq.

the same time, losses in transmission—due to both technical reasons and theft of electricity—remain a serious concern. Increasing efficiency in transmission and distribution is therefore a key objective of regional energy cooperation.

3.2.3.1 Development and State of Interconnection

The region comprising the territories of SADC Member States is characterized by large hydropower reserves in the northern parts, especially along the Zambezi River basin and the Inga in Congo, and extensive coal reserves in the southern regions of Botswana, South Africa and Zimbabwe. The power generation portfolio in the countries of the SADC reflects these resource endowments, with South Africa relying heavily on coal-fired generation and its northern neighbours mostly tapping into the hydropower reserves by building large dams and exchanging the electricity thereby generated. These resource endowments and the ensuing trading opportunities have predetermined much of the development in the expansion of the transmission network.[141]

The first plans to build cross-border electricity transmission lines in Africa date back to the beginning of the twentieth century. The mining industry located in the Witwatersrand Mountains in South Africa was seeking for the large-scale power generation necessary to allow the extension of its operations, and found it in the hydropower potential of the Victoria Falls in Southern Rhodesia (now Zimbabwe).[142] While the project failed mainly due to the technical limitations of long-distance transmission, the supply of electricity to the mining industry was the driving factor for many of the long-distance transmission projects that were realized in the region in the second half of the twentieth century. One of the first such projects was an HVDC transmission link from the Congo River in the DRC to the mines along the Katanga copper belt in Zambia.[143] Another large project involved the construction of the Kariba Dam on the river Zambezi and an adjacent hydropower station in the late 1950s. A 330 kV transmission line was built for this purpose between Zimbabwe and Zambia.[144] In the late 1970s, the Cahora Bassa HVDC transmission line realized the plan to deliver hydropower from the Cahora Bassa Dam on the Zambezi in Mozambique to the Johannesburg region in South Africa.[145]

These large-scale projects were not constructed with the establishment of a regional electricity market in mind but were aimed at delivering electricity from

---

[141] Ibid. See also Economic Consulting Associates, 'Regional Power Sector Integration: Lessons From Global Case Studies and a Literature Review' (ESMAP Briefing Note 004/10, June 2010) 2 http://www.esmap.org/sites/esmap.org/files/BN004-10_REISP-CD_The%20Potential%20of%20 Regional%20Power%20Sector%20Integration-Literature%20Review.pdf.

[142] Economic Consulting Associates (2010), p. 20.

[143] REN 21 (n 313), p. 22.

[144] Economic Consulting Associates (2010), p. 21.

[145] Ibid, at 20.

large generation sites to industrial consumption centres. During the years of the Apartheid regime in South Africa, grid interconnections were reinforced between Zambia, Zimbabwe, and Botswana mainly to reduce their dependence on electricity imports from South Africa.[146] At the same time and because of seasonal power shortages in the three countries, the South African electric utility Eskom was actively seeking to strengthen interconnections with the northern neighbours to allow for exports of electricity from coal-fired power plants.[147] Eskom has been an ardent supporter of a regional electricity network ever since, seeking the opportunities in the access of the hydropower resources in the northern SAPP Member States.[148] After the end of Apartheid in South Africa, cooperation in the electricity sector increased and several joint projects were engaged in by South Africa and its neighbours.[149]

While the transmission projects in the decades preceding the foundation of the SAPP demonstrated the advantages of pooling electricity generation from hydropower in the northern region and the large coal reserves in the southern part of the SADC, the interconnections between the two parts remained weak. In 1996, shortly after the SAPP was established, a 400 kV interconnector was constructed between Botswana and Zimbabwe. This further strengthened the electricity links between the northern and southern parts of the SADC.[150]

Several transmission projects have been brought underway in recent years as part of the SAPP cooperation. A 220 kV interconnector between the Victoria Falls in Zambia and Namibia, spanning a distance of 230 km, was commissioned in 2008.[151] Another important project under the auspices of the SAPP is the 400 kV ZIZABONA line, which is supposed to create a new 'western transmission corridor' among Zimbabwe, Zambia, Botswana and Namibia.[152] Further enlargement of the Western Corridor (involving a total of up to 3000 km of transmission lines between the Congo, South Africa and up to Angola) is under consideration, as well as a 220 kV Mozambique-Malawi interconnector and a link from the SAPP to Tanzania, a Member of the East African Power Pool (EAPP).[153]

3.2.3.2   The Regulatory and Institutional Framework

The energy sector has played an important role in the history of the SADC and its predecessor, the Southern African Development Coordination Conference

---

[146] Ibid, at 8.

[147] Ibid, at 1.

[148] Ibid.

[149] Economic Consulting Associates (2010), p. 22.

[150] REN 21 (n 313) 26.

[151] Economic Consulting Associates (2010), p. 27.

[152] Ibid.

[153] Ibid.

(SADCC).[154] Contributions by these organizations involved a series of transmission infrastructure initiatives and the implementation of specialized committees for sub-sectors like electricity, coal, and biomass.[155] The energy relations between the SADC Member States have been governed by the Energy Protocol, which entered into force in 1998.[156] Three subsidiary bodies have thus far been established by the SADC in the energy field: The SAPP, the Regional Energy Regulators Association (RERA) and the SADC Centre for Renewable Energy and Energy Efficiency (SACREEE).[157] The SAPP was legally established through a Memorandum of Understanding between the 12 governments of the non-island SADC Member States in 1995.[158] Out of these, nine members are part of the interconnected electricity grid in the region.[159] The SAPP is a clear testament to the importance of the energy sector for wider regional political integration, which some see as the principal purpose for its creation.[160]

The establishment and administration of the SAPP are governed by four documents: A Memorandum of Understanding between the participating governments; a Memorandum of Understanding between the electric utilities of the participating Member States; an 'Operating Agreement' and the 'Operating Guidelines'.[161] The SAPP provides a regional forum for cooperation on electricity generation, supply, and the coordinated planning and expansion of transmission capacity.[162] Among the goals explicitly stated in one of the founding documents, one can also find the improved use of hydroelectric energy.[163] The Executive Committee, composed of the Chief Executives of the utilities of the Member States, is the highest authority in the SAPP. While remaining under the supervision of the SADC Secretariat, the SAPP is vested with considerable autonomy with respect to the operation and technical aspects of the integrated electricity system.[164] Electricity markets in the region are characterized by vertically integrated electric utilities, most of which are state-owned and operate under monopolistic conditions.[165] The South African utility

---

[154] REN 21 (n 312), p. 25.

[155] Ibid.

[156] Protocol on Energy in the Southern African Development Community (SADC) Region (signed 24 August 1996) available at https://www.sadc.int/documents-publications/show/Protocol_on_Energy1996.pdf.

[157] REN 21 (n 312), p. 26.

[158] Bowen et al. (1999), pp. 83 et seq. The SAPP excludes the SADC Members of Madagascar, Mauritius and the Seychelles.

[159] Economic Consulting Associates (2010), p. 2.

[160] Ibid, at 23.

[161] Art. 2 SAPP Inter-Utility Memorandum of Understanding (7 December 1994) available at https://www.sadc.int/files/3013/5333/7979/MOU-_Southern_African_Power_Pool_Inter-Utility1994.pdf.

[162] Spalding-Fecher et al. (2017), p. 403.

[163] Art. 1 SAPP Inter-Utility Memorandum of Understanding (n 336).

[164] Economic Consulting Associates (2010), p. 38.

[165] REN 21 (n 312) 54.

Eskom has been instrumental in creating many cross-border transmission lines linking South Africa with its neighbours. It has played a leading role in the construction of the electricity systems of Botswana, Lesotho, Namibia and Swaziland, and exports to these countries have provided important market opportunities.[166] South Africa continues to play an important role as the driver of electricity market integration among the SAPP countries, only in more recent times, the focus has shifted to securing access to low-cost hydropower from the northern neighbours.[167]

While the short-term goals are of a cooperative nature, the establishment of a competitive electricity market for the SADC region remains a main objective of the SAPP.[168] Indeed, it is the intention of SAPP members to move from a 'cooperative pool'—with prices representing average costs of the exporter and avoided costs of the importer—to a 'competitive pool' with prices determined by market principles.[169] In terms of market arrangements, this development is characterised by progress from a near-exclusive reliance on bilateral contracts between SAPP utilities to a day-ahead market established in 2009, on which increasing amounts of the electricity generated in the region are traded. Between 2001 and 2007, the SAPP Members operated the Short-Term Energy Market (STEM). While members continued to rely on bilateral contracts for most of their electricity trade, 5–10% of the total electricity traded was sold via the STEM during the years of its operation.[170] The market was open only to utilities of the Member States and was mainly used to trade the surplus power that had not been covered by the bilateral contracts.[171] The total amount of electricity traded across borders was thus rather small during these years, amounting to only 7% of total electricity generation.[172] A more competitive market was introduced in 2009 with the Day-Ahead Market (DAM). The DAM involves utilities, independent power producers, transmission entities, and distributors.[173] The SAPP Coordination Centre operates the DAM and determines a market-clearing price based on the merit order of power plants.[174]

National regulators for electricity now exist in most SADC countries. Cooperation takes place through the Regional Electricity Regulators Association (RERA), founded in 2002. The role of RERA in electricity cooperation has been limited to facilitating regulatory cooperation, capacity building and information sharing but might evolve further with the growth of the SAPP.[175] In sum, one can conclude that

---

[166]Economic Consulting Associates (2010), p. 1.

[167]Ibid.

[168]Ibid, at 24.

[169]Ibid.

[170]Ibid, at 28.

[171]Ibid.

[172]Ibid.

[173]Ibid, at 29.

[174]Cf. Ibid.

[175]Ibid, at 40.

the SAPP is evolving in the direction of an increasingly liquid short-term electricity market, although bilateral longer-term contracts remain important.

3.2.3.3 Outlook

The Southern African region has a long history of bilateral power trading, the main driving factor being the export of hydropower generated along the large rivers to industrial and mining centres. Commercial arrangements have long been exclusively bilateral, and an electricity market was only established in 2001. While the commercial market arrangements are in place, the volumes of electricity traded on this market remain small for the time being. In comparison to the NAFTA Members' electricity trade relations, the Southern African region exhibits a rather advanced degree of cooperation and integration. The infrastructure needs major upgrades to accommodate more short-term trading in addition to the electricity sold under long-term bilateral contracts. The legal and institutional framework was strengthened somewhat through the creation of the DAM in 2009 but remains rather weak overall. It has been proposed to amend the SADC Energy Protocol modelled on other regional electricity governance experiences and to create a committee of high-level national energy officials.[176]

The massive potential of hydropower in the region will only be effectively developed under cooperative schemes, as demand in a single country is not sufficient to justify such projects.[177] Several of the large-scale infrastructure projects under construction and several more under consideration will lead to increased regional electricity trade. At the same time as these infrastructure projects are securing financing and construction permits, the SAPP Member States are making progress in the development of micro-grids and smaller-scale distributed energy.[178]

3.2.4 The West African Power Pool

The Economic Community of West African States (ECOWAS) is one of the better-known examples of regional economic integration in Africa. The stated overall objective of the 15-Member organization is to promote cooperation and integration, with a view to establishing an economic and monetary union.[179] Nigeria is a dominant player in the region in terms of size, population, and economic prowess,

---

[176] Castalia Strategic Advisors, 'International Experience with Cross-border Power Trading: Report to the Regional Electricity Regulators' Association (RERA) and the World Bank (2009), p. 10.

[177] Eberhard and Shkarathan (2012), p. 17.

[178] REN 21 (n 312), p. 10.

[179] ECOWAS, 'ECOWAS takes steps towards common Monetary Union' (3 April 2019) https://www.ecowas.int/ecowas-takes-steps-towards-common-monetary-union/.

and the ECOWAS Secretariat is located in its capital, Abuja. The other ECOWAS Members are Benin, Burkina Faso, Cape Verde, Gambia, Ghana, Guinea, Guinea-Bissau, Ivory Coast, Liberia, Mali, Niger, Senegal, Sierra Leone and Togo. In more recent times the ECOWAS Members have embarked on the path to electricity market integration. Its energy relationships are similar to the ones in the SADC, but the ECOWAS Member States have different resource endowments and, accordingly, a markedly different generation mix when compared with the Southern African countries. Especially the eastern ECOWAS Member States can count on rich oil and gas resources with Nigeria alone being able to provide gas supply for the whole region for about two decades.[180] In the Western part around Guinea, hydropower plays a more important role. This could be complemented by solar generation in the northern regions closer to the Sahel. In general, the countries with excess hydro capacity are complementary to the neighbouring countries exhibiting excess solar capacity. Most ECOWAS Members experience shortages of supply for a considerable period of the year. Interconnections between national transmission networks could help to level these differences and improve overall access to electricity, which is as low as 18% in Niger and 22% in Sierra Leone.[181] In general, access to electricity is a problem for the ECOWAS region as a whole and electricity consumption per capita is much lower than elsewhere.[182] Losses of electricity are a problem in several national systems.

3.2.4.1 Development and State of Interconnection

The region has a rather long history of cross-border electricity trading. Electricity supply from a hydro plant at the Volta River Dam in Ghana to Togo and Benin began in 1969. Similar to the SADC region, the infrastructure was developed following the conclusion of bilateral long-term supply contracts.[183] Nonetheless, at present electricity trading among ECOWAS member states is happening at quite low volumes, accounting for less than 10% of total energy generated in the region. The creation of the West African Power Pool (WAPP) has given new impetus to the development of transmission infrastructure between the ECOWAS Members.[184] This involves an 'upgrading' of the coastal backbone interconnector between Cote D'Ivoire and Ghana and an interconnector from Ghana to Mali via Burkina Faso. Both projects

---

[180] Castalia Strategic Advisors (2009), p. 50.

[181] According to numbers for 2019 by the World Bank and International Energy Agency. See World Bank, Sustainable Energy for All (SE4ALL) database from the SE4ALL Global Tracking Framework led jointly by the World Bank, International Energy Agency, and the Energy Sector Management Assistance Program, available at https://data.worldbank.org/indicator/EG.ELC.ACCS.ZS. In countries like Ghana and Nigeria, on the other hand, the access rate is much higher with 84% and 55%, respectively.

[182] Pineau (2008), p. 212.

[183] Castalia Strategic Advisors (2009), p. 48.

[184] Ibid.

were envisaged to be in their final stages by late 2021 but have experienced delays. This infrastructure is urgently needed as energy demand is expected to grow significantly over the coming years.[185] Moreover, new hydropower plants in the western part of the ECOWAS region and the exploitation of the vast natural gas resources located in coastal areas will require new transmission lines. The development of large generation plants in countries like Benin and Togo is only feasible if the countries have the possibility of exporting some of the electricity produced as domestic demand is too small to justify the required investments. The infrastructure development for the WAPP project involves identifying a list of priority projects for interconnection. So far, the WAPP Members have been quite successful in attracting funding for the cross-border electricity infrastructure projects.[186]

3.2.4.2 The Regulatory and Institutional Framework

The ECOWAS Treaty was signed in 1975 in Lagos, Nigeria and was revised in 1993.[187] The Treaty itself contains an Article on energy, based on which Members agree to co-ordinate and harmonize their policies and programs in the sector.[188] More specifically, the Members have agreed to 'harmonize their national energy development plans by ensuring particularly the interconnection of electricity distribution networks'.[189]

In 2003, the ECOWAS Members signed an Energy Protocol, aimed at establishing a legal framework for the long-term cooperation in the energy field.[190] Interestingly, the ECOWAS Energy Protocol is closely modelled on the Energy Charter Treaty.[191] The signatories of the Energy Protocol recognize that the ECT principles 'represent the leading internationally accepted basis for the promotion, cooperation, integration and development of energy investment projects and energy trade among sovereign nations'.[192] Just like the ECT, the ECOWAS Energy Protocol focuses on three broad areas: the protection of foreign investments, non-discriminatory trade in energy products, and the resolution of disputes between participating states as well as between foreign investors and host states.[193] By

---

[185] Castalia Strategic Advisors (2009), p. 49.

[186] Reportedly, they were able to raise around 10 billion USD.

[187] Revised Treaty of the Economic Community of West African States (ECOWAS), signed 24 July 1993, entered into force 23 August 1995.

[188] Ibid, Article 28.

[189] Ibid, Article 28 (2) (d).

[190] Cf Article 2 of the ECOWAS Energy Protocol, signed 31 January 2003 (entered into force after ninth ratification in accordance with Article 39 of the Protocol).

[191] Energy Charter Treaty (17 December 1994) 2080 U.N.T.S. 95. On the ECT see also below in Chap. 6, pp. 123 et seq.

[192] Preamble of the ECOWAS Energy Protocol (n 191).

[193] Castalia Strategic Advisors (2009), p. 52.

incorporating the ECT's trade and investment provisions, the Protocol aims at increased investment and facilitating energy trade in the West African Region.[194] The main provisions of the Protocol with respect to trade relate to open access to power generation and transmission facilities and freedom of transit. With respect to investment, the Protocol contains a no less favourable treatment clause and provides for a prohibition of nationalization and expropriation and access to national capital markets.

To create a common electricity market, 14 ECOWAS Members formally established the WAPP in 2006.[195] The WAPP is similar to the SAPP that came into operation a few years earlier.[196] Its aim is to coordinate electricity generation and transmission in the West-African sub-region.[197] While no clear future market structure has yet been agreed upon by the Members, it is not likely that the WAPP will be developed into a short-term market like the SAPP in the foreseeable future. Furthermore, there is a clear focus on providing incentives for the development of new generation and transmission infrastructure. The WAPP plays an active role in this development.[198]

While not all ECOWAS Member States have yet established an independent regulator for electricity, they have collectively established a regional regulator called ECOWAS Regional Electricity Regulatory Authority (ERERA). Among its main tasks are the contribution to creating favourable investment conditions in the region and to assist in the harmonization of national policies and power market structures.[199] To achieve this aim, ERERA can issue technical and commercial rules and resolve disputes among market participants. The establishment of ERERA constitutes an innovation as it is so far one of just two regional electricity regulators in the world.[200]

Markets in the ECOWAS Member States exhibit diverse structures, some characterized by vertical integration, others by partial unbundling. Nigeria has prescribed unbundling and the privatization of its formerly state-dominated electricity sector.[201] Cote D'Ivoire is another successful model for liberalization in the region, after its

---

[194]Cf. Article 2 of the ECOWAS Energy Protocol (n 191).

[195]Cf. the Articles of Agreement of the West African Power Pool Organization and Functions, available at https://erera.arrec.org/en/articles-of-agreement-of-the-west-african-power-pool-organi zation-and-functions/. The idea to establish a power pool in West Africa dates back to 1992 when it was first suggested within the ECOWAS bureaucracy. By 1999 the heads of the ECOWAS Member States had agreed to formally establish a power pool. The signing of the WAPP Articles of Agreement in July 2006 then marked the official inauguration of the project.

[196]Gnansounou et al. (2007), p. 4143.

[197]Ibid.

[198]Castalia Strategic Advisors (2009), p. 48.

[199]Supplementary Act A/SA.2/01/08 creating ERERA, available at https://erera.arrec.org/wp-content/uploads/2018/07/Resolution-No-011-ERERA-17_Rules-of-PracticeProcedures_ERERA.pdf.

[200]Ikeonu (2017), p. 8.

[201]Adhekpukoli (2018), pp. 1 et seq.

Electricity Code of 2014 formally ended the state monopoly on transmission and distribution as well as imports and exports and other activities.[202] It must be stressed that in some states, the regulators might not be endowed with sufficient powers to effectively oversee a liberalized electricity market. Moreover, some markets might simply be too small to successfully implement an unbundling regime. As a certain level of harmonization between these diverse markets was seen as desirable, the ECOWAS Council of Ministers adopted the Directive on the Organisation of the Regional Electricity Market (the 'Market Directive') in June 2013. It can be seen as the first step towards a future common market design, as it lays down some minimum market criteria to be adhered to by the ECOWAS Members.[203] The Directive also stipulates that market integration shall proceed in three phases. The first phase was finalized in 2012 and involves trading based on model bilateral contracts.

Transmission pricing takes place according to a regional transmission pricing methodology approved by ERERA. In the second phase, trading takes place on a combination of bilateral contracts and a short-term day-ahead market. The ECOWAS regional electricity market was officially launched in June 2018.[204] The third and final phase is envisaged to allow trading on the basis of a wholesale electricity market with sufficient liquidity to function efficiently.[205]

3.2.4.3   Outlook

The West African Power Pool is a rather ambitious example of regional electricity market integration. While at present cross-border electricity flows still mainly stem from bilateral exchanges and long-term contracts based on an ad hoc regulatory framework, the picture is slowly changing, as the contours of a common regulatory framework are emerging. Rules are already in place with respect to transmission pricing and priority for certain generators in cases of congestion.

Where the project will ultimately lead is uncertain as clear long-term objectives are currently missing. Short- and medium-term measures include improving the management of utilities and extending cross-border transmission infrastructure.[206] The latter would especially benefit the landlocked member states of ECOWAS which are experiencing generation shortages like Mali, Burkina Faso and Niger.[207]

---

[202] Along with Cape Verde, Cote D'Ivoire is the only WAPP member country with an electricity sector where private ownership prevails. See Adebayo and Adeniji (2018), p. 22.

[203] This concerns, among others, an unbundling of the accounts for the different segments of the market, access requirements for the transmission infrastructure and harmonization of contracts. Ikeonu (2017), pp. 10 et seq.

[204] Press Release, 'Launching of ECOWAS Electricity Market' (13 July 2018) http://www.ecowapp.org/en/events/press-release-%E2%80%93-launching-ecowas-electricity-market.

[205] Ikeonu (2017), p. 10.

[206] Pineau (2008), p. 221.

[207] Castalia Strategic Advisors (2009), p. 49.

The Energy Protocol, which borrows much from the ECT, is a comprehensive treaty laying down general principles of investment protection and non-discriminatory energy trade. This regulatory framework's focus on 'traditional' trade issues contrasts with other regional electricity integration initiatives, which lack rules for non-discrimination between states.[208] In the medium-term future, the WAPP infrastructure could be extended into central Africa (and thereby tapping into the electricity generated by the dams along the Inga River) and even as far as Morocco.

3.2.5   The Central American Power Market

Several countries of Central America are currently working together in the pursuit of a twofold objective: the creation of a competitive electricity market for the region and the development of the infrastructure required to connect all countries and allow for long-distance transmission of electricity.[209] The joint initiative, which is called *Sistema de Interconexión Eléctrica de los Países de América Central* (SIEPAC), comprises Guatemala, Panama, El Salvador, Honduras, Nicaragua and Costa Rica. Hydropower has been the prevalent source of electricity generation in the region and more recently fossil fuel-fired power plants have been added.[210] Most households in the region still use biomass for energy supply.[211] Ultimately, the initiative is envisaged to result in a Regional Electricity Market (Mercado Eléctrico Regional or MER), which is meant to contribute to bringing down consumer prices of electricity and to improving the security of supply.[212]

3.2.5.1   Development and State of Interconnection

Cross-border electricity interconnections in the Central American region already exist, but only allow for very small volumes of electricity to be transmitted between the countries.[213] The new SIEPAC transmission line, which is operating at 230 kV and spanning more than 1800 km, is envisaged to provide the backbone for regional transmission by allowing 300 MW of electricity to be transmitted in a first phase. The line will range from Panama to Guatemala and connect the markets of all Central American countries.[214] Anticipating future expansion of this network, tower

---

[208] Ibid, at 23.

[209] Prada and Bowman (2004), pp. 1 et seq.; Martin (2010), p. 5.

[210] Martin (2010), p. 2.

[211] Ibid.

[212] Ibid, at 5.

[213] Prada and Bowman (2004), p. 3.

[214] Martin (2010), p. 3.

infrastructure has been put in place to allow adding a second circuit at a later point.[215] This could enhance the capacity of the interconnection to 600 MW. The transmission circuit also includes 16 high voltage substations and allows for bi-directional transmission. Financing for the SIEPAC infrastructure was provided to a large part by the Inter-American Development Bank (IADB).[216]

The objectives of this interconnection initiative include enhancing the security of supply in the interconnected countries, lowering the costs of generation, and reducing the need for reserve capacities.[217]

The countries connected through SIEPAC will also be linked to the neighbouring Andean Electrical Interconnection System (SINEA) through a cross-border line between Panama and Colombia.[218] SINEA is comprised of Colombia, Ecuador, Peru, Bolivia and Chile.[219]

3.2.5.2 The Regulatory and Institutional Framework

The regulatory frameworks for the electricity sector differ considerably between the individual Central American countries. Some continue to operate under a single-buyer model; others have allowed a wholesale market with private generators to emerge.[220] To establish a regulatory framework for regional electricity trade, the 'Tratado Marco Del Mercado Eléctrico de América Central' (the 'Framework Treaty') was agreed upon in 1996 between Guatemala, El Salvador, Honduras, Nicaragua, Costa Rica, and Panama.[221] The Framework Treaty seeks to establish the conditions for integrating their national electricity markets into a regional one; allowing for more private participation in the electricity sector; establishing non-discriminatory and transparent conditions for participation; and ensuring that the benefits of regional integration reach all the inhabitants of the countries involved.[222] Article 4 of the Framework Treaty declares that 'the market should develop gradually from an initially limited situation towards a broader, more open and competitive situation underpinned by existing and future infrastructure'. The

---

[215] Ibid.

[216] The IADB reportedly issued a US$170 million loan to finance part of the total estimated cost of US$385 Million. See Castalia Strategic Advisors (2009), p. 40.

[217] Inter-American Development Bank, 'Energy Integration in Central America: Full Steam Ahead' (25 June 2013) https://www.iadb.org/en/news/webstories/2013-06-25/energy-integration-in-cen tral-america,10494.html.

[218] Ochoa et al. (2013), p. 268. The line is planned for commissioning in 2024.

[219] For a detailed description of the development of the SIEPAC project see Del Barrio et al. (2017).

[220] Prada and Bowman (2004), p. 2.

[221] Tratado Marco y Protocolo del Mercado Eléctrico de América Central (signed 30 December 1996), henceforth referred to as 'Framework Treaty', text available at https://www.enteoperador. org/archivos/document/Tratado-Marco-EOR-2019.pdf. The Framework Treaty became legally binding after sufficient ratifications in January 1998.

[222] Article 2 of the Framework Treaty (n 221).

Regional Electricity Market (MER) thus established is meant to be complementary to the existing national markets.[223]

There are three main bodies responsible for operating and governing the Market, all mandated by the Framework Treaty. One is the *Comisión Regional de Interconexión Electrica (CRIE)*, which functions as a regional regulatory body and which is responsible for setting the terms of the commercial relationships within the market.[224] With respect to the development, construction, ownership and operation of the cross-border infrastructure, the Empresa Proprietaria de la Red (EPR) is the responsible entity. The EPR is a consortium of public and private organizations from Central America, Mexico, Colombia and Spain established on the basis of the Framework Treaty in 1998.[225] A third important body is the Ente Operador Regional (EOR), the regional system operator. It is responsible for the dispatch of generation, financial settlements, and information exchange via the national system operators.[226] A further task is the formulation of an indicative regional expansion plan for generation and transmission.[227] Promising first steps have already been undertaken in this respect.

3.2.5.3 Outlook

The SIEPAC project is unique in several respects when compared with the other regional electricity market initiatives discussed here. It relies heavily on a single infrastructure project, the SIEPAC line. Market and regulatory arrangements have been designed around this infrastructure. As a rather advanced feature of regional electricity market integration, the SIEPAC Members have established a regional regulatory authority. This is a feature that is lacking in other regional arrangements like the SAPP. For these reasons, in the words of one author, 'the level of integration is exceptional in the region for any kind of activity'.[228] The project remains controversial, however. Critics doubt that the objective of lowering electricity generating costs and prices for all participating countries will be attained. It is also argued that new capacity will mainly, if not entirely, consist of large hydropower plants, with corresponding environmental and social challenges.[229] The role of Colombia and Mexico remains pivotal in the process and it is suggested that Mexico sees the SIEPAC as a major opportunity for electricity exports to Central

---

[223] Prada and Bowman (2004), p. 4.

[224] Ibid.

[225] Martin (2010), p. 4.

[226] Castalia Strategic Advisors (2009), p. 36.

[227] Ibid.

[228] Sempértegui (2017), p. 437.

[229] Martin (2010), p. 5.

America.[230] It will be interesting to see how the SIEPAC will relate to neighbouring electricity markets like the Andean electricity market of Colombia, Ecuador, Peru and Venezuela which has not reached the same level of integration as SIEPAC.[231]

3.2.6   Interim Conclusions on Regional Electricity Markets

Regional electricity markets have been emerging on four continents. While some of the cross-border electricity transmission projects predate the first attempts at regional economic and political integration in their respective regions, most of them have been seized and absorbed by those wider political integration efforts. The regional electricity integration initiatives differ markedly in terms of their ambition, stages of development, and the overall rate of success. Regional electricity integration ranks high on the political agenda of EU institutions and has been gaining importance in the context of the two African as well as the Central American initiatives discussed. In the North American context, it plays a less important role, but an increasing bilateral integration can be detected between the US and Canada. Differences between the regional electricity initiatives were also identified with respect to the two concrete dimensions analysed above—physical interconnection and regulatory development.

The regulatory arrangements are unique in each case. The WAPP is special in that it is the only example where an already existing international legal instrument, the ECT, has been used as a blueprint for the formulation of general rules of non-discriminatory trade and investment. In North America, Chapter 6 of the NAFTA Agreement provided an energy-specific regulatory frame for Canada, Mexico and the US until 2018, when the NAFTA was superseded by the CUSMA. Overall, there is a wide difference in regulatory 'depth' in the various regional projects, ranging from broad declarations of intent to the binding regulation of issues such as costs of hosting cross-border electricity flows, charges for access to the interconnectors, and congestion management.

The EU internal electricity market has made the furthest advances with regard to both infrastructure and regulation. Its regulatory framework has evolved from a regime focused on general transit provisions to common network codes dealing with complex technical issues and presupposing a high degree of cooperation between national system operators. A rather unique feature of the EU internal electricity market is that it started by prescribing a far-reaching liberalization of national electricity markets as a first step. The other regional initiatives did not adopt this approach, focusing instead on non-discrimination, congestion rules and in some cases technical harmonization. While in the EU the push towards transferring regulatory powers to a central regulatory authority like ACER has so far been

---

[230]Del Barrio et al. (2017), p. 126.

[231]As Sempértegui (2017), p. 433, notes, this is mainly due to concerns over sovereignty.

resisted by Member States, the WAPP and SIEPAC have successfully created regional regulatory authorities to oversee the integration of their respective electricity markets. With respect to the WAPP, the regional regulator (ERERA) has comparatively far-reaching powers which include intervention in domestic markets to ensure conformity with regional rules.[232]

Whether these regional markets could be linked up to form inter-continental transmission grids and a possible future 'global grid' is the subject of ongoing discussions.[233] Single intercontinental electricity lines already exist and several more are under consideration.[234] However, it should also be pointed out that a number of countries are still maintaining completely isolated systems without any interconnections to neighbouring countries.[235]

3.2.7 Steps Towards a Global Interconnection of Electricity Networks

While the twentieth century witnessed the construction of electricity transmission lines allowing electricity to be transmitted over ever-longer distances with increasing efficiency, electricity networks have remained confined to the continental level with very few exceptions.[236] From a theoretical point of view, the benefits of cross-border trade identified above (a better balance of demand and supply, the minimization of required reserves, alleviation of the storage problem) would apply in an amplified manner to electricity interconnection on a global scale.[237] Moreover, as the German Advisory Council on Global Change (WBGU) wrote in 2004, '[t]here is no doubt that in the long term, the use of renewable energy would require a more or less global

---

[232] Ikeonu (2017), p. 8.

[233] This is the explicit vision pursued by the Global Energy Interconnection Development and Cooperation Organization (GEIDCO), as outlined in the book of the former chairman of State Grid Corporation of China, Liu Zhenya. Liu (2015).

[234] Das Neves (2014), pp. 177 et seq.; Asian Development Bank, Power Interconnection Project to Strengthen Power Trade Between Afghanistan, Turkmenistan, Pakistan (ADB Press Release 28 February 2018) https://www.adb.org/news/power-interconnection-project-strengthen-power-trade between afghanistan turkmenistan pakistan.

[235] Apart from most island states, one prominent example is the Republic of Korea. See Energy Charter Secretariat (2015), p. 77.

[236] Cf. Chatzivasileiadis et al. (2013), p. 373 who remark that 'Comparing the electricity network with networks of similar magnitude, such as the transportation or the telecommunications network, one realizes that several of them have already managed to span the globe. It seems that the only network of similar size which does not form interconnections over the world is the electric power grid.'

[237] As Chatzivasileiadis et al. (2013), p. 379 have demonstrated for the US, importing renewable electricity from Europe via a submarine cable could be more economical under certain circumstances than continuing to operate domestic fossil-fuel power plants; See also Selivanova (2015), p. 1.

network for electricity to function efficiently.'[238] Indeed, a global electricity network tapping into the vast renewable energy resources located in remote regions of the world would theoretically promise to solve all of humankind's energy problems.[239] In contrast to these theoretical benefits, challenges abound with respect to technical, social, economic and legal issues. So far, therefore, the theoretical case for global interconnection has not translated into concrete projects reaching beyond the planning stages.

Several proposals have been advanced for developing a 'global grid'. Most of these build on already existing continental electricity networks.[240] The idea of a global power grid spanning all continents can be traced back at least to the 1970s.[241] It has since resurfaced in different contexts but has never received wide attention. Attempts to realize large-scale transcontinental infrastructure projects like the 'DESERTEC' initiative have so far failed, not least due to social and political issues.[242] The most recent initiative towards the development of a global grid is being advanced by a coalition of public and private actors under the leadership of the State Grid Corporation of China (SGCC). Its former chairman Zhenya Liu has outlined his vision of a 'Global Energy Interconnection' (GEI) in a book devoted specifically to the subject. In the words of Liu, '[t]he global development of electricity-oriented clean energy in the future will lead to the formation of global electricity trade and electricity markets and invoke new requirements on the global allocation of electric power.'[243] The main idea is to link remote renewable energy generation by long-distance, intercontinental ultra-high-voltage (UHV) lines. The GEI has been given an institutional arm through the Global Energy Interconnection Development and Cooperation Organization (GEIDCO). The initiative was presented at the UN Sustainable Development Summit in 2015 by China's President Xi Jinping, who proposed to 'discuss the construction of Global Energy Interconnection (GEI) to facilitate efforts to meet the global power demand with clean and green energy alternatives'.[244] It has not yet been embraced by other important political players on the global scene. One objective of the GEI is the replacement of fossil energy by electricity, i.e. instead of transporting oil and gas, electricity generated from renewable sources should be transmitted to the places of

---

[238] Selivanova (2015), citing Wissenschaftlicher Beirat der Bundesregierung Globale Umweltveränderungen (German Advisory Council on Global Change), World in Transition. Towards Sustainable Energy Systems (2004) 189. On the concept of a global grid, see also Rudenko and Yershevich (1991); Hammons et al. (1994).

[239] Liu (2015), p. 13.

[240] Chatzivasileiadis et al. (2013), p. 379.

[241] Abbott (2014), p. 1.

[242] On the DESERTEC project see Liliestam and Ellenbeck (2011); Backhaus et al. (2015).

[243] Liu (2015), p. 105.

[244] Jinping (2015).

consumption.[245] To achieve this, a 'global platform for electric power allocation' is envisaged.[246]

The construction of trans-continental electricity interconnections would not necessarily be an antidote to more decentralized and small-scale solutions in the electricity systems. Rather, trans-continental interconnections could complement these developments and serve as a reliable 'back-bone' infrastructure. A series of questions will have to be answered before the development of a global grid can seriously be considered. These concern topics such as financing, sharing of benefits, cybersecurity, and the geopolitical aspects pertaining to conflicts over resources and strategic infrastructure.[247] Most importantly for the focus of the present study, however, the legal framework governing an ever-more global electricity trade will have to be considered carefully by international institutions and states willing to engage further in the process.

References

Abbott F (2014) Transfer of technology and a global clean energy grid. Paper Prepared for the World Trade Forum, World Trade Institute

Adebayo A, Adeniji S (2018) Integrated power market in West Africa: an overview. J Public Policy Admin 2:20

Adhekpukoli E (2018) The democratization of electricity in Nigeria. Electricity J 31:1

Agora Energiewende (2015) The European Power System in 2030: flexibility challenges and integration benefits. https://www.agora-energiewende.de/fileadmin/Projekte/2014/Ein-flexibler-Strommarkt-2030/Agora_European_Flexibility_Challenges_Integration_Benefits_WEB_Rev1.pdf

Amundsen E, Bergman L, Andersson B (1998) Competition and prices on the emerging nordic electricity market. Stockholm School of Economics Working Paper Series in Economics and Finance, Working Paper No. 217. Stockholm School of Economics

Backhaus K, Gausling P, Hildebrand L (2015) Comparing the incomparable: lessons to be learned from models evaluating the feasibility of Desertec. Energy 82:905

Booz & Company (2013) Benefits of an integrated European Energy Market. Final Report prepared for the Directorate-General Energy of the European Commission. https://ec.europa.eu/energy/sites/ener/files/documents/20130902_energy_integration_benefits.pdf

Bowen BH, Sparrow FT, Yu Z (1999) Modelling electricity trade policy for the twelve nations of the Southern African Power Pool (SAPP). Utilities Policy 8:183

Cabrera-Colorado O (2018) Increasing U.S.-Mexico cross-border trade in electricity by NAFTA's renegotiation. Energy Law J 39:79

Cain C, Lesser J (2007) A common sense guide to wholesale electricity markets. Bates White Economic Consulting. https://www.bateswhite.com/media/publication/55_media.741.pdf

---

[245] Liu (2015), p. 83 f. As Liu points out, 'Currently, the allocation of capacity of the world's electric power is limited and can hardly satisfy the future development of clean energy. Compared with fossil energy, the current level of global electricity trade is minimal, representing approximately 80 million tons of standard coal or less than 2% of fossil energy trade.' Liu (2015), p. 60.

[246] Ibid.

[247] On the challenges, see also Chatzivasileiadis et al. (2013), p. 77.

Castalia Strategic Advisors (2009) International experience with cross-border power trading: report to the regional electricity regulators' Association (RERA) and the World Bank. https://documents1.worldbank.org/curated/en/843261468006254751/pdf/703710WP0P11140Border0Power0Trading.pdf

Chatzivasileiadis S, Ernst D, Andersson G (2013) The global grid. Renew Energy 57:372

Cohen M (2003) B.C. Hydro's Deep Integration with the U.S. through RTO West. BC Citizens for Public Power. http://www.sfu.ca/~mcohen/publications/Electric/hightens.pdf

Das Neves M (2014) Electricity interconnection and trade between Norway and Russia. Arctic Rev Law Politics 5:177

De Montravel G (2004) European interconnection: state of the Art 2003. In: Bielecki J, Desta MG (eds) Electricity trade in Europe: review of the economic and regulatory challenges. Kluwer Law International, Alphen aan den Rijn

Del Barrio Alvarez D, Komatsuzaki S, Horii H (2017) Regional power sector integration: critical success factors in the Central American electricity market. OIDA J Sustain Dev 7:119

Dralle T (2018) Ownership unbundling and related measures in the EU Energy Sector: foundations, the impact of WTO law and investment protection. Springer, Berlin

Eberhard A, Shkarathan M (2012) Powering Africa: meeting the financing and reform challenges. Energy Policy 42:9

Economic Consulting Associates (2010) Regional power sector integration: lessons from global case studies and a literature review. ESMAP Briefing Note 004/10. https://www.eca-uk.com/wp-content/uploads/2016/10/Regional-Power-Sector-Integration-Lessons-report.pdf

Energy Charter Secretariat (2015) The role of the ECT in fostering regional electricity market integration: lessons learnt from the EU and implications for Northeast Asia. https://www.energycharter.org/fileadmin/DocumentsMedia/Thematic/Northeast_Asia_Study_EN.pdf

Ferrero M (2012) The Andean electricity market: a competition law analysis. Wm Mary Environ Law 36:769

Fickling M, Schott J (2011) NAFTA and climate change. Peterson Institute for International Economics, Washington

Glachant J, Ruester S (2014) The EU internal electricity market: done forever? Utilities Policy 31:221

Gnansounou E, Bayem H, Bednyagin D, Dong J (2007) Strategies for regional integration of electricity supply in West Africa. Energy Policy 35:4142

Gottschal E (2009) the role of an energy agency in regulating an internal energy market: cross-border regulation across the line? In: Roggenkamp M, Hammer U (eds) European Energy Law Report VI. Intersentia, Cambridge

Hammons T, Falcon J, Meisen P (1994) Remote renewable energy resources made possible by International Electrical Interconnections – a Priority for all Continents' (1994) Power Generation. Technology. http://www.geni.org/globalenergy/library/geni/PowerGeneration/remote-renewable-energy%2D%2Dinternational-electrical-interconnections%2D%2Da-priority-for-all-continents/index.shtml

Hooper E, Medvedev A (2009) Electrifying integration: electricity production and the South East Europe regional energy market. Utilities Policy 17:24

Hufbauer G, Schott J (2005) NAFTA revisited: achievements and challenges. Columbia University Press, New York

Ikeonu I (2017) Perspectives on regulating a regional electricity market: the ECOWAS experience. https://erranet.org/wp-content/uploads/2017/09/Winner-2-Ikeonu_ECOWAS_ERRA-Award-2017-4.pdf

International Electrotechnical Commission (2016) Whitepaper: global energy interconnection. https://webstore.iec.ch/publication/26002

International Energy Agency (2014) Seamless Power Markets. https://www.iea.org/reports/seamless-power-markets

International Energy Agency (2020) Electricity Market Report December 2020. https://www.iea.org/reports/electricity-market-report-december-2020

Jinping X (2015) Remarks at the UN sustainable development summit on 26 September 2015, https://sustainabledevelopment.un.org/content/documents/20548china.pdf

Karova R (2011) Regional electricity markets in Europe: focus on the energy community. Utilities Policy 19:80

Keay M (2013) The EU "Target Model" for electricity markets – fit for purpose? Oxford Energy Comment. https://www.oxfordenergy.org/publications/the-eu-target-model-for-electricity-markets-fit-for-purpose

L'Abbate A, Migliavacca G, Calisti R, Martínez-Anido CB, Chaouachi A, Fulli G (2014) Electricity exchanges with North Africa at 2030. In: Cambini C, Rubino A (eds) Regional energy initiatives: MedReg and the energy community. Routledge, Milton Park

Lagendijk V (2008) Electrifying Europe: the power of Europe in the construction of electricity networks. Amsterdam University Press, Amsterdam

Lajous A (2014) Mexican Energy reform. Columbia Center on Global Energy Policy, 22 https://www.energypolicy.columbia.edu/research/reports-and-working-papers/mexican-energy-reform

Liliestam J, Ellenbeck S (2011) Energy security and renewable electricity trade — will Desertec make Europe vulnerable to the "Energy Weapon"? Energy Policy 39:3380

Liu Z (2015) Global energy interconnection. Elsevier, Amsterdam

Martin J (2010) Central America electric integration and the SIEPAC project: from a fragmented market toward a new reality? CIGRE Energy Cooperation and Security in the Hemisphere Task Force 5

Meeus L, Purchala K, Belmans R (2005) Development of the internal electricity market in Europe. Electricity J 18:25

Nakagawa J (2016) Free Trade Agreements and natural resources. In: Matsushita M, Schoenbaum TJ (eds) Emerging issues issues in sustainable development: International Trade Law and policy relating to natural resources, energy, and the environment. Springer, Berlin

Natural Resources Canada (2015) Energy Fact Book 2015–2016. https://www.nrcan.gc.ca/sites/www.nrcan.gc.ca/files/energy/files/pdf/EnergyFactBook2015-Eng_Web.pdf

Ochoa C, Dyner I, Franco C (2013) Simulating power integration in Latin America to assess challenges, opportunities, and threats. Energy Policy 61:267

Pineau P (2008) Electricity sector integration in West Africa. Energy Policy 36:210

Pineau P, Hira A, Froschauer K (2004) Measuring international electricity integration: a comparative study of the power systems under the Nordic Council, MERCOSUR, and NAFTA. Energy Policy 32:1457

Pollitt M, McKenna M (2014) Power pools: how cross-border trade in electricity can help meet development goals. World Bank Blog Post. https://beta-blogs.worldbank.org/trade

Prada J, Bowman D (2004) The regional electricity market of Central America. Paper presented at the CIGRE 2004 Session, Paris, France, September 2004

Renewable Energy Policy Network for the 21st Century (REN 21) SADC Renewable Energy and Energy Efficiency Status Report 2015 (REN 21 Secretariat 2015)

Rios-Herran R, Poretti P (2012) Energy Trade and Investment under the North American Free Trade Agreement. In: Selivanova Y (ed) Regulation of energy in International Trade Law. WTO, NAFTA and Energy Charter. Kluwer Law International, Alphen aan den Rijn

Rudenko Y, Yershevich V (1991) Is it possible and expedient to create a global energy network? Int J Global Energy Iss 3:159

Schwab A (2015) Elektroenergiesysteme: Erzeugung, Transport, Übertragung und Verteilung elektrischer Energie. Springer Vieweg, Berlin

Selivanova Y (2015) Clean Energy and access to infrastructure: implications for the global trade system. E15 expert group on clean energy technologies and the trade system think piece

Sempértegui L (2017) The legal framework for electricity transmission across boundaries in the Andean Region. J Energy Nat Resour Law 35:433

Spalding-Fecher R, Senatla M, Yamba F, Lukwesa B, Himunzowa G, Heaps C, Chapman A, Mahumane G, Tembo B, Nyambe I (2017) Electricity supply and demand scenarios for the Southern African power pool. Energy Policy 101:403

U.S. Department of Energy (2015) Quadrennial energy review: energy transmission, storage and distribution infrastructure. https://www.energy.gov/sites/prod/files/2015/04/f22/QER-ALL%20 FINAL_0.pdf

U.S. Energy Information Administration (2013) Mexico Week: U.S.-Mexico electricity trade is small, with tight regional focus. https://www.eia.gov/todayinenergy/detail.php?id=11311

U.S. Energy Information Administration (2015) Today in energy: U.S.-Canada electricity trade increases. https://www.eia.gov/todayinenergy/detail.php?id=21992

Verneyre F (2004) Regional electricity cooperation and integration. In: Bielecki J, Desta MG (eds) Electricity trade in Europe: review of the economic and regulatory challenges. Kluwer Law International, Alphen aan den Rijn

Wälde T, Gunst A (2004) International Energy Trade and access to networks. In: Bielecki J, Desta MG (eds) Electricity Trade in Europe: review of the economic and regulatory challenges. Kluwer Law International, Alphen aan den Rijn

Weekes J, Pearson D, Smith L, Kim M (2019) NAFTA 2.0: drilling down – the impact of CUSMA/ USMCA on Canadian Energy stakeholders. Energy Regul Q 7(1)

World Bank (2010) Regional power sector integration: lessons from global case studies and a literature review. Energy Sector Management Assistance Program (ESMAP), Briefing Note 004/10. https://openknowledge.worldbank.org/handle/10986/17507

WTO Secretariat (2010) World Trade Report 2010. World Trade Organization, Geneva

Chapter 4
Final Conclusions to Part I

The first part of this study has laid out the groundwork for the application of the rules of international economic law. The contours of contemporary electricity sectors have emerged as a basis on which to examine the suitability of the general and sector-specific trade rules in existence. It was shown that electricity shares some features with related economic sectors like the oil and gas industries, but also with telecommunications. At the same time, electricity is unique in many aspects and requires tailor-made regulatory solutions.

As the above chapters have described in detail, electricity trade is evolving from a local to a global phenomenon. The starting point was an electricity system that, aside from a few exceptions, remained confined to national or sub-national borders. The generation, transmission and supply functions were the responsibility of a single integrated undertaking, either in private hands or owned by the state. Tariffs for the different activities were regulated and the final electricity price reflected all the costs across the electricity supply chain. A 'market' for electricity transcending national borders, where suppliers and consumers from several countries could meet and a price would be defined according to supply and demand signals, did not exist.

A look at the contemporary electricity sector reveals that the picture has changed substantially. Restructuring and liberalization measures have been adopted in jurisdictions around the world. This has allowed independent generators to emerge and wholesale electricity markets to come into existence. More recently, regional electricity markets have emerged on several continents and the issue of interconnection is high on the energy policy agendas of many regional integration organizations and free trade areas. While regulatory arrangements are still in their infancy in some regions, in others electricity trade is being subjected to ever more sophisticated regulation and market rules.

Both trends—an increase in physical volumes of electricity exchanged across borders and further liberalization of national energy sectors—are expected to continue into the foreseeable future. Scenarios include the interconnection of regional electricity markets to allow intra-regional and ultimately inter-continental electricity

C. Frey, *World Trade Law and the Emergence of International Electricity Markets*, EYIEL Monographs - Studies in European and International Economic Law 25, https://doi.org/10.1007/978-3-031-04756-5_4

trade. This is already technologically feasible and has attracted high-profile political and business interest, with investments envisaged in the multi-billion-dollar range.

It is submitted that both the general market restructuring trends and the 'internationalization' of electricity trade will increase the potential for trade conflicts for the following three reasons: firstly, there is no level playing field: far from all countries have committed to liberalization at the domestic stage and the electricity sector remains one of the sectors most heavily influenced by strategic policy considerations and state influence. The transmission and distribution operations continue to be regulated as a natural monopoly and requirements for third-party access have not been adopted universally. Secondly, the restructuring of markets and the introduction of competition often entails more sophisticated regulation but not necessarily less regulation. The increasing depth of cross-border electricity trade regulation in markets like the European Union increases the potential for conflicts when foreign market actors find it difficult to comply with the requirements imposed on their operations and assets. As a recent WTO dispute concerning the regulation of infrastructure for natural gas trade between Russia and the EU illustrates, the precise design of an unbundling regime can lead to market access issues for foreign suppliers.[1] And finally, the need for exploitation of geographically concentrated new energy sources—mainly renewables like wind, solar PV or geothermal energy—could increase the potential for protectionism and profit-seeking as cooperation aspects which have traditionally been the underlying rationale of cross-border electricity trade recede into the background.

---

[1] WTO, *European Union and its Member States – Certain Measures Relating to the Energy Sector*, Request for the Establishment of a Panel by the Russian Federation (28 May 2015) WT/DS476/2. See also below in Sect. 5.1.2, p. 91.

Part II
World Trade Law and the Regulation of Electricity Trade

As long as electricity markets were confined to national borders and dominated by vertically integrated undertakings, the role of international trade law was limited. The existing interconnections between countries did not provoke significant trade frictions, because these interconnections usually benefitted both countries by allowing for emergency support. Cross-border commercial exchanges of electricity were at a minimum and traditional trade issues like discrimination among suppliers from different countries, protectionism through tariff policy or the adoption of non-tariff barriers hardly played any role.[1] The liberalization and restructuring efforts initiated by governments since the 1980s and the almost parallel evolution from national to regional and increasingly trans-continental electricity trade have changed this picture considerably. It is owing to these developments that international electricity trade has slowly entered the focus of world trade law.

Against this background, two main questions are sought to be answered in the present Part: how world trade law applies to the specific characteristics of the electricity sector; and whether the currently existing normative architecture of world trade law and the principles underlying it are well suited for application to trade in electric energy. These rules and principles are to be found primarily in the Agreements that were adopted within the framework and under the auspices of the WTO. Another relevant body of law is the Energy Charter Treaty (ECT), a treaty specific to the energy sector with a trans-regional membership. A third source of law can be found in the numerous bilateral and regional free trade agreements establishing preferential trading relations among their members (henceforth referred

---

[1] One important exception was the application of the principle of freedom of transit to electricity infrastructure, as the early efforts at codification of transit obligations relating to electricity transmission infrastructure show. See the Convention Relating to the Transmission in Transit of Electric Power, 9 December 1923, 58 LNTS 315. See also Gudas (2018), pp. 104 et seq. See also below in Chap. 12, pp. 197 et seq.

to as PTAs).[2] The membership of these three regimes taken together covers the vast majority of countries.[3]

Thus, the following chapters examine in more detail the three legal regimes which form the analytical framework of this study: the WTO, the ECT and PTAs. This analysis seeks to determine the position of electricity in the normative framework, examine the main principles laid down in the treaties and agreements, and draw lessons from the limited experience with electricity trade disputes at the international level.

Reference

Gudas K (2018) The law and policy of international trade in electricity. Europa Law Publishing

---

[2]For the purpose of the present study, PTAs are understood as agreements covering issues on a horizontal basis and not being of a sector-specific focus. Hence, the term as used here covers bilateral FTAs and the agreements designated in the WTO terminology as RTAs. The general understanding of a PTA is that of an agreement through which the contracting parties grant each other preferential conditions in deviation from the WTO standard of treatment. The ECT would thus also qualify as a PTA.

[3]Out of the 193 Members of the United Nations, 164 are currently Members of the WTO. Some countries like Turkmenistan, Uzbekistan and Belarus, which so far have not attained full WTO Membership, are Contracting Parties of the ECT.

Chapter 5
WTO Law and the Regulation of Electricity Trade

The WTO came into existence in 1995 and remains the only multilateral treaty-based negotiation forum for goods and services trade liberalization and regulation. As of May 2021, the WTO counted 164 members, among which the European Union as well as its Member States individually. Its founding document is the Marrakesh Agreement Establishing the WTO (hereinafter referred to as the WTO Agreement or WTOA).[1] Besides incorporating the General Agreement on Tariffs and Trade (GATT), which originally dates from 1947,[2] the WTO is also the umbrella organization for a number of other 'covered agreements', all of which are annexed to the WTOA.[3] These include the General Agreement on Trade in Services (GATS), the Agreement on Trade-Related Investment Measures (TRIMS), the Agreement on Technical Barriers to Trade (TBT) and the Agreement on the Application of Sanitary and Phytosanitary Measures (SPS). Furthermore, special rules on subsidies have been inscribed in the Agreement on Subsidies and Countervailing Measures (SCMA).

Besides providing the forum for the concerted elimination of trade barriers, the WTO hosts an adjudicatory system where Members are called upon to settle their trade disputes.[4] This dispute settlement mechanism has been used frequently by

---

[1] Agreement Establishing the World Trade Organization (15 April 1994) 1867 U.N.T.S. 154.

[2] The original GATT as such never entered into force. It was provisionally applied, however, by way of a Protocol of Provisional Application (UNTS Vol. 55 No. 814).

[3] The term 'covered agreements' comprises all multilateral Agreements that have been annexed to the WTOA. Cf. Palmeter and Mavroidis (1998), p. 399. The Appellate Body in *Brazil – Desiccated Coconut* clarified: 'The "covered agreements" include the WTO Agreement, the Agreements in Annexes 1 and 2, as well as any Plurilateral Trade Agreement in Annex 4 where its Committee of signatories has taken a decision to apply the DSU.' WTO, *Brazil – Measures Affecting Desiccated Coconut,* Report of the Appellate Body (21 February 1997) WT/DS22/AB/R, p. 13.

[4] Art. 3.2 of the Understanding on Rules and Procedures Governing the Settlement of Disputes reflects the aspiration ascribed by WTO Members to the dispute settlement mechanism as being a 'central element in providing security and predictability to the multilateral trading system.'

© The Author(s), under exclusive license to Springer Nature Switzerland AG 2022
C. Frey, *World Trade Law and the Emergence of International Electricity Markets,*
EYIEL Monographs - Studies in European and International Economic Law 25,
https://doi.org/10.1007/978-3-031-04756-5_5

WTO Members since its inception in 1995 and its decisions are followed in the large majority of cases.[5] The dispute settlement mechanism is governed by the Dispute Settlement Understanding (DSU), which lays down the procedures and principles for the settlement of trade disputes.[6] Notwithstanding the considerable and widely acknowledged success of the WTO dispute settlement system over the years of its existence, this very system has been facing an existential crisis. It became de facto non-functional in December 2019 when the terms of two of the last three remaining Members of the Appellate Body ended, making it impossible for the Appellate Body to hear any further complaints. Nominations of new Appellate Body Members have been blocked for several years by the US administration because of its discontent with the decisions of the body.[7] While it is not yet apparent if and how the current impasse will be overcome, the crisis could be a catalyst for reforms of the dispute settlement system or even of the wider WTO.[8]

A few general issues arising from the nature of WTO law merit mentioning at this point as they pose certain challenges for the application of WTO rules to the electricity sector. First and foremost, it is important to keep in mind that the WTO is a state-centred institution of public international law and its Agreements do not create direct rights or obligations for private enterprises or individuals.[9] How this fact relates to trade issues in the contemporary electricity sector is discussed in more detail below.[10] Secondly, it has been observed that the provisions of the WTO

---

[5]For a stocktaking and outlook on the dispute settlement system after 10 years of existence see McRae (2004).

[6]Understanding on Rules and Procedures Governing the Settlement of Disputes (15 April 1994) contained in Annex 2 to the Marrakesh Agreement Establishing the WTO, 1869 U.N.T.S. 401, 33 I.L.M. 1226.

[7]The Appellate Body hears appeals from reports issued by dispute settlement panels and, according to Article 17 (1) of the DSU, it is composed of seven persons, of which three will sit on an individual case. Thus, the current situation results in a paralysis of the Appellate Body. The (ad hoc) dispute settlement panels are still functional, but reports need to be adopted by the DSB in order to become operational. The DSB cannot adopt a report as long as an appeal is still pending before the Appellate Body. There is thus a threat for the wider system of dispute settlement at large resulting from the current situation: WTO Members can easily block the adoption of panel reports by lodging an appeal 'into the void'.

[8]Concrete proposals for reform have been submitted to the WTO by individual member governments already. See, e.g., WTO, Communication from the European Union, China, Canada, India, Norway, New Zealand, Switzerland, Australia, Republic of Korea, Iceland, Singapore and Mexico (26 November 2018) WT/GC/W/752.

[9]In a report, a WTO Panel contrasted the WTO with legal orders such as that of the European Community (now EU) where state obligations are construed as creating legally enforceable rights and obligations for individuals through the doctrine of direct effect. The fact that such direct effect had not yet been found to apply to WTO rules did not mean, in the eyes of the Panel, that 'in the legal system of any given Member, following internal constitutional principles, some obligations will be found to give rights to individuals.' WTO, *United States—Sections 301-310 of the Trade Act of 1947*, Report of the Panel (22 December 1999) WT/DS152/R [7.73].

[10]See below in Sect. 10.3, pp. 163 et seq. (for general considerations); Sect. 11.4.2.2, p. 187. (with respect to import and export restrictions; and in Sect. 12.3, p. 211 (with respect to transit).

Agreements, especially the GATT, reflect a normative bias towards disciplining import restrictions more than restrictions of exports.[11] This bias reflects the preference of most states for protecting domestic production by keeping competing foreign products out and at the same time encouraging exports of domestic products.[12] The main motivation for WTO Members to engage in reciprocal reductions of tariff and non-tariff barriers was market access for their domestic products abroad. At first glance, neither tariff protection of domestic production nor foreign market access for domestic producers have so far played a big role in the electricity sector. This preliminary observation and its consequences will be further elaborated on below.

5.1 The Status of the Energy Sector in the WTO Legal Order

Before looking specifically at how the WTO Agreements relate to electricity, it is necessary to locate the energy sector more generally within the WTO framework. Several factors have prompted commentators to question whether the energy sector is actually covered by the WTO Agreements, or whether it must be regarded as outside the domain of the WTO.[13] If the latter were found to be the case, the application of WTO rules to trade in electric energy more specifically would not have to be examined further. It is indeed noteworthy that, for example, no WTO complaint has ever been brought against the export-restrictive concerted practices of the OPEC.[14] As the UNCTAD has remarked with respect to trade in fossil fuels, 'the strategic importance of petroleum trade to the world economy has been such that in the past it has been treated as a special case, in a largely political context and not within the GATT multilateral framework of trade rules'.[15] Against this background, it is appropriate to analyse briefly whether and how the coverage of the WTO Agreements extends to the energy sector at large.

---

[11] See, e.g. Desta (2003), pp. 385 et seq.

[12] Ibid.

[13] See generally Marceau (2010); Yanovich (2012); Selivanova (2014), p. 275.

[14] Desta (2003), p. 388.

[15] UNCTAD, *Trade Agreements, Petroleum and Energy Policies* (United Nations 2000), p. 1.

5.1.1 The Absence of Energy-Specific Provisions in the WTO Agreements

Neither the GATT nor any of the other covered agreements of the WTO contain specific rules on energy trade.[16] The text of the GATS itself does not mention energy, but WTO Members have included commitments on a number of energy-related services in their schedules of concessions.[17] Despite its significance for the functioning of any modern economy and for the development of virtually all other goods and the provision of services, energy has no special status under the WTO Agreements.

This absence of energy-specific provisions in the WTO Agreements is neither exceptional nor surprising. The GATT and the GATS are, as their respective titles make clear, 'general' agreements and have no specific sectoral scope. The Agreements apply horizontally to all goods and the provision of services, respectively, for which no explicit exemptions have been adopted. Thus, the absence of provisions specific to the energy sector says nothing about the applicability of the rules of the GATT or any other covered agreement to energy trade.[18] More important is the fact that there is no carve-out for the energy sector to be found in any of the WTO Agreements.[19]

Another question worth considering is whether the drafting parties to the original GATT and to the later WTO Agreements can be reasonably assumed to have intended to exclude energy products from the scope of the Agreements. At the time of the drafting of the GATT 1947, infrastructure for the transport of electricity and gas was largely confined to national territories, and cross-border interconnections were very scarce.[20] With respect to fossil fuels, the situation had changed at the

---

[16] Indeed, the only direct reference to energy in the covered agreements is in a footnote in Annex II (on 'Guidelines on Consumption of Inputs in the Production Process') to the Agreement on Subsidies and Countervailing Measures. It reads 'Inputs consumed in the production process are inputs physically incorporated, *energy*, fuels and oil used in the production process and catalysts which are consumed in the course of their use to obtain the exported product' (emphasis added).

[17] For a comprehensive overview over energy services and the GATS see Cossy (2012).

[18] This seems to be the prevailing opinion among scholars. See e.g. Cottier et al. (2011), p. 212; Selivanova (2014), p. 280; Meyer (2017), p. 399.

[19] Although some exception provisions in the WTO Agreements are arguably of special relevance to energy trade, none of those were designed specifically with regard to the energy sector.

[20] During the negotiations leading to the original GATT 1947, energy played only a minor role. It was discussed superficially in the context of classification. In the New York Drafting Committee Report of the original GATT negotiations, it is noted that the general view in the room was that electric energy should not be classified as a commodity. This could be interpreted as an unwillingness among the international community to subject energy trade to substantive trade rules in general or simply as agreement that classification of energy in goods terms falling under the coverage of the GATT was not appropriate. See United Nations, Report of the Drafting Committee of the Preparatory Committee of the United Nations Conference on Trade and Employment (5 March 1947) available at http://worldtradelaw.net/misc/New%20York%20Draft.pdf.download. See also Selivanova (2014), p. 275.

time of the Uruguay Round negotiations which led to the creation of the WTO, as a global market for oil and natural gas had emerged. As a result, some WTO Members sought to address issues like export restrictions and dual pricing of fossil fuels in the WTO, without successfully triggering specific negotiations.[21] On the services side, some WTO Members undertook limited commitments on a few energy-related services during the Uruguay Round.[22] With respect to electricity, however, the situation at that time had changed only marginally, and in the mid-1990s it was still not envisaged that electricity trade could evolve into a global phenomenon. Indeed, the prevailing opinion has constantly been that electricity is a 'local' form of energy.[23] This could be one explanation for the absence of initiatives to discuss the electricity industry in the context of the goods-related WTO Agreements.[24]

Another factor which explains the long-standing lack of interest on the part of WTO Members in dealing with energy trade issues at the WTO is the vertically integrated structure of the energy sector and the considerable degree of state ownership. At the time of the Uruguay Round negotiations in the second half of the 1980s, there was still a widespread consensus about the benefits of these traditional market structures and the early examples of reform had not yet been widely adopted.[25] The consensus about the need for a state-dominated and vertically integrated structure to govern energy markets helps explain why specific liberalization initiatives at the international level were not actively pursued, and arguably the general rules of the GATT were relied on as being sufficient.[26]

To summarize, although the above considerations help to explain the lack of a special regime for energy trade within the WTO and the apparent lack of interest in seriously discussing the energy sector at the WTO negotiating table, they do not lead to the conclusion that the energy sector falls outside of the scope of the Agreements.[27] There is no convincing evidence to conclude that the general WTO rules should not be applicable to energy trade. Indeed, a whole range of commodities and products related to energy production falls under the purview of the Agreements. The raw materials used in the process of generating electricity must be treated as

---

[21] Selivanova (2014), p. 276 ff; Cottier et al. (2011), p. 212.

[22] These concerned services incidental to mining, services incidental to energy distribution and services related to the pipeline transportation of fuels. Specific commitments remained scarce during the Uruguay Round, however, and increased considerably with the accession of new members after 1995. Cf. Cossy (2009), p. 417.

[23] Cf. WTO, Council for Trade in Services, Energy Services—Background Note by the Secretariat (12 January 2010) S/C/W/311 ('electricity markets remain regional and depend on interconnection of the different national systems.'); see also Botchway (2001), p. 7.

[24] With respect to services, some countries submitted proposals on a new classification of energy services and proposed a 'Reference Paper' for energy services. See also below in Sect. 14.3.2.2, pp. 247 et seq.

[25] On Chile as a pioneer and role model for electricity market reform see above in Sect. 2.2.1, p. 26.

[26] Cottier et al. (2011), p. 212.

[27] In the same vein Marceau (2010), p. 25; Crosby (2012), p. 325; Boute (2016) [3.60]; Desta (2003), p. 388; Matsushita et al. (2015), p. 734.

goods and as such their trade falls under the GATT. This is true for oil, gas, coal and uranium. Trade in the equipment used in power plants is also subject to WTO rules, as several cases concerning components of solar modules and wind turbine parts have illustrated. On the services side, limited commitments on energy services can be observed. There is no specific chapter devoted to energy services in the classification instruments relied on by WTO Members, but several sub-sectors do refer to energy services.[28] Regulatory measures in the energy sector must also comply with the TBT Agreement, to the extent that they prescribe technical regulations. Investment measures relating to energy trade must conform to the TRIMS Agreement, and the subsidization of energy goods or production methods must be in line with the provisions of the SCMA.[29] With respect to the electricity value chain, however, open questions remain concerning the classification of goods and services. The answer to whether 'electric energy' is a good, a service, or possibly both, is not at all straightforward and this issue is discussed in detail further below.[30]

5.1.2   The Energy Sector in WTO Dispute Settlement

Despite historically accounting for a significant share of world commodity trade, WTO disputes involving trade in energy sources are rare.[31] Nevertheless, throughout the history of WTO dispute settlement, a number of cases have touched on energy issues. The second WTO dispute on record and the first ever report issued by the Appellate Body concerned the regulation of the composition and emission effects of gasoline in the US, a practice that Brazil and Venezuela considered to violate provisions of the GATT.[32] More recently, the treatment of imports of biodiesel in several countries was at issue in WTO dispute settlement.[33] Considering the volume of world oil and gas trade, however, the overall lack of disputes concerning these two

---

[28] See below in Sect. 5.2.7, pp. 107 et seq.

[29] Claims with regards to both the TRIMS and the SCMA were at issue in the *Canada – Feed-In Tariff Program* Case which involved local content measures in the renewable energy regulations of the Canadian province of Ontario. See also below in Sect. 5.1.2, p. 91.

[30] See below in Sect. 5.2, pp. 92 et seq.

[31] Both refined petroleum and crude petroleum are among the commodities most traded globally in terms of both volume and value. The former was only recently surpassed as the world's most traded commodity by passenger vehicles. Taken as a group, petroleum products made up 5% of global commodity exports in 2018. Cf. World Economic Forum, 'These are the world's most traded goods' (23 February 2018) https://www.weforum.org/agenda/2018/02/the-top-importers-and-exporters-of-the-world-s-18-most-traded-goods.

[32] WTO, *United States — Standards for Reformulated and Conventional Gasoline*, Report of the Appellate Body (29 April 1996) WT/DS2/AB/R.

[33] See WTO, DS 459, *European Union — Certain Measures on the Importation and Marketing of Biodiesel and Measures Supporting the Biodiesel Industry* (in consultations since May 2013) and DS 443, *European Union and a Member State — Certain Measures Concerning the Importation of Biodiesels* (in consultations since August 2012).

commodities is noteworthy.[34] Indeed, the first opportunity for a dispute settlement panel to present its views on measures restricting trade in energy goods as such reached the WTO Dispute Settlement Body (DSB) in April 2014, when the Russian Federation filed a complaint against alleged discriminatory treatment of Russian gas and gas suppliers through the application of the EU's Third Energy Package.[35] Russia has been exporting its natural gas to EU Member States for decades. EU energy market legislation requires Russian gas suppliers with commercial activities in the EU to 'unbundle' their operations, i.e. to engage in a separation of the generation, transmission and distribution functions.[36] Russia complained specifically that the EU rules on the restructuring of integrated energy companies (the unbundling requirements) disadvantaged the Russian gas producer and supplier, Gazprom.[37] Moreover, Russia complained about the fact that pipelines for gas imports from Russia into the EU were disadvantaged under EU law with respect to the support of strategic infrastructure.[38] The dispute demonstrates the potential for trade conflicts caused by domestic regulation in the energy sector, an issue expected to gain relevance in the future. It also illustrates how trade conflicts can arise where energy consumers are situated in liberalized and competitive markets and a supplier situated abroad is a state-owned vertically integrated energy company.

A different group of disputes involves the energy sector in the broader sense. The energy sector remained on the margins of WTO dispute settlement until 2010 when the EU complained against local content requirements of a feed-in tariff (FIT) scheme for renewable energy generation in the Canadian province of Ontario.[39] This was followed by similar complaints targeting support measures for renewable energy generation components in several countries.[40] This series of disputes concerned the modalities of the subsidization of renewable energy generation. Political economy arguments help best to explain why there seems to be a great interest for some WTO Members in pressuring others to openly design domestic support systems and allow companies from abroad to participate in the economic

---

[34] For possible explanations of this lack of fossil fuel disputes, see Meyer (2017), p. 391.

[35] WTO, *European Union and its Member States – Certain Measures Relating to the Energy Sector*, Request for Consultations by the Russian Federation (8 May 2014) WT/DS476/1.

[36] On unbundling and the application of international economic law rules to EU Energy Regulation see Dralle (2018).

[37] WTO, *EU – Energy Package*, Russia's Request for Consultations, p. 2.

[38] WTO, *European Union and its Member States – Certain Measures Relating to the Energy Sector*, Request for the Establishment of a Panel by the Russian Federation (28 May 2015) WT/DS476/1, p. 8.

[39] WTO, *Canada – Measures Relating to the Feed-in Tariff Program*, Report of the Appellate Body (6 May 2013) WT/DS426/19.

[40] These cases concern a complaint by the United States against China with respect to certain local content measures regarding wind power equipment (DS 419, in consultations since December 2010), a complaint by China against the European Union concerning certain local content measures in the renewable energy sector (DS 452, in consultations since November 2012) and a complaint by the United States against India concerning alleged local content requirements for solar cells and modules (DS 456, Appellate Body report circulated in September 2016).

opportunities which renewable energy development offers. The renewable energy industry is still relatively young, and a fierce global competition has emerged which leaves many companies behind. The issue lying at the heart of these disputes concerns the design of support schemes for renewable energy generation; not import or export restrictions for the electricity generated from renewable sources per se. A convincing explanation for the lack of disputes falling into the latter category is that countries are keen to uphold a secure supply of electricity and will thus refrain from restricting such imports. Electricity export restrictions are more common, but no such measure has yet been challenged before the WTO. Hence, the motivation for bringing the complaints in the renewable energy sector must be found in securing foreign market access for domestic solar cells and wind turbines, not for the electricity thereby generated.[41] The European Union has no interest in Canadian electricity and vice versa, because as of yet there is no common market and thus no direct competitive relationship. Thus, in contrast to the gas sector, where cross-border trade has been intensifying for decades as countries are looking to diversify their supplies and domestic reserves are declining, the first genuine electricity dispute has yet to reach the WTO stage.

5.2 Locating Electricity Within the Framework for Goods and Services

While the electricity sector as part of the wider energy sector is clearly covered by the WTO Agreements, the application of the existing norms sometimes causes confusion. The structure of the WTO Agreements shows a clear distinction between goods-related and services-related agreements. The GATT and a few other goods-related covered agreements in Annex I of the WTOA do not apply to trade in services. The GATS applies exclusively to measures affecting trade in services.[42] As electricity is neither specifically addressed in the goods-related WTO Agreements nor in the GATS, the applicability of the Agreements hinges on the classification issue.[43] It is owing to this inherent dichotomy in WTO law that commentators

---

[41] It is also not to target the renewable energy subsidy schemes per se, as some authors seem to suggest when they qualify the disputes as an 'attack on RE subsidies'. Meyer (2012), p. 5. Rather, WTO Members exporting renewable energy generation equipment want to participate in the eating of the subsidy cake.

[42] See Article I:1 GATS.

[43] The question whether a measure is covered by the GATT or the GATS is a threshold issue. Before consistency with the substantial obligations of the Agreements can be assessed, a dispute settlement Panel will have to determine whether the measure is covered by the respective agreements. The Appellate Body in *Canada-Autos* found that a Panel had erred in its interpretation of the GATS by arguing that a determination of whether a measure affected trade in services could not be made in isolation from examining whether the effect of such a measure was consistent with the Member's obligations and commitments under the GATS. WTO, *Canada—Certain Measures Affecting the*

have engaged in discussing whether electricity should be characterized as a good or a service, with widely differing outcomes. Some authors refer to the GATT negotiating history which allegedly confirms that at the time the general mood was that electricity should not be regarded as a commodity.[44] Indeed, the view that the GATT should not apply to electricity appears to have had some appeal among scholars writing on the subject until recently.[45] Today, however, there seems to be more willingness among academics to accept that electricity is subject to GATT rules.[46]

One might question why a deeper evaluation of this issue is important at all, especially since dispute settlement bodies have held that a single measure can be scrutinized under both the GATT and the GATS.[47] It is submitted that in a WTO dispute concerning trade in electric energy, a Member maintaining an alleged WTO-inconsistent measure might be inclined to argue that the GATT is not applicable by holding that electricity is not a good. Similar arguments were raised by parties in previous disputes with respect to audio-visual services and periodicals.[48] The reason for making this argument is obvious: While the substantial obligations of the GATT apply to trade in goods 'across the board', the applicability of most GATS provisions depends on specific concessions that Members have made with respect to particular services. The GATS thus leaves Members room to 'opt-out' of multilateral commitments vis-à-vis other Members for certain sensitive sectors. Due to the central significance of a reliable electricity supply, it must be assumed that this consideration applies to electricity as well.

Automotive Industry, Report of the Appellate Body (31 May 2000) WT/DS139/AB/R, WT/DS142/AB/R [150–152]. See also Zacharias (2008), p. 9.

[44] Jackson (1969), pp. 119 et seq. The Drafting Committee Report of the original GATT observes that 'as it seemed to be generally accepted that electric power should not be classified as a commodity, two delegates did not find it necessary to reserve the right for their countries to prohibit the export of electric power'. Report of the New York Drafting Committee, p. 31.

[45] Most of these authors then either implicitly or explicitly qualify electricity as a service instead. See, e.g., Plourde (1990), pp. 35 set seq.; Botchway (2001), p. 13, who bases his claim on the 'wide definition' of services ('any service in any sector') in Article 1 (3) (b) of the GATS; Cottier et al. (2011), pp. 222 et seq. Matsushita, Schoenbaum and Mavroidis also appear to share the view that electricity is a service. See Matsushita et al. (2015), p. 734.

[46] See Farah and Cima (2013) Fn. 14 ('We now agree that the production of primary and secondary energy does not constitute a 'service' and therefore is not subject to the GATS, but it rather results in goods, whose trade is regulated by GATT rules'); Espa (2017) applies several provisions of the GATT to electricity.

[47] The Appellate Body held that some measures 'could be found to fall within the scope of both the GATT 1994 and the GATS.' In the words of the AB, 'these are measures that involve a service relating to a particular good or a service supplied in conjunction with a particular good.' WTO, *European Communities – Regime for the Importation, Sale and Distribution of Bananas*, Report of the Appellate Body (9 September 1997) WT/DS27/AB/R [221]. Whether or not this is the case will depend on the nature of the measures at issue and must be determined on a case-by-case basis. Ibid.

[48] WTO, *China – Measures Affecting Trading Rights and Distribution Services for Certain Publications and Audiovisual Entertainment Products*, Report of the Panel (12 August 2009) WT/DS363/R [4.92]; WTO, *Canada – Certain Measures Concerning Periodicals*, Report of the Panel (14 March 1997) WT/DS31/R [3.33].

5.2.1   General Considerations: 'Goods' and 'Services' in the WTO Legal Framework

The WTO Agreements themselves provide no definition of the terms 'good', 'product', 'merchandise' and 'service' although all of these terms are used frequently throughout the covered agreements. In the absence of definitions in the WTO Agreements, the starting point to defining these terms should focus on their ordinary meaning in their context as foreseen by the Vienna Convention on the Law of Treaties (VCLT).[49] The dispute settlement bodies of the WTO, in seeking to determine 'ordinary meaning', frequently engage in textual interpretations of certain terms in the covered agreements.[50] While dictionary definitions of the terms 'good', 'product' and 'service' might not conclusively settle the question of whether for purposes of the application of WTO law electricity is to be qualified as either one or the other, these definitions provide the 'keystone upon which interpretation is built.'[51] A first important observation is that in the GATT, the term 'product' is used more often than 'good'. While some provisions refer exclusively to 'products' (Article I), others refer to both 'products' and 'goods' (Articles II, III, V). There seems to be implicit agreement that these two terms represent synonyms in the GATT context,[52] although the general understanding of 'good' and 'product' is certainly not identical. The Shorter Oxford English Dictionary, which is routinely referred to by the Appellate Body, defines the term product as 'a thing produced by an action, operation, or natural process' and more specifically 'that which is produced commercially for sale'.

---

[49]Cf. Article 31(1) of the Vienna Convention on the Law of Treaties (23 May 1969) 1155 U.N.T.S. 331. As international treaties, the GATT and the GATS are both subject to the customary rules of interpretation as codified in the Vienna Convention. This is also in line with Article 3.2 of the Dispute Settlement Understanding (DSU) which provides that existing provisions of the covered agreements be clarified by the dispute settlement system 'in accordance with customary rules of interpretation of public international law.' The rules of the VCLT and Article 31 in particular, have been repeatedly applied by the Appellate Body. See, e.g. WTO, *United States – Standards for Reformulated and Conventional Gasoline,* Report of the Appellate Body (29 April 1996) WT/DS2/AB/R, pp. 16 f; WTO, *Japan – Taxes on Alcoholic Beverages,* Report of the Appellate Body (4 October 1996) WT/DS8/AB/R, WT/DS10/AB/R, WT/DS11/AB/R, pp. 10 ff.; WTO, *European Communities – Customs Classification of Certain Computer Equipment,* Report of the Appellate Body (5 June 1998) WT/DS62/AB/R, WT/DS67/AB/R, WT/DS68/AB/R [84 ff.]; WTO, *United States – Import Prohibition of Certain Shrimp and Shrimp Products,* Report of the Appellate Body (12 October 1998) WT/DS58/AB/R [114 ff.]. For a discussion of treaty interpretation in the WTO framework see Van Damme (2009).

[50]For a critical view of the frequent use of dictionaries see Irwin and Weiler (2008), p. 90, who characterize the approach of the dispute settlement bodies as 'privileging the textual and contextual (the "ordinary meaning" of terms)' and only 'grudgingly and sparingly' considering the teleological. For a slightly differing view see Van Damme (2010), p. 621 ('The Appellate Body's apparently excessive attention to the words of the treaty language might seem overdone, but it is correct nonetheless').

[51]Van Damme (2010), p. 622.

[52]This must be inferred from the noticeable absence of dissent on the issue.

'Goods' on the other hand are defined as 'property or possessions, esp. movable property' and 'saleable commodities, merchandise'.[53] Goods are generally regarded as physical tangible objects. From a commercial point of view, they are 'appropriable and, therefore transferable between economic units.'[54] As it encompasses anything produced commercially for sale, movable or immovable, 'product' has a broader meaning than 'good'. Since the GATT uses the two terms interchangeably this widens the scope of application of the GATT disciplines. The Appellate Body also appears to use both terms without making a distinction as to their meaning in the GATT framework.[55] Commodities as a special category of goods,[56] and most natural resources more specifically, fall under the GATT disciplines.[57]

The drafters of the GATS equally refrained from providing a definition of the term 'service' and instead opted to subject to the provisions of the GATS four modes of 'trade in services' which are enumerated in Article I GATS.[58] These modes are cross-border supply, consumption abroad, commercial presence and the presence of natural persons. As Article I:3 lit. b clarifies, '"services" includes any service in any sector except services supplied in the exercise of governmental authority'. The understanding of services is in practice further informed by the inclusion of actual services in GATS Members schedules of concessions.

Turning again to the ordinary meaning of the term, provision of a service can best be described as an activity performed by one economic unit (the service supplier) for the benefit of another economic unit (the service consumer).[59] Besides their intangible nature, many services are also characterized by invisibility, lack of suitability for storage, or lack of transportability and coincidence of production and

---

[53] See Brown et al. (2002), p. 1125. One should also keep in mind that for the purposes of economic statistics, the term 'product' is used to refer to all goods *and services* that are the result of production. Cf United Nations and others, *System of National Accounts 2008* (United Nations 2009) [6.24] available at https://unstats.un.org/unsd/nationalaccount/docs/SNA2008.pdf.

[54] Hill (1977), p. 317. Black's Law Dictionary defines goods as '(t)angible or movable personal property other than money; esp., articles of trade or items of merchandise'.

[55] The Appellate Body in *Canada-Autos*, for example, consistently uses the term 'goods' when referring to Article III:4 GATT while the provision uses the term 'product'. WTO, *Canada — Certain Measures Affecting the Automotive Industry*, Report of the Appellate (31 May 2000) WT/DS139/AB/R, WT/DS142/AB/R [140].

[56] The term 'commodity', according to the Shorter Oxford English Dictionary, means 'a thing that is an object of trade, esp. a raw material or agricultural crop'. Brown et al. (2002).

[57] For natural resources, see WTO Secretariat (2010), pp. 46 et seq.

[58] The reason for the lack of a definition of services might be general disagreement among the contracting parties. Cf. Zacharias (2008) [11]. It is also true that new services keep emerging that continuously expand the precise scope of the concept of 'services'. Cf. Abu-Akeel (1999), pp. 190 et seq.

[59] The definition of a 'service' in Black's Law Dictionary is: 'A person or company whose business is to do useful things for others; an intangible commodity in the form of human effort, such as labor, skill or advice'. In the Shorter Oxford English Dictionary, the term 'services' is defined in economic terms as 'the sector of the economy that supplies the need of the consumer but produces no tangible goods'.

consumption.[60] While these properties may apply to a large number of services, they neither offer conclusive guidance nor are they suitable to accurately distinguish services from goods in all cases.[61] Against the background of these definitional concepts, the classification of electricity for the purpose of applying the GATT or the GATS deserves a deeper evaluation.

As a preliminary remark, it should be noted that trade in electric energy is not feasible in the absence of a large number of activities, which can easily be labelled 'services'. Indeed, the everyday usage of electricity depends on services such as network balancing and customer metering. This does not help much, however, in answering the question whether 'electric energy' as the result of a production process can be classified as a good or whether its nature mandates a more holistic view and consequently the classification as a service. Therefore, what follows is an attempt to categorize electricity for the purpose of the application of the WTO Agreements from different angles. After briefly reassessing the relevant physical and commercial traits of electricity in light of the interpretation given to the terms 'good', 'product' and 'service' as outlined above, the analysis will draw on existing dispute settlement practice, practice with respect to both domestic legal systems and international treaties and practice with respect to customs classification and classification for scheduling services.

5.2.2   The Physical Characteristics of Electricity

The physical characteristics of electricity have been described in some detail in Chap. 1 above. Electricity is the process of an electrical charge spreading over a conductor rather than a substance or a tangible object. Being of an intangible nature, electricity can only be measured in kilowatt-hours (kWh) or megawatt-hours (MWh) at the points of generation and consumption. On a wire, the only relevant attributes of electricity are voltage and frequency, and individual units of electricity are impossible to identify from the outside. The electrons present in a wire move at close to the speed of light and as of today, it is physically impossible to steer these electrons in the direction of a particular consumer in a targeted manner.[62] Electricity cannot yet be stored in large quantities at short notice, and it always requires an overall system balance. With that in mind, it is sometimes argued that electric utilities do not so much 'produce' electricity but rather provide for permanent

---

[60] Zacharias (2008) [16].

[61] As *Zacharias* rightly notes, these are not 'criteria that can be used in every case to describe services in a clear-cut manner'. Zacharias (2008) [17-19].

[62] Ferrey (2004), p. 1863. A debate is emerging in the energy industry about whether the application of the blockchain technology has the potential to fundamentally change these precepts. It is too early to make an informed judgment. Cf. Andoni (2019), pp. 143 et seq.

availability of electric power by maintaining the system balance and keeping generators running to match demand at all times.[63]

Based on all these characteristics, electricity bears more resemblance to a service than a good. Indeed, in some engineering textbooks, the authors plainly characterize electricity as a service. To illustrate, one standard textbook contains the following passage:

> In many texts, electric current is described as a physical flow of electrons. It is not. The electrons do not flow. Rather, electricity is a flow of energy as a result of electron vibrations. The mechanism is the transfer of energy from one electron to the other as they collide with each other. Electric power systems thus provide a service, the availability of energy, not a product, to consumers.[64]

In this respect, electricity resembles telecommunications, where voice or text is transmitted via electromagnetic waves between users. There is little ambiguity about the service character of telecommunications.[65] In sum, the physical characteristics clearly weigh against the classification of electricity as a good. This observation stands even in the light of the seemingly very broad interpretative scope of the terms 'good' and 'product' taken together.

5.2.3 Commercial Aspects of Electricity

From a commercial perspective, electricity shares many features with tradable commodities. The electricity industry has treated electricity as a product subject to commercial transactions by applying certain standards with regard to volume, time, and location.[66] For example, despite the impossibility of steering electrons in a meshed grid along a certain path, generation and consumption are matched by creating virtual accounts administered by so-called 'balancing groups'. Billing of the customer takes place with the help of electricity meters that measure the consumption in kWh.[67]

---

[63] See Müller (2001), p. 27 who argues that electricity utilities are tasked with constantly supplying voltage and current to consumers and thus delivering a service. Electricity, according to Müller, would thus have to be regarded as a service and not a good. ('Die Aufgabe der EVU besteht in der Verpflichtung den Kunden gegenüber, jederzeit Spannung und Strom zur Lieferung bereitzustellen, d.h. eine Dienstleistung zu erbringen. Elektrizität ist damit keine Ware, sondern eine Dienstleistung').

[64] Casazza and Delea (2010), p. 28.

[65] Ferrey (2004), p. 1863.

[66] International Energy Agency (2005), p. 87.

[67] In this context, one United States Court has argued that there had to be a delay between the point of consumption and metering for electricity to qualify as a good under the Uniform Commercial Code of the United States (U.C.C.). If consumption and metering happened at the same time (as is usually the case), the Court found, electricity could not be regarded as a good. See In re Great Atlantic & Pacific Tea Co. Inc, 12-CV-7629CS, 2013 WL 5212141 (S.D.N.Y. Sept. 16, 2013). See

The development of the electricity sector over the past decades has contributed to the visibility of electricity as a commercial product. The vertically integrated structure which persisted in the electricity sector of many countries until the first restructuring efforts were undertaken in the 1980s made the distinction between electricity as a good and the related services less prevalent.[68] Electricity supply was essentially regarded as one integrated activity. Transmission and distribution were usually provided on an in-house basis and not as separate commercial activities.[69] The whole exercise of liberalization and market reform was carried out with the idea in mind that electricity can be traded just like other goods—and thus treated independently from its transport and supply to final customers.[70] The unbundling of activities has made trade in electricity commercially and organizationally independent from its transportation and final supply to consumers. Unbundling has made possible the distinct treatment of different stages of the electricity supply chain, and thereby allowed some services to appear independently and others to newly emerge.[71] All of these developments contributed to the 'commoditisation' of electricity, as evidenced by, *inter alia*, the recent proliferation of electricity exchanges like the EEX, EPEX SPOT or Nord Pool Spot.[72] In sum, despite its unique features electricity is in fact produced commercially for sale and traded like many other commodities.

5.2.4   The Status of Electricity in Domestic Legal Systems

In most national legal systems, electricity is treated as a good. In commercial laws, electricity is often characterized as merchandise or a tradable good.[73] In Germany, Austria and Switzerland, for example, there is a clear inclination to consider

---

also Steinkamp, 'Is Electricity a Good or a Service? The Debate Charges On' (Stout Insights, 16 July 2014) https://www.stout.com/de-de/insights/article/electricity-good-or-service-debate-charges.

[68] Cottier et al. (2011), p. 213.

[69] Poretti and Rios-Herran (2006), p. 13.

[70] Crastan (2009), p. 89 f.

[71] Poretti and Rios-Herran (2006), p. 13. Among the 'new' services are those related to wholesale trading and brokerage. See also Gamberale (2001), p. 259.

[72] On the commoditisation of electricity see Clark et al. (2001), pp. 5 et seq. See also Albath (2005), p. 91.

[73] Section 2 (5) of Germany's Securities Trading Act reads: 'Commodities within the meaning of this Act mean economic goods of a fungible nature that are capable of being delivered; they include metals, ores and alloys, agricultural products and energy, *such as electricity*' (emphasis added). Section 2 (5) of the Securities Trading Act (Wertpapierhandelsgesetz, WpHG) of 9 September 1998, BGBl. I S. 2708 in its non-binding translation by the Federal Financial Supervisory Authority (BaFin), available at https://www.bafin.de/SharedDocs/Veroeffentlichungen/EN/Aufsichtsrecht/Gesetz/WpHG_en.html?nn=8379954#doc7856864bodyText3.

electricity as a commercial product falling under the sale of goods laws.[74] The treatment of electricity differs however in some Nordic countries, where electricity is regarded as a peculiar commodity and laws governing the sale of goods are not readily applicable.[75] In Ireland, electricity is treated as the supply of service under the 1980 Sale of Goods and Supply of Services Act.[76]

The European Court of Justice has been confronted several times with disputes involving electricity and the question of whether the EU Treaty provisions on the free movement of goods were applicable. The first such dispute reached the Court as a preliminary reference from a municipal court in Milan, Italy.[77] The national proceedings concerned non-payment of an invoice for electricity consumption. In its judgment, the European Court of Justice was not explicitly asked to rule on the classification issue. Some authors have nonetheless concluded that in this early judgment the Court implicitly decided that electricity was a 'good', as the Court elaborated on the free movement of goods in the context of state monopolies.[78] The Court for the first time explicitly accepted the notion that electricity is a good in its judgment in the *Almelo* case in 1994.[79] At issue in that case was the compatibility with the EU Treaties of an exclusive electricity-purchasing clause for a Dutch municipality, which effectively resulted in an import ban for local distributors. The Court elaborated: 'In Community law, and indeed in the national laws of the Member States, it is accepted that electricity constitutes a good within the meaning of Article 30 of the Treaty. Electricity is thus regarded as a good under the Community's tariff nomenclature.'[80]

---

[74]Electricity supply contracts in Germany are treated as contracts for the sale of goods according to §433 of the German Civil Code (BGB). In Austria, electricity qualifies as a thing under §285 of the Austrian Civil Code (ABGB) which admittedly has a very broad scope ('alles, was von einer Person unterschieden ist, und zum Gebrauche der Menschen dient'). In Switzerland, electricity supply contracts were interpreted by courts to be contracts for the sale of goods. See Schweizerisches Bundesgericht, BGE 48 II 370. See also Mäntysaari (2015), p. 76.

[75]See for further references to Swedish and Norwegian sources Mäntysaari (2015), p. 72.

[76]Cf. Section 40 (5) (a) of the Irish Sale of Goods and Supply of services Act, 1980.

[77]European Court of Justice, Case 6/64 *Costa v ENEL*, ECLI:EU:C:1964:66.

[78]See, e.g. Pierros and Nüesch (2000), p. 105. The European Court of Justice also shared this view in Case C-393/92 *Municipality of Almelo and others v NV Energiebedrijf Ijsselmij* [1994] ECR I-1477 [28] ('(. . .) in its judgment in Case 6/64 Costa v ENEL [1964] ECR 1141 the Court accepted that electricity may fall within the scope of Article 37 of the Treaty').

[79]European Court of Justice, Case C-393/92 *Municipality of Almelo and others v NV Energiebedrijf Ijsselmij* [1994] ECR I-1477.

[80]Ibid [28]. In light of the short survey with respect to the treatment of electricity in some EU Member States conducted above, the finding by the European Court of Justice does not seem entirely accurate. It is interesting to note that Advocate General *Darmon* in his opinion in the *Almelo* case, while 'having no doubt that electricity must be regarded as a good within the meaning of the Treaty', did not explicitly base his findings on the treatment in individual EU Member States. See European Court of Justice, Case C-393/92 *Municipality of Almelo and others v NV Energiebedrijf Ijsselmij*, Opinion of Advocate General Darmon (8 February 1994).

The *Almelo* judgment was confirmed by the Court in a case concerning the exclusive import and export rights of the Italian national energy company ENEL.[81] The Italian government had argued that the national provisions did not fall within the scope of the Treaty provisions on the free movement of goods, as electricity 'displays much greater similarity to the category of services.'[82] The Italian government advanced an interesting line of argumentation to support this claim, while also referring to the familiar characteristics of electricity (as an 'incorporeal substance which cannot be stored').[83] The starting point for Italy's argumentation was that electricity 'has no economic existence as such – it is never useful in itself but only by reason of its possible applications.'[84] Building further on this argument, the Italian government opined that the importation and exportation of electricity were 'merely aspects of the management of the electricity network which, by their nature, fall within the category of "services".'[85] By arguing thus, Italy sought to rely on earlier judgments to the extent that the Court had found that the import and export of goods for the sole purpose of providing services fall outside the free movement of goods provisions, as they form part of the services themselves.[86] In the *ENEL*-case before it, however, the Court distinguished the situation from its earlier judgment as the goods distributed in that case (lottery tickets and advertisements) had not been 'ends in themselves, their sole purpose being to enable residents of the Member States where those objects are imported and distributed to participate in the lottery [i. e the service provided].'[87] The situation in the case before it was reversed, as the Court made clear, declaring that the services associated with the import and export of electricity (especially transmission and distribution) 'merely constitute the means for supplying users with goods within the meaning of the Treaty.'[88]

The three cases presented here show that the European Court of Justice has confirmed the application of the free movement of goods to electricity imports and exports and thereby, albeit not always explicitly, rejected the application of the rules on free movement of services.[89]

In the United States, the classification question has been the subject of a considerable number of court proceedings in commercial cases and is of relevance, among

---

[81] European Court of Justice, Case C 158/94 *Commission v Italian Republic* [1997] ECR I 5789 [14 ff.].

[82] Ibid, at 14.

[83] Ibid.

[84] Ibid.

[85] Ibid.

[86] Italy specifically referred to Case C-275/92 *H. M. Customs and Excise* v *Schindler* [1994] ECR 1-1039 and Case C-260/89 *ERT v DEP* [1991] ECR 1-2925.

[87] European Court of Justice, Case C-158/94 *Commission v Italian Republic* [18].

[88] Ibid.

[89] Cf Pierros and Nüesch (2000), p. 105.

others, to contract law, tort law, bankruptcy law[90] and antitrust law.[91] As the definition of 'goods' in the Uniform Commercial Code (UCC) is 'all things... which are movable at the time of identification to a contract for sale',[92] courts have often focused on the question whether the electricity is 'movable' at the moment of metering at the final customer. This approach has led courts to assumptions—sometimes problematic—about the nature of electricity. To illustrate, one court found that metered electricity is a good because

> [it] does not simply reach a customer's meter and simultaneously cease to exist. Instead, it passes through, the meter. At the time the electricity is identified to the contract, it is literally moving, and it remains movable for some period of time thereafter. The electricity continues to move through the customer's electrical wiring until it is ultimately put to use. This process may occur at speeds so imperceptible that consumption appears to occur simultaneous with identification, but logic compels the conclusion that electricity is moving (and remains in motion) until it reaches the product sought to be electrified.[93]

So far, courts in the US seem unwilling to qualify electricity in all its forms as a good. Rather, distinctions—sometimes artificial—have been introduced by the courts into electricity that is metered and electricity that has not yet 'reached the meter'.[94] Based on these and other considerations, state courts in several US jurisdictions have reached different and inconsistent conclusions. While some courts have found that electricity can be regarded as a product, at least at the moment of its metering at the customer's destination,[95] others expressly found that electricity is not a good.[96] Some courts reaching the latter conclusion then found that electricity possesses the qualities of a service.[97]

While the overall picture of the jurisprudence regarding the classification issue is inconsistent, a majority of state courts in the US accept that at least for purposes of metering, electricity is a good, while a minority of courts find electricity to be a service.[98] Compared to the jurisprudence in the EU described above, US courts seem

---

[90] The classification question was at issue in a series of cases relating to § 503 (b) (9) of the US Bankruptcy Code. The classification becomes relevant in the context of this provision because sellers of 'goods' under certain conditions enjoy a priority status in bankruptcy proceedings which sellers of 'services' do not. Absent a definition of the terms 'good' and 'service' in the Bankruptcy Code, the Courts have had to fill the gap, mostly with recourse to the UCC definition of 'good'.

[91] Cf the overview over relevant case law in *GFI Wisconsin, Inc. v. Reedsburg Utility Com'n*, 440 B.R. 791, 797 f. (W.D. Wis. 2010).

[92] Uniform Commercial Code of the United States (UCC) § 2-105.

[93] *In Re Erving Industries, Inc.*, 432 B.R. 354, 370 (Bankr. D. Mass. 2010).

[94] For a critique of this reasoning see Ferrey (2004), p. 1888.

[95] *Cincinnati Gas & Elec. Co. v. Goebel*, 502 N.E.2d 713 (Hamilton County Mun. Ct. Ohio 1986); See also Ferrey (2004), p. 1869.

[96] See, among others, *Buckeye Union Fire Ins. Co. v. Detroit Edison Co.*, 196 N.W.2d 316 (Mich. Ct. App. 1972); *United States v. Consolidated Edison Co. of New York, Inc.*, 590 F. Supp. 266, 269 (S.D.N.Y.1984); *In re Pilgrim's Pride Corp.*, 421 B.R. 231, 239 (Bankr. N.D.Tex.2009).

[97] *Otte v. Dayton Power & Light Co.*, 37 Ohio St. 3d 33 (Ohio 1988).

[98] Ferrey (2004), p. 1877.

a bit more cautious to let electricity broadly fall into the goods category. One might speculate that this is because the U.C.C.'s definition of a 'good' is narrower than the understanding of goods for purposes of the application of the EU free movement provisions. In light of the wide interpretive scope of the relevant terms in the GATT, the US approach seems too narrow to follow at the multilateral level.

5.2.5 International Treaties and PTAs

While the treatment of electricity differs considerably between national jurisdictions, international treaties could provide evidence of a common understanding of the WTO Member States with respect to how electricity should be classified. Pursuant to Article 31 (3) lit c VCLT, the terms of a treaty can be interpreted by having recourse to 'any relevant rules of international law applicable in the relations between the parties'.[99] In order to qualify as 'relevant', the text referred to must deal with a similar subject matter.[100] There are two important caveats, however. The first is that according to the text of Article 31 (3) lit c the relevant rules of international law must be 'applicable *in the relations between the parties*' [to the treaty under interpretation]. The relevance of the provision thus depends on whether the term 'between the parties' requires all states that have ratified the treaty under interpretation to be contracting parties to the treaty relied on for interpretative guidance, or whether it suffices that only a part or the majority have ratified it. A WTO Panel ruling on the issue clearly leaned towards the former reading.[101] The second caveat is that, in order to qualify as a means of interpretation under Article 31 (3) lit c, an agreement

---

[99] When bi- or plurilateral PTAs or sectoral agreements were relied on by parties to a WTO dispute, past panels and the Appellate Body referred to these agreements in the context of subsequent practice or as supplementary means of interpretation pursuant to Article 32 VCLT. See WTO, *European Communities – Measures Affecting the Importation of Certain Poultry Products*, Report of the Appellate Body (13 July 1998) WT/DS69/AB/R [83], where the Appellate Body opined that the Oilseeds Agreement negotiated between the European Communities and Brazil may serve as supplementary means of interpretation for the interpretation of a WTO Member's schedule of concessions. More appropriately, however, international agreements would have to be qualified as relevant rules of international law in the meaning of Article 31 (3) lit c VCLT. Subsequent practice relates to the application of the specific treaty to be interpreted (i.e. the WTO covered agreement) while 'any rules of international law applicable in the relations between the parties' include agreements not directly related to the specific Treaty under interpretation.

[100] WTO, *European Communities and Certain Member States – Measures Affecting Trade in Large Civil Aircraft*, Report of the Appellate Body (18 May 2011) WT/DS316/AB/R ('A rule is "relevant" if it concerns the subject matter of the provision at issue'). See also Villiger (2009), p. 433; Dörr and Schmalenbach (2018) [102].

[101] WTO, *European Communities — Measures Affecting the Approval and Marketing of Biotech Products*, Panel Report (29 September 2006) WT/DS291/R [7.68] ('This understanding of the term "the parties" leads logically to the view that the rules of international law to be taken into account in interpreting the WTO agreements at issue in this dispute are those which are applicable in the relations between the WTO Members').

cannot be of a lower rank than the treaty under interpretation. A treaty which explicitly provides that provisions of the treaty under interpretation shall remain unaffected, or that explicitly foresees an adjustment to the rules of the treaty under interpretation, lacks the authority to be qualified as 'relevant'.[102] Even if these two qualifications taken together exclude a considerable number of international treaties as a means of interpretation under Article 31 (3) lit c, the jurisprudence of the WTO adjudicating bodies suggests that such treaties could be relied on as supplementary means of interpretation. The following considerations, therefore, provide a brief survey of 'relevant' international treaties and bilateral agreements.

In the ECT, the list of 'energy materials and products' to which the provisions of the Treaty apply includes 'electricity'.[103] Thus, the drafters of the ECT were clear in their classification: electricity should be treated as a good falling under the ECT rules incorporating GATT provisions.[104]

The NAFTA also treated electricity as a good, despite the equivocal signals coming from domestic jurisprudence in the US. For example, Article 602 (2) NAFTA establishing the scope of application of NAFTA's energy chapter with respect to energy goods expressly listed the electricity sub-heading from the harmonized system (HS).[105] This approach had already been followed by the US and Canada in their bilateral FTA (CUSFTA).[106]

A different approach is followed in some free trade agreements entered into by the EFTA countries (Iceland, Liechtenstein, Norway and Switzerland), as these agreements contain reservations by all or some members to the effect that, for purposes of

---

[102] WTO, *Chile – Price Band System and Safeguard Measures Relating to Certain Agricultural Products*, Panel Report (3 May 2002) WT/DS207/R [7.85].

[103] Energy Charter Treaty (17 December 1994) 2080 U.N.T.S. 95, Annex EM. While the ECT is certainly 'relevant' for classification of electricity in terms of the subject matter that it seeks to regulate, it also serves well to illustrate both challenges mentioned with respect to the application of Article 31 (3) lit c VCLT. All of the ECT's contracting parties with the exception of Turkmenistan are also members of the WTO, but they make up only about a third of the WTO Membership. One might find it incongruous to allow this group of WTO members to determine the interpretation of the WTO Agreements. Furthermore, the text of the ECT explicitly stipulates in Article 4 that 'nothing in this Treaty shall derogate, as between particular Contracting Parties which are members of the WTO, from the provisions of the WTO Agreement as they are applied between those Contracting Parties.' And finally, Article 3 of the 'Trade Amendment' to the ECT stipulates that ECT dispute settlement panels 'shall be guided by the interpretations given to the WTO Agreement within the framework of the WTO Agreement'.

[104] Lakatos (2004), pp. 124 et seq.

[105] Article 602 of the North American Free Trade Agreement (17 December 1992) 32 I.L.M. 289 (1993).

[106] Cf. Article 901(2) (a) of the Canada-United States Free Trade Agreement. As the energy chapter has been removed during the renegotiation of the former NAFTA, the provision ceased to apply between Canada, Mexico and the US at the entering into force of the new CUSMA. The electric energy heading of the HS still features in the individual tariff schedules of the three CUSMA signatories, however.

investment provisions, 'all activities in the power and energy sector (. . .) shall be treated as services under this Agreement.'[107]

The UN Convention on Contracts for the International Sale of Goods (CISG) does not apply to the sale of electricity.[108] According to the explanatory note to the CISG, electricity is part of a group of objects excluded from the scope as these are governed 'by special rules reflecting their special nature' in many states.[109] Other items excluded from the scope include stocks, investment securities, and money, but also ships, vessels and hovercraft. Thus, while the signatories of the CISG seem to agree that electricity is a special case, the exclusion of electricity from the scope of the Convention does not necessarily lead to the assumption that a majority of the CISG Members regard electricity as a service.

In sum, the above-mentioned regimes show a discrepancy in the various approaches to the question whether electricity is to be treated as a good or service. In public law regimes dealing with international trade issues, there seems to be a broader consensus that electricity should fall under trade in goods provisions, while in private commercial law settings electricity is often distinguished from other categories of products.

5.2.6   Treatment of Electricity in the Canada: Renewable Energy Dispute

WTO disputes take place between two or more Members and the findings contained in these reports are only binding upon the Members of the specific dispute. Reports of a panel or the Appellate Body and the reasoning contained therein do not formally constitute a binding precedent for subsequent WTO disputes. It is nonetheless likely that subsequent panels and the Appellate Body will refer to previous reports if interpretive questions come up which have previously been adjudicated or elaborated upon. This is also in line with the key objective of the WTO dispute settlement system as embodied in Article 3.2 DSU—to enhance the security and predictability of the multilateral trading system. The Appellate Body has not followed a Panel's reasoning according to which adopted panel reports constitute subsequent practice in the meaning of Article 31 (3) (b) VCLT in a specific case.[110] The Appellate Body has pointed out, however, that adopted panel reports create legitimate expectations among WTO Members and therefore they should be taken into account by

---

[107] See Appendix 1 to Annex XI (Reservation by all Parties to the investment part) to the Free Trade Agreement between the EFTA States and Singapore (26 June 2002).

[108] See Art. 2 (f) of the United Nations Convention on Contracts for the International Sale of Goods (CISG), 1489 U.N.T.S. 3, 19 I.L.M. 671 (11 April 1980). See also Mäntysaari (2015), p. 71.

[109] CISG (n 535), Explanatory Note.

[110] See WTO, *Japan – Taxes on Alcoholic Beverages*, Panel Report (11 July 1996) WT/DS8/R [6.10 *et seq.*] and the Report of the Appellate Body, WT/DS8/AB/R [108].

subsequent panels dealing with the same or a similar issue.[111] On a different occasion, the Appellate Body elaborated that 'panel reports in previous disputes do not form part of the context of a term or provision in the sense of Article 31 (2) of the Vienna Convention. Rather, the legal interpretation embodied in the adopted panel and Appellate Body reports become part and parcel of the WTO acquis and have to be taken into account as such.'[112]

In the only electricity-related dispute to date in the history of WTO Dispute Settlement, the question whether electricity must be regarded as a good or service was touched upon only in passing. The qualification was not a decisive issue because electricity did not lie at the heart of the GATT claims. Rather, the complainants claimed that electricity-generating equipment like wind towers manufactured outside the Canadian province of Ontario was discriminated against.[113] The measure at issue was a provision in the Feed-in Tariff (FIT) scheme, which the Ontario Power Authority had adopted in 2009 as part of the wider Green Energy and Green Economy Act of Ontario and Ontario's Long-Term Energy Plan.[114] This provision required that a certain minimum percentage of inputs for wind energy and solar facilities had to be produced in Ontario in order for the generators to qualify for the FIT remuneration.[115]

Despite the secondary importance of the classification issue for the dispute, the parties touched upon the question in their written submissions. The EU and Canada both took the position that electricity is to be regarded as a good. In their reasoning, they referred primarily to the practice of several WTO Members to undertake binding tariff commitments under the optional heading on electricity in the Harmonized System (HS).[116] While Japan expressly refrained from taking a conclusive position on this issue, it referred to electricity as a 'commodity' and recognized that it is treated as a good in the optional heading of the HS.[117] Furthermore, Japan did not dispute the classification of the FIT scheme in Ontario by Canada as government purchase of *goods*. The EU, in its written submission, took the view that electricity

---

[111] WTO, *Japan – Taxes on Alcoholic Beverages*, Report of the Appellate Body (4 October 1996) WT/DS8/AB/R, p. 14.

[112] WTO, *US – Anti-Dumping and Countervailing Duties* (China), Report of the Appellate Body (11 March 2011) WT/DS379/AB/R.

[113] Electricity as such was, however, at issue in the claims concerning the SCMA, as Canada contended that the measures challenged by Japan and the EU concerned the 'purchase of goods' by the government. Thus, Canada argued that the Feed-In Tariff, i.e., a fixed payment for a certain amount of electricity generated from renewable sources, qualifies as purchase of goods. As the Panel notes, Japan had not challenged this contention. See WTO, *Canada – Certain Measures Affecting the Renewable Energy Generation Sector*, Panel Report (19 December 2012) WT/DS412/R, footnote 46.

[114] Ontario Green Energy and Green Economy Act, 2009, S.O. 2009, c. 12 - Bill 150.

[115] For the detailed rules see Ontario Power Authority, Feed-In Tariff Program Rules (Version 1.5.1), available at http://www.ieso.ca/en/Sector-Participants/Feed-in-Tariff-Program/FIT-Archive.

[116] WTO, *Canada – Renewable Energy*, Panel Report, Footnote 46. On the significance of the HS, see below, pp. 107 et seq.

[117] Ibid.

generated through the FIT Contracts amounts to a 'product', rather than a service.[118] This claim was based on the FIT Contracts themselves, which used the term 'product' on several occasions when referring to electricity, and the observation that the generators benefitting from the FIT scheme did not engage in the distribution of electricity (a service), but the generation of electricity (the product concerned).[119] In sum, none of the Parties objected to the treatment of electricity as a good.

The Panel addressed the question only in a footnote as it was not central to the dispute. The Panel noted that the issue was uncontested among the parties who agreed that the result of the electricity generation process 'is a good and a product for the purpose of the covered agreements that are at issue.'[120] It is interesting to note that the Panel did not clearly distinguish between the three terms 'good', 'product' and 'commodity', but seemed to accept that electricity can be a good, commodity and product at the same time.[121] The classification issue was not submitted for review before the Appellate Body.

The Parties' submissions in the *Canada-Renewable Energy* dispute and the brief footnote-statement of the Panel provide a first taste of a possible approach to the classification issue for purposes of interpretation of the covered agreements of the WTO. One could interpret this as a tendency to qualify electricity as a good for WTO purposes. The actual significance of this cursory treatment of the issue for future disputes might be limited, however, especially when a Party will have a substantive legal interest in arguing that the rules of the GATT should not be applicable to the dispute.[122] The *Canada – Renewable Energy* dispute was framed as a goods-related case involving the GATT, the TRIMS and SCMA, and no services-related claims were put forward by the parties to the dispute. Considering the different approaches in WTO Members domestic legal systems and international agreements, the issue will have to be examined in more detail by future Panels or the Appellate Body.

---

[118] WTO, *Canada –Renewable Energy*, First written submission of the European Union (14 February 2012) Fn. 66.

[119] Ibid.

[120] WTO, *Canada – Renewable Energy*, Panel Report, Footnote 46.

[121] Ibid. In the words of the Panel: 'We note that it is not contested in these disputes that electricity produced from electricity generation facilities (what the parties refer to as "*commodity*" electricity) is a *good* and a *product* for the purpose of the covered agreements that are at issue.' (emphasis added).

[122] Mavroidis (2016), p. 141, stresses with respect to the classification issue that the Panel in *Canada – Renewable Energy* 'did not provide a definitive finding on the coverage of the GATT on this issue.' For a slightly different view see Sánchez Miranda (2015), p. 3 who points to the important role of precedent in WTO dispute settlement.

5.2.7 Treatment of Electricity in International Classification Instruments for Customs Purposes

Goods classification in international trade is mainly informed by the Harmonized Commodity Description and Coding System (also known as the HS system) administered by the World Customs Organization (WCO). The HS System is the 'common language' of goods trade and informs the interpretation of many GATT articles.[123] It entered into force in 1988 and is subject to amendments taking place roughly every 4–6 years to bring it in line with latest developments.[124] Importantly, the HS headings inform the schedules of tariff concessions in which WTO Members have registered their additional and specific commitments as a result of accession negotiations and trade rounds. They are also a point of reference for determining the scope of GATT obligations in Articles I, II and III GATT.[125] WTO panels and the Appellate Body have interpreted schedules as WTO treaty language in accordance with Article 31 VCLT by considering the schedules to be integral parts of the WTO Agreement.[126]

The HS System consists of codes of up to six standardized digits, which help to identify a product. The first two digits identify a chapter, the subsequent ones the heading and subheading. Beyond the six-digit classification, Members can introduce further subdivisions, a possibility that many countries make use of. 'Electric energy' is listed in the HS System under the HS code 2716.00 in Section V (Mineral Products), Chapter 27 (Mineral Fuels, Mineral Oils and Products of Their Distillation; Bituminous Substances; Mineral Waxes). The HS heading for electric energy is a special case, as it is the only optional heading in the HS. This means that WTO Members are not obliged to refer to it in their schedules of concessions and classify it as a commodity for tariff purposes.[127] Members are free to use a different description.[128] A few Members have indeed decided to refrain from including the electricity sub-heading in their respective schedules. A majority of WTO Members, however, has committed to tariffs under the heading.[129] The fact that a Member decides against including the HS heading for electricity in its schedule does not in and of itself mean that the coverage of the GATT is thereby limited, and the Member

---

[123] Feichtner (2008), p. 1481.

[124] Yu (2008), p. 1. The most recent revision of the HS entered into force on 1 January 2022.

[125] Feichtner (2008), p. 1482. See also Mavroidis (2016), p. 138 who states that 'the sum of classifications circumscribes (. . .) the coverage of the GATT'.

[126] WTO, *European Communities – Customs Classification of Certain Computer Equipment*, Report of the Appellate Body (5 June 1998) WT/DS62/AB/R [88].

[127] Zarrilli (2004), p. 243.

[128] Mavroidis (2016), p. 140.

[129] Lakatos (2004), p. 122.

escapes its obligations under the substantive GATT provisions with respect to electricity.[130]

The HS entry for electric energy and the practice of the large majority of WTO Members to base their tariff commitments on that entry advocate in favour of the classification of electricity as a good. Nevertheless, the optional nature of the heading attests to the existence of diverging views among countries on the adequacy of this classification.[131] Furthermore, the initial HS classifications stem from the old GATT 1947 era, at which point there were no services disciplines within the framework of the WTO.[132] Overall, it can be concluded that the harmonized system and WTO Members' practice of goods classification do not provide a secure enough foothold for the classification of electricity as a good.

5.2.8   Electricity in Services Classification Instruments

Similar to the HS System on goods classification, classification instruments also exist for services. The most important ones are the UN Central Product Classification (CPC)[133] and the Services Sectoral Classification List (hereafter referred to as the 'W/120').[134] A provisional version of the former was officially published in 1991 for statistical purposes. It includes a classification of goods *and* services. The latter was developed by the old GATT Secretariat before the WTO was established to facilitate negotiations on services and market access during the Uruguay Round negotiations. The W/120 is based on the CPC list. WTO Members frequently reference the lists in their schedules of commitments.[135] Members are not obliged to use these instruments, however, and the lists do not reflect all service aspects of modern economic activities.[136] While they neither provide an ultimate answer to the definition of 'services'[137] nor conclusive guidance as to whether a service falls within or outside the scope of the GATS,[138] at least the services included in the W/120 must be

---

[130]Mavroidis (2016), p. 141.

[131]Zarrilli (2004), p. 243.

[132]Cottier et al. (2011), p. 215.

[133]United Nations, Provisional Central Product Classification (1991) ST/ESA/STAT/SER.M/77.

[134]GATT Doc. MTN.GNS/W/120, Services Sectoral Classification List: Note by the Secretariat (10 July 1991).

[135]Cossy (2009), p. 153. The Council for Trade in Services recommends using the W/120, which is included as an attachment to the guidelines for the scheduling of specific commitments under the GATS.

[136]In fact, as Poretti and Rios-Herran (2006), p. 23 note, discontent with the current system of classification is widespread among the WTO Membership.

[137]WTO (2010) [53].

[138]Cossy (2009), p. 153.

regarded as defining the core of the sectoral coverage of the GATS.[139] This is especially relevant with respect to those horizontal commitments in the GATS which take effect independent of specific commitments by GATS Members, such as the MFN treatment provision.[140] The Appellate Body held that the W/120, together with the Scheduling Guidelines, constitute supplementary means of inter-pretation within the meaning of Article 32 VCLT.[141] Thus, in the determination of whether an economic activity constitutes a 'service' in a specific case, recourse can be had to the W/120 if the context and purpose are not conclusive.

The CPC has been updated from its provisional version to better reflect contem-porary developments with respect to the services industry. Updates of the CPC, however, do not automatically lead to modifications of the W/120. Changes to the WTO list will have to be agreed on by Members.[142] Thus it happens in practice that the CPC list is being modified to include new service entries or to add substance to existing divisions, while the W/120 remains 'locked in'. In fact, the WTO list has not been updated since it was first drafted in the context of the Uruguay Round in 1991.[143] This has specific relevance for the electricity sector, as will be discussed further below.

Neither of the two classification instruments includes a chapter specifically devoted to the energy sector.[144] Nonetheless, energy services are addressed in different chapters. The coverage of existing electricity services is certainly not

---

[139] In the words of *Adlung and Zhang*, the W/120 constitutes 'a (minimum) outer perimeter of the Agreement in terms of sectoral coverage.' See Adlung and Zhang (2012), p. 4. This does not seem to be academic consensus, however. Cf Cossy (2009), p. 153 who opines that 'classification instruments do not determine the scope of the Agreement: they are only tools to help Members establish their schedules of commitments.'

[140] Adlung and Zhang (2012), p. 4.

[141] WTO, *United States – Measures Affecting the Cross-Border Supply of Gambling and Betting Services*, Report of the Appellate Body (7 April 2005) WT/DS285/AB/R [197]. In the same Report, the Appellate Body discarded the Panel's approach to consider the W/120 and Scheduling Guide-lines as 'context' within the meaning of Article 31 (2) VCLT. The Appellate Body mainly based this finding on the fact that the W/120 was drafted by the GATT Secretariat rather than the Parties to the negotiations. In the words of the Appellate Body: 'Such documents can be characterized as context only where there is sufficient evidence of their constituting an "agreement relating to the treaty" between the parties or of their "accept[ance by the parties] as an instrument related to the treaty"'. Furthermore, the Appellate Body pointed out that 'although Members were encouraged to follow the broad structure of W/120, it was never meant to bind Members to the CPC definitions, nor to any other "specific nomenclature" (. . .).' Ibid [175].

[142] Adlung and Zhang (2012), p. 4.

[143] Zhang (2015), p. 8.

[144] WTO (2010) [42]. It has been speculated that this is because, during the Uruguay Round when the W/120 came into existence, the energy sector was still dominated by public ownership. See Cossy (2009), p. 152.

comprehensive,[145] especially with regards to those additional services which newly surfaced in the course of energy sector restructuring and liberalization.[146]

The W/120 includes three sub-sectors, which explicitly refer to energy. These are 'services incidental to mining'; 'services incidental to energy distribution'; and 'pipeline transportation of fuels'. Other individual activities which also apply to energy are scattered over other parts of the classification instrument.[147] 'Services incidental to mining' and 'transportation of fuels' have no specific relevance for electricity. The relevance of 'services incidental to energy distribution' is discussed below.

Based on this structure provided by the services classification instruments, it can be observed that for purposes of services classification, considering the entire electricity supply chain is much more crucial than for goods classification and that a clear line has to be drawn between the generation stage and the transmission and distribution stages. In this context, two controversial questions have presented themselves with respect to electricity. The first is whether and under what circumstances the generation of electricity can be regarded as a service. The second is whether transmission and distribution *per se* are covered, or only services *incidental to* these activities. Both issues will be discussed in turn.

5.2.8.1   The Classification of the Generation of Electricity

It is not an easy exercise to determine to what extent the generation of electricity falls within the scope of the GATS. Clearly, not all production services fall within the scope of either the CPC or the W/120. The WTO list includes a heading on 'services incidental to manufacturing'.[148] While this division includes a sub-heading on 'Petroleum, chemical and pharmaceutical manufacturing services'—which WTO Members have relied on to undertake commitments—no comparable entry exists for the generation of electricity. In the absence of specific electricity-related divisions in the classification instruments, the general entries for 'manufacturing services' could in principle apply to electricity nonetheless. Heading 88 on 'services incidental to manufacturing' has a corresponding entry in the old provisional CPC

---

[145]While Cossy (2009), p. 153 sees 'the entire chain of energy services' covered, Pineau (2004), p. 266 notes an 'absence of almost all energy services from the W/120 list'. The difference could stem from the narrower focus of *Pineau* on the electricity sector, while *Cossy* looks at the whole energy sector.

[146]Among many others, wholesale trading and retailing services, metering and billing of electricity were missing in the classification instruments. Cf Zarrilli (2004), p. 245; WTO (2010) [47]. Since updating it to Version 2.1, the CPC now includes an entry for 'wholesale trade services, except on a fee or contract basis, of electricity'. See United Nations Department of Economic and Social Affairs, Central Product Classification Version 2.1 (2015), p. 414.

[147]The most important ones are to be found in business services, construction, distribution and transport services. See also Cossy (2009), p. 153.

[148]See Heading No. 88 of the Services Sectoral Classification List W/120.

list, the explanatory note to which clarifies that this concerns only 'manufacturing services rendered to others where the raw materials processed, treated or finished are not owned by the manufacturer.'[149] In other words, 'services incidental to manufacturing' covers services rendered on a fee or contract basis,[150] i.e. outsourced production processes. The updated heading in the current version of the CPC makes it even clearer that ownership is the decisive criterion by referring to 'manufacturing services on physical inputs owned by others.' It follows from the above that the coverage of manufacturing services in the services classification instruments has an important limitation—the physical inputs of the production process must be owned by an entity different from the one supplying the manufacturing service.[151] When the inputs of production belong to the manufacturer, the production process does not qualify as a service within the scope of the GATS.[152] The resulting dichotomy between manufacturing services rendered on account of someone else and (in-house) production of a good leads to irrational results when applied to the electricity industry. Applying this reasoning to the generation segment of the electricity sector, it becomes clear that the ownership criterion is not appropriate to judge whether the generation must be qualified as a good or service. In most conventional power plants, the inputs of production—coal, uranium or gas—are purchased and thus owned by the operator of the plant. Under the definition suggested by the explanatory note, this would clearly not qualify as a service. Operators of most renewable energy facilities, on the other hand, cannot claim ownership over the inputs of production as sunlight and wind cannot be claimed as property. Thus, following the logic of the explanatory note to the CPC list, such type of electricity generation as a matter of fact could be carried out as a service. This outcome is unsatisfactory and appears to violate the principle of equal treatment. The focus on ownership as a criterion to determine whether an economic activity constitutes the provision of a service or the production of a good is a major weakness of the classification instruments relied on by WTO Members when applied to the electricity sector.

5.2.8.2   The Classification of Transmission and Distribution of Electricity

With respect to the transmission and distribution of electricity, the situation is as follows: The CPC category of 'services incidental to energy distribution' cover the transmission and distribution on a fee or contract basis of electricity to household, industrial, commercial and other users.[153] Whether this includes transmission and

---

[149] Cossy (2009), p. 151.

[150] This term is also used in the explanatory note.

[151] Cossy (2009), p. 151; Selivanova (2014), p. 295.

[152] Adlung and Zhang (2012), p. 9.

[153] See United Nations, Provisional Central Product Classification (1991) ST/ESA/STAT/SER.M/ 77, 48, 77.

distribution of electricity per se or just the services necessary to enable it remains disputed. As *Zarilli* notes,

> the original intent of that entry (CPC 88700) seems to have been those services – such as management, operation and repair of the network, and meter reading – necessary for the distribution and transmission of electricity on a fee or contract basis, but not transmission and distribution of electricity per se, since those activities were rarely undertaken on a fee or contract basis at the time when the classification list was established.[154]

Furthermore, the transport of energy goods 'in-house', i.e. produced by the same company, appears to fall outside the definition as it lacks the fundamental character of a service.[155] While the historical context—the original intent of the Parties—may well justify the distinction between services ancillary to the transmission and distribution of electricity and the transmission and distribution as separate activities, this distinction is artificial and does not do justice to the realities of the electricity sector. Management, operation, and repair of the network are precisely the services that together make up the commercial activities of transmission and distribution of electricity by network operators. Thus, nowadays there should be little ambiguity about the services character of all 'downstream' activities in the electricity sector, like transmission, distribution and supply. This view is in fact supported by more recent updates of the CPC. In its current version, it now also covers 'electricity transmission services' and 'transmission of electricity on own account'.[156] These improvements have not yet been reflected in the W/120, however.

The above considerations show that a realignment of the classification instruments with the physical and commercial realities in the electricity market is urgently needed. This fact has been recognized by several WTO Members and has found its way into GATS negotiations, but suggestions made by individual WTO Members never materialized.[157] At the same time, the significance of the services classification instruments should not be overstated, as they would not appear to constitute a formal impediment to market access negotiations.

---

[154]Zarrilli (2004), p. 245; see also WTO (2010) [47].

[155]Cossy (2009), p. 168.

[156]See codes 86311 and 69111 respectively of the CPC version 2.1. United Nations Department of Economic and Social Affairs, Central Product Classification Version 2.1 (2015) 114.

[157]The issue has been discussed within the Committee on Specific Commitments (CSC) since 1997. See Poretti and Rios Herran (2006), p. 23. In the early stages of the Doha negotiations, a group of WTO Members formed which called itself the 'Friends of Energy Services'. The group was advocating a more targeted classification of services in the energy sector but considering the current situation it must be concluded that their efforts were of limited effect.

5.2.9 Conclusions on the Classification of Electricity and Consequences for the Application of the GATT and the GATS

The above analysis makes it clear that the goods-services dichotomy so prevalent in international trade law poses a challenge when dealing with electricity trade disputes. The GATT does not exclusively refer to 'goods' but also to 'products' and moreover covers commodities. It has been argued that this widens the scope of application of the GATT. The nature of electricity does not correspond to dictionary definitions of the term 'goods'. A classification of electricity as a good thus to a certain extent disregards physical reality. This being said, future WTO adjudicators should not close their eyes to the object and purpose of the WTO Agreements and to commercial realities of the electricity industry by resorting exclusively to dictionary definitions. Electricity is treated and traded nowadays as a commodity on many national and some regional energy markets. The large majority of WTO Members treat electricity as a good in their tariff schedules. Practice and jurisprudence in other domestic and international legal frameworks also show an overall tendency to categorize electricity as a good.

Based on the foregoing, it can be concluded that electricity as the result of the generation process is a commodity subject to the rules of the GATT and other goods-related covered agreements.

Moving away from a narrow focus on electricity as the result of the process of generation, it can also be observed that a constant and secure supply of electricity, and indeed the commercial use of electric energy, depends on a large number of services. It seems likely that regulatory measures in the electricity sector which will be made subject to review by the WTO dispute settlement bodies will involve aspects of both goods and services, calling for the application of both GATT and GATS disciplines. As the Panel in *Canada-Periodicals* has already declared in 1997 (albeit probably not having electricity in mind), overlaps between the subject matters of the two agreements 'will further increase with the progress of technology and the globalization of economic activities.'[158]

Two major challenges for the classification of individual stages of the electricity value chain have been identified based on the treatment of electricity in the services classification instruments regularly relied on by WTO Members for scheduling commitments. The first relates to the generation process which, based on the language in explanatory notes to the classification instruments, only qualifies as a service if the inputs of production are not owned by the producer (i.e., a power plant). The second relates to the 'rendered on a fee or contract basis' requirement for the qualification of transmission and distribution as services. Both examples make it clear that the premises of services classification are out of touch with the

---

[158] WTO, *Canada – Certain Measures Concerning Periodicals*, Report of the Panel (14 March 1997) WT/DS31/R [5.18].

contemporary realities of the electricity industry. This state of affairs should be remedied for the sake of certainty and the visibility of services.[159]

In sum, for the purposes of applying the WTO covered agreements, it is sensible to follow many national courts and the European Court of Justice in applying the provisions on trade in goods to measures regulating the import or export of electric energy or its treatment once imported. At the same time, most 'downstream' activities in the electricity sector are services and the providers of these services are subject to GATS obligations such as national treatment and market access. This applies to the transmission and distribution of electricity and ancillary services relating to balancing, metering and other aspects usually carried out by system operators or distribution companies and suppliers. If WTO Members remain reluctant to undertake binding commitments on electricity services, however, market access will remain very limited for electricity service providers.

The example of electricity serves as evidence to support the claim that 'the distinction between services and merchandise trade has increasingly been rendered void', and that the WTO Agreements are not well equipped to deal with the challenges posed by contemporary economic realities.[160] A multilateral sectoral Agreement could remedy the identified shortcomings by either accepting the integrated nature of the electricity sector and providing for 'neutral' rules; or by providing clearer and more explicit classifications when subjecting electricity trade to the existing Agreements.[161]

5.3 Electricity As a Subject of WTO Accessions

Accession to the WTO involves negotiating the terms and conditions of membership and the relations with other Members. Accession takes place in line with Article XII of the WTO Agreement, according to which 'any State or separate customs territory (. . .) may accede to this Agreement, on terms agreed between it and the WTO.' The accession procedure is set in motion by a written request from a State or customs territory to the WTO Secretariat, which then forwards the request to all existing Members and the WTO General Council.[162] The General Council establishes a Working Party open to all interested WTO Members to deal with practical matters arising from the accession request. The process involves not just multilateral elements, but also bilateral discussions and negotiations. The final Working Party Report will contain the legally binding commitments negotiated between the

---

[159] See the proposals for a new 'classification list on electricity services' in Part IV below at pp. 229 et seq.

[160] Adlung and Mamdouh (2017), p. 22.

[161] For concrete proposals in this respect see below in Sect. 14.2.1, pp. 229 et seq.

[162] Milthorp and Christy (2012), pp. 266 et seq. For a profound analysis of the accession process see Geraets (2018).

existing Members and the State requesting accession.[163] Together with the Protocol
of Accession, which includes the specific terms of the accession, the Working Party
Report then becomes a part of the final Accession Package, which must be approved
by the General Council before an accession is finalized. The negotiated commitments as fixed in the Protocol are enforceable in WTO dispute settlement and add to
the obligations entered into under the WTO Agreements. The precise relationship
between a Protocol of Accession and the multilateral WTO Agreements is not easy
to determine. With respect to China's protocol of accession, the Appellate Body held
that China's accession protocol was an 'integral part' of the multilateral trade
agreements.[164] The Protocol of Accession will bind a WTO Member for the period
of membership unless otherwise agreed.

Several Protocols of Accession deal specifically with energy issues and the
energy sector plays an increasingly important role in accession negotiations.[165]
Long-standing WTO Members sometimes take the accession protocols as a welcome
opportunity to ask new members for concessions that they were not able to get in
multilateral negotiations.[166] More recent accessions of fossil fuel exporting countries
like Oman, Saudi Arabia and the Russian Federation have added some commitments
with respect to issues typically arising in oil and gas trade. Among these are pricing
policies, the treatment of state trading enterprises, licensing requirements, export
duties, and quantitative export restrictions and subsidization.[167] Mexico, in its 1986
Protocol of Accession, managed to negotiate an exemption from GATT rules by
preserving the right to maintain energy export restrictions.[168] With respect to pricing
policies, on the other hand, Mexico conceded that it would not apply price practices
in the energy sector which would amount to an export subsidy.[169] Saudi Arabia was
asked by WTO Members to abolish a dual pricing system for liquid natural gas
(LNG)—a system which had resulted in significantly higher prices for exports than
for internal sales.[170] The Saudi-Arabian accession was interesting also from a more
general perspective, as it implicitly confirmed the notion that energy trade falls
within the domain of the WTO.[171]

---

[163] Milthorp and Christy (2012), p. 268.

[164] WTO, *China – Measures Related to the Exportation of Rare Earths, Tungsten, and Molybdenum*, Report of the Appellate Body (7 August 2015) WT/DS431/AB/R [5.75].

[165] Meyer (2012), p. 145; Mathur and Mann note that most commitments in these sub-sectors have
been undertaken by recently acceded members. Mathur and Mann (2014), p. 92.

[166] Meyer (2012), p. 145.

[167] For an overview over all these issues see Mathur and Mann (2014), p. 75 ff.

[168] Meyer (2012), p. 146; citing Leal-Arcas et al. (2014), p. 125.

[169] WTO, Report of the Working Party on the Accession of Mexico (4 July 1986) GATT Document
L/6010 [54].

[170] Mathur and Mann (2014), p. 76.

[171] Milthorp and Christy (2012), p. 259 report that during a stakeholder meeting in Riyadh
preceding the WTO accession, it was claimed that the WTO lacks rules on energy, particularly
oil, and therefore 'has nothing to offer us'.

While most of the energy-related sections of accession working party reports and protocols of accession are motivated by interests in fossil fuel trade, the commitments included in them are relevant for electricity as well. This relates especially, but not exclusively, to topics such as the investment framework, competition law, state-trading and state-owned enterprises, transit provisions, and import and export restrictions like quotas and licensing requirements.

In the accession of Oman, pricing policies for electricity were at issue. Oman maintained maximum prices for electricity and other basic services and subsidized electricity consumption for private households. For industrial and commercial users, a maximum price was set at Baisa 24 per kWh in summer and Baisa 12 per kWh during the winter months.[172] Upon request of a WTO Member, Oman stated in the accession negotiations that the differentiation of electricity prices for private households had social reasons and that the maximum prices for industrial and commercial users were aimed at the development of infant industries.[173] The Omani representative also reported that harmonization of the prices and privatization of the electricity sector was under consideration and ensured that the pricing policy would be applied in a WTO-consistent manner.[174]

Saudi Arabia, in its working party report, informed the WTO Members about the state-owned Saudi Electricity Company (SEC). This entity was responsible for electric power services, domestic and foreign investments in the electricity sector and the import and export of electricity across Saudi Arabia's borders.[175] Saudi Arabia informed the WTO Members that the government did not play any role in the setting of company policy or in operational decisions and that the SEC did not enjoy any special or exclusive privileges.[176] Members made similar requests for information during Ukraine's accession with respect to the state-owned electricity company Energorynok.[177]

With respect to transit, the accession protocols of Ukraine and Russia are informative as they include an express commitment to apply domestic rules on the transit of energy goods in conformity with existing WTO transit provisions (Article V GATT).[178] This illustrates how provisions in the WTO Agreements with general coverage can be restated with a sector-specific focus in accession negotiations in order to mitigate the concerns of other members.

---

[172] WTO, Report of the Working Party on the Accession of the Sultanate of Oman, WT/ACC/OMN/26 (28 September 2000) [22]. Baisa is a unit of an Omani Rial, the official currency of the Sultanate of Oman.

[173] WTO, Report of the Working Party on the Accession of the Sultanate of Oman, WT/ACC/OMN/26 (28 September 2000) [23].

[174] Ibid [22-23].

[175] WTO, Report of the Working Party on the Accession of the Kingdom of Saudi Arabia, WT/ACC/SAU/61 (1 November 2005) [44 (iii)].

[176] Ibid.

[177] WTO, Report of the Working Party on the Accession of Ukraine, WT/ACC/UKR/152 (25 January 2008) [43-44].

[178] Mathur and Mann (2014), p. 92.

Accession negotiations have also contained commitments in the services sector. Accessions in the more recent past have generally included a higher number of concessions in relation to the energy sector.[179] These commitments concern most of the service sub-sectors discussed above.[180] The driving force behind most of these concessions were bilateral market access negotiations, where trading partners sought access to new markets for their energy service providers.[181] In sum, the evidence on record from the 36 accession protocols that have been negotiated so far shows that the energy sector features increasingly prominently.[182] It can also be assumed that, based on the commitments entered into by acceding countries, WTO accession can be a step on the way to the liberalization of the domestic electricity market of the acceding WTO Member. It remains to be seen whether future accessions will continue this trend or whether the electricity sector will perhaps play an even larger role.

5.4   Lessons from the Treatment of Electricity in WTO Dispute Settlement

As already mentioned, the electricity sector has not yet been the subject of a WTO dispute. No measure regulating trade in electricity has ever been challenged before the WTO. Two disputes came close, however. The first was the *Canada – Renewable Energy* case[183] and the second was *European Union – Measures Relating to the Energy sector*.[184] In the latter, Russia had initially included a number of regulatory instruments concerning the electricity sector in its request for consultations.[185] It later dropped the electricity-related claims, however, and focused exclusively on the gas sector in its request for the establishment of a Panel.[186] For this reason, this case will not be further discussed here.[187]

---

[179] Ibid.

[180] See above in Sect. 5.2.8, pp. 108 et seq.

[181] Mathur and Mann (2014), p. 92.

[182] The accession protocols concluded so far can be consulted on the WTO website at https://www. wto.org/english/thewto_e/acc_e/completeacc_e.htm.

[183] WTO, *Canada – Certain Measures Affecting the Renewable Energy Generation Sector*, Reports of the Appellate Body (6 May 2013) WT/DS412/AB/R; WT/DS426/AB/R.

[184] WTO, *European Union and its Member States – Certain Measures Relating to the Energy Sector*, Request for Consultations by the Russian Federation (8 May 2014) WT/DS476/1.

[185] Ibid.

[186] WTO, *European Union and its Member States – Certain Measures Relating to the Energy Sector*, Request for the Establishment of a Panel by the Russian Federation (28 May 2015) WT/DS476/2.

[187] For a discussion of the case and a critical appraisal of the Panel Report see Dralle and Frey (2018), pp. 445 et seq. See also Talus and Wüstenberg (2018).

Canada-Renewable Energy did not concern international trade in electricity as such. The case was confined to the electricity system of Ontario and whether any electricity had crossed the border to neighbouring countries was of no relevance to the case. Rather, the goods that were traded internationally and subject to alleged discriminatory treatment were wind power and solar PV technologies utilized in electricity generation facilities.[188] The claimants, Japan and the EU, have considerable export interests in these goods. Despite the fact that the claims brought under the GATT, the TRIMS and the SCMA did not concern electricity as such, the case is interesting and potentially relevant for the electricity sector. This is because the Panel and Appellate Body in their reasoning found it necessary to draw on the fundamentals of electricity sector regulation in general, and the specifics of such regulation in Ontario to properly evaluate the measures at issue in the case.[189] In the words of the Panel: 'the complexity of electricity systems and how electricity prices are determined in Ontario are germane to much of our analysis of the complainants' claims.'[190] To approach this 'complexity', the Panel relied on the report of an expert in electricity regulation. Both the Panel and the Appellate Body referred to the 'Hogan Report' named after its author on several occasions.[191]

The Panel engaged in a discussion of the typical features of electricity systems and explained the main concepts underlying electricity markets.[192] The Panel noted that electricity is characterized by special properties in comparison to other goods and explained that the electric system has to be kept in constant operation to ensure a reliable supply.[193] The Panel went on to note the intangibility of electricity and its non-storability and inferred that generation and consumption must happen simultaneously.[194] It then continued by introducing the concept of the electric grid with different voltage levels. Particular emphasis was put on the necessity of balancing generation and load and the serious consequences which can result when imbalances occur.[195] One implication, according to the Panel is that access to the grid 'has to be tightly controlled to ensure the integrity of the system as a whole.'[196] The Panel also noted the further interesting fact that due to the need to keep the entire system in continuous balance, 'uncoordinated bilateral trades between buyers and sellers of

---

[188] WTO, *Canada – Certain Measures Affecting the Renewable Energy Generation Sector*, Request for Consultations by the European Union (16 August 2011) WT/DS426/1.

[189] WTO, *Canada – Certain Measures Affecting the Renewable Energy Generation Sector*, Reports of the Panels (19 December 2012) WT/DS412/R; WT/DS426/R [7.9].

[190] Ibid.

[191] Hogan, 'Overview of the Electricity System in the Province of Ontario' ('The Hogan Report') (21 December 2011), Panel Exhibit CDA-2.

[192] WTO, *Canada – Renewable Energy*, Reports of the Panels [7.32-33].

[193] Ibid [7.11].

[194] Ibid.

[195] Ibid.

[196] Ibid.

electricity cannot take place.'[197] The Panel went further by stating that '(...) because of the nature of how electricity must be produced and consumed, it is generally not possible for an individual consumer to enter into an individual supply contract with one or more specific generators.'[198] This statement by the Panel is not entirely in line with more recent developments in the electricity sector, which is witnessing an increase in direct power supply contracts between companies and individual generators (so-called 'corporate power purchase agreements' or 'corporate PPAs').[199] Thus, the panel could have distinguished more clearly between contractual relations (which indeed often are bilateral) and actual physical delivery.

The Panel also noted the historical development of the electricity sector from vertical integration and the domination of state-owned enterprises or regulated private monopolies to restructured and more competitive markets.[200] A particular problem recognized by the Panel is that electricity markets are seldom perfect markets and almost never function without any state intervention. In this context, the Panel discussed the problem of 'missing money', a common theme in the academic literature on electricity markets. The core of the missing money problem is that in extreme situations or when regulated price caps do not allow the price to rise over a certain limit, the price signals may not be strong enough to incentivize investors to build new generation capacity.

This short summary of the most relevant statements of the Panel demonstrates that the special nature of electricity—and the resulting need for safety and central oversight (a 'central coordination mechanism' in the words of the Panel[201])—has been acknowledged by WTO Dispute Settlement organs. Some of the textbook explanations of the Panel seem to be a bit outdated and disregard the rapid evolution of electricity markets in the course of digitalization and the energy transition. The Appellate Body on appeal restated some of the more questionable points but remarked with a certain amount of caution that 'to the extent we reproduce the Panel's statements that seem to relate generally to electricity markets, we do so because we consider them to be of particular application to the circumstances of these disputes and not necessarily because we are of the view that they necessarily reflect the characteristics of all electricity markets.'[202]

---

[197] Ibid [7.12].

[198] Ibid.

[199] On the concept of PPAs see above in Sect. 2.2.6, pp. 35 et seq.

[200] WTO, *Canada – Renewable Energy*, Reports of the Panels [7.20].

[201] Ibid [7.12].

[202] WTO, *Canada – Renewable Energy*, AB Reports [4.1].

References

Abu-Akeel A (1999) Definition of trade in services under the GATS: legal implications. Geo Wash J Int Law Econ 32:189

Adlung R, Mamdouh H (2017) Plurilateral Trade Agreements: An Escape Route for the WTO? WTO Working Paper ERSD-2017-03

Adlung R, Zhang W (2012) Trade disciplines with a trapdoor: contract manufacturing. WTO Staff Working Paper ERSD-2012-11

Albath L (2005) Handel und Investitionen in Strom und Gas: Die internationalen Regeln. C. H. Beck, Munich, p 91

Andoni M (2019) Blockchain technology in the energy sector: a systematic review of challenges and opportunities. Renew Sustain Energy Rev 100:143

Botchway F (2001) International Trade Regime and Energy Trade. Syracuse J Int Law Commerce 1:1

Boute A (2016) Energy Trade and investment law: international limits to EU energy law and policy. In: Roggenkamp M et al (eds) Energy Law in Europe - National, EU and International Regulation, 3rd edn. Oxford University Press, Oxford

Brown L, Trumble W, Stevenson A (eds) (2002) Shorter Oxford English Dictionary Volume 1: A-M, 5th edn. Oxford University Press, Oxford

Casazza J, Delea F (2010) Understanding electric power systems: an overview of technology, the marketplace and government regulation. Wiley, Hoboken, p 132

Clark E, Lesourd J, Thiéblemont R (2001) International Commodity Trading: physical and derivative markets. Wiley, Hoboken

Cossy M (2009) The liberalization of energy services: are PTAs more energetic than the GATS? In: Marchetti JA, Roy M (eds) Opening markets for trade in services: countries and sectors in bilateral and WTO negotiations. Cambridge University Press, Cambridge

Cossy M (2012) Energy services under the general agreement on trade in services. In: Selivanova Y (ed) Regulation of energy in International Trade Law: WTO, NAFTA and Energy Charter. Kluwer Law International, Alphen aan den Rijn

Cottier T, Malumfashi G, Matteotti-Berkutova S, Nartova O, De Sepibus J, Bigdeli SZ (2011) Energy in WTO law and policy. In: Cottier T, Delimatsis P (eds) The prospects of International Trade Regulation: from fragmentation to coherence. Cambridge University Press, Cambridge

Crastan V (2009) Elektrische Energieversorgung. Springer, Berlin

Crosby D (2012) Energy discrimination and international rules in hard times: what's new this time around, and what can be done. J World Energy Law Bus 5:325

Desta M (2003) The GATT/WTO system and international trade in petroleum: an overview. J Energy Nat Resour Law 21:385

Dörr O, Schmalenbach K (2018) Vienna convention on the law of treaties: a commentary, 2nd edn. Springer, Berlin

Dralle T (2018) Ownership unbundling and related measures in the EU energy sector: foundations, the impact of WTO law and investment protection. Springer, Berlin

Dralle T, Frey C (2018) Der WTO-Panel-Bericht zum Dritten Energiebinnenmarktpaket. EnWZ 7: 445

Espa I (2017) The treatment of restrictions and financial charges on imports and exports of electricity under EU and International Law. In: Cottier T, Espa I (eds) International Trade in sustainable electricity: regulatory challenges in international economic law. Cambridge University Press, Cambridge

Farah P, Cima E (2013) Energy trade and the WTO: implications for renewable energy and the OPEC cartel. J Int Econ Law 16:707

Feichtner I (2008) The administration of the vocabulary of international trade: the adaptation of WTO schedules to changes in the harmonized system. German Law J 9:1481

Ferrey S (2004) Inverting choice of law in the wired universe: thermodynamics, mass and energy. Wm Mary Law Rev 45:1839

Gamberale C (2001) Energy services. In: WTO Secretariat (ed) Guide to the GATS: an overview of issues for further liberalization of trade in services. Kluwer Law International, Alphen aan den Rijn

Geraets D (2018) Accession to the World Trade Organization: a legal analysis. Edward Elgar, Cheltenham

Hill T (1977) On goods and services. Rev Income Wealth 23:315

International Energy Agency (2005) Lessons from liberalized electricity markets. https://www.iea.org/reports/lessons-from-liberalised-electricity-markets

Irwin D, Weiler J (2008) Measures affecting the cross-border supply of gambling and betting services. World Trade Rev 7:71

Jackson J (1969) World Trade and the law of GATT. Bobbs-Merrill Co., Indianapolis

Lakatos A (2004) Overview of the regulatory environment for trade in electricity. In: Bielecki J, Desta MG (eds) Electricity Trade in Europe: review of the economic and regulatory challenges. Kluwer Law International, Alphen aan den Rijn

Leal-Arcas R, Filis A, Abu Gosh E (eds) (2014) International Energy Governance. Edward Elgar, Cheltenham

Mäntysaari P (2015) EU Electricity Trade Law: the legal tools of electricity producers in the internal electricity market. Springer, Berlin

Marceau G (2010) The WTO in the emerging energy governance debate. In: Pauwelyn J (ed) Global challenges at the intersection of trade, energy and the environment. Center for Economic and Policy Research, Washington, D.C

Mathur S, Mann P (2014) GATT/WTO accessions and energy security. In: Mathur S, Mann P (eds) Trade, the WTO and energy security. Springer, Berlin

Matsushita M, Schoenbaum TJ, Mavroidis PC, Hahn M (2015) The World Trade Organization: law, practice and policy. Oxford University Press, Oxford

Mavroidis P (2016) The regulation of International Trade (volume I: GATT). Massachusetts Institute of Technology Press, Cambridge

McRae D (2004) What is the future of WTO dispute settlement? J Int Econ Law 7:3

Meyer T (2012) Explaining energy disputes at the World Trade Organization. Vanderbilt Law and Economics Research Paper No. 16-14

Meyer T (2017) Explaining energy disputes at the World Trade Organization. Int Environ Agreements Politics Law Econ 17:391

Milthorp P, Christy D (2012) Energy issues in selected WTO accessions. In: Selivanova Y (ed) Regulation of energy in International Trade Law: WTO, NAFTA and Energy Charter. Wolters Kluwer, Cambridge

Müller L (2001) Handbuch der Elektrizitätswirtschaft: Technische, wirtschaftliche und rechtliche Grundlagen, 2nd edn. Springer, Berlin

Palmeter D, Mavroidis P (1998) The WTO legal system: sources of law. Am J Int Law 92:398

Pierros P, Nüesch S (2000) Trade in electricity: spot on. J World Trade 34:95

Pineau P (2004) Electricity services in the GATS and the FTAA. Energy Stud Rev 12:258

Plourde A (1990) Canada's international obligations in energy and the free-trade agreement with the United States. J World Trade 24(5):35

Poretti P, Rios-Herran R (2006) A reference paper on energy services: the best way forward? Manch J Int Econ Law 3:2

Sánchez Miranda M (2015) Market access in international electricity trade: is the light on? Graduate Institute of International and Development Studies Research Paper

Selivanova Y (2014) The WTO agreements and energy. In: Selivanova Y (ed) Research handbook on International Energy Law. Edward Elgar, Cheltenham

Talus K, Wüstenberg M (2018) WTO panel report in the EU – energy package dispute and the European Commission proposal to amend the 2009 Gas Market Directive. J Energy Nat Resour Law 73:327

UNCTAD (2000) Trade Agreements, Petroleum and Energy Policies

Van Damme I (2009) Treaty interpretation by the WTO appellate body. Oxford University Press, Oxford

Van Damme I (2010) Treaty interpretation by the WTO appellate body. Eur J Int Law 21:605

Villiger M (2009) Commentary on the 1969 Vienna Convention on the Law of Treaties. Martinus Nijhoff, Leiden

WTO Secretariat (2010) World Trade Report 2010. World Trade Organization, Geneva

Yanovich A (2012) WTO rules and the energy sector. In: Selivanova Y (ed) Regulation of energy in International Trade Law: WTO, NAFTA and Energy Charter. Kluwer Law International, Alphen aan den Rijn

Yu D (2008) The harmonized system: amendments and their impact on WTO Members' Schedules. WTO Staff Working Paper, No. ERSD-2008-02 https://www.wto.org/english/res_e/reser_e/ersd200802_e.pdf

Zacharias D (2008) Article I GATS. In: Max Planck commentaries on World Trade Law, vol 6. Martinus Nijhoff Publishers, Leiden

Zarrilli S (2004) Multilateral rules and trade in energy goods and services: the case of electricity. In: Bielecki J, Desta MG (eds) Electricity trade in Europe: review of the economic and regulatory challenges. Kluwer Law International, Alphen aan den Rijn

Zhang R (2015) Covered or not covered: that is the question. WTO Working Paper ERSD-2015-11

Chapter 6
The Energy Charter Treaty and the Regulation of Electricity Trade

Almost in parallel with the establishment of the WTO, a sector-specific Agreement, the Energy Charter Treaty (ECT), was signed in December 1994 to deal with energy trade and investment issues.[1] The ECT entered into force in 1998 and, to the present day, has been signed by 54 states and international organizations (the EU and EURATOM).[2] The signatories have all become members of the Energy Charter Conference, an intergovernmental organization tasked with governing the Energy Charter Process and overseeing the implementation of the ECT. The timing of the ECT was not a coincidence. The Energy Charter process started immediately after the fall of the Berlin Wall with the signing of the Energy Charter Declaration in 1991. The main motive behind the Energy Charter was the desire on the side of Western Europe to unlock non-domestic energy resources and the need on the side of the former Soviet Republics to invest in and modernize the means of exploitation of their oil and gas reserves. The Energy Charter Treaty was meant to provide investors with rule of law guarantees and a legal framework for the east-west trade in energy products.[3] This is sought to be achieved through the protection and promotion of foreign investments in the energy sector by providing a mechanism for both investor-state and intra-state dispute settlement. By incorporating rules of the GATT, the ECT also seeks to provide a stable and predictable framework for trade in energy products. A further stated objective of the ECT is to ensure uninterrupted energy transit through the territories of ECT Member States. Finally, the ECT

---

[1] Energy Charter Treaty (17 December 1994) 2080 U.N.T.S. 95.

[2] Out of these 54, all but Australia, Belarus, Norway and the Russian Federation have ratified the ECT.

[3] Title 1 of the European Energy Charter states as the main objective of the energy charter process that Members are 'determined to create a climate favourable to the operation of enterprises and to the flow of investments and technologies by implementing market principles in the field of energy.'

© The Author(s), under exclusive license to Springer Nature Switzerland AG 2022   123
C. Frey, *World Trade Law and the Emergence of International Electricity Markets*,
EYIEL Monographs - Studies in European and International Economic Law 25,
https://doi.org/10.1007/978-3-031-04756-5_6

includes provisions on energy efficiency and environmental protection. Neither of these lays down binding commitments, however.[4]

The ECT has evolved past a regional Eurasian instrument in terms of membership as its signatories include Afghanistan, Australia, Japan and Turkey. International organizations, including ASEAN, the OECD, the World Bank, and the WTO are amongst the group of observers. However, the ECT lacks the support of some major players in international energy production and trade. Russia applied the Treaty provisionally until October 2009, but never ratified it. In January 2018, Russia officially confirmed its intention not to be considered as a signatory to the ECT and its Protocols. The US and Canada both signed the initial European Energy Charter in 1991 but never ratified the ECT. Italy decided to suspend its membership in the ECT and, from 1 January 2016, is no longer a contracting party.[5] China long remained outside the ECT framework but became a signatory of the International Energy Charter in 2015.[6] Most, but not all, ECT Contracting Parties are Members of the WTO. Only Azerbaijan,[7] Belarus,[8] Bosnia and Herzegovina,[9] Uzbekistan,[10] and Turkmenistan[11] have not yet concluded their WTO accession. Despite not amounting to a true multilateral forum yet, the Members, provisional appliers, and observers all attest to the attractiveness of a body of trade rules tailored specifically to energy products. In more recent times, however, discontent has been growing among several ECT Members because the Treaty and especially its provisions related to investment protection are seen as obstacles in regulatory responses to climate change. The Energy Charter Conference launched a discussion on the modernisation of the ECT in November 2017. The discussions have been proceeding in a working group and are currently in their twelfth negotiation round (April

---

[4]Belyi (2012), pp. 311 et seq. See also Energy Charter Secretariat (2001) [186-187] pointing out that the ECT provisions, specifically Articles 18 and 19 ECT, refer more explicitly than the WTO Agreements to the need to protect the environment in the energy sector.

[5]See Kustova (2016), p. 359.

[6]The International Energy Charter is a political declaration adopted in 2015 and signed by a total of 90 states and regional integration organizations. It aims at updating the initial European Energy Charter and at strengthening energy cooperation. It does not bear legally binding obligations. See International Energy Charter, agreed text for adoption in the Hague at the Ministerial Conference on the International Energy Charter on 20 May 2015, available at https://www.energycharter.org/fileadmin/DocumentsMedia/Legal/IEC_EN.pdf.

[7]On the current status of Azerbaijan's accession see the WTO website, https://www.wto.org/english/thewto_e/acc_e/a1_azerbaidjan_e.htm.

[8]On the current status of the accession of Belarus see the WTO website, https://www.wto.org/english/thewto_e/acc_e/a1_belarus_e.htm.

[9]On the current status of the accession of Bosnia and Herzegovina see the WTO website, https://www.wto.org/english/thewto_e/acc_e/a1_bosnie_e.htm.

[10]On the current status of Uzbekistan's accession see the WTO website, https://www.wto.org/english/thewto_e/acc_e/a1_ouzbekistan_e.htm.

[11]Turkmenistan has not yet initiated the WTO accession procedure.

2022).[12] While the focus of the modernisation efforts is on the investment provisions of the ECT, some general definitional questions and issues with respect to transit are also on the table.

6.1   The Relationship Between the ECT and the WTO Agreements

The ECT came into being at a time when multilateral trade negotiations entered the final phase of the Uruguay Round. It is not surprising therefore that the latter discussions substantively influenced the provisions of the ECT, which after all were meant to provide for an energy-specific trading framework complementary to the WTO. As the ECT was finally concluded while the last items on the Uruguay Round negotiator's list were still unresolved, it was agreed that there should be an amendment to the ECT once the new multilateral trade rules had entered into force.[13] Accordingly, about 3 years after the initial Treaty had been signed by the Contracting Parties, a 'Trade Amendment' was agreed upon in April 1998. After the provisional application for a period of 12 years, the Trade Amendment entered into force in January 2010 upon ratification by the thirty-fifth party.[14] The following considerations are based on the current text of the ECT after the implementation of the Trade Amendment.

Article 4 of the ECT stipulates that 'nothing in this Treaty shall derogate, as between particular Contracting Parties which are members of the WTO, from the provisions of the WTO Agreement as they are applied between those Contracting Parties.' This principle of non-derogation is one of the cornerstones of the ECT. As the text makes clear, this only applies to relations between Contracting Parties which are also WTO Members. Their relationship with regard to energy trade shall continue to be governed by WTO rules. However, as regards the relations between Contracting Parties at least one of which is not a WTO Member, the WTO rules with relevance for energy trade are incorporated by reference.[15] In other words, the few ECT Contracting Parties which are not yet WTO Members are treated as if they were

---

[12] For further information on the progress of the ECT modernisation process see https://www.energychartertreaty.org/modernisation-of-the-treaty/.

[13] Gundel (2004), p. 177; Konoplyanik and Wälde (2006), p. 542.

[14] Energy Charter Secretariat, 'The Trade Amendment of the Energy Charter Treaty Explained to Decision-Makers of Ratifying Countries' https://energycharter.org/fileadmin/DocumentsMedia/Thematic/Trade_Amendment_Explanations-EN.pdf.

[15] For this purpose, Article 29 (2) (a) ECT provides that 'Trade in Energy Materials and Products and Energy-Related Equipment between Contracting Parties at least one of which is not a member of the WTO shall be governed, subject to subparagraph (b) and to the exceptions and rules provided for in Annex W, by the provisions of the WTO Agreement, as applied and practiced with regard to Energy Materials and Products and Energy-Related Equipment by members of the WTO among themselves, as if all Contracting Parties were members of the WTO.'

already Members.[16] The underlying assumption is that all ECT Contracting Parties will gradually accede to the WTO and the ECT thus assumes a gap-filling role for the time being.[17] Consequently, the central non-discrimination obligations (MFN and national treatment) are applicable between ECT Members, just like many other provisions of the GATT and other WTO Agreements.[18]

There is, however, a long list of exceptions to the application of the WTO provisions as between ECT Contracting Parties one of which is not a WTO Member. Importantly, this concerns all of the WTO rules on trade in services as the entire GATS is not applicable in the ECT context.[19] With respect to the GATT, the principle of customs tariff bindings and the schedules drawn up on the basis of Article II GATT are not applicable. Customs tariffs are instead dealt with in a separate ECT provision which provides that 'each Contracting Party shall endeavour not to increase any customs duty or charge of any kind imposed on or in connection with importation or exportation.'[20]

The ECT, in its chapter II on trade, adds a few more specific provisions, some of which overlap with the substance of the WTO Agreements.[21] Article 7 ECT deals in some detail with transit issues.[22] The classification into goods and services which was identified above as a problem with respect to electricity trade is resolved in an intelligible way in the ECT: 'energy materials and products' to which the ECT provisions shall apply are listed exhaustively with reference to HS headings in an Annex to the ECT.[23] The list includes electric energy, making it clear that electricity is treated as a good in the ECT context.

WTO provisions on the settlement of disputes are only available between WTO Members. The ECT, in its Article 29 and the corresponding Annex D, provides for a separate dispute settlement mechanism for trade disputes among Contracting Parties, which involve a non-Member of the WTO. The procedure foresees a panel mechanism that is closely modelled on the WTO's DSU, but which is of a less formal

---

[16] Konoplyanik and Wälde (2006), p. 542.

[17] Ibid, at 541.

[18] Defilla (2003), p. 430.

[19] See Annex W to the Energy Charter Treaty

[20] Article 29 (4) of the Energy Charter Treaty; see also Energy Charter Secretariat (2001) [42]. Finally, with respect to customs duties, whilst the Trade Amendment has maintained the 'best endeavours' system described above (now also applied to energy-related equipment), it has introduced the possibility to progressively replace the pledge to maintain levels of tariffs by a binding customs tariff standstill regime. See the amended Article 29 (6) of the ECT (n 367).

[21] These concern trade-related investment measures (Article 5), competition (Article 6), transit (Article 7) and transfer of technology (Article 8).

[22] On the application of ECT provisions to issues arising from electricity transit see below in Sect. 12.4, pp. 211 et seq.

[23] See Annex EM I of the ECT. The categories are nuclear energy, coal, natural gas, petroleum products, electrical energy and other energy. See also Energy Charter Secretariat (2001) [46].

character.[24] The Trade Amendment introduced a link to WTO dispute settlement to the effect that 'panels shall be guided by the interpretations given to the WTO Agreement within the framework of the WTO Agreement (...)'.[25] Thus, decisions by panels and the Appellate Body as adopted by the DSB could in principle 'fertilise' the interpretation of the ECT.[26] However, given the limited experience with trade disputes involving electricity at the WTO level, this finding is of little relevance for the time being. Besides this WTO-like trade dispute resolution mechanism, special procedures are applicable to disputes relating to transit issues[27] and to investment disputes.[28] Furthermore, Article 27 foresees a state-to-state dispute settlement procedure, which applies to the ECT-specific trade provisions if at least one of the parties to a dispute is not a WTO Member.[29]

At the time of the drafting of the ECT, almost half of the prospective Contracting Parties had not ratified the GATT 1947, the WTO's predecessor.[30] The picture has changed dramatically and, as described above, only five out of the currently more than 50 ECT Contracting Parties have not acceded to the WTO in the meantime. Out of these, only Turkmenistan has not yet initiated the accession procedure. Considering the fact that an essential feature of the ECT has been to provide an interim step towards WTO Membership, one could question the continuing relevance of the Treaty Framework. Another factor possibly diminishing the relevance of the ECT in future is the proliferation of other regional regimes with significance for the energy sector, that can be seen as competing with the Energy Charter framework. Examples include the Energy Community,[31] a tool to 'export' the EU energy acquis to neighbouring countries in South-East Europe, and more general economic integration regimes with partial relevance for electricity like ASEAN, CETA or RCEP.[32]

However, in light of the current crisis of the WTO's dispute settlement system and the corresponding weakening of the WTO as an organization, one could also take the opposite view and expect the ECT to rise as an alternative forum for the resolution of disputes in the energy sector. Part III of this study will examine in more detail the substantial contribution the ECT provisions make to facilitating trade in electric energy and their additional value as compared with WTO disciplines.

---

[24] Marhold (2015), p. 413; Gundel (2004), p. 179.

[25] Article 3 of the Amendment to the Trade-Related Provisions of the Energy Charter Treaty, in Energy Charter Secretariat (2004), p. 177.

[26] Azaria (2009), p. 561.

[27] See below in Sect. 12.4, p. 215.

[28] Article 26 ECT. See also Hobér (2010).

[29] Gundel (2004), p. 179.

[30] Sakmar (2008), p. 99.

[31] Treaty Establishing the Energy Community (signed on 25 October 2005) OJ 2006/L 198/18.

[32] See also the late Thomas Wälde in the preface to his edited volume on the ECT who speculated that 'perhaps these forces will overshadow and deny to the Energy Charter Treaty any significant future growth'. Wälde (1996), Editors Preface.

References

Azaria D (2009) Energy transit under the Energy Charter Treaty and the general agreement on tariffs and trade. J Energy Nat Resour Law 27:559

Belyi A (2012) The energy charter process and energy security. In: Delvaux B, Hunt M, Talus K (eds) EU energy law and policy issues. Intersentia, Cambridge

Defilla S (2003) Energy Trade under the ECT and accession to the WTO. J Energy Nat Resour Law 21:428

Energy Charter Secretariat (2004) The Energy Charter Treaty and related documents, a legal framework for International Energy Cooperation. ECT Secretariat

Energy Charter Secretariat (2001) Trade in Energy – WTO rules applying under the Energy Charter Treaty. ECT Secretariat

Gundel J (2004) Regionales Wirtschaftsvölkerrecht in der Entwicklung: Das Beispiel des Energiecharta-Vertrages. Archiv des Völkerrechts 42:157

Hobér K (2010) Investment arbitration and the Energy Charter Treaty. J Int Dispute Settlement 1: 153

Konoplyanik A, Wälde T (2006) Energy Charter Treaty and its role in international energy. J Energy Nat Resour Law 24:523

Kustova I (2016) A Treaty a la Carte? Some reflections on the modernization of the energy charter process. J World Energy Law Bus 9:357

Marhold A (2015) Fragmentation and the Nexus between the WTO and the ECT in Global Energy Governance – a legal-institutional analysis twenty years later. J World Invest Trade 16:389

Sakmar S (2008) Bringing Energy Trade into the WTO: the historical context, current status, and potential implications for the Middle East Region. Ind Int Comp Law Rev 18:89

Wälde T (1996) Editors preface. In: Wälde TW (ed) The Energy Charter Treaty: an east-west gateway for investment and trade. Kluwer Law International, Alphen aan den Rijn

Chapter 7
Electricity in Other Preferential Trade Agreements

Other than in the ECT, trade in energy—and electric energy more specifically—has also been made subject to specific rules in many bilateral and regional preferential trade agreements (PTA). Subject to certain conditions laid down in Article XXIV GATT, PTA members can grant each other preferential treatment in deviation from the MFN principle.[1] Such preferential trade agreements have proliferated recently and more than 300 are currently in force.[2] As of 2017, all WTO Members were parties to at least one such agreement.[3] More recently and due mainly to the standstill in multilateral trade negotiations, Members have engaged in the negotiation of large plurilateral trade agreements which have been labelled as 'mega-regionals'.[4] Examples are the Comprehensive Economic and Trade Agreement (CETA) between Canada and the EU,[5] and the Comprehensive and Progressive Agreement for Trans-Pacific Partnership (CPTPP).[6] Because of the tolerated deviation from the

---

[1] Art. XXIV GATT applies to 'customs unions' and 'free trade areas'. With respect to the latter category, it is stated that 'a free-trade area shall be understood to mean a group of two or more customs territories in which the duties and other restrictive regulations of commerce (. . .) are eliminated on substantially all the trade between the constituting territories in products originating in such territories.'

[2] WTO Secretariat, Regional Trade Agreements, https://www.wto.org/english/tratop_e/region_e/regfac_e.htm.

[3] Ibid.

[4] For a comprehensive account of the phenomenon of 'mega-regionals' see Rensmann (ed.) (2017). See also Griller et al. (eds) (2017).

[5] Comprehensive and Progressive Economic and Trade Agreement between the European Union and Canada – Consolidated text (2016), available at https://www.international.gc.ca/trade-commerce/trade-agreements-accords-commerciaux/agr-acc/ceta-aecg/text-texte/toc-tdm.aspx?lang=eng.

[6] Comprehensive Agreement for the Trans-Pacific Partnership (signed 8 March 2018, entry into force 30 December 2018) text available at https://www.dfat.gov.au/trade/agreements/in-force/cptpp/official-documents.

© The Author(s), under exclusive license to Springer Nature Switzerland AG 2022
C. Frey, *World Trade Law and the Emergence of International Electricity Markets*,
EYIEL Monographs - Studies in European and International Economic Law 25,
https://doi.org/10.1007/978-3-031-04756-5_7

MFN principle, the proliferation of regional trade agreements has been interpreted as a potential threat to the applicability of the multilateral obligations contained in Agreements such as the GATT and GATS.[7] One of the conditions that Article XXIV GATT imposes on regional economic integration is therefore that these agreements eliminate tariffs and other trade barriers 'with respect to substantially all the trade' between the parties.

In practice, regional trade agreements often entail obligations going beyond the standard provided for by the WTO Agreements. Regarding the energy sector, only a small number of PTAs contain meaningful 'WTO-plus' commitments.[8] Electric energy features as an entry in many schedules of tariff concessions in PTAs, but multilaterally-bound customs tariffs for electricity are already low on average. On the services side, commitments in PTAs sometimes provide for a greater level of access than the multilateral commitments inscribed in the WTO Members' GATS schedules.[9] *Cossy*, based on a survey of more than forty PTAs with regard to services commitments, concludes that while the situation varies considerably from one agreement to another, agreements using the negative-listing approach usually represent further-reaching commitments than positive list agreements.[10] Moreover, GATS-plus commitments in the agreements surveyed were mostly undertaken by developing countries.[11] Conversely, one will also frequently find reservations with regard to trade in services related to electricity in these Agreements. Singapore maintains restrictions on trade in the services of electricity transmission and distribution in its FTA with the United States,[12] just as Japan does in its Agreement with Mexico.[13]

In some more recent agreements, members have paid specific attention to the energy sector. The way energy is dealt with ranges from a single article on cooperation in energy matters[14] to comprehensive chapters providing for very specific aspects of non-discrimination in the electricity, oil and gas sectors. An example of

---

[7] See Bhagwati (2008).

[8] Pineau (2004), p. 272. The NAFTA Agreement, with its Chapter 6 on energy, was a prominent exception. See above in Sect. 3.2.2.2, pp. 55 et seq.

[9] WTO, Council for Trade in Services, Energy Services – Background Note by the Secretariat (12 January 2010) S/C/W/311 [84 ff.].

[10] See Cossy (2009), p. 432.

[11] Ibid, at 433.

[12] Annex 8A of the United States – Singapore Free Trade Agreement (6 May 2003) 35, https://ustr. gov/sites/default/files/uploads/agreements/fta/singapore/asset_upload_file999_4045.pdf. See also Cossy (2009), p. 423.

[13] Annex 7 of the Free Trade Agreement between Japan and the United Mexican States for the Strengthening of the Economic Partnership (17 September 2004) 1160, https://www.mofa.go.jp/region/latin/mexico/agreement/annex7.pdf.

[14] In the Korea-Singapore FTA, for example, one finds a dedicated article on energy cooperation, which, *inter alia*, provides for the development and promotion of co-operative activities in the energy sector in the form of sharing experiences in the field of electricity restructuring. See Article 18.12 of the Korea – Singapore Free Trade Agreement (4 August 2005).

the latter is the Enhanced Partnership and Cooperation Agreement between the EU and Kazakhstan (EPCA), which entered into force in March 2020.[15] The Agreement features a chapter on 'raw materials and energy' and a chapter on 'cooperation in the area of energy'. Overall, a number of WTO-plus and even ECT-plus provisions can be identified in the EPCA.[16] These concern positive obligations with respect to granting access to high-voltage transmission lines,[17] the establishment of independent regulatory authorities,[18] a prohibition against maintaining export monopolies,[19] as well as a transit clause.[20] The EU-Georgia Association Agreement includes similar provisions, albeit with different nuances.[21] In the North American context, Canada and the US have agreed on bilaterally applicable disciplines related to energy regulatory measures and transparency in a side letter to the CUSMA. The disciplines include a commitment to maintain or establish independent regulatory authorities[22] and a provision requiring each party to grant access to electricity transmission facilities and pipeline networks on non-discriminatory terms.[23]

Based on this brief survey of regional PTAs, some conclusions can be drawn. First of all, the readiness to agree on WTO-plus provisions in the energy sector in such agreements has traditionally been rather limited. Reservations with respect to services in the electricity sector are not uncommon. The EU, in some more recent agreements with its trading partners, has started to include provisions with respect to electricity trade which clearly go beyond anything in the existing multilateral and regional instruments. However, it has not followed this approach consistently with countries with which it has recently concluded free trade agreements. Georgia and Kazakhstan, while not sharing a direct border with an EU Member State, could both theoretically be reached by high-voltage transmission infrastructure and might therefore be of strategic interest for electricity trade in the future. This might help explain why the EU has opted to include in these Agreements access and transit provisions with respect not just to oil and gas, but also for electricity. The same objective must be assumed to underlie the bilaterally agreed-upon provisions between Canada and the US in the context of the CUSMA.

---

[15] Enhanced Partnership and Cooperation Agreement between the European Union and the Republic of Kazakhstan (21 December 2015), OJ 2016/L 29/3.

[16] These are included in Chapter 9 of the Agreement.

[17] Enhanced Partnership and Cooperation Agreement between the European Union and the Republic of Kazakhstan (21 December 2015), OJ 2016/L 29/3, Article 145.

[18] Ibid, Article 146.

[19] Ibid, Article 140.

[20] Ibid, Article 143.

[21] Association Agreement between the European Union and the European Atomic Energy Community and their Member States, of the one part, and Georgia, of the other part (27 June 2014) OJ 2014/L 261/4, 86. The provisions relevant for international electricity trade will be discussed in Part III below in the context of concrete trade issues.

[22] Canada-United States-Mexico Agreement, Article 4.

[23] Ibid, Article 5.

References

Bhagwati J (2008) Termites in the trading system: how preferential agreements undermine free trade. Oxford University Press, Oxford

Cossy M (2009) The liberalization of energy services: are PTAs more energetic than the GATS? In: Marchetti JA, Roy M (eds) Opening markets for trade in services: countries and sectors in bilateral and WTO negotiations. Cambridge University Press, Cambridge

Griller S, Obwexer W, Vranes E (eds) (2017) Mega-regional trade agreements: CETA, TTIP, and TiSA – new orientations for EU external economic relations. Oxford University Press, Oxford

Pineau P (2004) Electricity services in the GATS and the FTAA. Energy Stud Rev 12:258

Rensmann T (ed) (2017) Mega-regional trade agreements. Springer, Berlin

Chapter 8
Final Conclusions to Part II

The above analysis leads to a finding that, despite its special nature and occasional assertions to the contrary, trade in electricity is covered by the WTO Agreements. Hence, a multilateral framework is in existence stipulating non-discriminatory trade in goods and services. What is more, the electricity sector has found its way into the jurisprudence of the WTO dispute settlement system and the special nature of electricity has been recognized by a panel. An opportunity has not yet presented itself, however, for WTO adjudicators to apply GATT or GATS provisions to regulatory instruments specific to the electricity sector. The fact that WTO Members have not yet referred such a complaint to the WTO—and that Russia dropped electricity-related issues from its complaint before it reached the Panel stage— reflects the traditional view that electricity is not an international commodity but a source of energy with a geographically limited reach. As this notion is currently changing, it could only be a matter of time until the first genuine electricity dispute is referred to the WTO.

The fact that electricity is not excluded from the coverage of the WTO Agreements does not mean that actual barriers to free trade in electricity can be dealt with satisfactorily on the basis of the existing provisions. As the experiences of domestic electricity regulation and of the developing EU electricity market show, electricity trade depends on proactive legislation to remove structural challenges to cross-border trade.[1] Partly liberalized energy sectors are often heavily regulated to ensure the reliable functioning of systems wherein liberalized and natural monopoly segments continue to coexist. The degree to which WTO provisions can be relied on to deal with existing barriers will be analyzed in Part III below.

---

[1] In fact, owing to the complex realities of electricity markets, ensuring competition after the breaking-up of vertically integrated monopolies regularly requires re-regulation rather than deregulation. See also WTO, Council for Trade in Services, Energy Services—Background Note by the Secretariat (09 September 1998) S/C/W/52 [64].

© The Author(s), under exclusive license to Springer Nature Switzerland AG 2022   133
C. Frey, *World Trade Law and the Emergence of International Electricity Markets*,
EYIEL Monographs - Studies in European and International Economic Law 25,
https://doi.org/10.1007/978-3-031-04756-5_8

Another challenge in applying the concrete rules of the WTO framework to measures regulating trade in electricity emanates from the structure of the WTO Agreements which are dealing with either trade in goods *or* services. The application of this framework to the electricity sector poses its own challenges. Looking beyond pure dictionary definitions and engaging in a more holistic assessment incorporating other international treaties as well as WTO Members' practice allows for the conclusion that electricity can be regarded as a commodity falling under GATT rules. At the same time, numerous services covered by the GATS are fundamental to electricity being brought from the site of generation to the final consumer. WTO Members have been reluctant to liberalize services in the energy sector, however, thereby largely limiting the current significance of the GATS to those horizontal commitments which apply irrespective of a country's specific commitments as identified in its GATS schedule.

With respect to certain segments of the electricity value chain, uncertainty persists concerning classification as a service. An analysis of services classification instruments has revealed that their methodology is not well suited to be applied to the realities of the contemporary electricity sector, and a strict adherence to these instruments would indeed lead to untenable results. These instruments should be updated and brought in line with commercial and technological realities.[2]

Coming into existence around the same time as the WTO, the Energy Charter Treaty has been providing a sector-specific rulebook for energy trade and investment. With respect to the classification issue, the ECT negotiators have offered a significant improvement by clearly listing electric energy as part of a group of energy products and thereby removing doubts as to the applicability of the goods-related rules of the ECT. The practical consequences of this definitional improvement are limited, however, because the ECT trade rules only apply as between two Contracting Parties at least one of which has not yet acceded to the WTO.

Importantly, the ECT does not cover trade in services and will therefore be inapplicable to a large number of issues in electricity trade. Moreover, despite its continuously growing membership, the ECT has not received a truly global following and is currently undergoing a modernisation process.[3]

A third source of legal obligations is provided by the numerous regional trade agreements concluded between neighbouring countries and, increasingly, between trading partners at greater distances. While the NAFTA stood out as an early example of energy-specific rules, two rather recent agreements the EU has negotiated with its eastern trading partners provide some meaningful provisions with specific application to electricity trade.

---

[2]For concrete suggestions to this effect see below in Sect. 14.2.1, pp. 229 et seq.

[3]This point is discussed further below in Sect. 14.3.1, pp. 242 et seq.

The three different regimes discussed reveal a certain regulatory fragmentation that adds to the existing frameworks for regional electricity markets which were analysed in Part I. It is therefore submitted that future interconnection and increased trade and cooperation in electricity would benefit from an overhaul of the parallel regimes currently in place. This could only be achieved in a meaningful way by a multilateral endeavour.

Part III
Barriers to Electricity Trade and the Role of World Trade Law

In the previous chapter, the conclusion was reached that the rules of world trade law are generally applicable to trade in electric energy, albeit with some caveats. The following considerations will focus on specific trade barriers that exist in the electricity sector and potential trade conflicts arising from the interconnection of electricity systems across countries and regions. Rather than aiming for an exhaustive analysis of all trade barriers, the focus will be on those ones that are deemed most relevant for the further integration of electricity markets and the successful interconnection of more national transmission systems. It is expected that the assessment will allow for a substantiated judgment about the readiness of world trade law to deal with the major challenges to a seamless international electricity trade. The analysis will proceed in three steps. It will first identify the nature of barriers existing in international electricity trade. It will then analyse the disciplines world trade law imposes with respect to the identified trade issues. Finally, it will make an assessment about whether or not the existing disciplines are well suited to deal adequately with the issues identified. In the absence of disputes concerning the treatment of electricity brought so far before multilateral trade dispute settlement bodies, the analysis draws in part on the existing experiences with bilateral and regional cross-border electricity trade.[1] It focuses on the relevant provisions of the WTO Agreements, as well as on additional commitments under the ECT and PTAs, where such exist. Where GATT provisions are applicable without modifications between ECT Contracting Parties, the findings reached for the GATT are valid for the ECT as well.[2]

---

[1] Where examples stemming from the EU are employed to explain the practical relevance of a certain trade issue, this is mainly because the EU internal energy market represents the most advanced example of regional electricity integration.

[2] On the general relationship between WTO and ECT rules, see above in Sect. 6.1, pp. 125 et seq.

Chapter 9
A Typology of International Trade Issues in the Electricity Sector

International commercial exchanges of electric power give rise to a number of issues, which form the substance of the following considerations. A delineation can be drawn between two sets of issues: One relates to the preconditions of trade in electric energy, and the other relates to the treatment of goods and services once cross-border trade is established. Regarding the first set of issues, challenges include developing the required infrastructure, like high-voltage lines and substations. Typical issues which present themselves at this stage concern the siting and construction of transmission lines (and associated problems of a social and environmental nature); establishing an appropriate investment and institutional framework; and the mechanism for sharing the financial burdens and benefits of interconnection. On the face of it, world trade law has a rather limited role to play in solving issues related to this 'pre-trade' stage. Questions regarding the siting of infrastructure, environmental regulations and impact assessments, as well as public acceptance aspects pertain to national planning laws and permitting procedures. Financial and risk-sharing aspects will have to be settled contractually among the stakeholders of a specific project. This, of course, does not mean that this preparatory stage is excluded from coverage of the rules of world trade law. To give an example: The construction of electricity transmission lines by a network operator from country A in the territory of country B (whether supplied cross-border or through the establishment of the operator abroad) could be subject to GATS disciplines if the Contracting Parties have entered into specific commitments in this field.[1] Likewise, providers of wholesale trading services (e.g. operators of an energy market platform) might want to enter new markets via commercial presence abroad. Rules on the planning and permitting of energy infrastructure can also come under the purview of GATT disciplines when they alter the competitive opportunities to the detriment of goods from other WTO Members.

---

[1] WTO Members have entered into commitments for services such as engineering, technical testing and analysis, maintenance and repair of equipment and general construction work for civil engineering. See the discussion of energy-related services at Cossy (2012), p. 159.

© The Author(s), under exclusive license to Springer Nature Switzerland AG 2022
C. Frey, *World Trade Law and the Emergence of International Electricity Markets*,
EYIEL Monographs - Studies in European and International Economic Law 25,
https://doi.org/10.1007/978-3-031-04756-5_9

This was illustrated by the WTO dispute between Russia and the European Union in which the EU regime for the development and financial support of Trans-European Energy Networks was portrayed as discriminatory by the Russian Federation.[2]

The second set of issues relates to the treatment of goods and services once the physical infrastructure is in place and electric energy is subject to cross-border commercial transactions. It is only with the rather recent advent of international electricity trade and the possibility to connect regions with different resource endowments and cost structures that these more traditional trade issues have become increasingly relevant.[3] Pertinent questions concern the granting of non-discriminatory conditions for imports, exports, sales, and the marketing of electricity; the transit of electricity; and the subsidization of certain modes of generation. Due to the natural monopoly character of the electricity transmission segment of the market, non-discriminatory conditions for network access and transparent mechanisms for the allocation of existing capacity are important instruments to prevent restrictive business practices and vertical foreclosure.[4] The structure of the electricity market itself can of course also pose an important barrier to international trade. The degree of vertical integration and the influence of the state over generation, transmission and distribution often directly reflect upon the openness to trade in electricity with other countries.

While customs duties have traditionally stood at the centre of attention of negotiations within the WTO and still play a major role in trade policy, tariffs are notably low on electricity imports. Applied tariffs for electricity stand at 2.5% on average among WTO Members.[5] The average bound tariff is considerably higher and currently stands at 22%. Major industrialized countries maintain low bound tariffs of below 5%, but some African countries maintain tariffs of 70 or even up to 100%.[6] Furthermore, as the subheading for electricity in the harmonized system is optional, a small group of Members have left their schedules blank.

The following analysis focuses on three topics that are considered particularly relevant for international electricity trade: The structure of electricity markets; import and export restrictions; and transit. While all of the other issues identified above would in principle also deserve a deeper evaluation, the application of world trade law disciplines to electricity customs duties, subsidies in the electricity sector or the provision of manufacturing services for transmission networks does not seem to pose very specific challenges and is therefore not subject to this study.

---

[2] WTO, *European Union and its Member States – Certain Measures Relating to the Energy Sector*, Request for the Establishment of a Panel by the Russian Federation (28 May 2015) WT/DS476/2.

[3] Hunt (2002), p. 39.

[4] WTO, Council for Trade in Services, Energy Services – Background Note by the Secretariat (09 September 1998) S/C/W/52 [37].

[5] Sánchez Miranda (2018), p. 95.

[6] Ibid.

References

Cossy M (2012) Energy Trade and WTO rules: reflexions on sovereignty over natural resources, export restrictions and freedom of transit. In: Hermann C, Terhechte J (eds) European Yearbook of International Economic Law. Springer, Berlin

Hunt S (2002) Making competition work in electricity. Wiley, Hoboken

Sánchez Miranda M (2018) Liberalization at the speed of light: International Trade in electricity and interconnected networks. J Int Econ Law 21:1

Chapter 10
Market Structure As an Impediment to International Trade in Electricity: Vertical Integration, Monopolies and State Ownership

Electricity sectors in countries around the world were long characterized by state ownership and vertically integrated, monopolistic structures.[1] Liberalization and privatization in electricity sectors started in the 1980s and have since become a major trend. This entails, *inter alia*, the disintegration of the generation, transmission and distribution segments (a process called 'unbundling') and the privatization of formerly state-owned electricity companies. A look at the current structure of electricity markets, however, reveals that the transition phase is still ongoing. Vertical integration remains a common feature in electricity markets around the world. The same applies to state ownership over the different segments of the electricity market. Some countries do not show any inclination to abolish state or quasi state-owned monopolies in the near future.[2]

It is important to point out that the legal liberalization of electricity markets is mostly not sufficient to bring about real competition.[3] While the formal abolition of monopolies and the introduction of independent power production are prerequisites for competition, they cannot guarantee that a market actually develops into a competitive one and that foreign providers of goods and services are not de facto barred from entering the market. Even where formal liberalization measures have been carried out de jure, the former monopolies often remain de facto intact. The incumbents continue to exert market power simply because of their size and control of strategic infrastructure assets. Some electricity utilities are responsible for more than 90% of a country's power supply.[4] In the EU Member States, even after several legislative initiatives for liberalization and the breaking up of existing monopolies,

---

[1] See above in Sect. 2.2.1, pp. 25 et seq.

[2] Among many others, this is the case in China. Cf. Yi-Chong (2017), pp. 180 et seq.

[3] See, e.g. Wälde and Gunst (2004), p. 193.

[4] EUROSTAT, 'Electricity Production, Consumption and Market Overview' (July 2018) https://ec.europa.eu/eurostat/statistics-explained/index.php/Electricity_production_consumption_and_market_overview#Electricity_generation.

© The Author(s), under exclusive license to Springer Nature Switzerland AG 2022
C. Frey, *World Trade Law and the Emergence of International Electricity Markets*,
EYIEL Monographs - Studies in European and International Economic Law 25,
https://doi.org/10.1007/978-3-031-04756-5_10

the degree of market dominance is still remarkable. In 2016, in at least 15 out of the 28 EU Member States, the largest electricity generator had a market share corresponding to the OECD dominance threshold of 40%.[5] In seven Member States, the market share exceeded 70%. This number had slightly reduced until 2019, when the remaining five Member States with a market share of the main electricity generating company above 70% were Croatia, France, Estonia, Malta and Slovakia.[6] While the market share of the largest generator in the electricity market in 2019 was still 100% in Cyprus, it was 86% in Latvia and 80% in Croatia. Because of the natural monopoly character of transmission and distribution, competition is the rare exception in these segments of the market.

One often overlooked issue is that the difference in the market opening between two countries establishing trade relationships can itself lead to trade frictions. This was illustrated by the *EU—Energy Sector* case. The gas supplier from Russia was a vertically integrated undertaking and its customers were located in the liberalized markets of the European Union. Accordingly, the EU subjected the Russian supplier to unbundling and other rules which Russia claimed were unduly discriminatory and in violation of the GATT and GATS. Energy trade between Russia and Kazakhstan encountered similar problems. Kazakhstan had allowed independent energy production, established a wholesale electricity market, and transmission system operators were charging transparent tariffs while there was a vertically integrated monopoly on the Russian side. The Kazakh grid operator complained about major problems for electricity transit from Kazakhstan through Russia.[7]

Market foreclosure and other barriers to competition based on market structure and monopolies come in different forms. One of these is the granting of exclusive import or export rights to a designated entity, e.g. a monopolistic network operator. Subjecting trade among generators and distribution companies to the prior agreement of the network operator is also not uncommon.[8] In many partially liberalized markets, designated entities act as single buyers and resellers of electricity (e.g. to distribution companies and exporters). As will be shown, single buyers can abuse their dominant position in a number of ways.

State ownership is another feature still prevailing in the different segments of the electricity market. At the generation stage, state-owned companies were responsible for more than 60% of the additions in new conventional power plant capacity on a

---

[5] Based on data provided by EUROSTAT.

[6] EUROSTAT, Electricity Market Indicators, available at https://ec.europa.eu/eurostat/statistics-explained/.

[7] Lakatos (2004), footnote 83 on p. 150.

[8] Energy Charter Secretariat, 'Regional Electricity Markets in the ECT Area' (Paper Submitted for the Energy Charter Seminar 'Liberalizing Trade and Investment in the Eurasian Power Sector', 3 October 2002, Brussels) 35, available at https://energycharter.org/fileadmin/DocumentsMedia/Events/20021003-EPS_Seminar_ECS_Regional_Electricity_Markets.pdf.

global scale in 2015.[9] For ownership of transmission, this number is considerably higher. While almost 100 countries around the globe have unbundled their formerly integrated utilities, only 16 of those countries have privatized transmission operations. With one exception, all of these are located in high-income countries.[10]

The market power of remaining monopolies and the vertically integrated structure of many electricity markets are potentially problematic issues for international trade in electricity. Indeed, the ECT Secretariat has characterized this industry structure as 'the most restrictive among all barriers' to electricity trade.[11] While this is certainly true with respect to the provision of cross-border electricity services, the record is less clear for trade in electric power itself.[12] Nonetheless, the potential for anti-competitive behaviour is evident, especially in cases where the volumes of cross-border electricity trade are increasing significantly.[13] Some suppliers exert influence beyond national borders, extending their dominant position into neighbouring markets. The South African utility ESKOM, the shares of which are entirely owned by the government, generated roughly 45% of the electricity consumed on the entire African continent in 2017.[14] The vertically integrated company acts as the dominant buyer and seller of electricity in the Southern African Power Pool. ESKOM has faced numerous allegations of anti-competitive behaviour like excessive pricing on the domestic market, the delayed building of infrastructure, and it has had to apply load shedding,[15] all of which are typical behavioural traits of an incumbent monopolist. Furthermore, there have been reported instances of the refusal on the part of ESKOM to enter into direct power purchase agreements (PPAs) with certain generators.[16] Such a practice is not uncommon in partially liberalized markets with a single buyer model, which allows the existence of independent power producers but

---

[9] International Energy Agency, *World Energy Investment 2016* (IEA 2016), p. 116. The number includes fossil fuel, nuclear and hydropower plants. With respect to new wind and solar PV capacity, the picture is more diverse and state ownership less prevalent.

[10] See Boulle (2019).

[11] Energy Charter Secretariat, *Regional Electricity Markets in the ECT Area* (ECT 2003), p. 84. See also Dralle (2018), p. 324.

[12] While in other sectors, the vertically integrated and monopolistic structure of markets has hindered imports through measures like the imposition of very high retail prices, the problem seems to have had less significance in the electricity sector in the past. This is likely due to the strategic importance of a reliable and secure supply with electric power for each country individually and the historically very limited degree of interconnection which easily arrives at maximum capacity.

[13] The gas sector, where international trade has been firmly embedded for decades, offers evidence. The first WTO dispute on trade in natural gas was brought by Russia against the EU in 2014.

[14] Government of South Africa, *Official Guide to South Africa 2017/18: Energy and Water* (Government Communication and Information System 2018) https://www.gcis.gov.za/sites/default/files/docs/resourcecentre/pocketguide/09-Energy%20and%20Water-1718.pdf.

[15] Load shedding refers to an intentional interruption of electricity delivery in certain parts of a system. It is used as a last resort measure to avoid larger blackouts and occurs mainly in systems where generation is insufficient or where the infrastructure is poorly managed.

[16] Nicholls (2019).

obliges them to sell their electricity to one designated off-taker. Single buyers can often exert market power and, depending on the regulatory framework, influence prices.[17]

A major challenge with respect to incumbent operators, especially vertically integrated utilities, is the granting of access to existing networks. Monopolistic market structures can also pose serious obstacles to the cross-border provision of electricity-related services. One example is the development of new interconnectors by merchant transmission companies. This segment is sometimes foreclosed by the monopoly of a TSO that only allows developments of new transmission in partnerships.[18] Where statutory obligations to build new interconnectors or provide access to existing ones are lacking, incumbent monopolists might abuse their discretion and discriminate against certain operators requesting access.[19]

While state ownership is not in and of itself a barrier to cross-border electricity trade, decisions of enterprises owned or controlled by the state are not always motivated by purely economic considerations. Based on close ties with governments, operations of state enterprises can be supported through hidden subsidies or a number of other advantages.[20] Some commentators go so far as to state that 'virtually all energy monopolies have been involved in corrupt relationships with politicians.'[21] It is indeed not uncommon for officials to get appointed to managing boards of energy utilities after their life in politics.[22]

One final observation is warranted. The degree to which the market structure and a possible legal or factual foreclosure of market access actually impede competition depends to a large extent on the existence of functioning regulatory agencies for the energy sector. While some regulators work rather successfully to ensure competition in the electricity market, weak regulators lacking the necessary authority can exacerbate the situation.

---

[17] Energy Charter Secretariat (2003), p. 100.

[18] *Maria Das Neves* reports about the situation in Norway, where the private development of merchant interconnections was only possible in partnership with the TSO Statnett. Das Neves (2014), p. 197.

[19] To give an example, in Mexico until the electricity reforms of 2013, interconnection requests had to be directed to the state utility CFE and there was no statutory obligation on CFE to grant interconnection. See Cabrera-Colorado (2018), p. 93.

[20] Energy Charter Secretariat (2003), p. 97.

[21] Wälde and Gunst (2004), p. 182.

[22] Ibid, 193.

10.1 Applying the Legal Disciplines: State-Owned Enterprises and Beyond

The GATT, GATS and most other WTO Agreements do not provide for comprehensive rules on competition.[23] Hence, the role of the multilateral trade provisions in challenging vertically integrated and monopolistic electricity sectors as such must be considered to be limited. While multilateral trade rules have little to offer for challenging vertical integration and state ownership per se on electricity markets, world trade law does impose certain boundaries concerning the conduct of monopolistic actors. Primarily, this entails the obligation to respect the non-discrimination principle as laid out in the MFN and NT obligations. The most directly relevant norms in the WTO Agreements are Article XVII GATT and Article VIII GATS. Although the general obligations assumed under these articles are similar, some differences in their scope are worth exploring in more detail.

10.1.1 Article XVII GATT

Article XVII GATT is addressed to 'state trading enterprises' (STEs). No definition of this term is provided in the Article itself. The text of the provision only makes clear that apart from 'state enterprises', (all) enterprises that have been granted *exclusive or special privileges* by the government of a contracting party are covered. An understanding of the interpretation of this provision offers a working definition for the purpose of notification of STEs to the WTO Council for Trade in Goods. According to this definition, the notification requirement applies to 'governmental and non-governmental enterprises, including marketing boards, which have been granted exclusive or special rights or privileges, including statutory or constitutional powers in the exercise of which they influence through their purchases or sales the level or direction of imports or exports.'[24] As the Understanding is relevant only for the specific purpose of notification of an STE to the WTO, it does not comprehensively delineate the scope of coverage of Article XVII.[25] Nonetheless, based on both the text of Article XVII and the addition in the Understanding, it can be concluded that undertakings fall into the STE category if they are either (a) state-owned

---

[23]Mavroidis (2016), p. 173.

[24]WTO, Understanding on the Interpretation of Article XVII of the General Agreement on Tariffs and Trade 1994 [1].

[25]The 'added value' of the working definition seems to lie in the fact that it requires exclusive or special rights or privileges to have been granted to any kind of undertaking, while this does not follow from the text of Article XVII itself. State enterprises are covered by the general definition absent the granting of exclusive or special rights or privileges. Following the working definition, there does not appear to be an obligation to notify state enterprises which are not recipients of such privileges or rights while these types of entities continue to be covered by Article XVII. Cf. Mattoo (1998), p. 38.

enterprises; (b) (privately-owned) enterprises to which the government has granted *special privileges*; or (c) entities to which an *exclusive privilege* has been granted.[26] An exclusive privilege can result in a monopoly position, but this is not a legal requirement.[27] While state-owned companies along the electricity supply chain (whether or not they exhibit a vertically-integrated structure) clearly fall within the scope of Article XVII, private utilities and system operators are only covered if they have been granted a statutory monopoly or other special rights or privileges like exclusive import or export licenses.

In essence, the GATT discipline on STEs seeks to ensure that the rules of the Agreement are not circumvented by government-owned or government-controlled commercial actors to which the WTO commitments do not typically apply.[28] The main obligation assumed under Art. XVII GATT to achieve this goal is the observation of the non-discrimination principle. Article XVII:1 (b) GATT adds two more concrete categories of sub-obligations, namely, to behave in accordance with 'commercial considerations' and to afford other companies adequate opportunities to compete.[29] As the Appellate Body has made clear, the latter two requirements should not be read as self-standing legal obligations but rather serve 'to clarify the scope of the requirement not to discriminate in subparagraph (a)'.[30]

Observation of the non-discrimination obligation entails MFN treatment (no discrimination between imports from or exports to different WTO Members through state trading enterprises). Whether it also entails a national treatment obligation (no discrimination between imported and domestic products) is disputed.[31] The latter becomes relevant when the STE is acting not just as an importer

---

[26]Cf. WTO, 'Technical Information on State Trading Enterprises' (WTO Website), https://www. wto.org/English/tratop_e/statra_e/statra_info_e.htm. The Working Party on STEs has drafted an illustrative list. Where a dispute arises as to the question whether or not an entity qualifies as an STE, it will ultimately be up to WTO dispute settlement to decide on the matter. See also Mavroidis (2016), p. 405.

[27]WTO, 'Technical Information on State Trading Enterprises' (WTO Website), https://www.wto. org/English/tratop_e/statra_e/statra_info_e.htm.

[28]In the words of the Panel in *Canada — Wheat Exports and Grain Import*, the object and purpose of Article XVII is 'to prevent WTO Members from doing indirectly through STEs that which they have contracted not to do directly under the GATT 1994'. WTO, *Canada – Measures Relating to Exports of Wheat and Treatment of Imported Grain*, Report of the Panel (30 August 2004) WT/DS276//R [4.224]; See also Energy Charter Secretariat (2001) [140].

[29]Mavroidis (2016), p. 405.

[30]WTO, *Canada – Measures Relating to Exports of Wheat and Treatment of Imported Grain*, Report of the Appellate Body (30 August 2004) WT/DS276/AB/R [89].

[31]For the affirmative view see WTO, *Korea – Measures Affecting Imports of Fresh, Chilled and Frozen Beef*, Report of the Panel (31 July 2000) WT/DS161/R, WT/DS169/R [7.53]; GATT, *Canada – Import, Distribution and Sale of Alcoholic Drinks by Canadian Provincial Marketing Agencies*, Report of the Panel (22 March 1988) L/6304 - 35S/37 [4.26] ('the Panel saw great force in the argument that Article III:4 was also applicable to state-trading enterprises at least when the monopoly of the importation and monopoly of the distribution in the domestic markets were combined (. . .)'); Energy Charter Secretariat (2001) [149]; Defilla (2003), p. 434. For the opposing view see GATT, *Canada – Administration of the Foreign Investment Review Act*, Report of the

of electricity, but as a domestic distributor of the imported electricity as well. This is clearly the case as regards most 'traditional' energy utilities. Observing the national treatment obligation as laid down in Article III GATT would require the STE owning the networks to grant access to the transmission and distribution infrastructure to foreign suppliers. Deprived of this obligation, Article XVII GATT is rendered virtually meaningless for tackling vertical foreclosure of the electricity market of a given WTO member and for enabling the participation of foreign electricity generators and transmission operators.[32] While disagreement prevails in the academic literature, the better arguments speak against limiting the coverage of Article XVII GATT to MFN. The text of Article XVII offers a first point of orientation. It requires from contracting parties that their STEs 'act in a manner consistent with the general principles of non-discriminatory treatment *prescribed in this Agreement* [. . .]'.[33] It is widely agreed upon that Article I and III GATT are the cornerstones of the non-discrimination principle in world trade law.[34] This was also confirmed by the Panel in *Korea – Beef*, which considered that 'this general principle of non-discrimination includes at least the provisions of Articles I and III of GATT.'[35] Another question is whether or not Article XVII GATT was initially designed to operate as an anti-circumvention provision and whether it should consequently be held to have broad coverage. Such a reading would make intuitive sense inasmuch as the provision was inserted to prevent WTO Members from using STEs in order to discriminate in ways that would be prohibited if they were undertaken directly by the Members.[36] The Appellate Body in *Canada – Wheat Exports* expressly accepted this reading of Article XVII GATT by stating that subparagraph (a):

> seeks to ensure that a Member cannot, through the creation or maintenance of a state enterprise or the grant of exclusive or special privileges to any enterprise, engage in or facilitate conduct that would be condemned as discriminatory under the GATT 1994 if such conduct were undertaken directly by the Member itself. In other words, subparagraph (a) is an 'anti-circumvention' provision.[37]

Only the first of three Panel reports dealing with the issue leaned towards excluding national treatment from the scope of Article XVII GATS, although without taking a

---

Panel (7 February 1984) L/5504 - 30S/140 [5.16]; Jackson (1991), p. 284; Dralle (2018), pp. 291 et seq.

[32] As Tilman Dralle points out, if the vertically integrated undertaking controlling the transmission networks was only required to provide MFN treatment, 'this would hardly be of any value, given that the TSO could deny network access to all foreign energy products'. See ibid at 291 f.

[33] Article XVII:1 GATT (emphasis added).

[34] See, e.g., Mitchell et al., (2016); Diebold (2011). See also WTO, 'Principles of the Trading System' (WTO Website) https://www.wto.org/english/thewto_e/whatis_e/tif_e/fact2_e.htm.

[35] WTO, *Korea – Measures Affecting Imports of Fresh, Chilled and Frozen Beef*, Report of the Panel (31 July 2000) WT/DS161/R, WT/DS169/R [7.53].

[36] WTO, *Canada — Wheat Exports and Grain Imports*, AB Report [98].

[37] Ibid [85].

final position.[38] Commentators have pointed to the negotiating history of the GATT 1994, which demonstrates that Members opposed a proposal to explicitly subject STEs to national treatment.[39] This only shows, however, that it was not desired to be more specific than necessary. It does not inevitably reflect a majority view to the effect that the coverage of Article XVII GATT should not extend to national treatment.

The text of Article XVII GATT does offer one important limitation to the national treatment obligation, however. An STE is required to act in accordance with the non-discrimination principles only 'in its purchases or sales involving either imports or exports.' Thus, only certain types of transactions, namely purchases or sales on the domestic market of goods either imported or destined for export are subject to national treatment.[40] If a vertically integrated utility qualifying as an STE favoured domestically produced electricity over imported electricity in its purchases or sales, it would be in violation of Article XVII. With respect to vertically integrated utilities, the practical consequences of this limitation are minor because such entities almost per definition generate electricity in-house and only in exceptional circumstances (e.g. in the case of a technical problem with power plants) do they purchase on the market. With respect to unbundled transmission system operators acting as STEs, however, the effect of the limitation is indeed an important one. The 'purchases or sales involving either imports or exports' limitation seriously reduces the relevance of Article XVII vis-a-vis unbundled transmission system operators because these entities usually neither purchase nor sell electricity involving imports or exports. The only exception would appear to be the procurement of balancing energy for purposes of safeguarding the system.[41] Balancing energy could in principle be provided by generators located abroad and thus imported. Hence, a system operator qualifying as an STE must adhere to the national treatment principle when purchasing electricity for balancing purposes. As was stated above, this entails behaving in accordance with commercial considerations and offering competitors adequate opportunities to compete. Summing up, the non-discrimination principle enshrined in Article XVII GATT entails both an MFN and a national treatment requirement, but its effect for electricity STEs is seriously hampered by the limitation that the obligations must only be observed in the purchases or sales involving imports or exports of an STE.

Apart from imposing non-discrimination obligations, Article XVII GATT imposes notification (XVII:4 (a)) and transparency (XVII:4 (b)) requirements on

---

[38] GATT, *Canada – Administration of the Foreign Investment Review Act*, Report of the Panel (7 February 1984) L/5504 - 30S/140 [5.16].

[39] See the Report of the first session of the Preparatory Committee held in London in 1946, EPCT/33 ('London Report'), p. 32. See also Petersmann (1998), p. 71.

[40] *Tilman Dralle* argues that based on this limitation in the text of Article XVII GATT, the provision does not include a national treatment obligation because an STE does not have to comply with the general non-discrimination principles with respect to purely domestic transactions. See Dralle (2018), p. 292.

[41] Balancing energy refers to the procurement of electricity from generators at short notice to balance unplanned fluctuations and deviation from forecasted generation or load.

WTO Members administering STEs.[42] While the substantial significance of these requirements is limited, they do provide the WTO Membership with some visibility on state trading practices. Most existing notifications of WTO Members concern agricultural commodities, but some energy-specific notifications can also be identified. Several countries have notified STEs with respect to trade in fossil fuels.[43] With respect to electricity, Mexico and the US have made relevant notifications. The US has identified a number of 'power (marketing) administrations' as STEs with respect to trade in the product 'electrical energy' as listed in HS heading 2716.[44] Power marketing administrations are mainly tasked with the marketing and sale of hydro-electric power from certain large-scale projects. This also involves imports and exports of electricity (effectively only to and from Canada).[45] Mexico notified its state-owned electricity producer and supplier, CFE as an STE. As far as the author is aware, this is the only electricity utility currently notified to the WTO.[46]

Considering the large number of existing vertically integrated and state-owned electricity utilities with major market power, it can be assumed that there is some 'untapped potential' around for future notifications.[47] The actual effectiveness of the transparency disciplines of Article XVII with respect to vertically integrated STEs must therefore be questioned.

Apart from the general STE provision of Article XVII GATT, references to STEs are found in a few other places in the Agreement. With respect to tariffs, it is made clear that the bound tariffs of a WTO Member are not to be circumvented through the practice of import monopolies.[48] Furthermore, there is an explicit clarification in the

---

[42] The STEs currently notified can be consulted on the WTO website at https://www.wto.org/english/tratop_e/statra_e/statra_e.htm.

[43] Countries like India, Jordan, Mexico, Uruguay and Venezuela have notified STEs in the oil sector. See also Mathur and Mann (2014), p. 82.

[44] Power Marketing Administrations (PMA) are federal agencies within the U.S. Department of Energy and have been tasked primarily with the marketing of hydropower and constructing the necessary infrastructure to transmit the electricity. There are currently four PMAs, all of which were notified as STEs to the WTO: The Bonneville Power Administration and the Southeastern, Southwestern and Western Area Power Administrations, respectively. Only Bonneville and the Western Area PMA engage in exports and imports of electricity. See also Campbell (2019).

[45] WTO, Working Party on State Trading Enterprises, New and Full Notification Pursuant to Article XVII:4(a) of the GATT 1994 and Paragraph 1 of the Understanding on the Interpretation of Article XVII – United States (10 April 2017) G/STR/N/16/USA.

[46] Mexico's energy sector underwent major reforms and liberalization. The reforms did not entail privatization of state-owned enterprises, however. See above in Sect. 3.2.2.2, pp. 56 et seq.

[47] Cf. Mathur and Mann (2014), p. 82; Energy Charter Secretariat (2003), p. 8.

[48] Art. II:4 GATT reads, in relevant part: 'If any contracting party establishes, maintains or authorizes, formally or in effect, a monopoly of the importation of any product described in the appropriate Schedule annexed to this Agreement, such monopoly shall not, except as provided for in that Schedule or as otherwise agreed between the parties which initially negotiated the concession, operate so as to afford protection on the average in excess of the amount of protection provided for in that Schedule.' Article II:4 GATT thus restricts import monopolies to the extent that once the WTO Member maintaining the monopoly has committed to a tariff binding on electricity, the entity may not go beyond what is provided in the schedule in protecting domestic electricity producers.

Interpretative Note to Articles XI, XII, XIII, XIV and XVIII to the effect that throughout these articles, the terms 'import restrictions' and 'export restrictions' include restrictions made effective through state trading entities.[49] Therefore, import or export restrictions might still be contrary to the GATT even if not imposed directly through governmental regulation but through the regulations, purchases or sales of a state trading enterprise. One example would be a quota system for a certain amount of imported electricity, which is imposed through an STE.[50] For the sake of completeness, it should be mentioned that Article XX (d) contains a general exception for measures necessary to secure compliance with laws or regulations that are not inconsistent with the provisions of the GATT. This applies to, among others, 'the enforcement of monopolies operated under paragraph 4 of Article II and Article XVII'.

10.1.2   Article VIII GATS

On the services side, Article VIII GATS deals with 'monopoly suppliers of a service'. The text of Article VIII:1 GATS reads: 'Each Member shall ensure that any monopoly supplier of a service in its territory does not, in the supply of the monopoly service in the relevant market, act in a manner inconsistent with that Member's obligations under Article II and specific commitments'. The term 'monopoly supplier' is defined in Article XXVIII lit. h as 'any person, public or private, which in the relevant market of the territory of a Member is authorized or established formally or in effect by that Member as the sole supplier of that service'. Based on Article VIII:5 GATS, the obligations that apply to monopoly service suppliers apply also to 'exclusive service suppliers' where two conditions are met.[51] The scope of Article VIII is explicitly targeted at monopolies and *exclusive* service suppliers and therefore arguably narrower than that of Article XVII GATT (applying to state enterprises with exclusive or special privileges).[52] What is clear is that the provision aims at disciplining monopolies regardless of whether these are

---

This becomes relevant with respect to sales of electricity on the domestic market. In addition to the level of the tariff binding the WTO Member has committed to, the import monopoly can only apply a 'mark-up' representing reasonable profit margin and costs associated with the marketing of imported electricity. See Energy Charter Secretariat (2001), pp. 145–147.

[49] WTO, General Agreement on Tariffs and Trade, Ad Note to Articles XI, XII, XIII, XIV and XVIII.

[50] Energy Charter Secretariat (2001), p. 153 which applies the same example to the case of natural gas.

[51] The obligations apply if the WTO Member concerned, formally or in effect, (a) authorizes or establishes a small number of service suppliers and (b) substantially prevents competition among those suppliers in its territory. See WTO, *China – Certain Measures Affecting Electronic Payment Services*, Report of the Panel (16 July 2012) WT/DS413/R [7.587].

[52] Willemyns (2016), p. 664.

private or public entities, as long as the entity is the sole supplier of a service in the relevant market.[53] Nevertheless, the wording 'established formally or in effect' also makes clear that in order to qualify as a monopoly for the purposes of the application of Article VIII there must be some sort of action by the government.[54] Merely tolerating the monopolistic status of a service supplier does not seem enough to trigger the application of Article VIII. Accordingly, a natural monopoly that remains in existence 'without any facilitating government action' would fall outside the scope of Article VIII GATS.[55] The exact threshold is very difficult to determine in practice, however.

In the electricity supply world of the past, many vertically integrated utilities were statutory monopolies. This is still the case in a considerable number of jurisdictions. A different situation arises, however, regarding entities operating as the sole suppliers of a service after formal liberalization of the sector.[56] There are good reasons to suggest that these incumbent natural monopolists, due to the absence of facilitating government action, do not qualify as monopoly service suppliers and accordingly are not covered by the Article VIII GATS commitments.

Turning now to the substantive obligations that Article VIII imposes on monopoly service suppliers, these are similar to the GATT obligations for STEs. First and foremost, compliance with the MFN obligation as enshrined in Article II GATS is required following Article VIII:1 GATS.[57] Moreover, specific commitments entered into by WTO Members in their GATS schedules must be respected by monopoly service suppliers. This concerns market access (Art. XVI GATS) and the national treatment obligation (Art. XVII GATS). Contrary to Article XVII GATT, the obligation to ensure that a monopoly supplier does not act inconsistently with these obligations extends only to services supplied 'in its territory'. Thus, the provision does not cover extraterritorial actions of a monopoly service supplier.

In Article VIII:2 GATS, WTO Members are called upon to ensure that monopoly suppliers do not abuse their position regarding the provision of a service subject to specific commitments *outside of the scope of their monopoly rights*, i.e. on

---

[53] Bigdeli and Rechsteiner (2008) [4].

[54] Ibid [5].

[55] Ibid [5] citing Mattoo (1998), p. 39.

[56] The German transmission system is a case in point. In Germany, four transmission system operators each administer a separate control area corresponding to different geographical parts of the country. The four TSOs emanated from former vertically integrated energy companies as part of the fulfilment of their unbundling obligations. The TSOs were never granted explicit statutory rights by the German government, but they were granted a permit to operate the transmission network. The reason why these regional transmission monopolies continue to operate without competition is mainly technical and economical. The assets are owned by the TSO and there is no incentive to divest from all or parts of the network.

[57] Article VIII:1 GATS reads: 'Each Member shall ensure that any monopoly supplier of a service in its territory does not, in the supply of the monopoly service in the relevant market, act in a manner inconsistent with that Member's obligations under Article II and specific commitments.'

neighbouring markets.[58] Based on this drafting, it has been held that Article VIII GATS is particularly aimed at avoiding cross-sectoral spillovers of monopoly power.[59] A typical example of such a constellation is the abuse by a vertically integrated electricity company of its dominant position on the (natural monopoly) transmission market through its anti-competitive behaviour either upstream (in the liberalized generation segment) or further downstream (in the distribution segment).[60] With respect to competitive suppliers in the generation segment of the market, concrete actions that could be disciplined through Article VIII GATS are the refusal to enter into contracts and the exercise of buyer power in contract negotiations.[61] Regarding the downstream segments, the natural monopoly infrastructure is a necessary input ('bottleneck') to downstream services which could be supplied competitively.[62] A company holding a monopoly in transmission might cross-subsidize its activities in distribution or retailing, in which it possibly competes with service suppliers from abroad.

Article VIII:2 GATS could also be applied to the refusal to grant necessary access to the transmission infrastructure. In this context, the doctrine of 'essential facilities' is sometimes discussed, according to which the granting of access to facilities that cannot easily be duplicated becomes mandatory if this can be feasibly realized.[63] In the EU, obstructing access to transmission infrastructure for new entrants through granting priority access rights for long periods was found by the European Commission to amount to an abuse of dominant position, and the granting of access was effectuated through litigation.[64] With respect to both the exercise of monopoly power on upstream and downstream markets in general, and the granting of access to electricity networks in particular, Article VIII could thus in principle be an

---

[58] WTO, Council for Trade in Services, Energy Services – Background Note by the Secretariat (09 September 1998) S/C/W/52 [39] (emphasis added).

[59] Adlung (2006), p. 473.

[60] WTO, Council for Trade in Services, Energy Services – Background Note by the Secretariat (09 September 1998) S/C/W/52 [39].

[61] Dee and Findlay (2008), p. 351.

[62] Ibid, at 343.

[63] Bigdeli and Rechsteiner (2008) [25 ff.] citing Lipsky and Sidak (1999), pp. 1190–1191. The doctrine has been developed to a large extent by U.S. case law, see *United States v. Terminal Railroad Association,* 224 U.S. 383 (1912). This line of jurisprudence developed a 'four elements test' under which the liability of the monopolist for abuse of its dominant position has to be analyzed. According to this test there has to be (a) control of an essential facility by a monopolist, (b) a competitor's inability to practically duplicate the facility, (c) denial of the use of that facility to a competitor and (d) the feasibility of providing the facility. See Poretti and Rios Herran (2006), p. 35. The essential facilities doctrine has also found its way into the EU legal order and has developed there with slightly different nuances. See for two leading judgments of the European Court of Justice Joined Cases C-241/91 P and C-242/91 P, *Radio Telefis Eireann v Commission* [1995] ECLI:EU:C:1995:98 and Case C-418/01, *IMS Health GmbH & Co. OHG v NDC Health GmbH & Co. KG* [2004] ECR 2004 I-05039. As to the energy sector see Talus (2011).

[64] De Hautecloque and Talus (2012), pp. 210 et seq. The authors refer to the 'litigation approach' by the EU Commission to tackle grandfathering rights prevalent in EU Member States.

effective tool to discipline vertically integrated monopolies. However, the lack of more concrete sectoral commitments for electricity impedes the enforcement of mandatory access. To awaken the 'sleeping potential' of Article VIII:2 GATS two things will be necessary: (a) a concerted initiative to liberalize specific services in the electricity value chain and (b) defining more concrete terms of access following the approach of the telecommunications reference paper.[65]

Apart from the substantive MFN obligation for monopolies in Article VIII:1 and the prohibition against abusing a monopoly position with respect to sectors subject to specific commitments in Article VIII:2 GATS, the provision on monopolies and exclusive service suppliers contains some further elements. At the request of a WTO Member, the Council for Trade in Services may require a Member administering monopoly suppliers to provide specific information regarding the relevant operations.[66] Furthermore, Article VIII:4 GATS requires WTO Members to notify the Council for Trade in Services of any intention to grant monopoly rights concerning the supply of a service for which a Member has entered into specific commitments.[67] This notification requirement applies only to monopoly rights granted after the entry into force of the WTO Agreement.[68]

The effectiveness of Article VIII GATS with respect to eliminating anti-competitive practices arising from vertical foreclosure of the electricity market is limited by several factors in addition to the already mentioned narrow definition of the term 'monopoly supplier'. The most important of these limitations is that the scope of application of Article VIII, in areas other than MFN, depends crucially on the extent to which WTO Members have entered into specific commitments concerning relevant services.[69] Another limitation arises out of the general exclusion of governmental service suppliers from the scope of the GATS as foreseen by Article I:3 (b). According to Article I:3 (c) GATS, a 'service supplied in the exercise of governmental authority' means 'any service which is supplied neither on a commercial basis, nor in competition with one or more service suppliers.' Taken cumulatively, these requirements however make for a narrow definition of governmental services and only very few public monopolies in the energy sector will escape GATS coverage on this ground.[70] Finally, as already mentioned, the scope of Article VIII GATS does not include extraterritorial anti-competitive behaviour of monopoly service suppliers as indicated by the words 'in its territory'. Thus, if a monopoly

---

[65] Reference Paper on Basic Telecommunications Services (24 April 1996) 36 I.L.M. 367 (1997). The Reference Paper on Basic Telecommunications includes rules regarding transparency concerning such issues as terms of access. See also Bigdeli and Rechsteiner (2008) [31].

[66] See Article VIII:3 GATS.

[67] See Article VIII:4 GATT. In case other Members raise concerns, Article XXI GATS applies which foresees provisions on modification and withdrawal of commitments.

[68] Bigdeli and Rechsteiner (2008) [34].

[69] The relevant services would concern services outside the scope of the monopoly rights of a Member's monopoly.

[70] See also Krajewski (2003a), pp. 341 et seq. With respect to the energy sector see Dralle (2018), p. 91.

undertaking or exclusive service supplier in the electricity transmission business owns a part of a network outside of the territory where it is located, denial of access to this part of the network would not be covered by the disciplines of Article VIII GATS.

10.1.3   Article XVI:2 (a) GATS

Article XVI GATS, on market access, is one of the central GATS provisions. It requires WTO Members to accord services and service suppliers from other Members treatment no less favourable than that specified in their schedules of concessions. Its positioning in Part III of the GATS and the repeated reference to Members' schedules in the text make it clear that the scope of Article XVI crucially rests on the extent to which Members have entered into commitments regarding specific services. The provision indicates a willingness of the drafters of the GATS to move beyond non-discrimination and tackle certain restrictive domestic services regulations.[71] This can be taken as a testament to the general appetite for liberalization and deregulation during the second half of the 1980s when the Uruguay Round started.[72]

After the first paragraph of Article XVI sets out the general rule that services and service suppliers of other Members may not be accorded treatment inferior to what WTO Members have conceded in their schedules, the second paragraph specifically and exhaustively defines the measures that a Member must not adopt unless otherwise specified in its schedules.[73] For the present discussion, Article XVI:2 (a) is the most significant. It provides in relevant part that

> in sectors where market access commitments are undertaken, the measures which a Member shall not maintain or adopt [. . .] unless otherwise specified in its Schedule, are defined as: a) limitations on the number of service suppliers whether in the form of numerical quotas, *monopolies, exclusive service suppliers* or the requirements of an economic needs test.[74]

The difference in scope compared to Article VI:4 and VI:5 on domestic regulation is that Article XVI relates to quantitative limitations only, meaning restrictions on the supply of services expressed in numbers, and not qualitatively.[75] Monopolies established by the government or those to which the government grants statutory

---

[71] Krajewski (2005), pp. 430 et seq.

[72] *Krajewski* ascribes this also partly to lobbying efforts of the telecommunications industry that advocated strongly for making the GATS a vehicle for deregulation and privatization. Ibid, at 430.

[73] WTO, *United States – Measures Affecting the Cross-Border Supply of Gambling and Betting Services,* Report of the Panel (10 November 2004) WT/DS285/R [6.318]. See also WTO, *China – Measures Affecting Trading Rights and Distribution Services for Certain Publications and Audio-visual Entertainment Products*, Report of the Panel (12 August 2009) WT/DS363/R [7.1353].

[74] Emphasis added.

[75] Pauwelyn (2005), p. 153 citing WTO, *US – Gambling,* Panel Report (10 November 2004) [6.327].

rights clearly fall within the scope of Article XVI:2 GATS. The public energy utilities still prevalent in some countries could thus be disciplined by Article XVI:2 (a) GATS so long as Members have undertaken specific market access commitments with respect to one or more of the services supplied by such undertakings and unless Members have specifically 'opted out' in their schedules. Similarly, and under the same conditions, the granting of licenses for exclusive service suppliers, a prevalent practice vis-à-vis energy utilities in a number of countries, could be scrutinized. Members have scheduled both public energy utilities as well as private entities as market access restrictions in their schedules of concessions.[76]

Article XVI was applied by dispute settlement bodies for the first time in the *US-Gambling* dispute, which concerned the cross-border provision of online gambling services.[77] The Panel and Appellate Body rulings have been critically assessed by some scholars mainly with regard to their extensive interpretation of the term 'in the form of numerical quotas'. With respect to limitations in the form of 'monopolies' and 'exclusive service suppliers', the Appellate Body concluded that these 'encompass limitations that are *in form or in effect* monopolies or exclusive service suppliers'[78] (emphasis added). In its reasoning, the Appellate Body referred to the definitions in Articles XXVIII (h) and VIII:5 GATS, respectively.[79] This reading by the Appellate Body appears to suggest that the market access obligation comprises not just legal monopolies but also de facto monopolies which came into existence absent government involvement, and that Article XVI could thus be interpreted as a general prohibition against maintaining monopolies in those sectors where the respective Member has undertaken commitments on market access.

This does not mean, however, that Article XVI:2 obliges governments to take action against private monopolies which come into existence absent government involvement.[80] As *Krajewski* points out, 'only monopolies depending on intentional government encouragement and support fall within the scope of Article XVI:2 (a)'.[81] Thus, natural monopolies whose monopolistic position is not explicitly supported by the behaviour of governments do not fall under the purview of Article XVI:2 GATS. Whereas a government's express choice not to apply its competition laws to a

---

[76] Krajewski (2003b), p. 87.

[77] WTO, *United States – Measures Affecting the Cross-Border Supply of Gambling and Betting Services*, Report of the Appellate Body (7 April 2005) WT/DS285/AB/R.

[78] Ibid [230]. The US had argued in this case that only numerical limitations, i.e. those limitations specifically expressed in numbers, could be subject to subparagraphs (a) or (c) of Article XVI GATS. The AB rejected these arguments and found that measures not dressed in numbers but amounting to a 'zero quota' would also be covered by the scope of the provision. The decision has been discussed critically by several authors. See, e.g. Ortino (2006), p. 136 who criticizes the AB for insufficient methods of treaty interpretation.

[79] Article XXVIII (h) GATS, which was referred to above, defines a monopoly supplier as a person which 'is authorized or established formally or in effect by that member as the sole supplier of that service'.

[80] Krajewski (2003b), p. 87.

[81] Ibid.

monopoly in a given situation could amount to the establishment of a monopoly supplier, assuming an obligation to enact competition legislation for sectors where such legislation is not yet in place would be going too far.[82]

With respect to PSOs, it should be noted that WTO Members remain free in principle to entrust an electricity utility with such obligations.[83] The substantial market access obligations in Article XVI GATS, and especially the prohibition against maintaining monopolies contained in Article XVI:2 (a) GATS, somewhat limit WTO Members' abilities to delegate public service obligations to undertakings qualifying as monopolies or exclusive service suppliers. Once a WTO Member has entered into specific commitments on market access or national treatment, entities entrusted with public service obligations have to respect these commitments. It has been pointed out that the scope and functions of entities entrusted with PSOs are often not clearly defined and therefore give rise to discretionary interpretation.[84] Based on this insight, special conditions for the imposition of 'universal service obligations' have been elaborated with respect to the telecommunications sector.[85] Possible ways in which the Reference Paper approach could be adopted for the electricity sector will be explored in Part IV below.[86]

10.1.4   Additional Disciplines in the ECT and PTAs

Like the GATT and GATS, the ECT does not contain a prohibition against maintaining monopolies. On the contrary, the ECT Secretariat has explicitly clarified that 'it is for governments to define the structure of their national energy sector.'[87] The ECT both incorporates Article XVII GATT and contains a specific provision in Article 22 with regard to state enterprises.[88] This specific provision calls on ECT Contracting Parties to ensure that such state enterprises act in a manner consistent with the provisions of the ECT. As the rules of the GATS are not applicable under

---

[82] Ibid.

[83] Cf. WTO, Council for Trade in Services, Energy Services – Background Note by the Secretariat (09 September 1998) S/C/W/52 [70]; for a general discussion see Adlung (2006), p. 455. On the concept of PSOs see above in Sect. 2.2.3, pp. 29 et seq.

[84] Lakatos (2004), p. 145.

[85] According to the Telecoms Reference Paper, 'any member has the right to define the kind of universal service obligation it wishes to maintain. Such obligations will not be regarded as anti-competitive per se, provided they are administered in a transparent, non-discriminatory and competitively neutral manner and not more burdensome than necessary for the kind of universal service defined by the Member.' See Reference Paper on Basic Telecommunications Services (24 April 1996) 36 I.L.M. 367 (1997).

[86] See below in Sect. 14.3.2.2, pp. 247 et seq.

[87] Energy Charter Secretariat, 'Frequently Asked Question about the Energy Charter Process' http://www.energycharter.org/process/frequently-asked-questions/. See also Dralle (2018), p. 308.

[88] The term used in the ECT is 'state and privileged enterprises'.

the ECT, the substantive obligations arising in the WTO framework from Article VIII GATS are absent from the ECT framework. This finding is not altered by Article 22 (1) ECT, which provides that 'each Contracting Party shall ensure that any state enterprise which it maintains or established shall conduct its activities in relation to the sale or *provision* of goods *and services* in its Area in a manner consistent with the Contracting Party's obligations under Part III of this Treaty.'[89] As Part III deals with the promotion and protection of investments, Article 22 ECT has only an indirect importance for electricity trade.

The ECT represents only an insignificant step forward with respect to positive obligations when compared with the WTO Agreements. It is specifically stated in the preamble of the ECT that access to markets 'should take account of the need to (. . .) promote competition.' On competition specifically, Article 6 ECT calls on the contracting parties to 'work to alleviate market distortions and barriers to competition in economic activity in the energy sector.' Besides calling on parties to work together by exchanging information and providing technical assistance to less experienced members, Article 6 provides for the right of a Contracting party to request the enforcement of competition rules by another Contracting Party.[90] This request has to be accorded 'full consideration' on the side of competition authorities in deciding whether or not to initiate an enforcement action. While the record is scarce, this 'soft' obligation does not seem to have had a significant impact so far.

STEs have played a comparably prominent role in several WTO accessions. This mainly concerns trade in fossil fuels, where both WTO-plus and WTO-minus commitments can be found.[91] STEs have also received attention in various PTAs. With respect to definitional scope, some agreements adopt the GATT terminology of 'state trading enterprises'[92] while others use different terminology, like 'state-owned enterprises'[93] or 'designated monopolies and government enterprises'.[94] Considering the fact that the term 'state trading enterprises' as used in the WTO context also covers private entities, the choice of the term 'state-owned' must be interpreted as a desire to limit the coverage to those entities in which the state has a decisive stake or complete control.

Concerning the material scope, the range reaches from affirming the existing rights and obligations as contained in Article XVII GATT and calling for 'maximum

---

[89] Emphasis added.

[90] Article 6 (5) ECT.

[91] See the overview in Marhold and Weiss (2019), pp. 61 et seq.

[92] See Article 2.13 of the Free Trade Agreement between the European Union and South Korea (16 September 2010) OJ 2011/L 127 (entered into force on 1 July 2011).

[93] See Article 22.1 of the Canada-United States-Mexico Agreement, titled 'state-owned enterprises and designated monopolies'.

[94] Article 12.8 of the United States – Singapore Free Trade Agreement (6 May 2003) 42 I.L.M. 1026 (entered into force 1 January 2004).

transparency' with respect to information requests in individual cases[95] to more substantial deviations from the WTO rules.[96]

Some more recently concluded PTAs also include positive elements addressing non-discrimination obligations specifically for the energy sector. Notably, this is the case in the EU-Georgia Association Agreement which entered into force in 2016. Its Article 217 provides for a third party access obligation for energy transport facilities to be implemented on the territories of the parties to the Agreement.[97] Implementing TPA was meant to prepare Georgia for membership in the Energy Community, which requires the adoption of the entire energy acquis of the EU.[98] A similar yet more detailed provision can be found in the EU-Kazakhstan EPCA.[99] The provision applies not to 'energy transport facilities' in general but more specifically to 'high-voltage electric energy transmission grids and lines'. With respect to this type of infrastructure, Article 145 of the EPCA spells out an obligation to

> provide the enterprises of the other Party, established as juridical persons in the territory of the Party granting the access, with non-discriminatory access to high-voltage electric energy transmission grids and lines, which are partly or fully owned and regulated by the Party granting the access within the available capacities of such grids and lines.[100]

Finally, Article 140 of the EPCA provides that the 'Parties shall not maintain or establish a trading or export monopoly for raw materials *or energy goods*' (emphasis added).

The EU has also negotiated third-party access provisions in its FTAs with Mexico and Vietnam. In the former, the relevant obligation reads:

> Each Party shall ensure that owners or operators of transmission networks in its territory grant non-discriminatory access to the energy infrastructure for the transport of gas and electricity of any entity of the Parties. Access to the energy infrastructure shall be granted within a reasonable period of time from the date of the request for access by that entity.[101]

---

[95] See Article 2.13 of the EU-Korea FTA.

[96] An example is the US-Singapore FTA. It comprises a number of provisions which go further than the non-discrimination standard at the WTO level and are also more detailed. Its provisions apply to 'designated monopolies and government enterprises'.

[97] Article 217 (1) Association Agreement between the European Union and the European Atomic Energy Community and their Member States, of the one part, and Georgia, of the other part (27 June 2014) OJ 2014/L 261/4, 86.

[98] Georgia has been a Member of the Energy Community since July 2017.

[99] Enhanced Partnership and Cooperation Agreement between the European Union and the Republic of Kazakhstan (21 December 2015), OJ 2016/L 29/3, Art. 145.

[100] EU – Kazakhstan Enhanced Partnership and Cooperation Agreement above, Article 145(1).

[101] Article 7 (1) of the Chapter on Energy and Raw Materials of the new EU-Mexico FTA as published by the European Commission, available at https://trade.ec.europa.eu/doclib/docs/2018/april/tradoc_156800.pdf. The EU and Mexico in April 2018 reached 'agreement in principle' on a new bilateral trade agreement replacing its predecessor which came into force in 2000. The Agreement has not yet been signed by the Parties and the text may thus be subject to further modifications.

After thus affirming the general principle of third-party access to transmission grids, both parties reserve the right to introduce or maintain 'a limited list of derogations'. Such derogations have to be based on objective criteria and they have to be necessary to fulfil a legitimate policy objective.[102] A third paragraph in the TPA provision complements the obligation on owners and operators of transmission networks of the first paragraph cited above with a slightly more concrete call on the EU and Mexico to

> [E]nsure that entities of the Parties are accorded access to and use of energy transport infrastructure for the transport of gas and electricity on reasonable and non-discriminatory terms and conditions, including non-discrimination between types of energy, and at cost-reflective tariffs. Each party shall publish the terms, conditions and tariffs for the access to and use of energy transport infrastructure.[103]

The access obligation in the EU-Vietnam FTA is located in Chapter 7 on '[n]on-tariff barriers to trade and investment in renewable energy generation'.[104] The objective of the Chapter is the promotion of the generation of energy from renewable sources through facilitating trade and investment.[105] To implement that objective, Article 7.4 (e) provides that parties to the Agreement shall 'ensure that the terms, conditions and procedures for the connection and access to electricity transmission grids are transparent and do not discriminate against suppliers of the other Party.'[106] Despite the location of this provision in the chapter on renewable energy generation, nothing in the text suggests that the access obligation is meant to apply only to electricity from renewable sources.

10.2 Conclusions on Market Structure As an Impediment to International Electricity Trade

The existing provisions of world trade law do not incentivize proactive regulation to abolish anti-competitive behaviour on domestic markets. More concretely, multilateral trade rules do not establish a prohibition against maintaining dominant undertakings or a general obligation to abolish existing monopolies. Nor do the multilateral trade provisions set down an obligation to privatize state-owned enterprises enjoying a monopoly status.[107] Finally, no direct obligation to unbundle a

---

[102] Ibid, Article 7 (2).

[103] Ibid, Article 7 (3).

[104] Free Trade Agreement between the European Union and the Socialist Republic of Vietnam (12 June 2020) OJ 2020/L 186/3.

[105] Ibid, Article 7.1.

[106] Ibid, Article 7.4.

[107] Nor, in principle, are governments under an obligation to act or provide useful remedies against private operators that engage in restrictive practices. See United Nations Conference on Trade and Development, 'WTO Core Principles and Prohibition: Obligations Relating to Private Practices,

vertically integrated undertaking by demanding a change in its ownership structure can be inferred from world trade law.[108]

Hence, the structural trade barriers posed by vertical integration, continuing exertion of monopoly power, and to a lesser extent state ownership cannot be effectively tackled through the analysed norms of world trade law. Neither the GATT nor the GATS brings about an obligation on incumbent network owners to establish an access regime guaranteeing the right to use the bottleneck facility on reasonable terms.[109]

This does not mean however that vertically integrated utilities and transmission system operators enjoying a monopoly can abuse their dominant position without limits. As long as these companies fall under the specific categories of entities to which the analysed GATT and GATS provisions apply, they have to abide by the general non-discrimination principles entailing MFN and national treatment. The latter implies that a WTO Member would violate Article XVII GATT if a vertically integrated STE were simply to deny access to electricity from abroad. A serious limitation derives from the narrow personal scope of application of Article XVII GATT, which is specifically targeted at STEs. The actual degree to which WTO Members make use of STEs in the electricity sector is not transparent, as notifications of such entities are very rare.

After privatization, formerly state-owned companies will only be subject to the obligations of Article XVII GATT if they are endowed with special or exclusive privileges. Similarly, incumbent system operators owning and administering the transmission network might escape the definition of a monopoly service supplier due to the lack of pro-active government involvement and will thus not be subject to the commitments under Article VIII GATS. If an entity does fulfil the requirements to qualify as a monopoly service supplier, compliance with the MFN principle and a Member's specific commitments is required by Article VIII GATS.

Another major problem is that the effectiveness of the analysed GATS disciplines rests crucially on the degree to which Members have scheduled commitments. As commitments in sensitive sectors like energy are comparatively rare, many monopoly suppliers and system operators will not be subject to GATS market access and national treatment obligations.[110]

Outside the WTO, notably in the ECT and PTA frameworks, modest progress has been made towards more positive regulation of competitive conditions in the electricity sector. One of the most notable examples is an access obligation in the EU-Kazakhstan EPCA which could be mirrored in future PTAs and a possible future multilateral agreement.

National Competition Laws and Implications for a Competition Policy Framework' (United Nations 2003) [6], available at https://unctad.org/en/Docs/ditcclp20032_en.pdf.

[108] See also Dralle (2018), p. 324.

[109] Dee and Findlay (2008), p. 354.

[110] Willemyns (2016), p. 667.

All of the above makes the electricity sector one of the areas that would benefit greatly from sector-specific pro-competitive rules and functioning regulatory agencies to oversee the observance of such rules.[111]

10.3 Interlude: The Role of Private Actors in the Electricity Sector and the Application of WTO Law

Before continuing to analyse the remaining substantive trade issues identified as particularly relevant for electricity trade—quantitative restrictions and transit—it is necessary to briefly shed light on a matter of importance for both of these issues: The question to what extent conduct by private actors can be disciplined under the rules of world trade law other than in cases where non-governmental entities are directly addressed (as is the case in the context of Article XVII GATT).

One notable feature concerning (possibly trade-restrictive) measures applied in the electricity sector is that they are often put into effect by non-state actors. This is specifically relevant with regard to the conduct of privatized system operators in liberalized electricity markets. As system operation is a natural monopoly and since usually no alternative routes to a given transmission network exist, the conduct of system operators can have serious consequences for the possibilities for import, export and transit, among others. As liberalization and privatization continue in electricity sectors around the world, the relevance of the conduct of private actors will increase rather than decrease. It is therefore warranted to briefly examine the role of private actors for the application of provisions like Article XI (on quantitative import and export restrictions) and Article V GATT (on transit).

It is generally accepted that only measures taken by governments can be the object of complaints under the WTO Agreements.[112] Indeed, measures coming under the purview of WTO rules and dispute settlement proceedings are 'in the usual case, the acts or omissions of the organs of the state'.[113] The issue of whether measures taken by non-state actors can still be scrutinized under the substantive WTO law disciplines is one of attribution.[114] The standard applied by WTO dispute settlement bodies to discern attribution is generally whether there is 'sufficient

---

[111]See also WTO, Council for Trade in Services, Energy Services – Background Note by the Secretariat (09 September 1998) S/C/W/52 [6].

[112]Article 3.3 of the DSU allows WTO contracting parties to resort to the dispute settlement system of the WTO in 'situations in which a Member considers that any benefits accruing to it directly or indirectly under the covered agreements are being impaired by *measures taken by another Member*' (emphasis added).

[113]WTO, *United States – Sunset Review of Anti-Dumping Duties on Corrosion-Resistant Carbon Steel Flat Products from Japan*, Appellate Body Report (15 December 2003) WT/DS244/ [81].

[114]In *US – Corrosion Resistant Steel Sunset Reviews*, the Appellate Body held that 'in principle, any act or omission attributable to a WTO Member can be a measure of that Member for purposes of dispute settlement proceedings.' See ibid [81].

government involvement' in play.[115] However, based on this standard, it is still not an easy exercise to carve out precisely how far the involvement of the government needs to extend to trigger attribution. The Panel in the *Kodak/Fuji* case confirmed this, by observing that 'it is difficult to establish bright line rules' and pointing out that this determination was a case-by-case exercise.[116]

Taking a rather extreme standpoint, one could argue that governmental involvement already exists when the measures taken by private actors conform to the official policy preferences of a government.[117] This would, however, go significantly beyond the principles of the law of state responsibility in customary international law as codified in the ILC Articles on State Responsibility.[118] The latter require 'acting on the instructions of, or under the direction or control of' a state for conduct to be considered an act of a state.[119] Recourse to the ILC Articles as relevant sources of international law thus suggests that purely private conduct which merely confirms policy preferences of a government is not, in the absence of any government action, sufficient to trigger attribution.

Several scenarios have been examined by WTO dispute settlement panels and the Appellate Body with respect to attribution. Broadly speaking, three scenarios can be distinguished: (a) a government specifically directs a private entity to adopt certain conduct; (b) a government creates incentives for the adoption of certain conduct; and (c) the conduct is based entirely on decisions by a private entity and the government has omitted to act against this conduct. While in the first two cases attribution has been confirmed in disputes, mere failure to act has not met the necessary standard for attribution. Measures have been attributed to a government if private actors were induced or encouraged to take certain decisions[120] and where the government provided incentives to act accordingly.[121] In *Japan-Semiconductors*, the Panel found that legally binding obligations on private actors were absent, but that 'this amounted to a difference in form rather than substance because the measures were operated in a manner equivalent to mandatory requirements.'[122]

In *China – Raw Materials*, the question of delegation was at issue. China had delegated implementing authority to the China Chamber of Commerce of Metals, Minerals and Chemicals Importers and Exporters (CCCMC) for the coordination of export prices for certain raw materials which were under review in the dispute. One

---

[115]WTO, *Japan – Measures Affecting Consumer Photographic Film and Paper* (Kodak/Fuji), Report of the Panel (31 March 1998) WT/DS44/R [10.56].

[116]Ibid.

[117]Zedalis (2007), pp. 357 et seq.

[118]International Law Commission (ILC), Draft Articles on Responsibility of States for Internationally Wrongful Acts, with commentaries (2001) YBILC 2001/II(2).

[119]Ibid, Article 8.

[120]WTO, *United States – Certain Country of Origin Labelling* (COOL) Requirements, Reports of the Appellate Body (29 June 2012) WT/DS384/AB/R, WT/DS386/AB/R [291].

[121]GATT, *Japan – Trade in Semi-Conductors*, Report of the Panel (4 May 1988) L/6309 - 35S/116 [109].

[122]Ibid [117].

should be cautious to draw the general conclusion from this Report that delegation can always trigger attribution to a government. The Panel did not elaborate in sufficient detail on why it was 'satisfied that the measures at issue (. . .) are measures 'attributable' to China'.[123] Moreover, the CCCMC is a subordinate unit of the Ministry of Commerce of China and therefore more directly related to the government than, say, an electricity system operator in the hands of private shareholders.

Based on this short survey of the treatment of conduct of non-state actors in WTO dispute settlement and the references to relevant sources of general international law, the exact circumstances under which WTO provisions apply to private conduct remain ringed with shadow. One safe conclusion, however, is that purely private conduct does not trigger attribution if there are no sufficient incentives or disincentives by the government. In other words, there has to be some affirmative conduct by the government. It is not sufficient that private measures 'coincidentally track [a] desired government policy.'[124]

Undertakings in the electricity sector come in different shapes and forms—some exercise elements of governmental authority, others are fully independent in their decisions and owned by private shareholders. It must be observed that, once privatization has taken place, the electricity system operators continue to act in a tightly regulated framework and with a clear mandate: to safeguard the operation and permanent balance of the system. While this is not in itself sufficient to trigger the application of GATT provisions, the societal circumstances, the general degree to which enterprises can act free from guidance by the administration and similar factors should be taken into account in each case. The determination remains a case-by-case exercise and will be discussed individually below with respect to the specific trade issues.

References

Adlung R (2006) Public services and the GATS. J Int Econ Law 9:455

Bigdeli S, Rechsteiner S (2008) Article VIII GATS. In: Wolfrum R, Stoll P, Feinäugle C (eds) Max Planck commentaries on World Trade Law, vol 6. Martinus Nijhoff Publishers, Leiden

Boulle M (2019) Global experience of unbundling national power utilities. University of Cape Town Research Paper. https://www.gsb.uct.ac.za/files/Global_experiences_of_unbundling_national_utilities_MBoulle.pdf

Cabrera-Colorado O (2018) Increasing U.S.-Mexico cross-border trade in electricity by NAFTA's renegotiation. Energy Law J 39:79

Campbell R (2019) The power marketing administrations: background and current issues. Congressional Research Service. https://sgp.fas.org/crs/misc/R45548.pdf

Das Neves M (2014) Electricity interconnection and trade between Norway and Russia. Arctic Rev Law Politics 5:177

---

[123] WTO, *China – Measures Related to the Exportation of Various Raw Materials*, Reports of the Panel (5 July 2011) WT/DS394/R; WT/DS395/R; WT/DS398/R [7.1006].

[124] Zedalis (2007), p. 357.

De Hautecloque A, Talus K (2012) Capacity to compete: recent trends in access regimes in electricity and natural gas networks. In: Delveaux B, Hunt M, Talus K (eds) EU energy law and policy issues, vol 3. Intersentia, Cambridge

Dee P, Findlay C (2008) Trade in infrastructure services: a conceptual framework. A handbook of international trade in services. Oxford University Press, Oxford

Defilla S (2003) Energy trade under the ECT and accession to the WTO. J. Energy Nat Resour Law 21:428

Diebold N (2011) Standards of non-discrimination in International Economic Law. Int Comp Law Q 60:831

Dralle T (2018) Ownership unbundling and related measures in the EU energy sector: foundations, the impact of WTO law and investment protection. Springer, Berlin

Energy Charter Secretariat (2001) Trade in energy – WTO rules applying under the Energy Charter Treaty. ECT Secretariat

Energy Charter Secretariat (2003) Regional electricity markets in the ECT Area. https://www.energycharter.org/fileadmin/DocumentsMedia/Thematic/Regional_Electricity_Markets_2003_en.pdf

Jackson J (1991) The World Trading System: law and policy of International Economic Relations. MIT Press, Cambridge

Krajewski M (2003a) Public service and trade liberalization: mapping the legal framework. J Int Econ Law 6:341

Krajewski M (2003b) National regulation and trade liberalization in services: the legal impact of the General Agreement on Trade in Services (GATS) on National Regulatory Autonomy. Kluwer Law International, Alphen aan den Rijn, p 87

Krajewski M (2005) Playing by the rules of the game? Specific commitments after US – gambling and betting and the current GATS negotiations. Legal Iss Econ Integr 32:417

Lakatos A (2004) Overview of the regulatory environment for trade in electricity. In: Bielecki J, Desta MG (eds) Electricity trade in Europe: review of the economic and regulatory challenges. Kluwer Law International, Alphen aan den Rijn

Lipsky A, Sidak G (1999) Essential facilities. Stand Law Rev 51:1187

Marhold A, Weiss F (2019) Energy and fossil fuels as a topic of WTO accession protocols. In: Bungenberg M, Krajewski M, Tams C, Terhechte J, Ziegler A (eds) European yearbook of International Economic Law. Springer, Berlin

Mathur S, Mann P (2014) GATT/WTO accessions and energy security. In: Mathur S, Mann P (eds) Trade, the WTO and energy security. Springer, Berlin

Mattoo A (1998) Dealing with monopolies and state enterprises: WTO rules for goods and services. In: Cottier T, Mavroidis PC (eds) State trading in the twenty-first century. University of Michigan Press, Ann Arbor

Mavroidis P (2016) The regulation of International Trade (Volume I: GATT). Massachusetts Institute of Technology Press, Cambridge

Mitchell A, Heaton D, Henckels C (2016) Non-discrimination and the role of regulatory purpose in International Trade and Investment Law. Edward Elgar, Cheltenham

Nicholls D (2019) Op-Ed: what caused the current ESKOM crisis? ESI Africa. https://www.esi-africa.com/industry-sectors/generation/op-ed-what-caused-the-current-eskom-crisis/

Ortino F (2006) Treaty interpretation and the WTO appellate body report in US – gambling: a critique. J Int Econ Law 9:117

Pauwelyn J (2005) Rien Ne Va Plus? Distinguishing domestic regulation from market access in GATT and GATS. World Trade Rev 4:131

Petersmann E (1998) GATT law on state trading enterprises: critical evaluation of Article XVII and proposals for reform. In: Cottier T, Mavroidis PC (eds) State trading in the Twenty-First Century. University of Michigan Press, Ann Arbor

Poretti P, Rios-Herran R (2006) A reference paper on energy services: the best way forward? Manch J Int Econ L 3:2

Talus K (2011) Just what is the scope of the essential facilities doctrine in the energy sector? Third party access-friendly interpretation in the EU v. contractual freedom in the US'. Common Market Law Rev 48:1571

Wälde T, Gunst A (2004) International Energy Trade and access to networks. In: Bielecki J, Desta MG (eds) Electricity trade in Europe: review of the economic and regulatory challenges. Kluwer Law International, Alphen aan den Rijn

Willemyns I (2016) Disciplines on state-owned enterprises in International Economic Law: are we moving in the right direction? J Int Econ Law 19:657

Yi-Chong X (2017) Sinews of power: the politics of the state grid corporation of China. Oxford University Press, Oxford

Zedalis R (2007) When do the activities of private parties trigger WTO rules? J Int Econ Law 10:2

Chapter 11
Quantitative Import and Export Restrictions

Cross-border trade in electricity is gaining relevance owing to the developments outlined in previous chapters. It is therefore important to examine in detail how import and export restrictions are applied in the electricity sector and to have a closer look at the disciplines world trade law imposes. As will be seen, the typical import and export restrictions often used as trade policy measures in other economic sectors are not very prevalent in electric energy trade. This applies not only to customs duties but also to export taxes or production quotas. Rather, the electricity sector features some 'atypical' import and export restrictions, many of which can be explained by the technical specificities of electricity.

Cross-border electricity trade differs in procedure from trade within a purely domestic transmission system. The main reason is that interconnector capacity is limited and very often not all requests for trading can be accommodated. Therefore, the available interconnector capacity will have to be explicitly considered in the trading process unlike for domestic electricity trade, which does not usually take into account network constraints.[1] One way to do justice to the limitations in available interconnector capacity is to apply an allocation mechanism called pro-rata rationing. Pro-rata means that all scheduled transactions are curtailed in proportion to the total requested capacity. An alternative method is to allocate capacity on a first-come-first-serve basis. Increasingly, however, transmission rights are allocated via market-based mechanisms, especially auctions. In most systems, the system operator is the responsible entity for carrying out such auctions, as it usually owns the transmission assets.

Due to the characteristics of electricity as a network-bound form of energy and the safety and balancing considerations prevalent in any electricity network, the restriction of cross-border flows is not as straightforward as trade restrictions in other

---

[1] KU Leuven, 'Cross-border electricity trading: Towards flow-based market coupling' (KU Leuven EI-Fact-Sheet 2015-02) 1, available at https://set.kuleuven.be/ei/factsheets.

C. Frey, *World Trade Law and the Emergence of International Electricity Markets*,
EYIEL Monographs - Studies in European and International Economic Law 25,
https://doi.org/10.1007/978-3-031-04756-5_11

sectors. Most actions concerning cross-border flows will require close cooperation between system operators on both sides of the border to avoid technical problems. Moreover, in meshed electricity networks, not all electricity flows are equal. It is important at the outset to distinguish between trade flows and physical flows.[2] They are almost never identical, as the exact flow of electricity in an interconnected power grid is not controllable and the electrons cannot be directed with precision along a predetermined path.[3] Trade flows are usually scheduled in advance according to standard procedures called capacity calculation and capacity allocation. This is done based on available capacity on a cross-border interconnector. Physical flows on the other hand can be unscheduled and 'accidental'. The precise physical flows of electricity depend on a range of factors, like changes in consumption or the influence of weather on renewable energy output.[4] Furthermore, changing flow patterns in one region of the transmission network can instantaneously exert impacts on other regions of the same interconnected network.[5]

A particular case of an unscheduled physical flow pattern is a loop flow. A loop flow can be defined as 'the physical flow on a line where the source and sink are located in the same zone and the line or a part of that line is located in a different zone'.[6] In other words, a loop flow occurs when internal trade flows between two points of a domestic network induce physical flows over parts of a foreign network. Because of this phenomenon, physical flows between two countries frequently exceed commercial flows over the existing interconnectors between the same two countries. As a consequence, the unscheduled flows reduce the overall available capacity for cross-border trade.[7] One could therefore argue that a restriction of physical 'loop flows' in certain cases allows for more trading capacity to be made available.[8] Not every restriction of physical flows should thus be regarded as an import or export restriction.

---

[2] Cf. Kunz (2018), p. 199.

[3] Ibid, at 198.

[4] Mäntysaari (2015), p. 349.

[5] Kunz (2018), p. 198.

[6] This definition is taken from ENTSO-E Joint Task Force on Cross-Border Redispatch, 'Flow Definitions' available at https://www.entsoe.eu/publications/market-reports/.

[7] Kunz (2018), p. 198.

[8] The TSOs of several Eastern European countries publicly complained about loop flows through their domestic networks as a result of commercial transactions between Germany and Austria. Indeed, before the issue was tackled by splitting the former common market bidding zone between Germany and Austria, about half of the commercially scheduled transactions between the two countries took the path over other countries' networks. See Singh et al. (2016), pp. 287 et seq.

11.1   Electricity Import Restrictions

While primary energy goods like oil and gas are imported by most countries and exported in large quantities by only a few, the importation of electricity has been much less relevant in the past. Most countries have sufficient domestic power generating capacity to satisfy demand throughout the largest part of the year.[9] Only a few countries permanently rely on the importation of electricity because of insufficient domestic generating capacity. Other countries display a negative trade balance for electricity because of high domestic prices and the possibility of cheaper imports from adjacent countries.[10] It should be noted that for some countries, the picture varies significantly over the course of a year, as certain forms of generation (like hydropower) can experience significant seasonal differences in output. Accordingly, a country with a high share of these generating sources can be a net importer during one period of the year and a net exporter during another. Countries such as Australia, Japan, Iceland[11] and New Zealand currently neither import nor export electricity due to their geographical location as island states and long distances to neighbouring countries. Where electricity interconnections exist, e.g. in the European Union or between the NAFTA/CUSMA Members, there is usually a robust economic interest in the exchange of electricity, either because of temporal differences in generation or load between the countries, or because of price differentials. Nonetheless, countries sometimes restrict electricity imports for various reasons, as will be shown below.

11.1.1   Reasons for Restricting Electricity Imports

Electricity import restrictions are implemented for a variety of reasons. Three main categories can be distinguished: reasons of political economy; system security reasons; and public policy goals. Each of these will be discussed in turn.

---

[9]Bielecki (2004), p. 11.

[10]Examples of net importers include Belgium, Finland, Italy, the Netherlands, Morocco, the United States and Namibia, among many others. Cf International Energy Agency, Monthly Electricity Statistics, available at https://www.iea.org/reports/monthly-oecd-electricity-statistics.

[11]Iceland might in the near future export power to mainland Europe or the UK. The construction of a subsea cable, possibly to the UK, has been discussed for some time. Iceland has generation capacities largely exceeding domestic consumption, mainly because of its geothermal and hydropower potentials. Cf Schumpeter, 'Power under the Sea: Could a Power Cable from Iceland solve Britain's Energy Problem?' *The Economist* (20 January 2014) available at https://www.economist.com/schumpeter/2014/01/20/power-under-the-sea.

11.1.1.1 Political Economy Reasons: Safeguarding the Competitiveness of Domestic Generation

Electricity import restrictions of a quantitative nature based on economic reasons have rarely been applied until today. It would not seem impossible, however, to impose such restrictions in order to support the competitiveness of domestic electricity generators that produce at a higher cost than their foreign competitors do. Different generation portfolios between neighbouring countries with interconnected electricity systems can lead to significant variations in the costs of production. High volumes of wind and solar PV generation installed in one country, for example, can result in zero or even negative wholesale electricity prices when the conditions favour high generation output of these technologies. Such a situation could incentivize the 'dumping' of excess generation onto neighbouring markets. To avoid losses for domestic generators, governments might then be tempted to prevent such excess electricity from being imported.

Governments might also be interested in requiring a degree of market openness resembling their own standards and transparency from their electricity trading partners to provide for a level playing field. EU energy law specifically allowed Member States to refuse access to suppliers from other Member States that did not provide for the same degree of access for foreign suppliers.[12] This 'reciprocity clause' was meant to avoid imbalances in the gradual opening of electricity markets across the EU. It expired after a period of 9 years after the 1996 Electricity Directive entered into force. A number of EU Member States made use of the exception from domestic treatment granted by the Directive and adopted reciprocity clauses in domestic legislation for a limited period.[13]

11.1.1.2 System Security Reasons

More frequently than for purely economic reasons, import restrictions are applied to safeguard the domestic network against imbalances. The causes for imbalances in the network are numerous, and a distinction can be drawn between structural imbalances and short-term imbalances. Structural imbalances can occur, e.g., because of loop flows.[14] In an energy system with generation located mainly in one geographical area and large industrial load mainly in another, the national transmission system might not be ready to accommodate the resulting physical electricity flows. When internal lines experience structural congestion, electricity

---

[12] See Article 19 of Directive 96/92/EC of the European Parliament and of the Council concerning common rules for the internal market in electricity (19 December 1996) OJ 1997/L 27/20.; see also Lakatos (2004), pp. 135 et seq.

[13] The Member States temporarily adopting the reciprocity clause were Austria, Belgium, Germany, Italy Luxembourg, The Netherlands, Portugal, Spain and the UK.

[14] See above at p. 170.

will pass through neighbouring electricity systems on its way from source to sink.[15] Germany and its 'electricity neighbours' provide for a case study. The high penetration of wind energy installations in Northern Germany and the fact that industrial centres are located predominantly in South-western Germany coincided with an insufficient internal transmission network reinforcement. This caused considerable loop flows over the transmission networks of Poland and the Czech Republic, among others, increasing the need for balancing efforts by the Polish network operators. The Polish and German TSOs agreed on a common technical approach to alleviate the problem of structural loop flows between the two countries and installed devices called phase-shifting transformers.[16] While not blocking off all electricity flows between two areas of an interconnected network, phase shifters can reduce the load on critical lines by changing the pattern of physical flows in the grid.[17] While the installation of phase-shifting transformers will usually be carried out as a coordinated action between TSOs, they can also be installed as a unilateral measure.[18]

The need for restricting imports for technical reasons can also arise more spontaneously, for example when sudden and unforeseen spikes in generation occur on one side of the border. In such situations, network operators have a 'toolbox' of measures at hand that can help to mitigate the resulting stress to the network. Among these measures are counter-trading[19] and re-dispatching of generating installations.[20] As a last resort measure, curtailment of capacity on interconnectors will have to be considered by network operators.

---

[15] Loop flows occur mainly in synchronized electricity systems spanning several jurisdictions. As will be obvious, they are not an issue in isolated long-distance transmission lines that do not connect to the meshed grid.

[16] The strain over loops flows between Germany and its Eastern Neighbours and the installation of phase shifters were widely reported. See, e.g. Zeke Turner, 'In Central Europe, Germany's Renewable Revolution Causes Friction' The Wall Street Journal (16 February 2017) available at https://www.wsj.com/articles/in-central-europe-germanys-renewable-revolution-causes-friction-1487241180.

[17] Thema Consulting Group, 'Loop Flows – Final Advice' (Report prepared for the European Commission October 2013) available at https://ec.europa.eu/energy/sites/ener/files/documents/201310_loop-flows_study.pdf.

[18] Ibid, p. 13.

[19] In case of congestion of a line, the system operator can execute commercial transactions which would induce flows in the opposite direction of the flows causing the line to be congested. This 'countertrading' is a short-term measure and does not solve structural congestion issues.

[20] Redispatching refers to a change in the existing generation portfolio by interfering with the actual output of generators. In case of congestion, the system operator can request certain generators on one end of a congested line to reduce their output and those on the other end to increase their output.

11.1.1.3   Public Policy Goals

Because of the vital importance of electricity supply as the lifeblood of economies and the various societal and environmental impacts of electricity generation, governments strive to impose certain standards to protect their citizens and to pursue environmental or security agendas. Three main policy areas that can directly impact electricity imports and exports are discussed in the following paragraphs.

11.1.1.4   Environmental Protection and Public Health

In the past, several countries have adopted and maintained provisions requiring the imported electricity to fulfil certain conditions with respect to the environmental or human health impact of electricity generation. Section 13 of Austria's 1998 Electricity Act serves as an example. It provided that electricity supply contracts were not permissible when they involved the purchase from third countries in which plants were in operation that either did not 'comply with the state of the art' or the operation of which jeopardized the life or health of persons, animals or plants in Austria.[21] Supply contracts were also impermissible when the proper disposal of waste resulting from the generation of electricity could not be demonstrated.[22] Similar provisions were included in other EU Member States' energy laws.[23] The European Parliament in 2000 passed a resolution demanding that EU law require electricity imported from third countries to meet environmental and social standards similar to those applicable in the EU.[24] As the electricity mix of countries is gradually becoming cleaner and the concern for air quality is moving up the political agendas, governments could consider curtailing the import from those neighbouring electricity systems where generation is still largely based on power plants emitting hazardous substances like sulphur dioxide or carbon monoxide.

11.1.1.5   Climate Change

Import restrictions might become especially important in the context of climate-related energy policies. Different ambitions with respect to the transition from a mainly fossil-fuel-based energy sector to a low-carbon electricity supply mainly made up of renewable energy generation could tempt countries to restrict the

---

[21] §13 (1) of Austria's 1998 Electricity Act (Elektrizitätswirtschafts- und Organisationsgesetz (ElWOG), BGBl I Nr. 143/1998).

[22] Ibid, §13 (2).

[23] Among these other countries were the Czech Republic, Hungary, Italy and Luxembourg. See Bielecki and Ervik (2003), p. 415.

[24] European Parliament, Resolution on the Commission's second report to the Council and the European Parliament on the state of liberalisation of the energy markets (adopted 6 July 2000) [19]. See also Bielecki and Ervik (2003), p. 415.

importation of electricity from neighbouring countries where less ambitious policies are pursued. The announcement of the European Commission in late 2019 to impose a carbon border tax on certain imports into the EU shows the willingness to integrate climate protection into trade policy and to tackle the problem of carbon leakage.[25] The legislative proposal for a Carbon Border Adjustment Mechanism (CBAM) tabled by the European Commission in July 2021 indeed includes electricity as one of a small group of products to which the Mechanism will apply.

If one were to look for a hypothetical but not entirely unrealistic case, one could also take the example of Costa Rica. The country is on the path to complete decarbonisation and already generates around 98% of domestic electricity consumption from renewable sources. Sustainability is a major factor for Costa Rica's tourism industry and policies on climate change and environmental protection have contributed to the positive image of the country in the world.[26] The electricity system of Costa Rica is however interconnected with Nicaragua on the one side and Panama on the other. All three countries are Members of the regional electricity market project SIEPAC.[27] In Nicaragua, more than 50% of total electricity production is currently generated from fossil fuels, the largest part of which is provided by petrol.[28] While in Panama hydropower plays a larger role and the need for fossil fuels in electricity generation is reduced, the share of oil in the generation mix is still around 25%.[29] It would not be unthinkable for Costa Rica, therefore, to seriously consider curtailing electricity imports from one or both neighbouring countries to become '100% renewable' and safeguard its green public image.

11.1.1.6   National Security

Apart from environmental considerations, countries might also implement import or export restrictions due to concerns over national security or in times of open military conflict as a measure to cut off their neighbours' electricity supply. A recent spill-over of a general diplomatic crisis on the electricity system occurred in the context of a dispute between Kosovo and Serbia in 2018. As the entities responsible for the balancing of the network did not meet their obligations regarding system security,

---

[25] European Commission, Communication: The European Green Deal (11 December 2019), COM (2019) 640, p. 5.

[26] See, e.g. The New York Times, 'Tiny Costa Rica has a Green New Deal, too. It Matters for the Whole Planet' (12 March 2019) https://www.nytimes.com/2019/03/12/climate/costa-rica-climate-change.html.

[27] On SIEPAC, see above in Sect. 3.2.5, pp. 70 et seq.

[28] Meza et al. (2017), p. 495.

[29] International Renewable Energy Agency (IRENA), *Renewables Readiness Assessment Panama* (IRENA 2018).

widespread consequences for the whole European interconnected electricity transmission system followed.[30]

India and Pakistan agreed in 2014 to start the construction of an electricity interconnector between the two countries to export electricity from India.[31] While this announcement can be seen as a sign of 'neighbourly goodwill', considering the fragile relations between the two countries, future diplomatic conflicts could potentially spill over into the common management of the infrastructure.

11.2   Means of Restricting Cross-Border Electricity Flows

Electricity import or export restrictions, if the term is understood in a broad sense, can be applied in a variety of ways. Due to the character of electricity as a network-bound form of energy, the most obvious way is to simply refrain from constructing (or expanding) electricity interconnectors between two countries. Network expansion usually falls within the responsibility of system operators, like TSOs in Europe. The development and operation of interconnectors are often managed via a system of exclusive concessions. If these concessions are refused, market participants will be affected in their ability to import or export electricity. In this context, the case of Norway's regime for interconnector licensing has aroused suspicion concerning its compatibility with free movement of goods provisions in the EEA Agreement.[32] In addition to licensing for the development and construction of interconnectors, licensing regimes are also in place for the importation and/or exportation of electricity itself. An example of such a requirement can be found in the Electricity Act of the Republic of South Africa. It provides in relevant part that 'no person may, without a licence issued by the Regulator in accordance with this Act (. . .) import or export any electricity.'[33] Similar measures can be found in several electricity sector laws and regulations, e.g. in Canada,[34] the US[35] and Uganda.[36] The potential for restrictions on imports because of political or security interests or for other reasons is apparent.

---

[30] David Meyer, 'How a Mysterious Case of "Missing Energy" Caused Europe's Clocks to Run 6 Minutes Slow' *Fortune* (8 March 2018) available at https://fortune.com/2018/03/08/kosovo-serbia-energy-grid-frequency/.

[31] Ankit Panda, 'Pakistan Will Import Electricity From India' *The Diplomat* (22 March 2014) available at https://thediplomat.com/2014/03/pakistan-will-import-electricity-from-india/.

[32] See below at p. 178. See also Das Neves (2014), pp. 196 et seq.

[33] Section 8 of the Electricity Regulation Act, Act 4 of 2006 of the Republic of South Africa.

[34] See Part III.1 of Government of Canada, National Energy Board Act (NEB), R.S.C., 1985, c. N-7 (last amended on 29 March 2019) available at https://laws-lois.justice.gc.ca/PDF/N-7.pdf.

[35] See Section 202 (e) of the Federal Power Act, 16 U.S.C. 791, 824.

[36] See Part VI of Chapter 145 of Uganda's 1999 Electricity Act, available at https://uegcl.com/about/electricity-act/file.html.

When interconnectors have been established and their terms of use are non-discriminatory and transparent, restrictions of imports can still be carried out in several ways. These restrictions can be directed at transaction volumes, the capacity allocated to market participants on interconnectors, and the physical electricity flows resulting from market transactions. This order roughly corresponds to the timeframe in which these measures are applied, from weeks or even months ahead to real-time. A distinction can also be drawn between unilateral measures applied internally by system operators and cooperative measures applied cross-border and involving two or more system operators.[37]

The calculation of available capacity on interconnectors is a crucial exercise as it defines the trading possibilities between two zones. The determinants for cross-border electricity trade volumes are called 'net transfer capacity' (NTC) and 'available transfer capacity' (ATC). The NTC denotes the maximum allowable transfer capacity which can be made available for trading on an interconnector. The NTC value can be understood as the total technically available capacity after deduction of a security margin reserved for emergency situations.[38] The ATC is what is finally available for trade (usually on the day-ahead market) and is calculated by subtracting the volumes already reserved through long-term nominations from the NTC value.[39] Reductions of either the NTC or the ATC value which are not based on either the technical availability (NTC) or the economic values (ATC) should be regarded as import restrictions.[40]

After capacity *calculation*, capacity can be *allocated* by different means. Allocation can be realized through bilateral contracts between the network operator and the user of the capacity, but more advanced interconnections tend to allocate capacity via auctions.

Capacity allocation and congestion management are two sides of the same coin. The procedures for congestion management can result in restrictions of imports or exports similar to the capacity allocation methods. In emergency situations, network operators might have to curtail already allocated capacity on interconnectors.[41] In some jurisdictions, express provisions for such situations are in place providing for compensation of the affected market participants. In the EU, the principle of firmness of transmission rights is enshrined in law.[42] According to Article 15 (2) of the EU Electricity Regulation, 'transaction curtailment procedures shall only be used in

---

[37]Thema Consulting (2013), p. 12.

[38]KU Leuven, 'Cross-border electricity trading: Towards flow-based market coupling' (KU Leuven EI-Fact-Sheet 2015-02) 1, available at https://set.kuleuven.be/ei/factsheets, p. 3.

[39]Ibid.

[40]Cf Espa (2017), p. 242. Espa argues that as the NTC calculation by the domestic TSO 'is critical for exploiting the full potential of the interconnections to safely develop cross-border trade', it is important 'that TSOs assess the NTC in a transparent way and that the calculations are not manipulated in such a way as to de facto restrict cross-border electricity trade.'

[41]See also ibid, at 243.

[42]Cf. Article 69 ff of the Commission Regulation (EU) 2015/1222 establishing a Guideline on Capacity Allocation and Congestion Management (of 24 July 2015) OJ 2015/L 197/24.

emergency situations where the transmission system operator must act in an expeditious manner and re-dispatching or countertrading is not possible'. Furthermore, 'any such procedure shall be applied in a non-discriminatory manner'.[43] A second sentence adds that 'except in cases of force majeure, market participants who have been allocated capacity shall be compensated for any curtailment.'[44]

11.3 Restrictions on Exports of Electricity

On various occasions in the past countries have limited the trade in electricity with other countries. Export restrictions were implemented mainly to uphold the security of supply for domestic electricity consumers and to maintain the balance of supply and demand in critical periods of increased electricity demand or following the loss or failure of certain generators. Electricity export restrictions operate similar to the ones discussed for imports in that they consist in alteration of the market-based allocation procedures for cross-border capacity or in interfering directly with bilateral contracts.[45]

On a more general level, licensing requirements are in place in a number of countries regulating exports through licensing only one or a few entities for electricity exports. A case was opened in the EFTA context against Norway in December 2009 due to an assumed infringement of the prohibition of quantitative restrictions on exports in EU law (and measures having an equivalent effect). Norway required both a licence for the construction and operation of transmission lines and a 'Foreign Trade Licence' to physically import or export electricity.[46] The purpose of this requirement, according to the Norwegian Government, was to ensure the efficient and secure import and export of electrical energy. The criteria for granting the licence included security of supply, environmental protection, and resource management. The only license holders were the Norwegian network operator Statnett, and Nord Pool, a power exchange. In its justification of the measure, Norway argued that the quantity of imports and exports to and from Norway was not restricted by the licensing system, but by the physical transmission capacity and by other limitations in the power grid.[47] The Directorate of the EFTA Surveillance Authority argued that Norway should have focused on the application of market-based mechanisms and

---

[43] Article 16 of Regulation 2019/943 of the European Parliament and of the Council on the internal market for electricity (5 June 2019) OJ 2019/L 158/54.

[44] Ibid.

[45] Espa (2017), p. 240.

[46] See Section 3-1 (Construction and operating license) and Section 4-2 (Foreign Trade License) of the Norwegian Energy Act, Act no. 50 of 29 June 1990: Act relating to the generation, conversion, transmission, trading, distribution and use of energy etc.

[47] Statement of the Norwegian Ministry of Petroleum and Energy to the EFTA Surveillance Authority (3 February 2010) on Foreign Trade License – Section 4-2 of the Norwegian Energy Act (copy on file with the author).

emergency safeguards available to the system operator to ensure efficient and secure cross-border electricity transmission and safeguard the public policy goals already mentioned, and that the licensing requirements were therefore unnecessary.[48] To the best of the author's knowledge, no infringement proceedings were ultimately opened against Norway and the case was closed in 2013.

Lastly, export restrictions are also imposed to relieve critical supply situations. The limitations on exports of electricity enacted by Bulgaria in the winter of 2011/ 2012 may serve as an example. According to the government of Bulgaria, the restrictions were imposed due to a state of emergency on local electricity markets.[49] Bulgaria had experienced a season-specific spike in electricity demand that occurred in conjunction with low water levels of rivers and supply shortages of coal and natural gas.[50] The Energy Charter Secretariat investigated the Bulgarian export restrictions after it was informed of the measures by the Bulgarian government. The Secretariat called for full transparency and reiterated 'that the measures applied to prevent or relieve critical shortage of electricity on domestic markets should be the least restrictive and should not be employed for periods longer than is necessary to achieve that objective.'[51]

11.4 Applying the Legal Discipline: Article XI GATT

Import and export restrictions are subject to strict disciplines in the GATT. Article XI GATT deals with quantitative restrictions concerning imports and exports. The potential scope of application of Article XI is broad, and only those aspects most relevant to the electricity sector will be discussed here. While the delineation between Article XI GATT and Article III GATT is sometimes difficult in practice, most of the issues discussed in the following paragraphs deal with restrictions aimed

---

[48] EFTA Surveillance Authority, Reply to the Norwegian Ministry of Petroleum and Energy in Case No 66755 (Foreign Trade License – Section 4-2 of the Norwegian Energy Act) (5 November 2010), copy on file with the author. The EFTA Surveillance Authority argued as follows: 'in the Norwegian regulatory framework for electricity, security of supply concerns are mainly a task of the system operator, to be fulfilled to the greatest possible extent with instruments based on market principles, with the possibility to resort to various safeguard mechanisms in emergency situations. It is difficult to see why those subsequent procedures, which, for the main part, are based on non-discriminatory market-based mechanisms, cannot achieve the aim of an efficient and secure power transmission between Norway and third countries, safeguarding common public interests such as security of supply, the environment and resource management. So for that reason as well, it would therefore appear that the restriction of free movement entailed by this licence goes beyond what is necessary in order to attain the objectives put forward by Norway'.

[49] Espa (2017), p. 240.

[50] Energy Charter Secretariat, 'Restrictions on export of electricity in the Balkan region – update' (ECT Website News Item, 22 February 2012) available at https://energycharter.org/media/all-news/.

[51] Ibid.

directly at the importation of electricity and not the treatment of electricity once imported, and therefore would appear to fall under Article XI GATT.[52] Nonetheless, it is important to draw the conceptual line between the two provisions before examining the different categories of import and export restrictions more closely.

11.4.1   The Relationship Between Articles XI and III GATT

Imports and exports can be restricted by a variety of measures and many of these measures have been the subject of WTO dispute settlement procedures. One recurring difficulty is the drawing of the boundary between different categories of measures affecting imported products. In principle, Article XI deals with measures aimed at the importation or exportation itself, while Article III covers measures that are aimed at products after importation (technically speaking, after they have cleared customs). In other words, while measures falling under Article III are applied 'behind the border', Article XI measures are 'at-the-border measures'.[53] This conceptual delineation is not always conclusive in practice, however. An ad note to Article III addresses the relationship in an attempt to further clarify the matter. According to this note, 'any internal tax or other internal charge, or any law, regulation or requirement [...] which applies to an imported product and the like domestic product and is collected or enforced in the case of an imported product at the time or point of importation' should be regarded as an internal measure.[54] Thus, despite being applied at the border, these generally applicable measures remain outside the scope of Article XI.[55] Typical examples are safety requirements or environmental product regulations that apply across the board for a certain group of products. They will be covered by Article III even if compliance is checked at the border and import is prohibited as a result.[56] Measures directed at imports only with no equivalent for domestic products, on the other hand, are covered by Article XI.

Despite this attempt at clarifying the relationship between these two provisions, difficulties persist in practice as regards domestic measures applied at the border. It also cannot be ruled out that a situation may arise in which a measure has aspects to it that amount to a border measure and other aspects that would have to be qualified as

---

[52] The Panel in *Dominican Republic – Import and Sale of Cigarettes* referred to 'those measures which affect the opportunities for importation itself' as falling into the ambit of Art. XI GATT. WTO, *Dominican Republic – Measures Affecting the Importation and Internal Sale of Cigarettes*, Report of the Panel (26 November 2004) WT/DS302/R [7.261].

[53] Espa (2015), p. 67.

[54] Ad note to Article III GATT. See also Wolfrum (2011), p. 293.

[55] Mavroidis (2016), p. 99.

[56] Energy Charter Secretariat (2001) [122].

internal measures.[57] The Panel in *India-Autos* acknowledged this possibility by stating that

> [I]t therefore cannot be excluded a priori that different aspects of a measure may affect the competitive opportunities of imports in different ways, making them fall within the scope either of Article III (where competitive opportunities on the domestic market are affected) or of Article XI (where the opportunities for importation itself, i.e. entering the market, are affected), or even that there may be, in perhaps exceptional circumstances, a potential for overlap between the two provisions (. . .).[58]

One should not conclude from this, however, that the *same aspect* of a measure could simultaneously fall under the realm of both Articles III and XI GATT.[59]

An important difference in the treatment of measures exists between Article III and Article XI GATT. While Article III only disciplines measures that are applied discriminatorily (as between imported and domestic products), Article XI subjects border measures to an outright prohibition, only justifiable through the exceptions foreseen in Article XI itself and the general exceptions of the GATT.[60] One would therefore expect that a WTO Member would try to portray an allegedly GATT-inconsistent measure as an internal measure under Article III GATT rather than a quantitative restriction under Article XI GATT.[61] On the other hand, parties administering an allegedly Article XI-inconsistent measure can draw from a longer list of exceptions than in the case of Article III.[62] Under the usual sequence of legal review, Article XI would be applied only after a finding that the measure is not within the scope of Article III.[63] It is not always the case that WTO Members invoke both provisions, however.

11.4.2 Article XI GATT

Article XI GATT, the heading of which reads 'General Elimination of Quantitative Restrictions', subjects import and export restrictions other than duties, taxes or other charges to a general ban, allowing only narrow exceptions. In contrast to what the

---

[57] Mavroidis (2012), p. 66.

[58] WTO, *India — Measures Affecting the Automotive Sector*, Reports of the Panel (21 December 2001) WT/DS146/R; WT/DS175/R [7.224].

[59] Mavroidis (2016), p. 99.

[60] Wolfrum (2011), p. 293.

[61] Mavroidis (2016), p. 66 who states that 'one could hardly envisage a scenario where a WTO Member expresses a measure in terms of an import quantitative restriction rather than a domestic instrument'. For a similar view see Pauwelyn (2005), p. 142, who finds that 'for measures applied to both imports and domestic products, a preference is given to Article III over Article XI.'

[62] Other than by having recourse to the general exception provision of Article XX, Article XI-inconsistent measures can be justified by Art. XI:2, Art. XII (Safeguarding of balance of payments) and Art. XIV GATT (exceptions to the rule of non-discrimination).

[63] Wolfrum (2011), p. 293.

heading might suggest, Article XI:1 does not comprise restrictions in the form of numerical quotas only. As the text of the provision contains many crucial elements for its interpretation and application, it is useful to reproduce the first paragraph in its entirety. Article XI:1 reads as follows:

> No prohibitions or restrictions other than duties, taxes or other charges, whether made effective through quotas, import or export licences or other measures, shall be instituted or maintained by any contracting party on the importation of any product of the territory of any other contracting party or on the exportation or sale for export of any product destined for the territory of any other contracting party.

WTO adjudicating bodies have consistently interpreted Article XI:1 as being broad in scope.[64] The collective scope of the terms 'prohibitions' and 'restrictions' indeed comprehensively prohibits measures restricting imports and exports of products with the exception of those measures falling under paragraph 2 of Article XI or the general exceptions of Article XX GATT.[65] The Panel in *Colombia – Ports of Entry* summarized the wide interpretation by earlier panels by stating: '(…) a number of GATT and WTO panels have recognized the applicability of Article XI:1 to measures which create uncertainties and affect investment plans, restrict market access for imports or make importation prohibitively costly, all of which have implications on the competitive situation of an importer.'[66] In its Report in *China – Raw Materials*, the Panel even went as far as to 'consider the very *potential* to limit trade is sufficient to constitute a 'restriction [. . .] on the exportation or sale for export of any product' within the meaning of Article XI:1 of the GATT 1994.'[67] Even assuming a very broad scope of application, one should be cautious about claiming that any measure that *potentially* affects the volume of imports or exports will fall within the scope of Article XI. The important test is still whether it is a measure imposed on or directed at importation or exportation, i.e. whether it is a 'border measure'.[68] Panels have also continuously based their decisions on the design of the measure as opposed to examining in detail the actual impacts of the measure on cross-border trade.[69] In other words, panels look at the legal and regulatory situation of a WTO Member rather than at concrete trade transactions.[70]

Based on the text of Article XI:1 and the foregoing remarks it is clear that a complete trade ban (i.e. a 'prohibition' of imports or exports) is inconsistent with

---

[64] WTO, *India — Quantitative Restrictions on Imports of Agricultural, Textile and Industrial Products,* Report of the Panel (6 April 1999) WT/DS90/R [5.128].

[65] Mavroidis (2016), p. 77.

[66] WTO, *Colombia – Indicative Prices and Restrictions on Ports of Entry, Report of the Panel* (27 April 2009) WT/DS366/R [7.240].

[67] WTO, *China – Measures Related to the Exportation of Various Raw Materials,* Reports of the Panel (5 July 2011) WT/DS394/R; WT/DS395/R; WT/DS398/R [7.1081] (italics in original).

[68] Mavroidis (2012), pp. 77 et seq.

[69] The Panel in *Colombia – Ports of Entry* based its conclusion that the measure at issue was not a quantitative restriction on both the 'fundamental thrust and effect of the measure' and its 'design, architecture and revealing structure'. WTO, *Colombia –Ports of Entry*, Panel Report [4.156].

[70] Cf Wolfrum (2011), p. 285.

Art. XI:1 GATT. The Panel in *Canada-Periodicals* has expressly confirmed this.[71] It would seem that directing market actors to set their electricity cross-border trading schedules to zero by interfering with capacity allocation on interconnectors results in a 'prohibition' of trade and therefore clearly falls under Article XI:1 GATT. As was discussed above such measures are more common for exports than for imports of electricity.

With respect to 'restrictions' there is more room for interpretation than with respect to 'prohibitions'. The term 'restriction' must be understood in its ordinary meaning as a 'limitation on action, a limiting condition or regulation.'[72] It covers, in the words of one commentator, 'all measures which make export or import more difficult without making it impossible.'[73]

Despite the wide scope of the quantitative restrictions referred to in Article XI, it cannot be overlooked that three categories of measures are explicitly mentioned in the text of the provision: 'Quotas'; 'import or export licenses'; and 'other measures'. In light of the references in other parts of the GATT to the first two terms, little doubt should exist as to their meaning. At the same time, through the term 'other measures' the drafters of the GATT introduced a broad residual category justifying the already mentioned wide scope of application.[74] While measures of the first category, quotas, have generally been among the more prominent trade restrictive measures, they do not play a major role in electricity trade. The other two categories, licensing systems and 'other measures' are more important for electricity and will be discussed separately below.

11.4.2.1 Import and Export Licensing

Apart from 'quotas' and 'other measures', the text of Article XI:1 GATT specifically refers to import and export licenses. Licensing denotes an administrative procedure that requires the submission of a specific application or other documentation to the relevant administrative body as a condition for obtaining approval for importation or exportation.[75] While no specific rules exist for export licensing, import licensing is

---

[71] WTO, *Canada – Certain Measures Concerning Periodicals*, Report of the Panel (14 March 1997) WT/DS31/R [5.5].

[72] WTO, *India – Quantitative Restrictions on Imports of Agricultural, Textile and Industrial Products*, Report of the Panel (6 April 1999) WT/DS90/R [5.128] citing New Shorter Oxford Dictionary (1993) at p. 2569.

[73] Wolfrum (2011), p. 286.

[74] Mavroidis (2012), p. 82 citing WTO, *Argentina – Measures Affecting the Export of Bovine Hides and the Import of Finished Leather*, Report of the Panel (19 December 2000) WT/DS155/R [11.17].

[75] Cf Art. 1 of the Agreement on Import Licensing Procedures (15 April 1994), Legal Instruments of the Uruguay Round vol. 1, 33 I.L.M. 1154.

subject to a lex specialis regime—the Agreement on Import Licensing Procedures (ILA).[76]

A panel under the old GATT found that import or export licensing systems that are non-automatic or constitute a significant administrative or monetary impediment to cross-border trade violate Article XI:1 GATT, while automatic licensing systems would have to be regarded as compatible with that provision.[77] Subsequent case-law has confirmed this finding.[78] An import licence granted on the fifth working day after application was deemed to have been automatically granted.[79] Non-automatic licensing usually involves a number of mandatory requirements to be fulfilled before a licence can be granted. Such requirements can entail considerable additional costs and the validation period can be disproportionately long, resulting in negative impacts on export volumes or even having the same effect as an import or export ban.[80] An export licensing system for semiconductors administered by Japan was held by a GATT Panel to be inconsistent with Article XI:1 because the administrative procedures were responsible for delays in exports of semiconductors to WTO Members other than the US of up to 3 months.[81] Apart from the delay in time until a final decision is taken, another factor for distinguishing WTO-compatible from unlawful licensing is the exercise of discretion on the side of authorities and the resulting uncertainty for traders.[82]

Automatic licensing procedures are consistent with the obligations of WTO Members under Article XI GATT and the Agreement on Import Licensing when the rules are 'neutral in application and administered in a fair and equitable manner.'[83] This provision concerns the application and administration of such import

---

[76] Ibid. The relationship between the Agreement on Import Licensing, as lex specialis, and Article XI:1 GATT was touched upon marginally by the AB in *Argentina – Import Restrictions*. The AB subtly criticized the Panel in a footnote for having started the analysis with the more general Article XI GATT. See WTO, *Argentina – Measures Affecting the Importation of Goods*, Report by the Appellate Body (22 August 2014) WT/DS438/AB/R [5.253].

[77] GATT, *European Community – Programme of Minimum Import Prices, Licenses and Surety Deposits for Certain Processed Fruits and Vegetable*, Report of the Panel (18 October 1978) (L/4687 - 25S/68 [4.1]. The Panel in *China – Raw Materials* confirmed this finding by stating: 'The Panel concludes above that licences that are granted without condition or those that implement an underlying measure that is justified pursuant to another provision of the WTO Agreement, such as GATT Article XI:2, XII, XVIII, XIX, XX or XXI, may be consistent with Article XI:1, so long as the licence does not by its nature have a limiting or restrictive effect. Conversely, a licence requirement that results in a restriction additional to that inherent in a permissible measure would be inconsistent with GATT Article XI:1. Such restriction may arise in cases where licensing agencies have unfettered or undefined discretion to reject a licence application.'

[78] Wolfrum (2011), p. 287.

[79] GATT, *Japan – Trade in Semi-Conductors*, Report of the Panel (4 May 1988) L/6309 - 35S/116 [118].

[80] Espa (2015), p. 93.

[81] GATT, *Japan – Semi-Conductors,* Panel Report [118]. See also Nedumpura (2014), p. 25.

[82] WTO, *China – Raw Materials*, Panel Report [7.959].

[83] Article 1.3 of the Import Licensing Agreement.

licensing systems which in principle can be considered GATT-compatible, and not the licensing rules per se.[84] Article 1.4 of the Import Licensing Agreement furthermore requires Members to make available and publish all rules and information concerning the administrative procedures for the applications for import licenses 'in such a manner as to enable governments and traders to become acquainted with them.'

The licensing requirements for the construction of electricity interconnectors applicable in several countries fall outside the scope of the ILA and, consequently, Article XI GATT as long as they aim only indirectly at the process of importation and exportation of electricity. This finding appears to stand even considering the fact that interconnectors are a prerequisite for international trade in electricity. In comparison, most licensing schemes for the importation and exportation of electricity itself must be regarded as covered by the disciplines of Article XI:1 and the ILA.

Import licensing schemes appear to be less prevalent in practice for electricity trade. A non-automatic import licensing scheme for electric energy was administered by India between 2009 and 2012.[85] Import licenses were issued by the Directorate General of Foreign Trade (DGFT) in consultation with the Ministry of External Affairs and the Ministry of Power, among others.[86]

Licensing requirements applied to electricity exports are mostly non-automatic licensing systems. This is because authorities want to retain a certain amount of discretion to consider, among other things, the effects on the security of domestic power supply and the environment. The licensing systems pertaining to electricity exports of North American countries are illustrative. Exports of electricity from Canada are prohibited unless either a permit or a licence has been issued. A range of criteria apply for both permits and licences and the entity responsible for issuing these documents (the National Energy Board) enjoys discretion in its decision.[87] This is demonstrated by the fact that the Governor in Council may make an order designating an application for exportation of electricity as an application in respect of which a licencing requirement (as opposed to a permit) applies, with different sets of criteria. Furthermore, in many jurisdictions, only one or two entities are licence holders with respect to the import and export of electricity. Considering the disciplines on automatic and non-automatic licensing in the ILA and the experience from adjudication in the WTO, the non-automatic licensing schemes in the electricity sector must be held to constitute export restrictions within the meaning of Article XI

---

[84] WTO, *European Communities – Regime for the Importation, Sale and Distribution of Bananas*, Report of the Appellate Body (9 September 1997) WT/DS27/AB/R [197 f].

[85] European Commission, 'Overview of Potentially Trade Restrictive Measures Identified Between 2008 and end 2015' (European Commission May 2016) 11, available at http://trade.ec.europa.eu/doclib/docs/2016/may/tradoc_154568.pdf.

[86] Ibid.

[87] See Part III.1 of Government of Canada, National Energy Board Act (NEB), R.S.C., 1985, c. N-7 (last amended on 29 March 2019) available at https://laws-lois.justice.gc.ca/PDF/N-7.pdf.

GATT and would therefore have to be justified by having recourse to one of the grounds of exception foreseen in the GATT.[88]

11.4.2.2   'Other Measures'

In the absence of a generally agreed-upon definition or clearly defined scope of the term, GATT and WTO panels have qualified a number of individual measures as 'other measures'. Examples include data collection and monitoring requirements;[89] a prohibition to import copyrighted works not manufactured domestically;[90] a requirement of security deposits to guarantee an undertaking to effect imports;[91] and import prohibitions based on process and production methods.[92] The extent to which indirect effects on imports and exports are sufficient to trigger the application of Article XI GATT is not entirely clear. It is sometimes argued that even the regulation of the internal marketing and sales of a product, like a restriction on advertising, can qualify as an 'other measure'.[93] This would, however, cast the net too wide. It would also put into question the meaning of the non-discrimination obligation of Article III GATT, which should be clearly delimited from quantitative restrictions on imports and exports in the way elaborated above. What is clear is that the broad scope of 'other measures' encompasses de facto measures as well as the contents of a single decision. Thus, an 'other measure' can concern a once-off decision of individual application (like the decision to grant an exemption in a specific case) and does not need to be of general application.

Considering the broad scope of the provision as confirmed by several GATT and WTO panels, a large number of measures restricting the volume of electricity trade flows across national borders could amount to a quantitative restriction. This is specifically true for any alterations of capacity calculation and capacity allocation procedures, if these result in a decrease in import or export volumes of electricity.[94] Ex-ante reductions of capacity to be made available for trading on an interconnector and interfering with capacity auctions can be subsumed under 'other measures' in the same way as the curtailment of electricity flows. The unilateral installation of

---

[88] See below in Sect. 11.4.3, pp. 187 et seq.

[89] GATT, *Japan – Trade in Semi-Conductors*, Report of the Panel (4 May 1988) L/6309 – 35S/116 [118].

[90] GATT, *The United States Manufacturing Clause*, Report by the Panel (15 May 1984) L/5609 – 31S/74.

[91] GATT, *European Community Programme of Minimum Import Prices, Licences and Surety Deposits for Certain Processed Fruits and Vegetable*, Report of the Panel (18 October 1978) L/4687 - 25S/68.

[92] WTO, *United States – Import Prohibition of Certain Shrimp and Shrimp Products*, Report of the Appellate Body (12 October 1998) WT/DS58/AB/R. See also Wolfrum (2011), p. 288.

[93] Wolfrum (2011), p. 288.

[94] See above in Sect. 11.2, pp. 176 et seq.

phase-shifting transformers to tackle the problem of loop flows could in principle also fall under a broad interpretation of 'other measures'.

Measures requiring reciprocity in market opening or in the standards maintained with respect to environmental protection which have the effect of reducing imports are also covered by Article XI GATT. Mandatory environmental standards for both domestic and imported electricity would, however, have to be analysed under Article III GATT, even if they have the effect of limiting imports.[95]

As measures with respect to cross-border electricity trade are often put into effect by private actors, one must look closely at the legal requirements for capacity calculation, capacity allocation, and congestion management, and the degree of discretion these laws or regulations leave for individual applications. This will be a case-by-case exercise and general conclusions are difficult to draw.[96] The installation of phase-shifting transformers on the German-Polish border, for example, was a cooperative initiative between German and Polish TSOs. The available evidence does not reveal that this measure was induced or directly incentivized by either the Polish or German government. It is therefore hard to see why this should be disciplined by Article XI GATT. Taking the opposite view, one could argue that these entities are statutorily tasked with the administration and operation of the transmission network for which the government has delegated authority to the TSOs. This involves taking all necessary measures to keep the network stable and to maintain the operating frequency in the grid. On balance, in the absence of affirmative government behaviour in the specific case, the delegation of the broad task of securing system operation is not sufficient to trigger attribution to the government. To find that a measure put into effect by a private system operator is not compatible with Article XI, it would thus have to be proven that the measure is based on some kind of affirmative governmental conduct.

11.4.3   Exceptions: Article XI:2 and Article XX GATT

Having found that a measure amounts to an import or export restriction, several grounds for justification of such a measure are available in Article XI:2 GATT itself,

---

[95] See above in Sect. 11.1.1.4, p. 174.

[96] WTO, *Japan – Measures Affecting Consumer Photographic Film and Paper*, Report of the Panel (31 March 1998) WT/DS44/R [10.56] as confirmed by the Panel in *Argentina – Hides and Leather* ('we recall the statement of the Panel in Japan – Measures affecting Consumer Photographic Film and Paper to the effect that: "Past GATT cases demonstrate that the fact that an action is taken by private parties does not rule out the possibility that it may be deemed governmental if there is sufficient government involvement with it. It is difficult to establish bright-line rules in this regard, however. Thus, that possibility will need to be examined on a case-by-case basis."'). WTO, *Argentina – Measures Affecting the Export of Bovine Hides and the Import of Finished Leather*, Report of the Panel (19 December 2000) WT/DS155/R [11.17]. See for general considerations above in Sect. 10.3, pp. 163 et seq.

as well as in the general exception clause of Article XX GATT. Article XXI GATT (allowing measures necessary to uphold national security) could theoretically also become relevant. As it is focused primarily on military conflicts, however, it will not be further analysed here.

11.4.3.1   Article XI:2 GATT

The second paragraph of Article XI provides for a number of exceptions from the prohibition of quantitative restrictions. Of the three subparagraphs of Article XI:2 which each contain a separate ground for carving out a measure from GATT scrutiny, only the first is relevant for the present analysis and it applies exclusively to *exports*. According to Article XI:2 (a), the prohibition of quantitative restrictions as enshrined in Art. XI:1 shall not extend to 'export prohibitions or restrictions temporarily applied to prevent or relieve critical shortages of foodstuffs or other products essential to the exporting contracting party'. Accordingly, in order for an export restriction to be covered by the exception in Article XI:2 (a), there needs to be (a) a 'critical shortage' of (b) an 'essential product' and the measure may only be (c) 'temporarily applied'. Unfortunately, none of these three criteria is further defined in the provision itself.[97] The meaning of the term 'essential product' was at issue in the *China – Raw Materials* dispute. The Panel regarded a product as 'essential' if it is 'important', 'necessary' or 'indispensable' to a WTO Member.[98] Substitutability is a factor that, in the opinion of the Panel, can speak against the essential character of a product.[99] In *China – Raw Materials*, China argued that its restrictions on the export of bauxite should be exempted based on Article XI:2 (a) as the measures were held to be necessary to address a critical shortage of an essential product. The Panel and Appellate Body both accepted that the term 'other products' was sufficiently wide for bauxite to be regarded as an 'essential product'. The Panel also explicitly acknowledged that an 'essential product' need not be the final product, but could as well be an input product.[100] Based on the foregoing, it is submitted that electricity, considering its vital significance for modern societies and virtually any industrial production process, can regularly be regarded as an essential product.

The term 'critical shortage' was defined by the Appellate Body in *China – Raw Materials* as 'those deficiencies in quantity that are crucial, that amount to a situation of decisive importance, or that reach a vitally important or decisive stage, a turning point.'[101] The Appellate Body also pointed to the slight difference in wording as compared to paragraph (j) of Article XX that only speaks of 'short supply', omitting

---

[97] Karapinar (2012), p. 446, qualifies this as a 'major weakness' of the provision.

[98] WTO, *China – Raw Materials*, Panel Report [7.282].

[99] Ibid [7.341 ff].

[100] WTO, *China – Raw Materials*, Panel Report [7.340].

[101] WTO, *China – Measures Related to the Exportation of Various Raw Materials*, Reports of the Appellate Body (30 January 2012) WT/DS394/AB/R; WT/DS395/AB/R; WT/DS398/AB/R [324].

the term 'critical'.[102] For the Appellate Body, it followed from this that coverage of Article XI:2 (a) is narrower than that of Article XX GATT.[103]

When an export restriction concerns an 'essential product' which indeed is in critical shortage, measures to relieve this critical situation may only be applied temporarily. Hence, Article XI:2 (a) does not allow measures permanently applied to deal with chronic shortages of essential products.[104] It is thus of a different character than Article XX (g) GATT, which allows measures relating to the conservation of exhaustible natural resources to be permanently applied.[105] Depending on the electricity generation mix and the availability of short-term reserves in a given country, situations of 'critical shortage' regarding electricity supply can and do occur. The breakdown of large power plants or exceptionally low water levels in hydro reservoirs could both lead to a 'critical shortage' of domestic electricity generation capacity in certain countries. In such situations, recourse to Article XI:2 (a) is permitted. Measures must, however, be temporary and must be removed as soon as the critical situation has passed.[106]

Finally, it should be noted that it is the defendant who carries the burden of proof regarding the applicability of one or more of the grounds for an exception in Article XI:2 GATT.[107] When recourse to Article XI:2 is unsuccessful, the defendant can still invoke Article XX GATT, whereas when the requirements of Article XI:2 (a) have been met, such recourse is not possible.[108]

11.4.3.2 The General Exceptions in Article XX GATT

The Article XX GATT exceptions have been invoked on several occasions to defend export restrictions based on national sustainable development policies, albeit not yet with respect to electricity. It is well established that the application of Article XX GATT (titled 'General Exceptions') follows a sequence whereby the specific grounds for justification in paragraphs (a) to (j) are to be analysed in a first step and the conditions of the so-called 'chapeau' (the introductory paragraph) of Article XX in a second step.[109] Of the former, paragraphs XX (b) and (g) could be especially

---

[102] Ibid [325]. See also Mavroidis (2016), p. 100.

[103] Ibid.

[104] WTO, *China – Raw Materials*, Panel Report [7.297].

[105] Ibid [7.349]; WTO, *China – Raw Materials*, AB Report [339-340].

[106] Mavroidis (2016), p. 102.

[107] Ibid at 103.

[108] WTO, *China – Raw Materials*, AB Report [334].

[109] See, e.g. WTO, *Brazil – Measures Affecting Imports of Retreaded Tyres*, Report of the Appellate Body (3 December 2007) WT/DS332/AB/R [139]. For a measure to be judged compatible with the GATT, it must pass a two-tiered test and meet both the requirements of the respective subparagraph (s) and the requirements of the chapeau. See also WTO, *US – Gasoline*, AB Report p. 22. If recourse to one of the specific grounds of justification is not successful, there is no need to proceed to

relevant for justifying electricity import restrictions based on public policy. Article XX (b) allows measures necessary to protect human, animal or plant life or health while subparagraph (g) allows measures relating to the conservation of exhaustible natural resources.

Import restrictions taken with reference to health concerns fall under Article XX (b). They must be 'necessary' to achieve the protection of human health. A measure is more likely to be judged as necessary the more it is specifically suited to contribute to the attainment of the objective sought.[110] An import restriction on electricity could only be judged necessary for the protection of the health of humans in the exceptional circumstance that a power plant is situated in close proximity to a border and the plant generates electricity mainly for export to the country implementing the import restriction. Otherwise, the measure will not be suitable to realize the objective sought because the power plant will simply keep producing electricity for consumption elsewhere.

Measures taken in pursuit of climate policies can be considered under Article XX (g) if a convincing case can be made that the atmosphere is an 'exhaustible natural resource'. Support can be found in the dictum of the Appellate Body in the *US – Shrimp* dispute, according to which the term exhaustible natural resources 'must be read by a treaty interpreter in the light of contemporary concerns of the community of nations about the protection and conservation of the environment.'[111] In the same report, the Appellate Body also pointed out that the term 'natural resources' in Article XX (g) is not 'static' in its content or reference, but rather is 'by definition, evolutionary.'[112] The concern for the effects of climate change ranks among the most pressing issues in current international relations. The fact that climate researchers and international expert bodies like the Intergovernmental Panel on Climate Change (IPCC) have been expressing the diminishing room for action in terms of a 'carbon budget' also supports a finding that stable atmospheric conditions can be subsumed under the term 'exhaustible natural resources'.[113] It should be noted that electricity itself cannot be qualified as an 'exhaustible natural resource' even though this is sometimes claimed.[114] As the product of a conversion process, electricity lacks the qualities of a *natural* resource. Recourse to paragraph (g) of

---

examine the consistency of a measure with the chapeau. WTO, *China – Raw Materials*, AB Report [7.469].

[110] WTO, *Korea – Measures Affecting Imports of Fresh, Chilled and Frozen Beef*, Report of the Appellate Body (11 December 2012) W/DS161/AB/R [163].

[111] WTO, *United States – Import Prohibition of Certain Shrimp and Shrimp Products*, Report of the Appellate Body (12 October 1998) W/DS58/AB/R [84].

[112] Ibid [130].

[113] Cf. the IPCC Special Report 'Global Warming of 1.5° C' which refers to the remaining carbon budget (i.e. the amount of global anthropogenic emissions which can be emitted to stay within a 1.5 ° C scenario) at several points. IPCC, 'Global Warming of 1.5 ° C' (2018) available at https://report.ipcc.ch/sr15/pdf/sr15_spm_final.pdf.

[114] Albath (2005), p. 121.

Article XX to justify an export restriction taken due to a shortage of electricity supply would therefore be fruitless.

An additional requirement in Article XX (g) GATT is that the measure which is sought to be justified must have been made effective in conjunction with restrictions on domestic production or consumption. It is not necessary that the domestic and trade-restrictive measures be identical. The standard developed by dispute settlement bodies is one of 'even-handedness'. As the Panel held in *China – Rare Earths*, '[t]he measures should "work together" in the sense of forming together a rational system that works to further a stated objective.'[115] Thus, a WTO Member invoking Article XX (g) GATT with reference to climate protection will have to show that it has adopted climate change legislation of a similar character on the domestic level.

Finally, the measure must be primarily aimed at the objective pursued, i.e. the protection of the exhaustible natural resource. This was the definition given to the terms 'relating to' by the Panel in *Canada – Herring and Salmon*.[116] The party invoking Article XX (g) must show that a 'close and genuine relationship' exists between the ends and the means.[117]

After having found that a measure falls within one of the categories discussed, the measure will also have to satisfy the conditions of the chapeau of Article XX GATT. The chapeau requires that a measure does not constitute 'a means of arbitrary or unjustifiable discrimination between countries where the same conditions prevail, or a disguised restriction on international trade.' The purpose of the chapeau is to prevent the exceptions in Article XX from being abusively invoked by Members.[118] It furthermore seeks to strike a balance between the right of a Member to invoke an exception and the substantive rights of other Members under the GATT.[119] Based on these general considerations, it has been held that there needs to be a rational connection between the measure and the objective pursued.[120] Furthermore, in *US-Gasoline* the Appellate Body held that the existence of less restrictive alternatives will also be examined in the context of the chapeau of Article XX GATT.[121]

To summarize, WTO Members will have a difficult time trying to justify import restrictions of electricity under Article XX (b) GATT based on the protection of

---

[115] WTO, *China – Measures Related to the Exportation of Rare Earths, Tungsten, and Molybdenum*, Panel Report (26 March 2014) WT/DS431/R [7.302].

[116] GATT, Canada – Measures Affecting Exports of Unprocessed Herring and Salmon, Report of the Panel (22 March 1988) L/6268 - 35S/98 [3.24 ff].

[117] WTO, *China – Measures Related to the Exportation of Rare Earths, Tungsten, and Molybdenum*, Report of the Appellate Body (7 August 2015) WT/DS431/AB/R [5.90].

[118] WTO, *United States – Standards for Reformulated and Conventional Gasoline*, Report of the Panel (29 January 1996) WT/DS2/R, p. 22.

[119] WTO, *US – Shrimp*, AB Report [156].

[120] WTO, *Brazil – Retreaded Tyres*, AB Report [227].

[121] This test is similar to the one applied in the context of the 'necessity' requirement in Article XX (b) GATT. An evaluation of alternatives under the chapeau will thus often not be necessary if this has already been done under the specific ground of justification. In the context of paragraph (g), the reasonably available alternatives will be evaluated under the chapeau.

public health. Invoking paragraph (g) with reference to the mitigation of climate change is more likely to pass the scrutiny of Article XX GATT if the WTO Member invoking the provision can substantiate that climate change is an objective also pursued internally and the trade-restrictive measure is part of a wider policy agenda to tackle climate change.

11.4.4 Notification and Administration of Quantitative Restrictions

Quantitative restrictions falling under the scope of Article XI GATT which can be maintained on the grounds of one of the provisions discussed in the previous part must be administered in accordance with the special regime of Article XIII GATT and have to be notified to all WTO Members.

Article XIII GATT provides that quantitative restrictions on imports or exports shall be administered in a non-discriminatory manner. More specifically, Article XIII:1 GATT requires WTO Members to apply the MFN principle when maintaining import and export prohibitions or restrictions. Article XIII:2 adds to this that 'in applying import restrictions to any product, contracting parties shall aim at a distribution of trade in such product approaching as closely as possible the shares which the various contracting parties might be expected to obtain in the absence of such restrictions (. . .).' This wording aims in the first place at the allocation of quotas among all WTO trading partners, which should be oriented towards achieving the shares in trade that would occur absent the imposition of the quota.

In order to increase the transparency concerning the imposition of import and export restrictions, the WTO Members agreed to establish a notification procedure for measures falling within the scope of Article XI GATT. Since 2012, all notifications are compiled in a publicly accessible database. The only quantitative restriction notified in the field of electricity is the non-automatic licensing regime for imports of electric energy administered by India.[122]

11.5 Additional Disciplines in the ECT and PTAs

The ECT incorporates Article XI GATT by reference and provides little additional value. In PTAs, one can find minor deviations from the general ban on quantitative restrictions to the effect that these Agreements either allow for more exceptions than the GATT (WTO-minus) or fewer exceptions than the WTO disciplines (WTO-plus). The OECD surveyed a total of 93 regional trade agreements to assess

---

[122] As retrieved from WTO online database, available at https://www.wto.org/english/tratop_e/implic_e/implic_e.htm. See also above in Sect. 11.4.2.1, p. 185.

their provisions on export restrictions. Most of the agreements analysed did not deviate from the GATT standard, but the OECD found that there is a tendency towards WTO-plus provisions in agreements concluded in more recent times.[123] Twenty-two of the surveyed agreements contained provisions on export restrictions which the OECD qualified as WTO-minus while 15 contained WTO-plus provisions.[124] The Agreements falling below the WTO standard mostly allow export restrictions for certain categories of (valuable) products like fuels or certain metals and stones. WTO-plus types of provisions either contain a limitation (i.e. they impose conditions) on the exceptions the WTO allows for or simply allow for fewer exceptions than in the WTO framework.[125] A total of 12 WTO-plus agreements surveyed by the OECD admitted fewer exceptions to the export restriction discipline when compared with the WTO standard.[126] Among the Agreements with the fewest exceptions were the Trade, Development and Co-operation Agreement between the EU and South Africa, the EU-Israel Association Agreement, and the Central European Free Trade Agreement.[127] Most of these WTO-plus agreements surveyed provided for elimination of the GATT Article XX (j) exception which would have allowed restrictions 'essential to the acquisition or distribution of products in general or local short supply.'[128] Notably, a number of agreements either eliminate the exception in Article XI:2 for products in 'critical shortage' entirely or limit its application to foodstuffs only, while eliminating the other 'essential products' formulation.[129]

As far as can be ascertained, there are as of yet no explicit provisions with respect to electricity import or export restrictions in these agreements. This might change in the future given the increasing global relevance and visibility of electricity trade.[130]

11.6 Conclusions on Import and Export Restrictions

Import and export restrictions in the electricity sector can be instituted by different means and at different moments in time. A survey of relevant practice proves the hypothesis that countries are less inclined to restrict imports of electricity than

---

[123] Korinek and Bartos (2012), p. 34.

[124] Ibid, at 34.

[125] Ibid, at 23.

[126] Ibid.

[127] Ibid.

[128] Ibid.

[129] The EU and South Africa, for example, opted to strike the shortage exception from the text of the Agreement. The same approach was followed in the Trade Agreement between the EFTA and Chile. In the Agreements between the EU and the CARIFORUM countries and between the EU and Cote d'Ivoire, the shortage exception is restricted to foodstuffs only.

[130] See above in Part I.

exports of electricity. It is submitted that import restrictions might become more pertinent in the context of accelerating renewable energy ambition and the explicit choice of countries for or against certain forms of electricity generation. Total bans of actual electricity imports, however, are still hardly applied in practice.

Licensing systems for both electricity imports as well as exports are administered by many countries engaging in cross-border electricity trade with neighbours. Licensing for energy trade and investments into the sector has been seen as an important instrument to exercise sovereignty over resources and energy supply. Non-automatic export licensing systems as maintained by several WTO Members constitute export restrictions within the meaning of Article XI:1 GATT and require justification. Licensing systems are also in place for interconnectors. While electricity trade crucially depends on the construction of interconnectors, the respective licensing schemes are not challengeable under Article XI as they do not pertain to the traded commodity as such.

When applying the disciplines on import and export restrictions in world trade law to electricity, the physical properties of electricity flows must be taken into account. Electricity has the exceptional quality of spreading along a grid according to physical laws. Commercial transactions have an influence on the general direction of electricity flows, but the precise path cannot be predetermined if more than one line is available to transmit the electricity from its source of generation to its sink. The example of interconnected electricity grids in the EU illustrates that not all electricity flows over a domestic network stem from commercial transactions originating in or destined for that same country. These unscheduled flows reduce the capacity available to accommodate flows resulting from commercial transactions between two countries. National TSOs in some European countries have therefore resorted to installing phase shifters, which in effect reduce the amount of electricity entering the domestic part of the interconnected grid. Based on an analysis of Article XI GATT, such reduction qualifies as an import restriction and would thus have to be justified. It is submitted that safeguarding the security of the national electricity system does not fall under the rather narrowly defined grounds of the exception provided for in Article XI:2 GATT. In comparison, export restrictions taken to relieve critical situations with respect to the supply of electricity fall under the 'critical shortage' exception.

Based on the foregoing, it is submitted that there is a need to explicitly clarify that not every reduction in the volume of cross-border electricity flows should be regarded as a 'restriction' within the meaning of Article XI or to alternatively expand on the existing exceptions. System operators need a certain amount of flexibility to apply their tools in critical situations. Curtailment of capacity should remain a measure of last resort and subject to the compensation of traders. One general threshold question is whether it can be held that there is sufficient government involvement in measures ultimately carried out by private system operators. In the light of the existing WTO case law and relevant sources of general international law, this will have to be denied as long as governments do not actively induce the relevant conduct on private actors.

Measures restricting electricity imports or exports to protect the environment and to tackle climate change are gaining in importance. Measures aimed at reducing emissions and thus contributing to official decarbonization objectives will be easier to justify under the GATT's Article XX than restrictions based on public health concerns, as long as they are applied in a non-discriminatory and non-arbitrary way.

One final interesting question concerns the delineation between measures falling into the scope of Article XI GATT as import or export restrictions and those pertaining to transit, and not to import or export per se. The transit disciplines in world trade law are the subject of the discussion which follows below.

References

Albath L (2005) Handel und Investitionen in Strom und Gas: Die internationalen Regeln. C. H. Beck, Munich

Bielecki J (2004) Electricity trade: overview of current flows and infrastructure. In: Bielecki J, Desta M (eds) Electricity trade in Europe: review of the economic and regulatory challenges. Kluwer Law International, Alphen aan den Rijn

Bielecki J, Ervik L (2003) Environment-related restrictions to electricity trade. J Energy Nat Resour Law 21:413

Das Neves M (2014) Electricity interconnection and trade between Norway and Russia. Arctic Rev Law Politics 5:177

Energy Charter Secretariat (2001) Trade in Energy – WTO rules applying under the Energy Charter Treaty. ECT Secretariat

Espa I (2015) Export restrictions on critical minerals and metals. Cambridge University Press, Cambridge

Espa I (2017) The treatment of restrictions and financial charges on imports and exports of electricity under EU and international law. In: Cottier T, Espa I (eds) International Trade in sustainable electricity: regulatory challenges in International Economic Law. Cambridge University Press, Cambridge

Karapinar B (2012) Defining the legal boundaries of export restrictions: a case law analysis. J Int Econ Law 15:443

Korinek J, Bartos J (2012) Multilateralising regionalism: disciplines on export restrictions in regional trade agreements. OECD Trade Policy Papers, No 139. https://www.oecd-ilibrary.org

Kunz F (2018) Quo Vadis? (Un)scheduled electricity flows under market splitting and network extension in Central Europe. Energy Policy 116:198

Lakatos A (2004) Overview of the regulatory environment for trade in electricity. In: Bielecki J, Desta MG (eds) Electricity Trade in Europe: review of the economic and regulatory challenges. Kluwer Law International, Alphen aan den Rijn

Mäntysaari P (2015) EU Electricity Trade Law: the legal tools of electricity producers in the internal electricity market. Springer, Berlin

Mavroidis P (2012) Trade in goods. Oxford University Press, Oxford

Mavroidis P (2016) The regulation of International Trade (Volume I: GATT). Massachusetts Institute of Technology Press, Cambridge

Meza C, Amado N, Sauer I (2017) Transforming the Nicaraguan Energy mix towards 100% renewable. Energy Procedia 138:494

Nedumpura J (2014) Energy security and the WTO agreements. In: Mathur S (ed) Trade, the WTO and Energy Security: mapping the linkages for India. Springer, Berlin

Pauwelyn J (2005) Rien Ne Va Plus? Distinguishing domestic regulation from market access in GATT and GATS. World Trade Review

Singh A, Frei T, Chokani N, Abhari R (2016) Impact of unplanned power flows in interconnected transmission systems – case study of the Central Eastern European Region. Energy Policy 91: 287

Thema Consulting Group, 'Loop Flows – Final Advice' (Report prepared for the European Commission October 2013). available at https://ec.europa.eu/energy/sites/ener/files/docu ments/201310_loop-flows_study.pdf

Wolfrum R (2011) Article XI GATT. In: Wolfrum R, Stoll P, Hestermeyer H (eds) WTO – trade in goods. Max Planck Commentaries on World Trade Law, vol 5. Martinus Nijhoff Publishers, Leiden

Chapter 12
Transit of Electricity

Transit, for the purposes of this study, can be defined as a transport process across the territory of a state which is neither the state where the transport begins nor where it ends. The decisive element is the 'passage' through the transit state, as opposed to import, export or purely domestic transport.[1] One major issue is to find a balance between the principle of freedom of transit and the sovereign interests of the transit state. While the states where the process originates and ends are interested in an efficient delivery of products to the final destination, the transit state might experience the operationalization of the transit as a burden and demand a form of compensation. Thus, one recurring theme—and source of disagreement—is precisely how far the transit obligation extends. The need for regulation of transit in international trade was recognized at the multilateral level as early as 1921 when the General Conference on Freedom of Communications and Transit was held in Barcelona.[2] Remarkably, one of the outcomes of the General Conference was the 1923 Geneva Convention on Electricity Transit, which codified the main principles on the transit of electric energy.[3] Not just since the days of the Barcelona Conference, the freedom of transit has been a cornerstone of international trade law and is currently enshrined in the GATT as well as a number of regional and sector-specific agreements. Transit issues have also played a major role in the Energy Charter process, as transit disputes surfaced repeatedly after the dissolution of the Soviet

---

[1] On the topic of transit generally see Huarte Melgar (2015). For the transit of (fossil) energy goods see Azaria (2015).

[2] General principles of transit can be traced back to Grotius' stipulation of a general right of transit in the interest of the community of nations. See also Roggenkamp (1995), Fn. 35.

[3] Convention Relating to the Transmission in Transit of Electric Power, 9 December 1923, 58 LNTS 315. See also Gudas (2018), pp. 104 et seq.

© The Author(s), under exclusive license to Springer Nature Switzerland AG 2022
C. Frey, *World Trade Law and the Emergence of International Electricity Markets*,
EYIEL Monographs - Studies in European and International Economic Law 25,
https://doi.org/10.1007/978-3-031-04756-5_12

Union in 1991.[4] These mainly concerned the transit of natural gas rather than electricity, but the latter has started to come into the focus more recently.[5]

Electric energy, on its way from generation to consumption, increasingly crosses state borders. Harnessing renewable energy resources in remote world regions will require long-distance transmission of electricity, passing through several different national jurisdictions on the way to consumption centres. Electricity transmission lines will extend over land or across the territorial sea of transit states. Before analysing the legal framework established by WTO and other trade rules, it is necessary to carve out the distinguishing features of transit through electricity transmission lines as opposed to more traditional means of goods transit.

12.1 Special Features of Electricity Transit

Transit of electric power is different from other kinds of transit in at least two important respects: The first distinguishing factor is the reliance of electricity transit on fixed infrastructure. The second distinguishing factor is the physical phenomenon that electricity in an interconnected network will take the path of least resistance when moving from the point of entry into the grid to the point of exit from the grid. Both of these factors each have several important consequences, which will be briefly discussed in turn.

The fixed infrastructure determinant implies that the means of transportation are extremely limited and inflexible when compared with transportation of other products. Traders in agricultural products, textiles or other merchandise can choose between transportation by truck, train or airplane and switch between the one and the other rather spontaneously. Trade in electricity can only be realized via an existing transmission infrastructure and, prospectively, via newly-built lines. The electricity transmission systems of most countries were not designed to accommodate significant transit flows in addition to the electricity generated domestically or imported from power plants in neighbouring countries.[6] For this reason, it is pertinent to define the terms of transit and especially the terms of access to the transmission grid of the country hosting the transit flow. In addition, network reinforcements and the construction of new transmission lines are necessary to make optimal use of a world region's renewable energy sources.

Transit of electric power can be carried out either through isolated long-distance lines merely spanning over a territory, or by making use of the entire interconnected

---

[4]Roggenkamp (1995), p. 119.

[5]See, e.g., Kamila Aliyeva, 'Uzbekistan, Turkmenistan Agreed on Electricity Transit' *Azernews* (23 May 2017) available at https://www.azernews.az/region/113666.html.

[6]Such transit flows constitute problems when they imply that security margins are threatened in the host area, requiring costly measures to be implemented by system operators. See Thema Consulting Group (2013), p. 4.

network of the transit state.[7] A look at the first multilateral codification of electricity transit in the 1923 Geneva Convention reveals that the traditional understanding covers only the first alternative. The text of Article 2 of the Convention reads: '[e] lectric power shall be considered as transmitted in transit across the territory of a Contracting State when it crosses the said territory *by means of conductors erected for this purpose alone without being wholly or in part* produced, utilized or *transformed* within such territory' (emphasis added). This definition clearly does not cover the transit via meshed grids where electricity is transformed to higher or lower voltages. The issue of how the contemporary WTO and ECT transit disciplines deal with this issue is analysed in the next section.[8] Considering the central importance of infrastructure for enabling electricity trade, another important question is to what extent the transit principles in world trade law offer any incentives or even obligations to expand existing infrastructure. This question will be discussed below.

With respect to the second determining feature of electricity transit, it was already discussed that electricity spreads over a network according to the path of least resistance and not according to the exact location of buyers and sellers of electricity. As a consequence, in *technical* definitions electricity transit is often characterized as an 'unscheduled' flow and not as a scheduled trade flow. A further distinction is usually made within the category of unscheduled flows into transit and loop flows. While transit flows derive from trade between two countries (A-B-C), loop flows are a result of purely domestic trade flows (A-B-A).[9] In this respect, it is worth exploring whether the multilateral transit rules indeed cover only 'voluntary' transit, i.e. transit flows resulting from scheduled trade transactions or also 'involuntary' transit in the form of unscheduled transit or loop flows. If the latter were not included in the multilateral transit rules, the multilateral obligations could not be invoked against a state which obstructs such flows or requires disproportionally high compensatory fees.

Just like foreign trucks transporting goods over the roads of the transit state, electricity in transit will further reduce the limited capacity of the existing network. Moreover, such flows are a major source of uncertainty for grid operators when calculating the amounts of energy that can be exchanged with adjacent countries.[10]

---

[7] Research is currently being carried out on meshed HVDC grids which could combine the positive features of AC and DC transmission. See the EU-funded research project 'Progress on Meshed HVDC Offshore Transmission Networks' (PROMOTioN), https://www.promotion-offshore.net/.

[8] See below in Sect. 12.2, pp. 201 et seq.

[9] A being the country of origin, B the transit country and C the country of destination.

[10] The Belgian grid operator Elia explains with respect to the Belgian network that 'Belgium's central position in the European transmission system means it has to cope with significant unscheduled physical flows (i.e. energy exchanges which are not governed by a commercial agreement between countries, but are simply due to the fact that energy moves freely through the grid without stopping at borders). Such flows are a major source of uncertainty for Elia when calculating the amount of energy that can be exchanged with neighbouring countries.' This statement is taken from the Elia website at http://www.elia.be/en/grid-data/interconnections.

Nonetheless, for transit to be carried out in a meaningful way it is essential to provide non-discriminatory access to the networks of the transit state. Furthermore, transit flows of electricity regularly stem from trade between neighbouring countries and not only between two non-adjacent countries.[11] This case is a rare exception in the transit of other products.

One regional setting where the regulation of international electricity transit is rather advanced is the EU internal energy market. Special provisions on the compensation of costs associated with hosting transit flows are contained in the so-called Inter-Transmission System Operator Compensation (ITC) mechanism.[12] It provides, *inter alia*, how the amount of transit is to be calculated, namely on an hourly basis, 'by taking the lower of the absolute amount of imports of electricity and the absolute amount of exports of electricity on interconnections between national transmission systems'.[13] On this basis, the ITC prescribes that TSOs shall receive compensation for costs incurred as a result of making infrastructure available to host cross-border flows.

12.2 Applying the Legal Discipline: Article V GATT

Article V GATT is entitled 'Freedom of Transit'. This heading clearly indicates the basic objective of the provision: to establish and ensure free transit as a cornerstone of international trade in goods. The structure of the provision is as follows: Paragraph 1 comprises a definition of transit, paragraphs 2 to 6 entail separate obligations with respect to transit and paragraph 7 contains the only explicit exemption from coverage of Article V. Before analysing the substance of the transit provision, it is helpful to examine its exact scope with respect to the described specifics of electricity transit. The definition in Article V:1 GATT is as follows:

> Goods (including baggage), and also vessels and other means of transport, shall be deemed to be in transit across the territory of a contracting party when the passage across such territory, with or without trans-shipment, warehousing, breaking bulk, or change in the mode of transport, is only a portion of a complete journey beginning and terminating beyond the frontier of the contracting party across whose territory the traffic passes. Traffic of this nature is termed in this article 'traffic in transit'.

Until recently, transit disputes at the WTO level were quite rare and only in 2007 did a WTO Panel have the first opportunity to provide some clarity on the interpretation of Article V GATT. The first transit dispute to reach the panel stage, *Colombia –*

---

[11] As an example, trade between Germany and Austria will regularly result in increased electricity flows over the domestic grids of Poland and the Czech Republic.

[12] Commission Regulation (EU) No. 838/2010 on laying down guidelines relating to the inter-transmission system operator compensation mechanism and a common regulatory approach to transmission charging [2010] OJ L 250/5.

[13] Ibid, Annex Part A at 1.6.

Ports of Entry, was submitted to a Panel in October 2007.[14] The Panel noted that its task of interpreting Article V GATT was 'arduous' since 'it will be necessary to interpret Article V of the GATT 1994 without any meaningful guidance.'[15] A second opportunity for a Panel to interpret certain elements of Article V GATT presented itself in September 2016 when Ukraine brought a complaint against the Russian Federation.[16] While the parties to the two disputes addressed central concepts of the GATT transit discipline, far from all questions of specific relevance for electricity transit were argued. These questions must therefore be assessed in the absence of specific adjudicatory guidance.

Based on the text of Article V:1 GATT reproduced above, the first important observation is that the wording does not preclude transit through fixed infrastructure like electricity transmission lines.[17] The term 'means of transport' is sufficiently broad so as to encompass pipelines or electricity grids. As several commentators rightly argue, the fact that these modes of transport are not explicitly mentioned in the provision should not be interpreted as an exclusion from its scope.[18] Taking into account the object and purpose of the provision and the Agreement in which it is embedded supports a broad reading of the term 'means of transport'. In the preamble of the WTO Agreement, the Parties recognize that their economic and trade relations 'should be conducted (. . .) with a view to (. . .) expanding the production of and trade in goods and services.' The preamble of the GATT includes a corresponding wording with respect to the expansion of the production and exchange of goods. A narrow reading of 'means of transport' and a consequential exclusion of a whole group of commodities (i.e. those dependent on the transport through fixed infrastructure) from the coverage of the 'freedom of transit'[19] would not be in harmony with the purpose as expressed in the preambular language cited.

A second observation is that the definition of 'traffic in transit' appears to cover both transit through long-distance HVDC lines without ties to the local network as well as transit through the meshed network of the transit state. The definition in Article V:1 explicitly mentions four operations as forming part of the passage through the transit state, among which is 'change in transport mode'. What this inclusion makes clear is that it is not necessary for the transiting goods to exit the

---

[14]WTO, *Colombia – Indicative Prices and Restrictions on Ports of Entry*, Report of the Panel (27 April 2009) WT/DS366/R. An earlier transit dispute concerning the trans-shipment and warehousing of Swordfish by European fishermen in Chilean ports was brought by the European Communities before a Panel in 2000 but was discontinued after an agreement between the Parties.

[15]Ibid [7.388].

[16]WTO, *Russia — Measures Concerning Traffic in Transit*, Request for Consultations by Ukraine (21 September 2016) WT/DS512/1.

[17]This corresponds with the majority of commentators on the issue. See Gudas (2018), p. 115; Azaria (2009), p. 576; Ehring and Selivanova (2011), p. 60.

[18]Ehring and Selivanova (2011), p. 60; WTO Secretariat (2010), p. 167.

[19]On the notion of 'freedom of transit' see below in Sect. 12.2.1, pp. 203 et seq.

transit country in exactly the same shape or condition as they entered.[20] For the transit of electricity, this can thus be interpreted to include the transformation to higher or lower voltages in the transit country. This assessment is not altered by the fact that once the electricity has entered into the stream of the transmission grid of the host state, it cannot be physically traced to the 'exit point'. Nothing in the text of Article V GATT suggests that products in transit have to be visibly identified during the transit process. Thus, it would appear to be sufficient that the amounts of electricity 'in transit' can be identified through a statistical exercise by looking at the total amounts of imports and exports of electricity.

Another aspect worth mentioning is that the freedom of transit provision covers not only the transported 'goods' themselves, but also baggage and, more importantly, vessels and other means of transport. Indeed, the means of transport will also be deemed 'traffic in transit'. The question arises how this is to be interpreted with respect to transport via fixed infrastructure like energy pipelines and electricity transmission networks. Most commentators have rightly argued that the immovable and location-specific energy infrastructure cannot itself be in transit, but only the goods—oil, gas, and electricity—transported via this infrastructure.[21]

Article V GATT also covers the situation where the journey starts and ends in the same country.[22] According to the text of Article V:1 GATT, what matters is that the passage across the territory of the transit state is only a portion of the complete journey. Hence, Article V does not require that more than two WTO Members are involved. For trade in electric power, this means that the 'freedom of transit' in the GATT covers both the situation of transit flows as well as loop flows.[23] Furthermore, nothing in the text of Article V:1 GATT suggests that all states involved in the journey must be WTO Members. Read together with paragraph 2 of Article V it suffices that the transit state and either the state of departure or the final destination of the traffic in transit are Contracting Parties.[24]

More difficult to answer is whether because of their involuntary or 'accidental' character, unscheduled loop and transit flows should escape the scope of 'traffic in transit'. If this were not the case, measures to curtail such unscheduled flows could

---

[20] As *Ehring and Selivanova* note, there are instances where the whole purpose of the transit exercise is precisely to carry out one of the above, for example warehousing frozen fish before trans-shipment to other vessels. Ehring and Selivanova (2011), p. 57, citing WTO, *Chile – Measures affecting the Transit and Importing of Swordfish*, Request for Consultations submitted by the European Communities (19 April 2000), WT/DS193 (withdrawn on 28 May 2010).

[21] Cf. Ehring and Selivanova (2011), p. 57.

[22] This issue was (first) discussed at the Havana Conference at which GATT Members negotiated the creation of an International Trade Organization (ITO), which never came into existence. The Parties at the Conference agreed that a movement between two points in the same country had to be regarded as "in transit". Havana Reports, U.N. Doc. ICITO/1/8, p.71, para.10. See also Huarte Melgar (2015), p. 120.

[23] On this distinction see above in Sect. 12.1, p. 199.

[24] While the relevant formulation in Article V:1 GATT is 'across the territory of a contracting party', paragraphs 2 to 5 speak of traffic to *or* from the territory of other contracting parties. See also Ehring and Selivanova (2011), p. 56; Energy Charter Secretariat (2001) [91]; Bhala (2005), p. 472.

violate substantial obligations with respect to transit. The installation of phase shifters could then also be construed as a transit problem because these devices are installed at interconnectors with the explicit aim of curtailing loop flows. Nothing in the text of Article V:1 GATT appears to suggest that it only covers traffic in transit which is explicitly scheduled in advance for such transit. The provision requires no such thing as a pre-notification. One must acknowledge, however, that electricity is unique in this respect and unscheduled electricity flows might not have been considered when the transit provision was drafted. Despite the lack of evidence from the GATT negotiations, it can be argued that the Contracting Parties did not intend to extend the freedom of transit guarantee to involuntary or 'accidental' instances of transit as the phenomenon of loop flows was not an issue when the GATT was negotiated. Nonetheless, based on a textual interpretation of Article V:1 GATT, transit flows stemming from internal domestic electricity transactions would also be covered by the definition of 'traffic in transit' and accordingly have to be treated like any other traffic in transit. An interpretation taking into account the purpose of the provision (to ensure 'freedom of transit') also supports this finding. Loop flows are a corollary of transport between two points of a domestic network (a situation covered by Article V GATT) and the curtailment of loop flows will reduce the capacities for trade within one country.

Turning now to the substantive obligations imposed by Article V GATT, two main principles can be inferred from paragraphs 2 to 6 of the Article. The first is a broad obligation not to hinder traffic in transit and the second is an MFN treatment requirement with respect to goods in transit to or from other WTO Members.[25] The respective paragraphs and the corresponding trade issues will now be discussed in more detail.

12.2.1   Article V:2: 'Freedom of Transit (. . .) Via the Routes Most Convenient'

Article V:2 GATT stipulates 'freedom of transit' for traffic in transit to or from other Contracting Parties 'via the routes most convenient' for this transit. Furthermore, the paragraph contains an MFN-style obligation that encompasses the flag of vessels, place of origin, departure, entry, exit or destination, or 'any circumstances relating to the ownership of goods, of vessels or of other means of transport.' The term 'freedom' was defined by the Panel in *Colombia – Ports of Entry* to mean 'the unrestricted use of something'.[26] The Panel thereby adopted, as a basis, a broad interpretation of what the 'freedom' of transit entails.

---

[25] Neufeld (2002), p. 3.

[26] WTO, *Colombia – Ports of Entry*, Report of the Panel, citing the New Oxford Dictionary of English (Clarendon Press, 2nd Ed. 2001), p. 730.

This rather broad reading of the basic principle is somewhat tempered by the additional terms in Article V:2 GATT, first and foremost by the term 'route most convenient'. The obligation to guarantee transit on the most convenient route establishes neither an unconditional nor an absolute guarantee of transit. As the Panel in *Colombia-Ports of Entry* argued, a Member is not required to guarantee transport on necessarily any or all routes in its territory, but only the ones 'most convenient' for transport through its territory.[27] The added significance of the formulation 'via the routes most convenient' in Article V:2 GATT for electricity trade initially appears to be limited considering the impossibility of pre-determining a certain route for electricity flows along existing networks. However, one could question whether this formulation implies an obligation to allow the planning and construction of new infrastructure if the existing capacity is not sufficient to accommodate transit. A related question concerns a potential obligation to grant third party access on national transmission lines for countries that have not yet established such a system. Both points will be discussed in turn in the following paragraphs, starting with the establishment of new capacity.

12.2.2 Capacity Establishment

Opinions diverge on this point, but most commentators deny an unconditional obligation on the side of the transit state to allow capacity establishment in its territory.[28] The point was also discussed among the WTO Members during the Doha Round negotiations on trade facilitation. Some Members apparently wished to explicitly exclude capacity establishment and third-party access for energy transit but they were not successful in their endeavour.[29]

The term 'routes most convenient' in the first sentence of Article V:2 must not be understood to include only existing routes. The term 'route' is broad enough to encompass yet-to-be-established transport infrastructure and it would have been an easy task for the drafters of the provision to textually clarify a desired limitation in

---

[27] Ibid [7.401]. See also Neufeld (2002), who considers the formulation 'via the routes most convenient' to be an important limitation of the freedom of transit. G/C/W/408, 4.

[28] Cf Azaria (2009), p. 571; Cossy (2012), pp. 298 et seq; Rakhmanin (2010), p. 124. None of these commentators, however, writes with specific reference to electricity and most with respect to pipeline capacity. A slightly more affirmative view is presented by Roggenkamp (1994), pp. 72 et seq who ponders the idea that 'route most convenient' in Article V GATT can include the establishment of additional pipeline capacity.

[29] In the draft consolidated negotiating text of the WTO Negotiating Group on Trade Facilitation of October 2011 it is clearly stated that Article V GATT should neither be construed to require a Member to 'build infrastructure of any kind in its territory, or to permit the building of infrastructure by others, in order to facilitate the transit of goods' nor to 'provide access to any infrastructure for transit unless such infrastructure is open to general use by third parties'. WTO Secretariat, 'Negotiating Group on Trade Facilitation – Draft consolidated negotiating text' (7 October 2011) TN/TF/W/165/Rev.11, comments on Article 11, p. 22.

this respect.[30] At the same time, reading an unconditional capacity establishment obligation into the 'freedom of transit. . . .via the routes most convenient' wording would be going a step too far. It would therefore be wrong to assume a positive obligation on the transit state to construct transmission networks. This does not mean, however, that the transit state is at liberty to frustrate the construction of power lines necessary for realizing transit. On a more concrete level, the transit state would violate its obligation arising from Article V:2 by discouraging investments in transmission projects or by applying national planning and permitting regulations in an obstructive manner to new transmission projects. On the overall scale of things, a certain amount of cooperation by the transit state in the development of new infrastructure is necessary.[31]

Another problematic issue that presents itself based on the text of Article V:2 is who should bear the responsibility for determining what the 'most convenient' route is. This cannot be left to the discretion of the transit state alone, as that would seriously reduce the effectiveness of the 'freedom of transit' obligation.[32] On the other hand, delegating this responsibility in its entirety to the party relying on the transit would unduly restrict the sovereignty of the transit state, e.g. with respect to national environmental, planning and permitting laws.[33] Rather, the 'convenience' should be determined holistically, balancing the interest in a swift and economic transit with the legitimate claim to safeguard the domestic interests of the transit state.[34] In most jurisdictions, system operators determine the course of an electricity transmission line and the exact siting of poles, transformers, and other infrastructure components in accordance with applicable regulations and taking into account public consultations and results of impact assessments. The role of public authorities in applying spatial planning to new transmission infrastructure for transit and the degree to which authorities interfere with the development of such infrastructure is crucial for determining whether 'freedom of transit' is granted 'via the routes most convenient'.

---

[30] This is argued by Martha Roggenkamp with reference to the differing text of the 1921 Barcelona Transit Convention which referred to routes 'in use'. Roggenkamp (1995); Selivanova disagrees by stating that only 'routes' that already exist can be 'convenient', and only one of several existing routes can be the 'most convenient' She later admits, however, that 'one may argue that "freedom of transit" should imply the possibility to create new infrastructure'. Selivanova (2014), p. 217.

[31] In this respect, Pogoretskyy has argued with respect to gas transport infrastructure that Article V GATT should be interpreted having recourse to general principles of international law, specifically the principles of effective right and economic cooperation. Pogoretskyy (2013), p. 349.

[32] Ehring and Selivanova (2011), p. 71; Pogoretskyy (2013), p. 322.

[33] Ehring and Selivanova (2011), p. 71.

[34] Pogoretskyy (2013), p. 340 finds 'broad discretion' on the side of the transit state with respect to the operationalization of expansion of infrastructure (the 'who will build, own and operate the pipeline'). He concludes that 'in the end, what appears to be of key importance for the effective implementation of the principle of freedom of transit is that gas transit *is* established on reasonable terms as opposed to *how* exactly this should be done (emphasis in the original).

12.2.3   Network Access

A related question with respect to the formulations in Article V:2 GATT concerns the access to existing electricity networks in the transit state. It is quite obvious, based on the text of Article V:2 GATT, that access needs to be granted to an existing line if this is the only possible transit 'route' for electricity. As discussed, transmission lines are capacity limited and the question thus becomes how to cope with parallel requests when there is congestion.[35] An obligation to grant mandatory third party access is denied by most commentators.[36] *Selivanova* rightly opines that the transit state must 'allocate scarce transport capacities in such a way that transit is possible.'[37] However, this finding does not help much when electricity in transit competes with domestically produced electricity for the limited capacity available. The question remains whether access must *always* be granted, which would imply precedence for electricity in transit over electricity pertaining to domestic transactions. The Panel in *Colombia – Ports of Entry* opined that the second sentence of Article V:2 ('no distinction. . .based on the flag of vessels. . .') implied that 'goods from all Members must be ensured an *identical level of access* and equal conditions when proceeding in international transit'.[38] Applied to electricity, this would mean that electricity in transit may not be accorded an inferior level of access to the grid than domestic electricity.[39]

To operationalise the standard of an identical level of access to the transmission network of the host state, domestic market rules, including capacity allocation and congestion management methods, must be applied in the same way to volumes of electric power that are in transit. Thus, to make 'freedom of transit' effective on the route most convenient, the transit state must be obliged to implement non-discriminatory procedures for the allocation of capacity and congestion management allowing electricity in transit to compete for capacity on equal terms with domestically produced electricity or electricity intended for import or export.[40] If capacity is allocated via auctions, as is the case in international electricity markets at rather advanced stages of integration, these auctions must be executed in a transparent and comprehensible manner, not putting electricity competing for transit capacity at a disadvantage. Clearly, a transit country would not be at liberty to stop electricity

---

[35] On congestion management see above in Sect. 11.2, p. 176.

[36] Azaria (2009), p. 572; Pogoretskyy (2013), p. 342; Wälde and Gunst (2004), p. 209.

[37] Selivanova (2014); see also Ehring and Selivanova (2011), pp. 70 et seq.

[38] WTO, *Colombia – Ports of Entry*, Report of the Panel [7.402] (emphasis added).

[39] Azaria opines that the 'identical level of access' standard cannot be reasonably applied to energy transit via fixed infrastructures as this would necessarily entail establishing a mandatory TPA regime, a requirement which, according to Azaria, cannot be inferred from Article V GATT. Azaria (2009), p. 572.

[40] Cf Azaria (2009), p. 572 ('The only way to apply the Panel's finding to carriage via fixed infrastructure is to interpret "identical level of access" as requiring the transit state to establish a procedure to allow the owners of goods identical possibilities to access the infrastructure.')

from being transmitted into its territory for transit purposes at the border unless it could evoke serious threats to the security of its domestic system.

12.2.4   The Second Sentence of Article V:2: 'No Distinction…'

With respect to the second sentence of Article V:2 GATT, the application to electricity transit is less controversial than the question of access to electricity networks. Distinctions based on the flag of vessels, place of origin, departure, entry, exit or destination are just as illegal as distinctions 'made on any circumstances relating to the ownership of goods, of vessels or of other means of transport.' The non-discrimination obligation expressed here entails an MFN treatment requirement, although the language differs from other MFN provisions in the WTO Agreements.[41] No distinctions are allowed among electricity in transit. Concerning the MFN obligation, the relationship with Article V:5 is quite interesting and there appears to be some overlap between these provisions.[42]

One could ask, based on the text of Article V:2, whether it also lays down a general national treatment obligation prohibiting less favourable treatment of transit as compared to domestic transport or imports and exports. The text of Article V:2, second sentence, itself is inconclusive in this respect, but the 'no distinction' formulation seems to suggest that *any* distinctions based on the character of the transport process are prohibited. Reading the second sentence in conjunction with the preceding words of Article V:2, however, would suggest that it is only concerned with different kinds of traffic in transit and not the relationship between transit and purely domestic transactions or traffic meant for import or export.[43] This contextual reading of the 'no distinction' standard is indeed more tenable than interpreting the formulation as establishing a national treatment requirement.

It should be noted that while WTO Members cannot apply less favourable treatment based on the ownership of products or vessels, they remain free in principle to favour one means of transportation over another.[44] At least on the surface, this problem seems to be of minor significance for the electricity sector as there is no alternative to electricity transmission lines. A difference in treatment could however be established between overhead and underground cables or with regard to the transmission technology (AC vs DC). Whether or not the choice for a certain means of transport to the exclusion of others could amount to de facto

---

[41] MFN treatment in the WTO Agreements is usually indicated by the words 'shall be accorded immediately and unconditionally (…).' Cf. Article I GATT, Article II GATS and Article 4 of the TRIPS Agreement.

[42] See below in Sect. 12.2.6, pp. 210 et seq.

[43] Ehring and Selivanova (2011), p. 65.

[44] Ibid.

discrimination would have to be assessed on a case-by-case basis taking into account the specific circumstances of a transit operation.

12.2.5   Article V:3 and V:4 GATT

Paragraphs 3 and 4 of Article V GATT contain special disciplines that go beyond the 'no distinction' requirement in the second sentence of paragraph 2. According to Article V:3 GATT, traffic in transit may not be exposed to unnecessary delays or restrictions in the transit state. The same paragraph also provides for a general prohibition on customs duties concerning goods entering the territory of a WTO Member for transit purposes. Finally, for the traffic in transit, no charges shall be applicable 'except charges for transportation or those commensurate with administrative expenses entailed by transit or with the cost of services rendered.' Article V:4 adds to this that all charges and regulations imposed on traffic in transit 'shall be reasonable, having regard to the conditions of the traffic.'

The two paragraphs under discussion thus make provision for both financial ('duties', 'charges') and non-pecuniary regulations (namely those which cause 'delays or restrictions'). As *Ehring* and *Selivanova* point out, the outright prohibition on customs duties for transit deviates from the general GATT approach to favour negotiation of tariff bindings for each WTO Member instead of outlawing customs tariffs altogether.[45]

More interesting for electricity transit are the rules on financial charges that may be applied to transit. The only charges that may be applied based on the text of Article V:3 are those '*for transportation*' or those '*commensurate with administrative expenses entailed by transit or the cost of services rendered.*' The first requirement is that these charges be 'commensurate with the cost of services rendered'. The additional requirement resulting from Article V:4 GATT is that these charges must be reasonable, 'having regard to the conditions of the traffic'. The exact boundaries of the formulations used in Article V:3 and V:4 have not yet been explored in dispute settlement. The WTO Secretariat, in a note on Article V, points out that as a general principle 'transit traffic shall not be a source of fiscal revenue.'[46]

For electricity transit, the relevant question is whether a network operator may apply generally applicable transmission fees (which at least with respect to private TSOs amount to fiscal revenue as they are profit-seeking enterprises) to traffic in transit or whether Article V GATT would require an exemption for electricity in transit. The latter cannot be inferred from Article V:3 or V:4 GATT and would imply an undue financial burden on domestic users. Rather, transmission fees must be

---

[45] Ibid, at 74. Of course, this is only sensible as the goods in transit are not destined for consumption in the transit country.

[46] Neufeld (2002), p. 8.

qualified as 'charges for transportation' compatible with paragraphs 3 and 4 as long as they are reasonable (which does not rule out a reasonable profit).

The relevant costs with respect to electricity transit do not differ from those for domestic transmission or imports and exports unless new infrastructure is built to host the transit. The costs a system operator incurs are mainly costs resulting from the depreciation of investments in the infrastructure; maintenance of the infrastructure; and operational management of the grid. All of these costs together contribute to the calculation of transmission tariffs which can also reflect a reasonable margin of profit.

However, in electricity transit, the costs for making infrastructure available are not the only issue. Possibly as important as these costs are the losses incurred as a result of hosting transit flows. On the transmission network of the host state, any amount of electricity 'in transit' claims a part of the limited available capacity which would otherwise be used for domestic trade flows and/or imports or exports. It is uncertain whether 'the costs of services rendered' could also include 'opportunity costs', i.e. financial losses incurred because of hosting transit flows. One might reason, a maiore ad minus, that this should be the case.

The legislator in the European Union has responded to some of these challenges by imposing an inter-TSO compensation scheme. Thus, in the EU the transit flows are calculated and compensated on the level of TSOs and not involving individual market participants. This reflects the principle that TSOs are responsible for optimizing the networks in their respective control areas according to the expected electricity flows based on supply and demand. The better the domestic network is optimized, the less compensation a TSO will be obliged to pay another TSO for hosting physical flows not corresponding to trade volumes.

Besides these provisions relating to financial charges, 'unnecessary delays or restrictions' are prohibited by Article V:3. Delays, which could occur for, e.g., purposes of inspections at the border, are hardly conceivable for electricity transit and can therefore be disregarded. Restrictions, on the other hand, could be implemented at various levels in connection with electricity transit. An example would be the reduction of transmission capacity on an interconnector used exclusively for electricity transit due to health or safety concerns in the host state. In line with GATT jurisprudence on the definition of the term 'necessary', which has mainly revolved around the occurrence of this formulation in Article XX GATT, restrictions must be regarded as 'unnecessary' if a less restrictive alternative measure is reasonably available that attains the legitimate objective in question.[47]

---

[47] With reference to the principle of effective treaty interpretation see Ehring and Selivanova (2011), pp. 76 et seq., citing WTO, *Korea – Measures Affecting Imports of Fresh, Chilled and Frozen Beef*, Reports of the Appellate Body (11 December 2000) WT/DS161/AB/R; WT/DS169/AB/R [165]; WTO, *European Communities – Measures Affecting Asbestos and Products Containing Asbestos* (12 March 2001) WT/DS135/AB/R; [170-171]; WTO, *Thailand – Customs and Fiscal Measures on Cigarettes from the Philippines*, Report of the Panel (15 November 2010) WT/DS371/R [75].

12.2.6   Article V:5 and V:6 GATT: The Transit MFN
Principles

Paragraphs 5 and 6 of Article V establish two distinct MFN treatment obligations for transit. Article V:5 requires MFN treatment with respect to charges, regulations, and formalities of all traffic in transit. Accordingly, treatment of transit originating in or destined for the territory of another Contracting Party may not be accorded treatment less favourable than the treatment accorded to traffic to or from any third country. An ad note to this provision specifies that with respect to transportation charges, the MFN principle refers to like products being transported on the same route under like conditions.[48] For electricity in transit, this means that the host state has to apply its regulations and formalities as well as charges in accordance with the MFN principle. With regard to the specific subset of MFN treatment for *transportation charges*, much seems to depend on how one interprets the three 'likeness' criteria mentioned in the ad note, namely 'like products', 'same route' and 'under like conditions'.[49] Electricity is a very homogenous good and electricity from different generation sources and countries of origin must therefore be regarded as like. With regard to the 'same route' criterion, however, things are less clear. Interpreting this criterion strictly would lead to the finding that electricity being transmitted via a long-distance 'point-to-point' line erected solely for this purpose could be made subject to different and possibly higher transportation charges because it does not take the same route as electricity from other countries. Hence, the host state of the transit part of a transmission line could establish an individual tariff regime for that transit line without being in violation of Article V:5 GATT.

Paragraph 6 calls for MFN treatment with respect to prior transit. Traffic in transit which has previously been in transit through the territory of another WTO Member has to be treated in accordance with the MFN principle. This also applies to the country of final destination of the transit journey, as the Panel has expressly confirmed in *Colombia-Ports of Entry*.[50] Furthermore, no distinction may be made between products which were in transit through the territory of a WTO Member prior to entering the host state and those products which were not in transit, i.e. which directly entered the host state from the exporting country.[51] This obligation can also be held against the state of final importation, not just against the transit state.[52] It is also worth mentioning that the MFN obligation in Article 6 does not require a likeness test for the goods in transit, which is rather unusual.[53]

---

[48] Note ad Article V GATT (1 January 1948) 55 UNTS 296.

[49] On these conditions see Bhala (2005), p. 473.

[50] Ehring and Selivanova (2011), p. 78.

[51] Cf Ibid, at 62; Bhala (2005), p. 474.

[52] Ehring and Selivanova (2011), p. 63; for a different view see Bhala (2005), p. 474.

[53] Bhala (2005), p. 474.

12.3 Transit Through Privately-Owned Electricity Infrastructure

The freedom of transit provision is only binding on WTO Members and does not create direct obligations for private actors. This poses a challenge, as transit can be obstructed through the conduct of private system operators, which often own the infrastructure and enjoy some discretion as to the conditions for transmission. Some authors characterize the principle to allow 'freedom of transit' as an obligation of result.[54] This would imply that a government is required to take appropriate measures against a system operator violating one of the concrete principles laid down in Article V GATT.

Holding governments accountable for not curtailing the conduct of private system operators would be going beyond principles of attribution in general international law and the current state of evolution of adjudication by WTO dispute settlement bodies.[55] Denying such an obligation, however, would render Article V GATT ineffective with respect to large parts of the electricity sector. This is indeed a strong argument, especially considering the rather unique wording 'there shall be freedom of transit' which differs markedly from other GATT provisions in its clear objective and mandate. It is therefore submitted that governments are obliged to work towards ensuring free transit over privately-owned transmission networks by setting the appropriate regulatory framework and taking measures against system operators restricting electricity transit.

12.4 Transit Disciplines in the ECT and PTAs

Considering the territorial scope of the ECT and the original purpose of the Energy Charter framework to build a Eurasian energy bridge, it is not surprising that transit is an important discipline in the Treaty. Transit has also been among the most contentious subjects and has led to several disputes since the ECT's inception. The ECT incorporates Article V GATT as one of the applicable GATT provisions by reference. The negotiation of the ECT, however, also presented an opportunity to redefine certain concepts of the GATT transit provision to adapt the 'freedom of transit' to the transit of energy products. The result, now codified in Article 7 ECT, has been qualified as 'one of the most innovative elements of the Treaty.'[56] Considering the challenges surrounding the application of some of the elements of Article V GATT to electricity transit, it is a worthwhile exercise to explore the substance and additional value of the 'younger sister' of Article V GATT.

---

[54] Azaria (2009), p. 67.

[55] See above in Sect. 10.3, pp. 163 et seq.

[56] Wälde and Gunst (2006), p. 216.

With regard to the material scope of the provision, Article 7 (5) ECT refers to 'Energy Transport Facilities', which are defined as including, among others, 'high-voltage electricity transmission grids and lines.'[57] Considering the uncertainty that the text of Article V GATT has brought about, this must be regarded as a major improvement. Whether transit for the purposes of Article 7 ECT includes both transit via isolated long-distance lines having their origin and destination outside the transit country *and* the transmission of transit electricity through the local network is not specifically addressed. Just like in the GATT context, this must be assumed to be the case.[58] Of added value when compared with Article V GATT is that transit originating in and ending in one and the same country is explicitly mentioned as one of the covered modes of transit.[59]

In the same way that Article V GATT applies to transit between WTO Members, the ECT transit provision will apply if the transit country and either the country of origin or destination of the electricity are ECT Contracting Parties.[60]

Insofar as concerns the substantive transit obligations, Paragraph 1 of Article 7 reads as follows:

> Each Contracting Party shall take the necessary measures to facilitate the transit of Energy Materials and Products consistent with the principle of freedom of transit and without distinction as to the origin, destination or ownership of such Energy Materials and Products or discrimination as to pricing on the basis of such distinctions, and without imposing any unreasonable delays, restrictions or charges.

The prohibition against imposing any distinctions as to origin, destination or ownership of energy, discriminating with regard to pricing and imposing any unreasonable delays, restrictions or charges bears a close resemblance to the GATT standard of transit. These similarities aside, the difference in wording is also immediately apparent: The GATT stipulation of 'freedom of transit' is only referenced in passing, while it is supplemented in the ECT by a more concrete call on Contracting Parties to take those measures which are necessary to facilitate energy transit. Opinions diverge on whether this constitutes an improvement[61] or a deterioration[62] with

---

[57] The definition of the term 'Energy Transport Facilities' can be found in Article 7 (10) (b) and reads in full: 'Energy Transport Facilities' consist of high-pressure gas transmission pipelines, *high-voltage electricity transmission grids and lines*, crude oil transmission pipelines, coal slurry pipelines, oil product pipelines, and other fixed facilities specifically for handling Energy Materials and Products (emphasis added).

[58] For the GATT, this finding was reached above in Sect. 11.2, pp. 201 et seq.

[59] See Article 7 (10) (a) (ii) ECT: 'Transit means (. . .) the carriage through the Area of a Contracting Party of Energy Materials and Products originating in the Area of another Contracting Party and destined for the Area of that other Contracting Party (. . .)'. However, ECT contracting parties are free to mutually exclude this from the operative definition of transit in the Treaty by recording this decision in a joint entry in an Annex. See Article 7 (10) (a) (ii) ECT. See also Fatouros (2008), p. 431.

[60] Ehring and Selivanova (2011), p. 83.

[61] Fatouros (2008), pp. 433 et seq; Wälde and Gunst (2006), p. 213.

[62] Roggenkamp (1995), p. 143 (pointing to the 'rather vague' formulation in the ECT provision).

respect to facilitating transit. It is submitted that irrespective of the omission of explicit wording, the principle of freedom of transit is incorporated in Article 7 ECT.[63] Furthermore, in contrast to Article V GATT, Article 7 ECT does not explicitly require transit to be granted on 'routes most convenient'. The drafters instead opted for enumerating more concretely obligations to grant the use of existing and, notably, the construction of new transport facilities.[64]

The measures necessary to facilitate transit are not exhaustively defined but are given some substance by paragraphs 2 to 4 of Article 7.[65] Article 7 (2) calls on Contracting Parties to '*encourage* relevant entities to cooperate' in a number of ways conducive to transit (emphasis added).[66] As this wording makes clear, however, these are 'soft' commitments and thus of little added value.

Article 7 (3) ECT provides for a national treatment style obligation. It is sensible to reproduce the paragraph in its entirety as it has aroused much controversy:

> Each Contracting Party undertakes that its provisions relating to transport of Energy Materials and Products and the use of Energy Transport Facilities shall treat Energy Materials and Products in Transit in no less favourable a manner than its provisions treat such materials and products originating in or destined for its own Area, unless an existing international agreement provides otherwise.

The requirement to treat transit no worse than other transportation extends to access to networks, allocation of capacity, and congestion management.[67] Disagreement among ECT Contracting Parties has revolved mainly around the words 'originating in or destined for its own Area.'[68] It is quite evident that this wording establishes a prohibition against treating transit less favourable than *imports into or exports from* the transit country. In this respect, the national treatment standard in the ECT is more clearly carved out than in Article V GATT. What is contested, however, is whether this also applies to the conditions of *domestic transportation* vis-à-vis those of transit. In the absence of jurisprudential guidance on this point, commentators have engaged in a textual and contextual analysis of the relevant wording, with the majority concluding that it indeed establishes a prohibition against treating transit

---

[63] Cf Wälde and Gunst (2006), p. 213; Azaria (2009), p. 581.

[64] Azaria (2009), p. 580.

[65] See also Ehring and Selivanova (2011), p. 85.

[66] The areas of cooperation mentioned are

(a) modernising Energy Transport Facilities necessary to the Transit of Energy Materials and Products;
(b) the development and operation of Energy Transport Facilities serving the Areas of more than one Contracting Party;
(c) measures to mitigate the effects of interruptions in the supply of Energy Materials and Products;
(d) facilitating the interconnection of Energy Transport Facilities.

[67] Azaria (2009), p. 581.

[68] Reportedly, this was one of the most contentious issues in the accession process of Russia.

traffic worse than domestic transportation.[69] The formulation 'originating in' is of such a broad scope that this seems to be the adequate interpretation.

Another important point of improvement is Article 7 (4) ECT, which provides that

> In the event that Transit of Energy Materials and Products cannot be achieved on commercial terms by means of Energy Transport Facilities the Contracting Parties shall not place obstacles in the way of new capacity being established, except as may be otherwise provided in applicable legislation which is consistent with paragraph (1).

This wording makes it clear that ECT Contracting Parties have to allow the establishment of additional capacity for the purpose of transit as long as developers comply with the applicable domestic laws and regulations.[70] Certainly, in light of Article 7 (1) applications for new transmission lines could not be refused based on the origin, destination, or ownership of energy.[71] Several limitations apply in addition to the reservation for domestic legislation consistent with the first paragraph, however. The limitation 'in the event that Transit (. . .) cannot be achieved on commercial terms' is important but often overlooked. This means that the transit state is under no obligation to allow the construction of new lines if the use of existing capacity is possible and the conditions of its use are reasonable in economic terms. The second limitation derives from paragraph 5 (b) of Article 7, according to which the obligation to allow new capacity to be built is not applicable when the transit state can demonstrate that such infrastructure 'would endanger the security or efficiency of its energy systems, including the security of supply.' It has been pointed out by commentators that there is uncertainty about the degree of discretion on the side of the transit state in making determinations about threats to the security or to the efficiency of its energy systems.[72] A fourth limitation is constituted by paragraph 9 of Article 7, which reads:

> This Article shall not be so interpreted as to oblige any Contracting Party which does not have a certain type of Energy Transport Facilities used for Transit to take any measure under this Article with respect to that type of Energy Transport Facilities. Such a Contracting Party is, however, obliged to comply with paragraph (4).

It is unclear exactly what the relationship between the two paragraphs is, especially in light of the 'back reference' to paragraph 4. The critical words seem to be 'which does not have a certain type of Energy Transport Facilities.' The provision thus seems to be safeguarding the sovereign right of the transit state to make a general decision about the *type* of infrastructure it wants to admit on its territory.[73] When

---

[69] See. e.g., Ehring and Selivanova (2011), p. 91.

[70] The understanding to Art. 7 (4) ECT specifies this as including provisions on environmental protection, land use, safety and technical standards. When developers comply with such regulations, it would seem that little scope remains for governments to refuse authorization or obstruct permitting for new network capacity. See Wälde and Gunst (2006), p. 213.

[71] Ehring and Selivanova (2011), p. 85.

[72] Ehring and Selivanova (2011), p. 84.

[73] Cf Fatouros (2008), pp. 435 et seq.

applied to electricity transit, a narrow interpretation could focus on the type of technology (e.g. AC vs HVDC) or the material infrastructure (underground cables as opposed to lines above ground).

Finally, a few words on the dispute settlement process concerning Article 7 ECT are warranted. The ECT, in Article 7 (7), foresees a special 'conciliation' procedure for disputes concerning transit. According to that provision, a Contracting Party can start the procedure by referring a dispute to the Secretary General who will then notify all Contracting Parties. The Secretary General will appoint a conciliator who shall seek agreement amongst the parties to the dispute. If this conciliation effort is not successful within the course of 90 days, the conciliator shall recommend a solution or a procedure to achieve a resolution and shall 'decide the interim tariffs and other terms and conditions to be observed for Transit from a date which he shall specify until the dispute is resolved.'[74] The appeal of the Article 7 (7) conciliation procedure is grounded in the requirement that, in the event of a dispute over 'any matter' arising from transit over the territory of a Contracting Party, existing transit flows shall not be interrupted or reduced.[75] While the scope is very broad ('any matter arising from transit'), in practice most disagreements arise concerning transit tariffs. The transit conciliation procedure was hailed as a noteworthy achievement[76] because of its pioneering character, but it has never been put to practical test by the ECT Contracting Parties. One caveat is that the procedure can only start after Contracting Parties have exhausted 'all relevant contractual or other dispute resolution remedies previously agreed' between themselves.[77] This requirement has mostly been read narrowly in the sense that it neither stipulates the exhaustion of domestic remedies nor requires previous recourse to the ECT's general dispute resolution provisions of Articles 26 (investor-state) and 27 (state-state).[78] The latter would appear to be applicable in parallel to Article 7 (7) however, and the three procedures do in fact complement each other. As Article 7 (7) only applies to disagreements over existing transit, Article 27[79] could be invoked, for example, in a dispute concerning the refusal of a transit request.[80] Similarly, an investor could invoke Article 26 if the transit state were in breach of an obligation under the investment part of the ECT. This could be the case if, for example, a merchant

---

[74] Article 7 (7) (c) ECT.

[75] This is codified in Article 7 (6) ECT, which reads: 'A Contracting Party through whose Area Energy Materials and Products transit shall not, in the event of a dispute over any matter arising from that Transit, interrupt or reduce, permit any entity subject to its control to interrupt or reduce, or require any entity subject to its jurisdiction to interrupt or reduce the existing flow of Energy Materials and Products prior to the conclusion of the dispute resolution procedures set out in paragraph (7), except where this is specifically provided for in a contract or other agreement governing such Transit or permitted in accordance with the conciliator's decision.'

[76] See, e.g. Fatouros (2008), p. 439.

[77] Cf the Understanding with respect to Article 7 (7) ECT.

[78] Ehring and Selivanova (2011), p. 93; Fatouros (2008), p. 437.

[79] Which applies to all disputes concerning the application or interpretation of the ECT.

[80] Ehring and Selivanova (2011), p. 92.

investor in an electricity transmission line were to be exposed to discriminatory treatment or expropriation.[81]

Apart from the ECT, many PTAs provide for general rules on transit, often echoing the GATT level of protection of transit. One exception which goes beyond the GATT level and provides for energy-specific transit provisions is the EU-Georgia Association Agreement. In Article 67 on applicable legislation and procedures, it is stipulated with regard to transit that

> [F]or the purposes of this Agreement, the transit rules and definitions set out in the WTO provisions, in particular Article V of GATT 1994, and related provisions, including any clarifications and amendments resulting from the Doha Round negotiations on trade facilitation shall apply. Those provisions also apply when the transit of goods begins or ends in the territory of a Party.[82]

Article 211 of the Agreement reads: 'The Parties shall ensure transit, consistent with their international commitments in accordance with the provisions of GATT 1994 and the Energy Charter Treaty.' Rather than merely referencing these two legal instruments, the EU and Georgia included a few additional transit-specific provisions. They start with the following definition:

> Transit means the passage of *energy* goods across the territory of a Party, with or without trans-shipment, warehousing, breaking bulk, or change in the mode of transport, where such passage is only a portion of a complete journey beginning and terminating beyond the frontier of the Party across whose territory the traffic passes."[83]

Interestingly, the EU and Georgia opted for slightly modifying the GATT wording instead of using the more energy-specific text of Article 7 ECT, although both the EU and Georgia are ECT Contracting Parties. Through Article 212 of the Association Agreement, the Parties commit themselves to 'take all necessary measures to prohibit and address any unauthorised taking of energy goods in transit through its territory by any entity subject to that Party's control or jurisdiction.' Article 213 defines more concrete conduct that Parties should take or refrain from in order to guarantee 'uninterrupted transit' and Article 214 requires Parties to ensure that operators of energy transport facilities in the respective Parties' territories 'minimize the risk of accidental interruption' and 'expeditiously restore the normal operation of transit' in case an interruption does occur.

The transit regime in the EU-Georgia Association Agreement represents an interesting 'third way'; referencing both the GATT and the ECT but at the same time transcending both the multilateral as well as the ECT regimes. The main motivation for paying such considerable attention to energy transit in this specific Agreement was most likely the significance of Georgia as a transit state for natural

---

[81] Cf ibid, at 94 f.

[82] Article 67 of the Association Agreement between the European Union and the European Atomic Energy Community and their Member States, of the one part, and Georgia, of the other part (27 June 2014) OJ 2014/L 261/4, 86.

[83] Ibid, Article 211 (emphasis added).

gas reaching the EU through pipelines from the Caspian Sea.[84] Despite this thematic focus on fossil fuels, the provisions are to be welcomed from the point of view of electricity transit as well.

12.5 Conclusions on Transit

Transit of electric energy differs in several respects from the transit of most categories of goods. The grid-bound nature of electricity transmission causes specific problems and issues that have to be accounted for when interpreting and further developing transit provisions. Article V GATT provides for a multilateral codification of the principle of freedom of transit. The concepts embodied in Article V GATT are expressed in rather broad terms and as WTO Members have hardly ever invoked the provision, there is little authoritative interpretation available from WTO Panels or the Appellate Body.[85] The ECT negotiators managed to include an energy-specific transit provision into the Treaty, which provides several clarifications and adds substance to the freedom of transit principle. It does not eliminate all uncertainties surrounding the application of the right to enjoy and the obligation to grant freedom of electricity transit, respectively. This only shows how technically complex the problems related to transit of grid-bound electricity are and how carefully provisions have to be designed. Some modern PTAs, most notably the EU-Georgia Agreement, add some additional helpful elements which can be further developed.

Fixed electricity transmission infrastructure is covered by the transit disciplines in public international law. This applies to both the existing grid of the transit state as well as to single lines spanning the transit state's territory from border to border only for transit purposes. The application of the substantive transit provisions does not require three states to be involved; it suffices that the electricity is reimported into the country of origin after transiting through a neighbouring territory. The clarification to this effect in Article 7 ECT is a welcome improvement.

It is not entirely clear how far the obligation to guarantee transit extends with respect to infrastructure that is not yet in existence. It is submitted that the obligation to grant transit on 'routes most convenient' can entail routes not yet established.

---

[84] In the preamble, the Parties stress their commitment to 'enhancing the security of energy supply, including the development of the Southern Corridor by, inter alia, promoting the development of appropriate projects in Georgia facilitating the development of relevant infrastructure, including for transit through Georgia, increasing market integration and gradual regulatory approximation towards key elements of the EU acquis, and promoting energy efficiency and the use of renewable energy sources'.

[85] Cf Azaria (2009), p. 573 ('The difficulty here is that necessity and reasonableness are both open-textured standards that can only be judged on a case-by-case basis. While this allows adaptability to deal with different circumstances, it opens the door to disputes, delay and inconsistency in application as well and creates opportunities for what might be criticised as "judicial activism". WTO Panels and the Appellate Body have dealt with the principles of necessity, reasonableness and proportionality in different contexts, but not with respect to GATT Article V').

Again, the ECT represents a small step forward by laying down at least a soft obligation not to hinder the construction of new facilities.[86] National authorities will have to show a certain degree of cooperation with respect to the planning and permitting of new transmission lines for transit purposes. With respect to access to existing grids, the transit state is not required to grant mandatory third party access in all cases, but has to ensure access on equal footing with electricity produced domestically. This means that capacity allocation and congestion management need to take place on the basis of non-discriminatory, objective, and transparent terms.

In order to effectuate 'freedom of transit' in the ways just described it is inevitable to engage system operators, whether in public or private hands. In this respect, the EU-Georgia Association Agreement represents a welcome improvement as it includes a transit obligation for all operators, irrespective of their public or private nature. This could and should be further developed and extended in a future multilateral regime on electricity trade.[87]

One major issue that is peculiar to the electricity sector is the occurrence of loop flows across borders. With rising shares of renewable energy generation entering the network, loop flows will likely increase. It must be assumed that, due to the state of technological development at the time, such 'accidental' transit flows were not envisaged during the drafting of the GATT. A teleological interpretation based on making the 'freedom of transit' effective would lead to an affirmative finding regarding coverage of loop flows by Article V. The ECT transit discipline does not provide a solution or clarification to the problem either. A clarification would be welcome to the extent that curtailments of loop flows should be permitted in exceptional circumstances, i.e. when the domestic network is seriously threatened by such flows.

References

Azaria D (2009) Energy transit under the Energy Charter Treaty and the general agreement on tariffs and trade. J Energy Nat Resour Law 27:559
Azaria D (2015) Treaties on transit of energy via pipelines and countermeasures. Oxford University Press, Oxford
Bhala R (2005) Modern GATT law: a treatise on the general agreement on tariffs and trade. Sweet & Maxwell, Mytholmroyd
Cossy M (2012) Energy Trade and WTO rules: reflexions on sovereignty over natural resources, export restrictions and freedom of transit. In: Hermann C, Terhechte J (eds) European yearbook of International Economic Law. Springer, Berlin
Ehring L, Selivanova Y (2011) Energy transit. In: Regulation of energy in International Trade Law: WTO, NAFTA and Energy Charter. Kluwer Law International, Alphen aan den Rijn, p 60

---

[86] Art. 7 (4) ECT; see also Konoplyanik and Wälde (2006), p. 543.
[87] See below in Sect. 14.2.2, pp. 234 et seq.

Energy Charter Secretariat (2001) Trade in energy – WTO rules applying under the Energy Charter Treaty. ECT Secretariat

Fatouros A (2008) The Energy Charter Treaty: a possible pattern of international cooperation? In: Hague Academy of International Law (ed) Collected courses of the Hague Academy of International Law, vol 332. Brill, Leiden

Gudas K (2018) The law and policy of International Trade in Electricity. Europa Law Publishing, Waterstraat

Huarte Melgar B (2015) The transit of goods in public international law. Brill, Leiden

Konoplyanik A, Wälde T (2006) Energy Charter Treaty and its role in international energy. J Energy Nat Resour Law 24:523

Neufeld N (2002) Article V of the GATT 1994 – scope and application. Note prepared by the GATT Secretariat, 10 September 2002, G/C/W/408

Pogoretskyy V (2013) Freedom of transit and the principles of effective right and economic cooperation: can systemic interpretation of GATT Article V promote energy security and the development of an international gas market? J Int Econ Law 16:313

Rakhmanin V (2010) Transportation and transit of energy and multilateral trade rules: WTO and Energy Charter. In: Pauwelyn J (ed) Global challenges at the intersection of trade, energy and the environment. Center for Economic and Policy Research, Washington

Roggenkamp M (1994) Implications of GATT and EEC on networkbound energy trade in Europe. J Energy Nat Resour Law 12:59

Roggenkamp M (1995) Transit of networkbound energy: a new phenomenon? World Compet 19: 119

Selivanova Y (2014) The WTO agreements and energy. In: Selivanova (ed) Research handbook on International Energy Law. Edward Elgar, Cheltenham

Thema Consulting Group, 'Loop Flows – Final Advice' (Report prepared for the European Commission October 2013). available at https://ec.europa.eu/energy/sites/ener/files/docu ments/201310_loop-flows_study.pdf

Wälde T, Gunst A (2004) International Energy Trade and access to networks. In: Bielecki J, Desta MG (eds) Electricity Trade in Europe: review of the economic and regulatory challenges. Kluwer Law International, Alphen aan den Rijn

Wälde T, Gunst A (2006) International Energy Trade and access to energy networks. Oil Gas Energy Law 36(2):191–218

WTO Secretariat (2010) World Trade Report 2010. World Trade Organization, Geneva

Chapter 13
Final Conclusions to Part III

International electricity trade is subject to some familiar issues of world trade law while at the same time evoking sui generis problems that challenge the existing multilateral trade rules. Neither tariff protection of domestic production nor foreign market access for domestic utilities and independent power producers play a big role in the electricity sector. In the context of accelerating renewable energy ambition and the explicit choice of countries for or against certain types of generation, import restrictions based on environmental grounds might become more pertinent. As of today, however, export restrictions are more common in practice because of the vital importance of a secure electricity supply.

The foreclosure of many national electricity markets and different degrees of market opening around the world pose an important structural barrier to cross-border electricity trade. Without a certain degree of liberalization and especially the granting of access to national transmission grids, international electricity markets will not develop their full potential. Provisions in the WTO Agreements on STEs and monopolies could theoretically be relied on for tackling discriminatory access rules and policies on grid tariffs, but their effectiveness is seriously impaired by a narrow personal scope of application and the lack of transparency and specific services liberalization commitments of WTO Members. The disciplines of world trade law do not incentivize 'positive' regulation to abolish anti-competitive behaviour on domestic electricity markets.

Restrictions of actual trade flows on cross-border electricity interconnectors are covered by the GATT disciplines on import and export restrictions and transit. Prohibitions of electricity exports, which countries impose in times of generation shortages, are justifiable if they are imposed transitorily. Import restrictions based on CO_2 emission thresholds for power plants stand a good chance to pass the scrutiny of WTO general exceptions when they are implemented in the context of an ambitious overall decarbonization policy.

The dependence of electricity trade on capacity-constrained interconnectors and the specific flow patterns of electricity in an interconnected grid are the two most

© The Author(s), under exclusive license to Springer Nature Switzerland AG 2022   221
C. Frey, *World Trade Law and the Emergence of International Electricity Markets*,
EYIEL Monographs - Studies in European and International Economic Law 25,
https://doi.org/10.1007/978-3-031-04756-5_13

important aspects to factor in when applying world trade rules on imports, exports and transit of electricity. With respect to the former, effectively addressing import and export restrictions and ensuring uninterrupted transit will often come down to the issue of granting access to existing transmission grids. Article V GATT, while not requiring the imposition of a third-party access regime, can be interpreted to require that access for electricity in transit must be granted on an equal footing with domestic electricity which WTO Members can bring about by applying methods for capacity allocation and congestion management objectively and non-discriminatorily to electricity from generators within and outside national borders.

Delaying or completely obstructing the construction of the necessary cross-border infrastructure could in principle also amount to a violation of the relevant GATT disciplines. This is especially true with respect to planned transmission lines spanning a country for transit purposes. Challenging licensing schemes for the construction of interconnectors will be more difficult because the import and export licensing disciplines are only applicable to licensing for the product sought to be imported, not the infrastructure for transporting the product.

The second determinant of electricity-related trade issues, the occurrence of electricity flows which only indirectly represent commercial transactions, starkly reveals the lack of sector-specific world trade rules for energy. When electricity trade flows are curtailed on interconnectors at national borders, this is often done to relieve stress on domestic networks and to enable, rather than restrict, more trade between two countries. A certain deference to measures taken in the interest of safeguarding the balance and security of electricity systems and room for justification of measures taken in their pursuit is appropriate. At the same time, it needs to be ensured that the imposition of such measures does not discriminate against a certain source of electricity, that the measure is justified, and that the conditions of the curtailment of capacity are made transparent.

Taking the findings of the second and third Parts of this book together, it can be concluded that the multilateral regulatory framework is at risk of not keeping pace with the 'internationalization' of trade in electricity. On the regional and bilateral levels, some gaps were sought to be filled by trading partners through energy-specific chapters in PTAs. The most advanced rules in this respect concern access to electricity transmission networks and have been negotiated by the EU in some of its more recent trade agreements. When viewed against the background of the varying degrees of liberalization of electricity sectors around the world, a basic set of principles agreed at the multilateral level could provide the regulatory foundation for future electricity market integration in regions where this is economically and politically feasible. The contours of such an 'electricity trade agreement' will be explored in the following and final part of this book.

Part IV
Towards a Coherent Regulatory Framework for International Electricity Trade

Chapter 14
The Road Ahead for Multilateral Electricity Trade Regulation

The preceding chapters have analysed the application of the existing normative framework of world trade law to trade in electric energy. It has been shown that while the Agreements concluded under the umbrella of the WTO are applicable to electricity trade and some PTAs add single important disciplines, the current regulatory framework causes uncertainty and exhibits significant regulatory gaps. Most importantly, the cross-sectoral rules provided by the GATT and the GATS often cannot provide adequate solutions for electricity-specific trade barriers. Another issue facing a more global electricity interconnection is the fragmentation of regulatory regimes. The regional electricity markets that have emerged exhibit a wide variety of regulatory arrangements. Relevant provisions in the patchwork of PTAs add to this fragmentation. More targeted and detailed sector-specific regulation at the multilateral level would be a better foundation on which to build and extend the existing electricity trade on a global scale. Starting from the shortcomings regarding specific relevant issues as identified in the previous chapters, the final part of this study will assess possible paths ahead for the multilateral regulation of electricity trade.

At the outset, it should be stressed that many issues are better left to regulation in other fora. The precise design of an international regulatory authority for electricity trade, for example, might intuitively seem desirable to address, but would appear unrealistic to be agreed upon at the multilateral stage. Similarly, while common technical regulations like electricity grid codes are useful and are increasingly defined in regional contexts, they are not an issue for world trade regulation. Specialized organizations like the International Electrotechnical Commission (IEC) offer a more appropriate forum.[1] Provisions concerning the planning and permitting of new transmission infrastructure should also be left to national and

---

[1] The IEC is the standardization organization for the electric and electronic industries. https://www.iec.ch/index.htm.

© The Author(s), under exclusive license to Springer Nature Switzerland AG 2022
C. Frey, *World Trade Law and the Emergence of International Electricity Markets*,
EYIEL Monographs - Studies in European and International Economic Law 25,
https://doi.org/10.1007/978-3-031-04756-5_14

regional regulation and would thus fall outside the scope of a multilateral electricity trade agreement.[2]

In the WTO framework, exploratory work on a better multilateral regulation of energy trade has already taken place within the services sphere. The WTO Secretariat, at the request of a group of WTO Members, identified a number of working questions with respect to a GATS Reference Paper on Energy Services. These questions, while neither comprehensive nor electricity-specific, can offer important guidance. They are as follows:

1) Would it be desirable from a trade liberalization point of view to classify energy services as one sector, or should different parts of it be classified under relevant sectors (transport, distribution, etc.)?
2) Is the WTO separation between goods trade rules (applying to trade in energy products per se) and services trade rules (applying to trade in transportation/ transmission and distribution of energy products) desirable in the electricity and gas sectors? Would it be more efficient to apply a single coherent set of trade rules to liberalization in these sectors, considering the structure of the industry and the existing WTO rules?
3) Do regional initiatives in the energy sector (EU, ECT, ASEAN, APEC, NAFTA) provide useful models for trade liberalization and pro-competitive regulation at the multilateral level?
4) Would it be desirable in the context of a negotiation on energy services to agree on a set of regulatory principles based on the example of the Telecoms Reference Paper?[3]

As a preliminary observation, an electricity trade agreement to be drafted at the multilateral negotiating table would need to tackle disciplines on both goods *and* services. An integrated approach provides an opportunity to overcome the strict divide between rules on goods and rules on services characteristic of the current WTO architecture. A different question is whether rules should be defined for all energy carriers or whether it makes more sense to look at electricity, oil, gas, and other energy carriers as isolated regimes. This question will be dealt with in a first step. In a second step, the necessary building blocks of a regulatory framework that does justice to electricity-specific trade challenges will be identified. Based upon the results of this examination, an attempt will be made to identify the appropriate forum to host multilateral rules for electricity trade in the future.

---

[2]For the opposite view, see Gudas (2018), p. 180, who explicitly recommends to 'establish an institutional framework for the development of cross-border electricity transmission projects' and 'aim to increase the transparency at the planning and development of electricity grids stages'.

[3]WTO, Council for Trade in Services, Energy Services – Background Note by the Secretariat (09 September 1998) S/C/W/52, pp. 4 et seq.

14.1 An Integrated Approach for the Energy Sector or Electricity-Specific Rules?

When calling for sector-specific disciplines outside of, or in addition to, existing multilateral disciplines on goods and services trade, one should tread carefully. Despite recurring frictions, the GATT has stood the test for almost 75 years, and the other covered agreements for a quarter-century.[4] At the same time, the widespread adoption among WTO Members of a special regime for the telecommunications sector during the Uruguay round negotiations proves that there is a certain readiness among states to agree on more targeted rules for a specific sector if this is deemed necessary. It therefore makes sense to carefully elaborate whether it is desirable to define rules specifically for electricity, or whether an integrated approach covering several or all energy sources would be preferable. The latter would imply defining common rules at least for oil, gas and electricity. Some eminent authors have spoken out in favour of such an integrated approach.[5]

One argument in favour of a comprehensive 'energy trade agreement' is that it would avoid further fragmentation caused by identifying new sector-specific rules for just one energy carrier.[6] Indeed, many of the considerations with respect to electricity doubtlessly apply to oil and gas trade as well. Markets for fossil fuels exhibit similarities with the electricity industry and some national energy utilities have a portfolio combining both electricity generation and oil or gas extraction and trade. Furthermore, oil, gas and electricity are all traded via fixed infrastructure—pipelines and power grids. Examples from domestic jurisdictions show that a number of issues (e.g. unbundling, network operation, and incentive regulation for system operators) can be dealt with through defining common rules for the electricity and gas sectors.[7]

Another point to consider is that electricity trade will become more similar to trade in other commodities like oil and gas in the future, at least in the following important respect. Traditionally, each country has sought to satisfy its electricity demand from domestic power plants, using the technology that most suited their

---

[4]Cf Albath (2005), p. 85.

[5]Cottier et al. (2011), p. 221, speak out in favor of a comprehensive 'sectoral agreement on energy' ('Energy requires an integrated approach and does not lend itself to sectoral negotiations, depending upon different forms of energy applied to competing energy sectors (...). All (these) forms of energy should be subject to the same rules and thus conditions of competition.'). Wälde and Gunst (2004), p. 208, propose a reference paper on energy services and opine that the rules 'should cover electricity, oil and gas transit; and formulate specific access rules and procedures for interconnectors, storage and transport facilities'. See also Cossy (2012), p. 177 ('The characteristics of the energy sector would ideally call for a separate WTO Agreement specifically dedicated to *energy* trade') (emphasis added).

[6]Cottier et al. (2011), p. 221.

[7]See, for instance, the Energy Industry Act of Germany (Energiewirtschaftsgesetz) which provides common rules for the gas and electricity sectors. Energy Industry Act of Germany (Energiewirtschaftsgesetz) (1935) RGBl. I S. 1451.

respective needs. The Ricardian model of comparative advantage was and remains of very limited relevance under these circumstances.[8] This precept will likely change in a future electricity system powered entirely by renewable energy. Countries are unevenly endowed with 'renewable energy resources'—high wind speeds, intense solar radiation and hydropower potential. Similar to crude oil, which is concentrated heavily in certain regions like the Middle East, West Africa, or the North Sea, the best renewable energy resources are located in regions like the Sahara Desert, the windswept North of Russia and the Canadian Arctic. Therefore, while countries will still strive for energy autarchy, more concentrated large-scale generation and transmission over long distances seem inevitable to reach a completely decarbonized global energy system. This will amplify the difference between 'producing' and 'consuming' countries. It is thus expected that trade in the commodity electricity will become more similar to trade in other energy commodities. All of the arguments mentioned here speak in favour of providing for common rules for trade in all energy sources including electricity.

Some powerful arguments support the opposite view, however. Based on the discussions in the preceding parts, it should be clear that not all energy is alike. While sharing many features with trade in oil or gas, electric energy differs in a number of important respects from other energy sources. The classification of natural gas and oil as goods, for example, seems to be much less controversial than with respect to electric energy. Indeed, the application of GATT rules to the gas sector in the *EU—Energy Package* case was undisputed in principle among the parties.[9] Unlike both oil and gas, and indeed unlike any product traded internationally today, electricity is not a physical substance but an invisible process that requires constant surveillance and balancing.[10] In its physical characteristics, electricity resembles telecommunications more than fossil energy sources.[11] While oil and gas traders can resort to other means of transport like shipping, electricity is the only traded commodity that cannot yet reach its consumers in the absence of a fixed infrastructure.

Another aspect to consider is that due to the lack of Ricardian trade incentives with respect to electric energy, the traditional logic of trade liberalization within the

---

[8] The British economist David Ricardo first described his theory of comparative advantage in 1817 in his book 'On the Principles of Political Economy and Taxation'. Comparative advantage, to Ricardo, implied that specialization and trade between nations under normal conditions raised the income of both. One conclusion deriving from this theory is that a country would only export those goods in which it has a comparative advantage over the country with which it engages in trade (the theory originally only took into account bilateral trade between two countries). A further somewhat paradoxical result is that a country exhibiting a general productivity advantage over the other country would still benefit from trade if it specialized and imported those goods in relation to which its advantage was comparably less pronounced.

[9] WTO, *European Union and its Member States – Certain Measures Relating to the Energy Sector*, Request for Consultations by the Russian Federation (8 May 2014) WT/DS476/1. See also above in Sect. 5.1.2, pp. 90 et seq.

[10] Ferrey (2004), pp. 1863 et seq. See also above in Sect. 2.1.1, pp. 10 et seq.

[11] Ibid, at 1927.

WTO is *currently* not applicable to electricity trade.[12] This is because in the traditional world of electricity utilities, national self-sufficiency and energy autarchy were the order of the day, with large-scale power plants located close to consumption centres. The nature of electricity as described earlier generally presupposes increased levels of cooperation between trading partners. Interruptions resulting from a lack of cooperation could have severe consequences for both trading partners. Although far from impossible, this makes disputes among countries over electricity trade less likely. One should also not disregard the fact that trade in fossil fuels is often subject to (geo-) political considerations and thus bears a special strategic sensitivity. This geopolitical dimension is much less pronounced in the case of electricity. Countries might therefore be less willing to enter into multilateral commitments regarding their energy sectors based on a source-neutral approach than purely with respect to electric energy.[13] Finally, it should be noted that the policy of international oil trade is dominated by the OPEC and it is highly unlikely that OPEC Members will give in to new multilateral rules on trade in oil under the roof of the WTO. In the electricity sector, no equivalent to the OPEC has yet been established. One can therefore expect less resistance among countries with regard to negotiations on electricity trade rules under the guidance of the WTO. Weighing the arguments for and against a source-neutral and a source-specific approach, it is submitted that at least in an initial phase new rules should be defined with specific application to electricity rather than treating electricity as just one among a group of energy sources.

14.2 Building Blocks of a Multilateral Regulatory Regime for Electricity Trade

14.2.1 Classification of Goods and Services Along the Electricity Value Chain

The current framework for goods and services classification offers an inadequate basis for defining further commitments to free and open trade in electricity and for further liberalizing national foreclosed electricity markets.[14] While classification

---

[12] This logic, in a somewhat simplified version, consists in reciprocal market access concessions where one country would request access abroad for its own products and in turn offers access for products which it cannot supply at the same rate or quality. This is also reflected in an important facet of WTO dispute settlement: If a dispute settlement organ finds that commitments with respect to a certain good were violated by country A, country B can lawfully retaliate by suspending concessions with respect to a different good. Timothy Meyer calls this 'a legalized system in which states hold market access to each other's products hostage.' See Meyer (2017), p. 16.

[13] Cf Zarrilli (2004), p. 253.

[14] See above in Sect. 5.2.8, pp. 108 et seq. This was also recognized by the European Union during the GATS negotiations after 2000. In a communication to the Council for Trade in Services, the EU

systems are not legally binding on states, they help to clarify the scope of commitments that are entered into.[15] When defining new rules for international electricity trade, electricity services should be classified as one sector. This classification should clearly represent the different stages of the electricity value chain and differentiate between generation, transport (transmission and distribution) and marketing of electricity. This could be achieved through common efforts to draft a new 'classification list on electricity services', an exercise which would not be unprecedented in the WTO.[16]

When modifying the existing classification of goods and services, contracting parties must proceed carefully as they shall not fundamentally alter the balance of rights and obligations that resulted from the Uruguay Round negotiations.[17] After all, the commitments entered into by WTO Members in their respective schedules are legally binding and an integral part of the GATT and GATS. When WTO Members enter into GATS commitments based on a new classification, these cannot undermine the existing commitments unless the procedure for modification of schedules as provided for by Article XXI GATS is followed.[18] The current level of commitments in the energy sector, which is low when compared with other sectors, makes the problem of possible alteration of existing commitments less pertinent.[19]

The sustained uncertainty with respect to the applicability of *goods*-related disciplines stems mainly from the optional nature of the electricity sub-heading in the harmonized system. As the nature of electricity, and especially its physical characteristics, speak against qualification as a 'good', a clear understanding within

---

stated that 'The lack of a comprehensive approach to the classification of energy services is particularly evident now that, after some experiences of liberalisation of energy services throughout the world, the sector is becoming more dynamic and competitive. See WTO, 'Communication from The European Communities and their Member States on GATS 2000: Energy Services' (23 March 2001), EU S/CSS/W/60 [I (3)].

[15]Zhang (2015), p. 14. This point was also stressed by Japan in a communication to the Council on Trade in Services: 'The lack of transparency in energy services regulations reduces predictability for trade in the sector. In addition, a system with insufficient transparency leads to increased doubts on the part of those from the outside as to whether trade barriers do exist, thus resulting in a deterioration of market confidence in the country concerned. Accordingly, it is in the interest of all Member Countries to improve the regulatory transparency of energy services.' WTO, 'Communication from Japan to the Council on Trade in Services: Negotiating Proposal on Energy Services' (4 October 2001) S/CSS/W/42/Suppl.3 [6].

[16]Zarrilli (2004), p. 246. Alternative classification instruments were introduced also during or immediately after the Uruguay Round negotiations, among others for financial, telecommunications and transport services. See Zhang (2005), p. 7.

[17]Poretti and Rios-Herran (2006), p. 26.

[18]Article XXI:1 (a) reads: 'A Member (referred to in this Article as the "modifying Member") may modify or withdraw any commitment in its Schedule, at any time after three years have elapsed from the date on which that commitment entered into force, in accordance with the provisions of this Article.' The following paragraphs of Article XXI provide for the procedure to be followed for modification or withdrawal.

[19]Poretti and Rios-Herran (2006), p. 26.

the framework of international product classification would be particularly relevant. Thus, it would be important to provide for a clarification to the effect that the Parties to an electricity trade agreement consider electric energy to be a good to which the substantial obligations with respect to trade in goods apply.[20] Inspiration could be drawn from the ECT which clearly lists electricity as one of the energy products to which its trade rules apply.[21]

With respect to services, inconsistencies and uncertainties arise from (a) the fragmentation within the energy services classification instruments; and (b) ambiguity as to the precise scope of the classified services with relevance for the electricity sector. During the Uruguay Round, the energy sector was not treated in its own right in services negotiations. As a result, services with significance for the electricity value chain are now scattered out over the classification lists. The WTO list W/120 has not been updated since 1991 and is of a rather aggregated nature. The current version of the CPC list spells services out more clearly (and can thus be regarded as an improvement) but does not solve all the electricity-related classification issues.

Two main services categories of major significance for electricity trade in the WTO list are manufacturing services and services incidental to energy distribution. With respect to the latter, the current version of the CPC spells out the transmission of electricity and distribution of electricity as proper services. Around these main services, a number of other services entries cover further aspects of the electricity value chain. Based on the results of the analysis in Part II, it is submitted that the exercise of clearly carving out the services relevant for electricity should be limited to 'core' services with direct relevance for the electricity value chain and should not be extended to 'related' services which are relevant for a number of other sectors as well. Examples of services falling into the latter category are construction, consulting, and engineering services. Their application to the construction of electricity networks is not in doubt.

Parties to an electricity trade agreement should strive to settle two concrete issues. The first concerns the generation stage and the second the transmission stage. With respect to generation, it is crucial to draw a dividing line between the generation of electricity as a 'normal' manufacturing process outside the scope of GATS and generation as a service. As discussed earlier, 'manufacturing services' are now commonly understood as manufacturing on a fee or contract basis and not provided 'in-house'.[22]

In its most recent version, the CPC list refers to 'manufacturing services on physical inputs owned by others' and thus clarifies that this applies to outsourced

---

[20] It should again be pointed out that this is contested among academics. For the different view see Cottier et al. (2011), pp. 222-223 who argue that 'Electricity is a typical network industry, the components of which can best be dealt with following the principles of progressive liberalization and conditionality available under the GATS agreement. It is submitted that electricity should be defined as a service and should no longer be treated as a good'.

[21] See above in Sect. 5.2.5, p. 103.

[22] See above in Sect. 5.2.8.1, pp. 110 et. seq.

production processes, an interpretation which is seemingly consensual among WTO Members.[23] This state of affairs conflicts with the realities of contemporary power sectors, however, and application of the ownership criterion would lead to unreasonable results.[24] Rather than making the input—ownership over the source of generation—the decisive criterion, the focus should be on what happens to the electricity once it is generated. In other words, one should look at the relationship between the entity generating the electricity and the off-taker of the electricity to assess whether the generation process constitutes the provision of a service. Based on the current state of development of electricity sectors, three relevant scenarios can be distinguished in this respect: (a) the electricity is produced 'in-house' by a vertically integrated utility which is also responsible for transmission and distribution; (b) the electricity is generated by an independent power producer, sold on the market or via a long-term off-take agreement and entering the stream of an (independent) transmission system operator and (c) The electricity is sold and transmitted via a direct physical connection to a (usually corporate) off-taker (the 'on-site corporate PPA' model).[25] If the owner of a power plant is a vertically integrated utility with ownership over transmission and distribution networks and with or without responsibility for electricity retail, then the generation of electricity cannot qualify as a service. This finding is valid irrespective of the ownership over the inputs. The same applies with respect to an independent power producer selling its electricity on a power exchange or other marketplace to an (unbundled) utility, large industrial customer, or a specialized broker. The operator of the power plant produces electricity for sale on the market and this transaction cannot at the same time qualify as the provision of a service subject to GATS commitments. In the third model, the generation of electricity is for direct supply to an industrial consumer like a factory, mine or data centre. Large corporate electricity consumers increasingly enter into power purchase agreements directly with independent power producers.[26] This arrangement intuitively looks more like the provision of service than the generation for sale on an electricity exchange. Indeed, such direct supply for a fixed-term and a set tariff per megawatt-hour of electricity could qualify as production 'on a fee or contract basis.' If the explanatory note to the CPC is taken seriously, however, then under the current framework generation of renewable electricity under such corporate PPAs falls outside the scope of 'manufacturing services' as the ownership over the raw materials in renewable energy generation does not pertain to the generator.

As energy markets have evolved considerably over the last decades, electricity can now be sold just like any other commodity. Based on the typology of generation arrangements developed above the starting point and main principle should be that the generation of electricity—irrespective of the ownership over the resources—

---

[23] Ibid.

[24] See above in Sect. 5.2.8, p. 111.

[25] On the concept of PPAs see above in Sect. 2.2.6, pp. 35 et seq.

[26] Ibid.

qualifies as the production of a good and that services disciplines are not applica-ble.[27] To accommodate for services-like contractual arrangements such as corporate PPAs, a distinction between electricity supplied to the market 'via the public grid' and direct supply of electricity to a final consumer could be considered. This could be achieved through a formulation like 'electricity generation shall not be qualified as a (manufacturing) service unless the electricity is contracted via a power purchase agreement directly between the generator and the end-consumer and the electricity is supplied via a direct physical connection.'

With respect to the downstream transport activities along the electricity supply chain—transmission and distribution—parties to an electricity trade agreement should make clear that they qualify as services unless provided on own account. Such in-house transmission and distribution lack the fundamental character of a service as the provision of an activity between separate economic units.[28] In practice, this would mean that transmission and distribution of electricity as individual services only appear after unbundling has been carried out and an independent system operator takes care of transmission and distribution. On the other hand, if both are carried out by a vertically integrated utility, they should not qualify as a service.[29]

The main transmission-related issue that was identified as problematic with respect to the current system of classification is that under the W/120 list it is unclear whether only 'services incidental to' transmission and distribution are covered or also transmission and distribution as services per se.[30] For the sake of clarity, parties to an electricity trade agreement should agree to classify both the transmission of electricity and the distribution of electricity as services. In addition, the specific ancillary services necessary for transmission should also be clearly addressed. This concerns, *inter alia*, operational management, frequency control, the provision of reactive power and the scheduling and dispatch of generators.[31] Spelling individual services out clearly in a disaggregated fashion has the major advantage of avoiding ambiguity as to the scope of commitments and allowing more transparent and

---

[27] Of course, one should be aware of the consequence that qualification of the generation process as production of a good would effectively extricate a trillion-dollar industry from services coverage and thereby from possible liberalization under the substantive GATS rules.

[28] For a definitional approach see above in Sect. 5.2.1, pp. 94 et seq.

[29] This seems to be the logic under the current system of the GATS. As Tilman Dralle argues, 'measures affecting the transport of energy are fully covered by the applicable GATS disciplines if the transport is carried out on behalf of a third party or third parties. In contrast, the transport of energy does not qualify as a service within the meaning of the GATS if it is merely an 'in-house' activity'. According to Dralle, 'in-house' would mean transportation within 'a vertically integrated undertaking that is organized as one legal entity', but not on behalf of a separate legal entity, even if belonging to the same vertically-integrated undertaking. Dralle (2018), p. 90.

[30] See above in Sect. 5.2.8.2, pp. 111 et seq.

[31] There does not appear to be a globally accepted common definition of which services exactly the category of 'ancillary services' for electricity transmission entails. For one categorization see the overview provided by Deutsche Energie-Agentur (DENA), available at https://www.dena.de/en/topics-projects/energy-systems/electricity-grids/ancillary-services/.

precise scheduling.[32] In addition to the headings and sub-headings of the proposed services, the adoption of explanatory notes should be considered, so as to leave no doubt about the exact scope of a particular service and thus facilitate the work of trade negotiators.[33] With respect to marketing, at least the services of wholesaling of electricity and retailing of electricity should be included in the proposed electricity services classification list, for which no entry currently exists in the classification instruments. At the end-consumer stage, metering and billing of electricity are two further candidates for inclusion.

14.2.2   Principles on Electricity Transit

Transit of electricity is a technically complex matter, and it should be acknowledged that not all transit-related issues can be comprehensively addressed multilaterally. An electricity trade agreement would nonetheless offer an opportunity to refine the freedom of transit principle in order to reduce uncertainty and give contracting parties increased visibility with respect to their obligations. The existing and established multilateral codification of transit could be taken as a starting point, but some adjustments are needed to better reflect the realities of cross-border flows of electric power.

14.2.2.1   Scope of Application

The first and most important modification concerns the scope of application. While a teleological interpretation of Article V GATT supports the application of the provision to fixed infrastructure, a clarifying statement to that respect would remove doubts. It should be made clear that the transit obligations apply to the transit of electricity via existing transmission lines erected solely for the purpose of transit *as well as* to transit via existing national grids. It might be recalled that the first multilateral codification of electricity transit only covered the former alternative.[34] A departure from the traditional understanding in the 1923 Barcelona Convention is warranted as the integration of electricity markets entails the interconnection of meshed national grids. Realities have changed in almost 100 years since the principles of electricity transit were first codified. If the transit provision only extended to electricity flows over isolated long-distance lines and not the interconnected national grid, this would discriminate against a rather common form of electricity transit.

---

[32] Cf Zhang (2005), p. 6.

[33] Ibid., at p. 5.

[34] See above in Sect. 12.1, p. 199.

For definitional purposes, contracting parties to an electricity trade agreement could borrow from ENTSO-E,[35] which provides a sensible definition of transit broad enough to cover the different scenarios. It defines transit as follows: 'An energy flow that occurs in a country, which is neither the source nor the sink of the energy flow. The energy flow arrives in the grid over one border and leaves the country over one or more borders'.[36] It is submitted that this formulation provides a good starting point. In order to leave no doubts, the second sentence could be slightly adapted to the following effect: 'The electricity enters and exits the national transmission grid without being consumed in the transit country or enters and exits the territory of the transit country via a single transmission line without connection to the national grid.'

14.2.2.2 MFN Treatment

Regarding the substantive obligations which give teeth to the freedom of transit principle, the existing disciplines offer a suitable point of departure. An MFN treatment requirement with respect to all transit is the minimum that should be agreed upon. Distinctions should neither be allowed with respect to electricity in transit from different origins nor concerning transit as opposed to electricity destined for import or export. This would apply to access to the grid, technical interconnectivity, certifications and network charges.

14.2.2.3 Transmission Tariffs and Compensation for Hosting Cross-Border Flows

In an Agreement, contracting parties might also want to make provision for compensation for costs of hosting transit flows. It is not finally settled to what extent adequate compensation can be claimed on the basis of Article V GATT.[37] As will be recalled, following Article V:3, transit from WTO Contracting Parties is exempt from all transit duties and 'other charges imposed in respect of transit' except transportation fees, administrative expenses and costs of services rendered. Article V:4 adds a 'reasonableness' requirement with respect to all charges and regulations. While it is important to ensure that 'transit traffic shall not be a source of fiscal revenue',[38] it is unclear whether the currently applicable transit provisions allow for adequate compensation of domestic system operators for hosting transit flows. In the EU, relevant legislation provides that 'TSOs should be compensated for

---

[35] On ENTSO-E, see above in Sect. 3.2.1.2, p. 50.

[36] ENTSO-E, 'Statistical Yearbook 2011: Glossary of Statistical Terms', available at https:// eepublicdownloads.entsoe.eu/clean-documents/pre2015/publications/entsoe/Statistical_Yearbook/ SYB_2011/121216_SYB_2011_5_Glossary_of_statistical_terms.pdf.

[37] See above in Sect. 12.2.5, p. 209.

[38] Neufeld (2002), p. 8.

energy losses resulting from hosting cross-border flows of electricity.'[39] It makes sense to replicate this approach and include a general principle on the adequate compensation of network operators responsible for accommodating transit flows in their networks.

14.2.2.4   Network Access

Efficient electricity transit cannot be realized absent access to existing networks. Thus, one cornerstone of a meaningful electricity transit provision is access to existing infrastructure.

Access to electricity networks has different dimensions. One of those is technical interconnectivity. It is equally important, however, that the available capacity is calculated by taking into account transit flows and that it is allocated in a non-discriminatory manner. If an insufficient national grid cannot host the required transit flows and new capacity becomes necessary, then the development of this new capacity should not be obstructed or made unreasonably difficult by the transit country. Article 7 (4) ECT provides a sensible formulation to the effect that, subject to environmental, safety or technical exceptions to be defined in legislation, ECT Contracting Parties 'shall not place obstacles in the way of new capacity being established.'[40]

The crucial role of private entities in granting uninterrupted transit is a potential challenge to the enforcement of transit obligations.[41] Against this background, it would be advisable to obligate states to ensure that system operators under their jurisdictions, whether public or private, do not interrupt transit.[42]

14.2.2.5   Dealing with Loop Flows and System Security Challenges

To account for the singular characteristic of electricity spreading over a grid according to Kirchhoff's Law, it should be clarified that the transit country can take measures to curb unwanted loop flows by curtailing electricity imports as a last resort measure. In doing this, authorities and grid operators of the exporting state and the transit state should work together, and unilateral measures should be avoided as far as possible. Furthermore, as loop flows are a result of insufficient interconnector capacity, parties subscribing to new electricity trade rules should acknowledge the

---

[39] Commission Regulation (EU) 838/2010 on laying down guidelines relating to the inter-transmission system operator compensation mechanism and a common regulatory approach to transmission charging (23 September 2010) OJ 2010/L 250/5.

[40] Energy Charter Treaty (17 December 1994) 2080 U.N.T.S. 95, Article 7 (4).

[41] See above in Sect. 12.3, p. 211.

[42] Cf. Article 214 of the Association Agreement between the European Union and the European Atomic Energy Community and their Member States, of the one part, and Georgia, of the other part (27 June 2014) OJ 2014/L 261/4, 86. See also above, in Sect. 12.4, pp. 211 et seq.

necessity to expand the existing cross-border electricity infrastructure and to undertake common efforts in this respect.

At a more general level and not limited to transit, Article 14 of the new EU Electricity Market Regulation could serve as a model. According to its second paragraph:

> Transaction curtailment procedures shall only be used in emergency situations where the transmission system operator must act in an expeditious manner and redispatching or countertrading is not possible. Any such procedure shall be applied in a non-discriminatory manner. Except in cases of force majeure, market participants who have been allocated capacity shall be compensated for any curtailment.[43]

Finally, it makes sense to provide for a general clause allowing the transit country to take measures to safeguard its electricity system. The electricity network requires constant supervision and an active balancing of supply and demand. Hence, interventions by system operators might become necessary during uncommon events like extreme weather or sudden and unforeseen spikes in consumption. Such interventions should, as far as possible, be carefully coordinated with responsible entities overseeing neighbouring electricity systems. To this effect, contracting parties could borrow from the EU-Kazakhstan EPCA, which provides in Article 150 that:

> Nothing in this Chapter shall be construed as preventing the adoption or enforcement by either Party of measures necessary for the safe operation of the energy infrastructure, including energy transport and the production facilities concerned, in the interest of national security or public safety, including the prevention of and reaction to an emergency situation, subject to the requirement that such measures are not applied in a manner which would constitute a means of arbitrary or unjustifiable discrimination between the products, service suppliers or investors of the Parties where the same conditions prevail, or a disguised restriction on trade and investment between the Parties.[44]

14.2.3   Basic Principles on Good Regulatory Practice

Individual countries have come a long way in terms of liberalization and restructuring of electricity sectors, at least on paper. Continuing this process is a precondition for efficient cross-border electricity trade. However, anti-competitive conduct by incumbent monopolists persists in practice in many formally liberalized sectors.[45] The lack of coherent and effective disciplines on competition and non-discriminatory regulation in world trade law is a major shortcoming. While it is unrealistic to expect multilateral competition law to emerge within the framework of the existing institutions like the WTO, the example of the telecommunication sector shows that some progress can be made within the existing framework.

---

[43] Regulation (EU) 2019/943 of the European Parliament and of the Council of 5 June 2019 on the internal market for electricity (5 June 2019) OJ 2019/L 158/54.

[44] Art. 150 of the EU-Kazakhstan EPCA.

[45] See above in Chap. 10, pp. 143 et seq.

The similarities between the electricity and the telecommunication sectors have already been touched upon at different points in this book. Both sectors were initially characterized by monopolies and eventually subjected to liberalization and privatization. The continued exercise of incumbents' dominant position after formal liberalization is also a shared experience of both sectors. Building upon what has been achieved in terms of structural reforms at the national level, pro-competitive principles agreed upon multilaterally would help to make the most out of the domestic reforms. Some WTO Members seemingly supported strengthened multilateral disciplines also in the energy sector. A statement accompanying the Japanese negotiating proposal on energy services illustrates this:

> There has been no perfect model for a successful introduction of domestic regulations and a competitive environment for the energy services sector. On the contrary, every country is progressing with regulatory reform and business reorganization in the energy market on a trial and error basis. Recognizing such circumstances, Japan believes that in the negotiations on energy services, *it would be useful to consider the effectiveness of frameworks for domestic regulation, which would contribute to the creation of a competitive environment taking into account the viewpoint of a non-discriminate, fair and transparent use of the networks*, with due consideration being given to a Member's obligation under Articles XVI (market access) and XVII (national treatment).[46]

This statement by the Japanese delegation can be interpreted as a willingness to engage in multilateral negotiations on pro-competitive disciplines in the energy sector. Before assessing the form these principles should take when adopted, it is necessary to determine the most important issues that should be addressed. Based on the conclusions of preceding chapters, the issues that are deemed most important are:

a. Engaging in a round of liberalization through commitments on the basis of the services classification defined above;
b. A further round of notifications of electricity suppliers as STEs;
c. Establishment of common principles for access to electricity networks;
d. A common commitment to establish an independent regulatory body for electricity on the national level and recognition of the need for cooperation among national regulators;
e. Common principles on the scope and limits of public service obligations in the electricity sector;
f. Transparency requirements.

While most of these points speak for themselves, each will be elaborated upon briefly in the following paragraphs.[47]

The degree to which further liberalization can be achieved in the electricity sector depends to a large extent on the willingness of WTO Members to enter into *specific commitments* on electricity-related services. During the Uruguay Round which brought about the GATS, the energy sector received little attention in the services

---

[46]WTO, 'Communication from Japan to the Council on Trade in Services: Negotiating Proposal on Energy Services' (4 October 2001) S/CSS/W/42/Suppl.3 (emphasis added).

[47]For a similar proposal see Selivanova (2014), p. 204.

negotiations.[48] That changed somewhat during the multilateral negotiations on services that were carried out under the GATS from 2000 onwards. During the first phase of negotiations, a total of seven proposals on energy services were submitted by individual Members to the WTO. These proposals came from Chile,[49] Cuba,[50] the European Communities,[51] Japan,[52] Norway,[53] the US[54] and Venezuela.[55] Norway and the US proposed a reference paper on energy services.[56] Most of the proposals pointed to the fact that the classification list used for scheduling does not include a comprehensive entry for energy services.[57] As was discussed above, the effectiveness of Article VIII GATS in disciplining incumbent network operators is in practice seriously thwarted by the lack of specific commitments in the energy sector.[58] The same is true with respect to Article XVI GATS, as commitments on market access in the electricity sector are very rare. The lack of commitments undertaken in the energy sector undermines the transparency, predictability, and stability of energy services trade.[59] A 'negotiating round on electricity-related services' would be helpful even if further liberalizing commitments are unrealistic: it could seek clarification on (technical) improvement of existing commitments.

With respect to the second issue, the importance of gaining *access to existing networks* in the electricity sector has been stressed repeatedly. Integrated incumbent operators with exclusive rights seriously impede the access of foreign electricity suppliers on reasonable terms to transmission and distribution networks. To enable non-discriminatory cross-border trade, network operators have to make their networks available under conditions no less favourable than those granted to

---

[48] Zarrilli (2004), p. 235.

[49] WTO, Communication from Chile. The Negotiations on Trade in Services, S/CSS/VV/88 (May 2001).

[50] WTO, Communication from Cuba. Negotiating Proposal on Energy Services, S/CSS/W/144 (March 2002).

[51] WTO, Communication from the European Communities and Their Member States. GATS 2000: Energy Services, S/CSS/W /60 (March 2001).

[52] WTO, Communication from Japan, Negotiating Proposal on Energy Services, Supplement, S/CSS/W/42/Suppl.3 (October 2001).

[53] WTO, Communication from Norway. The Negotiations on Trade in Services, S/CSS/W/59 (March 2001).

[54] WTO, Communication from the United States. Classification or Energy Services, S/CSC/W/27 (May 2000).

[55] WTO, Communication from Venezuela. Negotiating Proposal on Energy Services, S/CSS/W/69 (March 2001).

[56] UNCTAD, Energy and Environmental Setvices: Negotiating Objectives and Development Priorities (UN 2003) 52, available at https://unctad.org/system/files/official-document/ditctncd20033_en.pdf.

[57] Zarrilli (2004), p. 242.

[58] See above in Sect. 10.1.2, pp. 155 et seq.

[59] Cf Adlung et al (2011), p. 2.

subsidiaries.[60] This relates to access tariffs, capacity allocation, and the non-discriminatory application of last resort measures like curtailments of capacity. Inspired by the approach in the bilateral EU-Kazakhstan EPCA, a general access obligation in a multilateral instrument could take the following formulation as a point of departure:

> Each Party shall provide the enterprises of the other Parties, established as juridical persons in the territory of the Party granting the access, with non-discriminatory access to high-voltage electric energy transmission grids and lines, which are partly or fully owned and regulated by the Party granting the access within the available capacities of such grids and lines. The access shall be allocated in a fair and equitable manner.[61]

Importantly, any doubts should be removed as to the applicability of this provision to networks owned by private operators and not just limited to infrastructure in public hands. The above formulation should thus be slightly amended to the effect that access must be granted to grids and lines 'which are partly or fully owned *or* regulated' by the Party granting the access.

The precise design of the access regime, i.e. whether the access conditions are firmly set by the regulator or negotiated, does not have to be settled multilaterally. To make the access regime effective, it should be made subject to a dispute settlement procedure.[62]

The *establishment of an independent regulator* has already been touched upon in services negotiations at the WTO. The need to set up independent regulatory authorities for the energy sector is stressed in some services requests submitted by WTO Members.[63] Just like most other energy-specific requests, these demands were not met by any meaningful offers. Furthermore, it has been suggested that this topic might be in better hands within the WTO Working Party on Domestic Regulations.[64] Within a new electricity trade agreement, contracting parties should at least stress the importance of establishing a regulatory body independent from the actors along the supply chain. Furthermore, contracting parties should commit their regulators to cooperate with each other. With more international interconnections and cross-border trade in electricity, anti-competitive conduct of entities outside their domestic jurisdictions will be harder to monitor by national regulators.[65] The independence and impartiality of the regulatory bodies are also some of the central elements contained in the Reference Paper on Basic Telecommunications.[66] The respective provision in the Reference Paper reads as follows: 'The regulatory body is separate

---

[60] Simonetta Zarrilli, Managing Request-Offer Negotiations Under The GATS: The Case of Energy Services' OECD Trade Directorate TD/TC/WP (2003)24/FINAL, p. 21.

[61] EU-Kazakhstan EPCA, Article 145.

[62] Ibid.

[63] Zarrilli (2004), p. 253.

[64] Ibid.

[65] Dee and Findlay (2008), p. 353.

[66] Reference Paper on Basic Telecommunications Services (24 April 1996) 36 I.L.M. 367 (1997). See also Blouin (2000), p. 138.

from, and not accountable to, any supplier of basic telecommunications services. The decisions of and the procedures used by regulators shall be impartial with respect to all market participants.'[67]

In Part III of this book, it was demonstrated that only a very few *state-owned utilities* in the electricity sector have been *notified* to the WTO as STEs.[68] This is surprising considering the still widespread occurrence of state-owned and vertically integrated electricity suppliers operating in countries around the world. As a large number of these would qualify as STEs under the definition provided in Article XVII GATT, it must be assumed that countries do not take their notification obligation very seriously. This diminishes the transparency and the ensuing potential for negotiations on liberalization among WTO Members. It can be speculated that one of the reasons for the lack of existing notifications is the lack of 'peer pressure' on governments as long as the general level of notifications remains as low as it currently is. Hence, countries should collectively agree to notify their electricity utilities as STEs where appropriate.

Public service obligations are routinely introduced at the domestic and regional levels after liberalization, as liberalized markets cannot guarantee that the benefits of electricity supply for all parts of the society will be fully realized.[69] PSOs are imposed on private operators for a variety of reasons, among which are to safeguard the continuing supply of all consumers with electricity, specifically those most vulnerable and those located in remote regions. Therefore, multilateral instruments should be drafted in a way as to not undermine the legitimate right of contracting parties to an electricity trade agreement to impose such obligations on operators.[70] At the same time, common principles and minimum standards with respect to PSOs should be agreed upon to ensure that they are not used arbitrarily or to discriminate against foreign entities. As the GATS Secretariat has observed, rules on PSOs should be clearly defined, non-discriminatory, and transparent.[71] The telecommunications sector is once again a step ahead in this respect. The Reference Paper stipulates that it is up to Members to define the kind of 'universal service obligation' they feel necessary to maintain. The mere presence of such obligations will not be qualified as anti-competitive as long as the requirements are administered in a transparent, non-discriminatory, and competitively neutral manner and are not more burdensome than necessary for the kind of service defined by the Member.[72]

Finally, with respect to *transparency*, this is a category that is relevant for all the other issues identified for multilateral regulation. It necessarily entails timely access

---

[67] WTO Reference Paper on Telecommunications (1996), at point 5.

[68] See above in Sect. 10.1.1, pp. 150 et seq.

[69] On PSOs see above in Sect. 2.2.3, pp. 29 et seq.

[70] WTO, Council for Trade in Services, Energy Services – Background Note by the Secretariat (09 September 1998) S/C/W/52 [70].

[71] Ibid [70].

[72] WTO Reference Paper on Telecommunications (1996). See also Zarrilli (2004), p. 261.

to information concerning technical specifications of access, (network) tariffs, available transmission capacity and scheduled maintenance work on the network.

14.3   Finding the Right Forum: Where Should Electricity-Specific Trade Rules Be Defined?

Having identified the most pertinent issues which should be made subject to sector-specific multilateral regulation, the focus now turns to the question of where the negotiations should take place and which existing forum is best suited to 'host' these new rules.

14.3.1   A Reformed Energy Charter Treaty

Taking the Energy Charter Treaty as a basis and building further upon the existing text seems like an attractive option due to the sector-specific scope of the Treaty and its constituency, which as of February 2022 includes 52 Parties and a number of observers. The Membership has indeed constantly expanded and now transcends the territorial core of Eurasia on which it was initially focused. As two prominent commentators on the Energy Charter Framework have remarked, the Treaty 'constitutes a proto-constitutional order for a future (possible) global energy market'.[73] Based on the discussions in previous chapters of this thesis, it must indeed be concluded that the provisions of the ECT, when compared with the WTO rules, mark some progress with respect to the specific problems of energy trade.

The regulation of transit is probably the area where the most significant improvements can be detected. Importantly, the ECT includes various provisions on dispute settlement and arbitration and combines trade and investment disciplines in one treaty text. With respect to the resolution of transit issues, the ECT environment must be deemed to be a more appropriate forum in which to resolve energy transit disputes than the WTO as it offers more targeted remedies and provides for non-interruption of existing transit flows.[74] Furthermore, the ECT has played a proactive role in increasing the visibility of energy-specific trade problems and as a platform for discussing contemporary issues of international trade regulation. Its appeal is also demonstrated by the fact that at least one regional electricity market, the ECOWAS, modelled parts of its regulatory framework on the ECT.[75] The ECOWAS signatories recognized that the Treaty 'represent[s] the leading internationally accepted basis for

---

[73] Konoplyanik and Wälde (2006), p. 556.

[74] See above in Sect. 12.4, pp. 211 et seq. See also Azaria (2009), p. 596.

[75] See above in Sect. 3.2.4.2, pp. 67 et seq.

the promotion, cooperation, integration and development of energy investment pro-jects and energy trade among sovereign nations'.[76]

While the Energy Charter Treaty has thus been an important piece in the nascent global regulatory framework for energy trade, its suitability for resolving the electricity-related issues identified in this thesis must be questioned. Several factors suggest that the Energy Charter framework might not be the best forum to host new rules on international electricity trade.

The European Energy Charter of 1991, of which the ECT was a result, arose in a very specific regional context and the electricity sector was arguably only peripher-ally considered. The more important driving forces behind the Energy Charter Process were questions of access to and exploitation of oil and gas reserves in the former Soviet Union and guaranteeing uninterrupted transit of these energy sources to Central and Western Europe. While the ECT expressly acknowledges electricity as an energy product and refers to grid-bound transport on several occasions, the Treaty falls short of comprehensively addressing electricity trade issues. Looking back over the past two and a half decades, one can also notice that the focus of the ECT has been more on the investment side than on the trade aspects. One major deficiency of the ECT in its current design is that it is not applicable to services trade. While all of these points somewhat diminish the current relevance of the ECT for regulating international trade in electricity, it could be asked whether a reformed Treaty under the roof of the International Energy Charter might provide a promising way forward.

One main issue to consider is that the ECT arguably suffers from a legitimacy problem. At the time of the drafting of the ECT, almost half of the prospective Contracting Parties had not ratified the GATT 1947, the WTO's predecessor.[77] The picture has changed dramatically and as described above, only five out of the currently 52 ECT Contracting Parties still have not acceded to the WTO. Out of these, only one has not yet initiated the accession procedure.[78] Considering the fact that an essential feature of the ECT has been to provide an interim step towards WTO Membership, the continuing future relevance of the Treaty's trade-related provisions can be called into question.[79] Furthermore, regional regimes with significance for the energy sector are proliferating, possibly competing with the Energy Charter frame-work. Examples are the Energy Community, a tool to 'export' the EU energy acquis to neighbouring countries in South-East Europe, and regional integration efforts on a broader political level like the Association of Southeast Asian Nations (ASEAN) and the CPTPP.[80] More important than 'regulatory competition' from PTAs is the fact that, despite its ambition of evolving into an 'International Energy Charter', the ECT has not really been embraced on a global scale. It is specifically striking that the

---

[76]Ibid.

[77]Sakmar (2008), p. 99.

[78]This concerns Turkmenistan.

[79]Marhold (2015), p. 424.

[80]Comprehensive and Progressive Agreement for the Trans-Pacific Partnership.

Treaty has not been signed by any African state, despite the already-mentioned reference to the ECT in the context of West-African electricity integration. Hence, it must be concluded that the ECT has not managed to evolve into an instrument with a truly global reach. The fact that neither Canada nor the US has ratified the ECT further weakens the position of the ECT as a possible multilateral forum for hosting electricity-specific provisions. An additional issue worth mentioning is the particularly uneasy relationship of one large WTO Member with the ECT—Russia. The disagreement concerning the Transit Protocol led Russia to refrain from ratification and to stay on the side-lines, sometimes even taking a hostile approach toward the Treaty. The retreat of Italy from the ECT in 2016 is another example of the arguably decreasing relevance of the Treaty.

Thus, despite the superficial appeal of the ECT as a sector-specific forum for energy trade regulation, it remains to be seen what route the 'modernization process' will take which was initiated by the ECT Members in 2018.[81]

14.3.2 Accommodating Rules on International Electricity Trade in the WTO Framework

An alternative to pursuing new rules on international electricity trade in the ECT is to use the WTO as an already-existing multilateral negotiating forum.[82] This would not be without precedent, as a considerable number of sectors have received special attention and treatment in the context of WTO negotiations. It is indeed one of the WTO's principal functions to provide a forum for hosting negotiations.[83] As expressed in Article III:2 WTOA:

> The WTO shall provide the forum for negotiations among its Members concerning their multilateral trade relations in matters dealt with under the agreements in the Annexes to this Agreement. The WTO may also provide a forum for further negotiations among its Members concerning their multilateral trade relations, and a framework for the implementation of the results of such negotiations, as may be decided by the Ministerial Conference.

While the repeated use of the term 'multilateral' in the reproduced text indicates that negotiations should in principle include most if not all WTO Members, the provision is silent as to a particular venue to be followed. It thus appears that some flexibility is allowed with respect to the precise negotiating approach pursued and the legal form

---

[81] On the modernization process see above in Chap. 6, p. 124. See also Coop and Seif (2019).

[82] The former Secretary General of the WTO, Pascal Lamy, promoted this idea by stating: 'When thinking about how the WTO can most effectively contribute to the energy goals of the international community, the question is not whether the WTO legal framework is relevant and applicable to trade in energy goods and services, for it clearly is. Instead, we need to ask ourselves how the WTO's contribution can be further improved, given rapid changes in the energy policy landscape and the international community's goals regarding energy.' Lamy (2013), p. 121.

[83] Marhold (2015), p. 426.

of the outcome of these negotiations.[84] This idea also underlies Article II:3 of the WTOA on 'Plurilateral Trade Agreements', which can be read as an exception to the 'single undertaking approach' that governed the Uruguay Round negotiations. Under the latter, WTO Members committed to adopt all elements negotiated during the Uruguay Round as opposed to 'picking and choosing'. Art. II:3, however, carves out a space for 'Plurilateral Trade Agreements' that are binding on supportive Members only without creating rights or obligations for the rest of the Membership. These plurilateral agreements are included in Annex 4 of the WTOA. The only sectoral Agreement included is the Agreement on Trade in Civil Aircraft. This is a typical case of a plurilateral agreement as the material scope – trade in aircraft equipment—is of interest to only a very limited group of WTO Members.

Based on the legal framework and the existing experience with incorporating special disciplines under the umbrella of the WTO, the following venues could be pursued while staying within the bounds of the WTO: A new sectoral agreement; amendment of relevant provisions throughout the existing Agreements; an interpretative decision; and a reference paper. It must be noted that this list is not exhaustive, and neither are the different options mutually exclusive. To the contrary, as the experience in the telecommunications sector shows, several instruments can be used cumulatively to drive liberalization and provide for basic principles on competition. It is submitted here that while 'repairing' single existing provisions in the WTO Agreements via the amendment procedure will be a cumbersome and unrewarding exercise[85], all remaining options are worth exploring. They will each be presented briefly in the following paragraphs. It is clear that all of the above approaches require a group of progressive WTO Members willing to lay the groundwork for negotiations and provide the necessary input and expertise.[86]

14.3.2.1   A WTO Sectoral Agreement on Electricity Trade

Agreements with distinct disciplines now exist for, *inter alia*, civil aircraft,[87] textiles,[88] agriculture,[89] information technology products[90] and telecommunications.[91]

---

[84] Adlung and Mamdouh (2017), p. 7.

[85] Agreement Establishing the World Trade Organization (15 April 1994) 1867 U.N.T.S. 154, Article X.

[86] Adlung and Mamdouh (2017), p. 8.

[87] Agreement on Trade in Civil Aircraft, contained in Annex 4 to the WTO Agreement.

[88] Agreement on Textiles and Clothing, contained in Annex 1A to the WTO Agreement, 1868 U.N.T.S. 14 (terminated on 1 January 2005).

[89] Agreement on Agriculture, contained in Annex 1A to the Agreement establishing the WTO, 1867 U.N.T.S. 410.

[90] WTO, Information Technology Agreement – an Explanation, https://www.wto.org/english/tratop_e/inftec_e/itaintro_e.htm.

[91] See WTO, Decision on Negotiations on Basic Telecommunications (15 April 1994) LT/UR/D-5/4.

Some date back to the Tokyo Round, others were negotiated during or after the Uruguay Round. The latter category is of specific interest for the purposes of the present study. The post-Uruguay Round Agreements were negotiated as plurilateral agreements with a 'critical mass' of WTO Members on board. The Agreements operate under the premise that the resulting benefits of further liberalization are to be extended on an MFN basis. Furthermore, other interested Members can join the plurilateral agreement at any later stage. In this context, the Information Technology Agreement (ITA) has been hailed as a major achievement.[92] The ITA was concluded in December 1996 and represents the first agreement negotiated in the aftermath of the Uruguay Round, and thus outside of a multilateral trade round.[93] The constantly growing role of IT for the general global economic development was widely recognized in the 1990s and this contributed to the interest in liberalizing trade in the sector.[94] As of the current moment, the Members that have acceded to the ITA represent 97% of world trade in the products addressed in the Agreement. As tariffs on IT products were rather high at the beginning of the ITA negotiations, achieving mutually agreed-upon reductions of these tariffs was the main focus area of the negotiators. The Agreement provides for significant tariff reductions on a range of IT products. The ITA approach inspired subsequent negotiations on sectoral agreements.[95]

The next such Agreement was the Agreement on Basic Telecommunications Services, which was concluded in 1997. Negotiations on telecommunications services had already begun under the umbrella of the GATT in 1986.[96] However, similar to the case of goods tariffs in the IT sector, few commitments had been taken on basic telecommunication services by WTO Members during the Uruguay Round.[97] The Agreement then built on the foundations of the general agreement on services that the Uruguay Round brought into existence—the GATS.[98] The main pillars of the Basic Agreement were 55 schedules of specific commitments, representing a total of 69 countries with the EU administering a single schedule.[99] Commitments were made with respect to market access and national treatment of foreign telecom service providers. A large group of Members undertook commitments on a broad range of services in the sector. Another important outcome of the negotiations on basic telecommunications was the Reference Paper, a set of regulatory principles for the sector which can be referred to in WTO Members' schedules of commitments.[100] The Reference Paper on Basic Telecommunications provides a

---

[92] Adlung and Mamdouh (2017), p. 11; Mann and Liu (2008), p. 182.

[93] Mann and Liu (2008), pp. 188 et seq.

[94] Ibid, at 188.

[95] Ibid, at 193 f where it is observed that 'the ITA has been serving as a model for sectoralism.'

[96] Blouin (2000), p. 136.

[97] Ibid, at 135.

[98] Ibid, at 136.

[99] Ibid, at 137.

[100] Reference Paper on Basic Telecommunications Services (24 April 1996) 36 I.L.M. 367 (1997).

unique development in the formulation of competition-related principles. It has received a widespread adoption as the majority of the Members of the Basic Telecommunications Agreement referred to it in the additional commitments section of their schedules.[101]

The degree to which the Basic Agreement and Reference Paper constitute substantive progress is judged differently in practice. Commentators have pointed out that most commitments reflected the status quo at the time in industrialized countries and could thus be regarded as standstill commitments rather than a new impetus for liberalization.[102] Lack of precision and the vagueness of provisions in the Basic Agreement have also been cited as reasons for criticism. Taking the opposite view, one has to recognize that it is an achievement to subject an entire sector to subject-specific multilateral trade regulation and bringing this into the ambit of multilateral dispute settlement (the WTO DSU).[103]

The experience with plurilateral agreements shows that while trade liberalization and amendments to the existing architecture of WTO Agreements usually happen through concerted trade rounds—with the latest Doha Round having been suspended in 2006 after years of deadlock—it is not impossible to achieve progress outside of 'single undertaking' rounds. An electricity trade agreement would depart from both the telecommunications and the IT experience in one important respect: As discussed above, it would ideally entail both rules on goods (albeit not necessarily with respect to customs duties, which are already low) and services. It is submitted that a sectoral agreement would precisely allow this flexibility and thereby help to overcome the division into rules on goods and rules on services typical of traditional WTO law.

14.3.2.2 A Reference Paper on Services Related to Electricity

Considering the similarities between the electricity and telecommunication sectors it is only natural that calls for a reference paper on energy services have been voiced from both academia and the WTO Membership.[104] The GATS Secretariat also discussed such an approach in a background note from 2010.[105] A reference paper, while of limited use as a self-standing legal instrument, offers several benefits

---

[101] Blouin (2000), p. 137.

[102] Ibid, at 138 et seq, citing Drake and Noam (1998).

[103] Blouin (2000), p. 139 refers to the 'insurance policy aspect' created through the certainty and predictability provided by international rules when compared to liberalization at the domestic level alone.

[104] It was already pointed out above that Norway and the US each proposed such a reference paper in the request-offer process under the GATS after 2000. For academic commentators discussing a reference paper on energy services see Selivanova (2014), p. 297; Rios Herran and Poretti (2012), pp. 33 et seq; Cossy (2008), p. 168.

[105] WTO, Council for Trade in Services, Energy Services – Background Note by the Secretariat (12 January 2010) S/C/W/311.

when embedded in a broader set of rules for the sector. It specifically offers the advantage that adopting it through inclusion in a Member's schedule of concessions under the additional commitments rubric remains voluntary. An attempt to include such pro-competitive principles in a multilateral agreement with broader coverage might fail because it may be deemed to encroach on the sovereignty and regulatory autonomy of states. While the adoption of principles laid down in a Reference Paper remains voluntary in principle, the telecom experience shows that broad support and the willingness to be bound by a reference paper exists among the Members who participated in the drafting.

One advantage of the reference paper approach is that it makes it possible to address sector-specific challenges at a level of detail which would be unrealistic to attain within the framework of an actual 'agreement'. The reference paper approach provides an opportunity to sharpen the non-discrimination principles in the covered agreements and to provide some interpretative assistance for WTO dispute settlement panels and the Appellate Body.[106]

However, despite the similarities between the telecommunication and electricity sectors, differences continue to exist between the two sectors which cannot be disregarded. The Telecommunications Reference Paper therefore cannot be simply transposed to the electricity sector through a copy-and-paste approach. To give one example, the qualification of telecommunication companies as 'service providers' is much easier than in the case of entities involved in the electricity industry.[107]

The proposals for a reference paper on energy services submitted by Norway and the US were not met with enthusiasm by the rest of the WTO Membership.[108] Hence it could be argued that a renewed push for a reference paper on services in the energy sector would face a difficult start. As was generally observed above, however, engaging in negotiations on electricity separate from other energy sources provides the opportunity to overcome particularly sensitive (geo-) political interests associated with the fossil fuel industry.

14.4   Final Conclusions to Part IV

In an attempt to provide more clarity on rules for traders and to overcome the existing fragmentation, a multilateral agreement on common principles for trade in electric energy (henceforth called 'Electricity Trade Agreement') would be desirable. It is submitted that such an Agreement would not have to be designed by going back to the drawing board. Instead, it could build upon existing provisions as included in the Agreements examined in the preceding parts of this work.[109]

---

[106]Cf Blouin (2000), p. 140.

[107]Cf Selivanova (2015), p. 4.

[108]Rios Herran and Poretti (2012), p. 41.

[109]Cf Cottier et al. (2011), p. 222 who suggest a framework convention-style approach.

Some principles of particular importance which could provide the core of an Electricity Trade Agreement have been outlined. It has been noted that an agreement would need to tackle trade issues concerning both goods and services and thereby depart from most other sector-specific agreements currently in existence. Furthermore, the scope should be limited to the electricity sector as opposed to pursuing a broader agenda including other energy sources. One recommended element of a sectoral agreement is a new 'classification list on electricity services'. To remedy the definitional problems of the current system, electricity should be characterized plainly as a 'good' and the generation of electricity as production of a good and not as a service. Transmission and distribution of electricity should be classified as services unless carried out on own account. Ancillary services provided with respect to transmission should be spelled out in a disaggregated way. The same would apply to wholesaling, metering and billing of electricity at the end consumer.

With respect to an electricity transit regime, transit disciplines should be made more concrete in a number of areas. They concern the scope of application as well as the substance of the principle of freedom of transit. The former would ideally involve a clarifying statement regarding the applicability of transit provisions to transit via both isolated long-distance lines and meshed grids of the transit state. Regarding substance, MFN guarantees should be put in place for electricity in transit and electricity in transit vis-à-vis electricity destined for importation or exportation. Most importantly, MFN should not only be granted in relation to access to grids, but also to transmission fees and other charges. MFN should be granted for transit irrespective of the technology used in transmission.[110] With respect to yet-to-be established infrastructure, states should be obligated not to unduly obstruct efforts to plan and execute such important transmission projects and to ensure that other entities under their jurisdiction do not engage in such obstruction.

A core body of principles on good regulatory practice has been identified in this study as an additional pillar to a newly defined set of provisions at the multilateral stage. This involves, *inter alia*, access to grids, the establishment of a regulatory body for the electricity sector and some minimum requirements with respect to the imposition and administration of PSOs. Ideally, the parties would agree to take further liberalizing commitments on the newly defined services entries in the electricity sector.

The choice of the right forum for negotiations on international electricity trade requires careful consideration. Perhaps surprisingly, this study concludes that the WTO would be the most suitable venue despite its traditional lack of focus on energy issues. This does not mean that the ECT framework should be disregarded. On the contrary, the sector-specific progress made in the ECT context could fertilize an additional instrument within the WTO framework. The same holds for some of the regulatory "innovations" found in some more recent PTAs.

---

[110]Countries might be tempted to support HVDC transmission technology as opposed to AC technology or vice versa because of preferences of their domestic industry.

References

Adlung R, Mamdouh H (2017) Plurilateral Trade Agreements: An Escape Route for the WTO? WTO Working Paper ERSD-2017-03

Adlung R, Morrison P, Martin R, Zhang W (2011) Fog in GATS commitments — Boon or bane? WTO Working Paper ERSD- 2011-04

Albath L (2005) Handel und Investitionen in Strom und Gas: Die internationalen Regeln. C. H. Beck, Munich, p 91

Azaria D (2009) Energy transit under the Energy Charter Treaty and the general agreement on tariffs and trade. J Energy Nat Resour Law 27:559

Blouin C (2000) The WTO agreement on basic telecommunications: a reevaluation. Telecommunications Policy 24:135

Coop G, Seif I (2019) Modernization of the ECT: an institutional perspective. Transnational Dispute Manag

Cossy M (2008) The liberalization of energy services: are PTAs more energetic than the GATS? In: Marchetti JA, Roy M (eds) Opening markets for trade in services: countries and sectors in bilateral and WTO negotiations. Cambridge University Press, Cambridge

Cossy M (2012) Energy services under the general agreement on trade in services. In: Selivanova Y (ed) Regulation of energy in International Trade Law: WTO, NAFTA and Energy Charter. Wolters Kluwer, Alphen aan den Rijn

Cottier T, Malumfashi G, Matteotti-Berkutova S, Nartova O, De Sepibus J, Bigdeli S (2011) Energy in WTO law and policy. In: Cottier T, Delimatsis P (eds) The prospects of International Trade Regulation: from fragmentation to coherence. Cambridge University Press, Cambridge

Dee P, Findlay C (2008) Trade in infrastructure services: a conceptual framework. a handbook of international trade in services. Oxford University Press, Oxford

Drake W, Noam E (1998) Assessing the WTO agreement on basic telecommunications. In: Unfinished business: telecommunications after the Uruguay Round. Institute for International Economics, Washington

Dralle T (2018) Ownership unbundling and related measures in the EU Energy Sector: Foundations, the impact of WTO law and investment protection. Springer, Berlin

Ferrey S (2004) Inverting choice of law in the wired universe: thermodynamics, mass and energy. Wm Mary Law Rev 45:1839

Gudas K (2018) The law and policy of international trade in electricity. Europa Law Publishing, Waterstraat

Konoplyanik A, Wälde T (2006) Energy Charter Treaty and its role in international energy. J Energy Nat Resour Law 24:523

Lamy P (2013) The Geneva consensus – making trade work for all. Cambridge University Press, Cambridge

Mann C, Liu X (2008) The information technology agreement: sui generis or model stepping stone? In: Baldwin R, Low P (eds) Multilateralizing regionalism: challenges for the global trading system. Cambridge University Press, Cambridge

Marhold A (2015) Fragmentation and the nexus between the WTO and the ECT in Global Energy Governance – a legal-institutional analysis twenty years later. J World Invest Trade 16:389

Meyer T (2017) Explaining energy disputes at the World Trade Organization. Int Environ Agreements Politics Law Econ 17:391

Neufeld N (2002) Article V of the GATT 1994 – scope and application. Note prepared by the GATT Secretariat, 10 September 2002, G/C/W/408

Poretti P, Rios-Herran R (2006) A reference paper on energy services: the best way forward? Manch J Int Econ Law 3:2

Rios-Herran R, Poretti P (2012) Energy trade and investment under the North American free trade agreement. In: Selivanova Y (ed) Regulation of energy in international trade law. WTO, NAFTA and energy charter. Kluwer Law International

Sakmar S (2008) Bringing Energy Trade into the WTO: the historical context, current status, and potential implications for the Middle East Region. Ind Int Comp Law Rev 18:89

Selivanova Y (2014) The WTO agreements and energy. In: Selivanova Y (ed) Research handbook on International Energy Law. Edward Elgar, Cheltenham

Selivanova Y (2015) Clean energy and access to infrastructure: implications for the global trade system. In: E15 expert group on clean energy technologies and the trade system think piece

Wälde T, Gunst A (2004) International Energy Trade and access to networks. In: Bielecki J, Desta MG (eds) Electricity Trade in Europe: review of the economic and regulatory challenges. Kluwer Law International, Alphen aan den Rijn

Zarrilli S (2004) Multilateral rules and trade in energy goods and services: the case of electricity. In: Bielecki J, Desta MG (eds) Electricity Trade in Europe: review of the economic and regulatory challenges. Kluwer Law International, Alphen aan den Rijn

Zhang R (2015) Covered or not covered: that is the question. WTO Working Paper, ERSD-2015-11

Chapter 15
General Conclusions

International trade in electricity has become a contemporary reality. Regional electricity markets are now in operation on several continents while the technology for long-distance transmission is developing at an impressive pace. The vital importance of a secure electricity supply for the provision of the basic necessities of everyday life and the production of virtually any goods and services cannot be overstated. It is no surprise, therefore, that governments around the world have tightly regulated the electricity sector and free trade and competition are developing much slower than in most other industries. Nonetheless, liberalization of electricity markets is continuing and electricity is now widely regarded as a tradable commodity. At the same time, the energy world as we know it is undergoing its most radical transformation in more than a century. Conventional means of generation are being phased out and replaced by more sustainable ones. The traditional logic of placing power plants in close proximity to where electricity is consumed is changing radically and new—renewable—sources necessitate cross-border interconnections and long-distance transmission. Over the coming decades, trade in electric energy is therefore expected to develop into a global phenomenon. This development also has the potential to fundamentally change the character of international electricity trade which so far has evolved in a cooperative spirit and in parallel with a constant strive for national self-sufficiency. Not all countries have the same preconditions for large-scale renewable energy generation—some will develop into exporters of electricity, while others will increasingly rely on imports. At least in this respect, electricity trade is becoming more similar to trade in other energy commodities. Against this backdrop, this study has analysed the boundaries of application of the GATT and the GATS, as well as of the rules of the ECT and other PTAs to international trade in electricity. The main findings are presented in condensed form in the following conclusions.

1. The unique physical properties of electricity distinguish it from virtually all other goods and services and predetermine how electricity is traded. Consequently,

C. Frey, *World Trade Law and the Emergence of International Electricity Markets*, EYIEL Monographs - Studies in European and International Economic Law 25, https://doi.org/10.1007/978-3-031-04756-5_15

these features need to be taken into account when designing rules for international electricity trade. The most important of these features are the reliance on fixed physical infrastructure; the non-storability of electricity except in smaller quantities; a resulting need for constant surveillance and balancing of the electricity system; the natural monopoly character of the transmission business; the impossibility of targeted delivery of electricity from a certain source to a specific end-consumer in a meshed grid; and the occurrence of physical flows in a grid which do not correspond to trade flows. All of these characteristics test the general rules and principles of world trade as embodied in the WTO Agreements and regional and bilateral PTAs. Textual interpretation of relevant provisions in the GATT and the GATS is regularly not conclusive and interpretation therefore has to be fertilized by existing practice, technical feasibility and commercial realities.

2. National electricity sectors were long dominated by vertically integrated, monopolistic structures, public ownership of assets and tight government control. Liberalization and restructuring, especially unbundling, have been carried out by a considerable number of countries and the process is still ongoing. Governmental efforts to restructure electricity markets do not necessarily result in deregulation. On the contrary, the more liberalization is sought, the larger and more important the regulatory rulebook becomes. These rules seek to guarantee that the generation segment is opened for competition, and transmission capacity is allocated equitably to a large number of parties without risking technical problems or imbalances. The increasing depth of regulation in the electricity sector, while aiming to provide a more level playing field, paradoxically raises the potential for discrimination and trade conflicts more generally. Future WTO dispute settlement bodies will be required to decide on matters involving an increasingly sophisticated regulatory regime that goes beyond the more traditional trade matters.

3. Despite occasional assertions to the contrary by scholars and some national delegations during multilateral negotiations, the WTO Agreements are applicable to the energy sector in general and to electricity trade more specifically. Multilateral rules with specific application to the electricity sector have not yet been established. The ECT constitutes an improvement when compared with the WTO provisions, as it clarifies several aspects which are left unclear based on the GATT terminology. This includes the coverage of electricity as a good and the application of the transit provision to fixed infrastructure. On a continental scale, different regulatory frameworks for local electricity markets have emerged, reflecting differences in technical and economic realities and in the ambitions of various countries with respect to the level of integration. The European Union has arguably advanced furthest in integrating national electricity markets, but other regions exhibit their own regulatory innovations. It is especially noticeable that regional regulatory authorities for the electricity sector have successfully been established in Central America and West Africa.

4. The trade issues on which multilateral negotiations have traditionally focused are less relevant for the electricity sector because of the mutual interest in exchanges

of electricity and the necessity of technical and regulatory cooperation. One consequence is the generally low level of customs duties on electricity currently applied in practice. Another is that import restrictions are generally less of an issue than export restrictions. More relevant for the electricity sector is the possibility to apply measures restricting trade in emergency situations. Electricity networks are sensitive to the smallest deviations from the anticipated supply and demand and imbalances can cause widespread consequences involving a large geographical area. Furthermore, countries seek to safeguard the supply for their domestic market and hence prioritize domestic supply over trade with their neighbours.

5. 'Traditional' world trade law as embodied in the WTO Agreements cannot realistically serve as a catalyst for liberalization or positive regulation, but rather comes into play as a benchmark against which to assess the trade impacts of market regulation. The disciplines on STEs and monopoly suppliers could indeed constrain the behaviour of electricity utilities and transmission system operators administering a natural monopoly. The rather narrow personal scope of application combined with insufficient commitments by WTO Members in the services sphere, however, diminishes the practical effect of the analysed multilateral rules. The ECT and most bilateral and regional PTAs without sector-specific focus do not constitute major improvements. Like the analysed WTO provisions, they fall short of requiring pro-competitive regulation. The existing disciplines should nonetheless be taken as a point of departure and should then be complemented by a newly defined set of provisions for the electricity sector.

6. Market access in the electricity sector, like in telecommunications, means access to networks. When two or more formerly isolated national grids are connected, the interconnector will be the bottleneck for cross-border trade. As transmission capacity on lines cannot be scaled up indefinitely, transparent allocation rules have to be defined for the available capacity. Interconnectors over numerous borders are structurally congested, implying that congestion management becomes an issue of critical importance for cross-border electricity trade. It is therefore pertinent for capacity allocation and congestion management to happen in line with the principles of non-discrimination and transparency. WTO Members could invoke Article XI GATT in case another Member systematically disadvantages foreign entities requesting access to its transmission networks or excludes such entities from capacity allocation on interconnectors. However, if transmission networks are owned and operated by private entities, making a case against such practice will be more difficult. Whether or not the attribution to a government will be successful in such a case will depend on the degree to which such behaviour is incentivized by public authorities. An obligation on the side of a WTO Member to establish a system of third-party access to its networks can neither be inferred from WTO rules nor from ECT provisions. On the bilateral level, the European Union has started to enshrine access obligations with specific application to electricity transmission lines in some of its PTAs with third countries.

7. The dichotomy between rules on goods and rules on services is a disadvantage in present-day world trade law, especially WTO law. It is not a unique feature of the electricity sector that value chains include a variety of aspects of both goods and services character and that, depending on the context, the characterization of economic activities can oscillate between the production of goods and production of services rather frequently. Hence, the example of the electricity sector puts the spotlight on a structural problem in current WTO law: trade issues resulting from contemporary economic activities are not necessarily well represented in the current architecture, especially in the GATT and GATS. To exacerbate the problem, the classification of electricity based on the goods and services classification instruments currently in use is outdated and reliance on these instruments can lead to unreasonable results. While these classification instruments may not be legally binding, they constitute the 'common language' of international trade and are meant to provide transparency and visibility of the liberalization commitments. Hence, an updating of these instruments to reduce uncertainty and bring classification in line with contemporary realities of the electricity sector is warranted. A sectoral approach to the classification of electricity services should be followed focusing on the 'core' services specific to the electricity sector. An 'electricity services classification list' would provide for more visibility and certainty and thereby increase the willingness of parties to enter into further liberalizing commitments.

8. The identified limitations of world trade law in its present state should be remedied if countries are serious about further integrating their national electricity markets and enhancing cross-border trade. To this effect, an 'Electricity Trade Agreement' within the WTO framework is identified as a desirable innovation. Such an Agreement could build on, but would ideally transcend, previous efforts with respect to the telecommunications sector. Negotiating parties could avail themselves of certain provisions found in the ECT (e.g. with respect to transit) and the 'latest generation' PTAs concluded by the EU. This would imply transcending the economic incentive-driven focus on regional rules and multilateralizing commitments—admittedly not an easy task.

While the appetite for strengthening multilateral institutions and global cooperation has somewhat faded in recent years, it would be a rewarding and useful exercise to embark on a multilateral effort leading to coherency in the international regulation of electricity trade. The need for coordination and mutual management of common resources is bigger than ever. This should be interpreted as an opportunity for WTO Members to set the course for regulating trade on a future global network aimed at ensuring the security of supply and catering to the sustainable development of the world.

Case Law

WTO Panel and Appellate Body

- Argentina – Measures Affecting the Export of Bovine Hides and the Import of Finished Leather, Report of the Panel (19 December 2000) WT/DS155/R
- Argentina – Measures Affecting the Importation of Goods, Report by the Appellate Body (22 August 2014) WT/DS438/AB/R
- Brazil – Measures Affecting Desiccated Coconut, Report of the Appellate Body (21 February 1997) WT/DS22/AB/R
- Brazil – Measures Affecting Imports of Retreaded Tyres, Report of the Appellate Body (3 December 2007) WT/DS332/AB/R
- Canada – Certain Measures concerning Periodicals, Report of the Panel (14 March 1997) WT/DS31/R
- Canada – Certain Measures concerning Periodicals, Report of the Appellate Body (30 June 1997) WT/DS31/AB/R
- Canada – Certain Measures Affecting the Automotive Industry, Report of the Panel (11 February 2000) WT/DS139/R, WT/DS142/R
- Canada – Certain Measures Affecting the Automotive Industry, Report of the Appellate Body (31 May 2000) WT/DS139/AB/R, WT/DS142/AB/R
- Canada – Measures Relating to Exports of Wheat and Treatment of Imported Grain, Report of the Panel (6 April 2004) WT/DS276/R
- Canada – Measures Relating to Exports of Wheat and Treatment of Imported Grain, Report of the Appellate Body (30 August 2004) WT/DS276/AB/R
- Canada – Measures Relating to the Feed-in Tariff Program, Report of the Panel (19 December 2012) WT/DS426/R
- Canada – Measures Relating to the Feed-in Tariff Program, Report of the Appellate Body (6 May 2013) WT/DS426/19
- China – Measures Related to the Exportation of Rare Earths, Tungsten, and Molybdenum, Report of the Appellate Body (7 August 2015) WT/DS431/AB/R

© The Author(s), under exclusive license to Springer Nature Switzerland AG 2022
C. Frey, *World Trade Law and the Emergence of International Electricity Markets*,
EYIEL Monographs - Studies in European and International Economic Law 25,
https://doi.org/10.1007/978-3-031-04756-5

- China – Measures Related to the Exportation of Various Raw Materials, Reports of the Panel (5 July 2011) WT/DS394/R; WT/DS395/R; WT/DS398/R
- China – Certain Measures Affecting Electronic Payment Services, Report of the Panel (16 July 2012) WT/DS413/R
- Chile – Price Band System and Safeguard Measures Relating to Certain Agricultural Products, Panel Report (3 May 2002) WT/DS207/R
- China – Measures Affecting Trading Rights and Distribution Services for Certain Publications and Audiovisual Entertainment Products, Report of the Panel (12 August 2009) WT/DS363/R
- China – Measures Related to the Exportation of Various Raw Materials, Reports of the Panel (5 July 2011) WT/DS394/R, WT/DS395/R, WT/DS398/R
- China – Measures Related to the Exportation of Various Raw Materials, Reports of the Appellate Body (30 January 2012) WT/DS394/AB/R, WT/DS395/AB/R, WT/DS398/AB/R
- Colombia – Indicative Prices and Restrictions on Ports of Entry, Report of the Panel (27 April 2009) WT/DS366/R
- Dominican Republic – Measures Affecting the Importation and Internal Sale of Cigarettes, Report of the Panel (26 November 2004) WT/DS302/R
- European Union and its Member States – Certain Measures Relating to the Energy Sector, Request for Consultations by the Russian Federation (8 May 2014) WT/DS476/1
- European Communities – Measures Affecting the Importation of Certain Poultry Products, Report of the Appellate Body (13 July 1998) WT/DS69/AB/R
- European Communities – Regime for the Importation, Sale and Distribution of Bananas, Report of the Appellate Body (9 September 1997) WT/DS27/AB/R
- European Communities – Customs Classification of Certain Computer Equipment, Report of the Appellate Body (5 June 1998) WT/DS62/AB/R, WT/DS67/AB/R, WT/DS68/AB/R
- European Communities – Measures Affecting Asbestos and Asbestos-Containing Products, Report of the Panel (18 September 2000) WT/DS135/R
- European Communities and Certain Member States – Measures Affecting Trade in Large Civil Aircraft, Report of the Appellate Body (18 May 2011) WT/DS316/AB/R
- European Communities – Measures Affecting Asbestos and Asbestos-Containing Products, Report of the Appellate Body (12 March 2001) WT/DS135/AB/R
- European Communities – Measures Affecting the Approval and Marketing of Biotech Products, Panel Report (29 September 2006) WT/DS291/R
- India – Measures Affecting the Automotive Sector, Report of the Panel (21 December 2001) WT/DS146/R; WT/DS175/R
- India – Quantitative Restrictions on Imports of Agricultural, Textile and Industrial Products, Report of the Panel (6 April 1999) WT/DS90/R
- Japan – Taxes on Alcoholic Beverages, Report of the Appellate Body (4 October 1996) WT/DS8/AB/R, WT/DS10/AB/R, WT/DS11/AB/R
- Japan – Taxes on Alcoholic Beverages, Panel Report (11 July 1996) WT/DS8/R

- Japan – Measures Affecting Consumer Photographic Film and Paper, Report of the Panel (31 March 1998) WT/DS44/R
- Korea – Measures Affecting Imports of Fresh, Chilled and Frozen Beef, Report of the Panel (31 July 2000) WT/DS161/R, WT/DS169/R
- Korea – Measures Affecting Imports of Fresh, Chilled and Frozen Beef, Report of the Appellate Body (11 December 2000) WT/DS161/AB/R, WT/DS169/AB/R
- Mexico – Measures Affecting Telecommunications Services, Report of the Panel (2 April 2004) WT/DS204/R
- Russia – Measures Concerning Traffic in Transit, Request for Consultations by Ukraine (21 September 2016) WT/DS512/1
- Thailand – Customs and Fiscal Measures on Cigarettes from the Philippines, Report of the Panel (15 November 2010) WT/DS371/AB/R
- United States – Standards for Reformulated and Conventional Gasoline, Report of the Appellate Body (29 April 1996) WT/DS2/AB/R
- United States – Import Prohibition of Certain Shrimp and Shrimp Products, Report of the Panel (15 May 1998) WT/DS58/R
- United States – Sections 301-310 of the Trade Act of 1947, Report of the Panel (22 December 1999) WT/DS152/R
- United States – Sunset Review of Anti-Dumping Duties on Corrosion-Resistant Carbon Steel Flat Products from Japan, Report of the Appellate Body (15 December 2003) WT/DS244/AB/R
- United States – Anti-Dumping and Countervailing Duties (China), Report of the Appellate Body (11 March 2011) WT/DS379/AB/R
- United States – Measures Affecting the Cross-Border Supply of Gambling and Betting Services, Report of the Panel (10 November 2004) WT/DS285/R
- United States – Measures Affecting the Cross-Border Supply of Gambling and Betting Services, Report of the Appellate Body (7 April 2005) WT/DS285/AB/R
- United States – Certain Country of Origin Labelling (COOL) Requirements, Reports of the Appellate Body (29 June 2012) WT/DS384/AB/R, WT/DS386/AB/R

GATT

- Canada – Measures Affecting Exports of Unprocessed Herring and Salmon, Report of the Panel (22 March 1988) L/6268 - 35S/98
- Canada – Administration of the Foreign Investment Review Act, Panel Report (7 February 1984) L/5504 - 30S/140
- GATT, Canada – Import, Distribution and Sale of Alcoholic Drinks by Canadian Provincial Marketing Agencies, Report of the Panel (22 March 1988) L/6304 - 35S/37
- European Community – Programme of Minimum Import Prices, Licenses and Surety Deposits for Certain Processed Fruits and Vegetable, Report of the Panel (18 October 1978) L/4687 - 25S/68

- Japan – Trade in Semi-Conductors, Report of the Panel (4 May 1988) L/6309 - 35S/116
- The United States Manufacturing Clause, Report by the Panel (15 May 1984) L/5609 - 31S/74

European Court of Justice

- Case C-265/08 Federutility and Others v Autorità per l'energia elettrica e il gas [2010] ECR I-03377, Opinion of AG Ruiz-Jarabo Colomer
- Joined Cases C-241/91 P and C-242/91 P, Radio Telefis Eireann v Commission [1995] ECLI:EU:C:1995:98 and Case C-418/01, IMS Health GmbH & Co. OHG v NDC Health GmbH & Co. KG [2004] ECR 2004 I-05039
- Case C-158/94 Commission v Italian Republic, Judgment [1997] ECR I-5789
- Case C-275/92 H. M. Customs and Excise v Schindler, Judgment [1994] ECR 1-1039
- Case C-393/92 Municipality of Almelo and others v NV Energiebedrijf Ijsselmij, Judgment [1994] ECR I-1477
- Case C-260/89 ERT v DEP, Judgment [1991] ECR 1-2925
- Case C-260/89 ERT v DEP [1991] ECR 1-2925
- Case 6/64 Costa v ENEL, Judgment, ECLI:EU:C:1964:66

Decisions of Domestic Courts

United States

- Buckeye Union Fire Ins. Co. v. Detroit Edison Co., 196 N.W.2d 316 (Mich. Ct. App. 1972)
- Cincinnati Gas & Elec. Co. v. Goebel, 502 N.E.2d 713 (Hamilton County Mun. Ct. Ohio 1986)
- GFI Wisconsin, Inc. v. Reedsburg Utility Com'n, 440 B.R. 791, 797 f. (W.D. Wis. 2010)
- In Re Erving Industries, Inc., 432 B.R. 354, 370 (Bankr. D. Mass. 2010)
- In re Pilgrim's Pride Corp., 421 B.R. 231, 239 (Bankr. N.D.Tex.2009)
- Otte v. Dayton Power & Light Co., 37 Ohio St. 3d 33 (Ohio 1988)
- United States v. Consolidated Edison Co. of New York, Inc., 590 F. Supp. 266, 269 (S.D.N.Y.1984)
- United States v. Terminal Railroad Association, 224 U.S. 383 (1912)

Switzerland

- Schweizerisches Bundesgericht, Elektrizitätswerke des Kantons Zürich gegen Renold, BGE 48 II 366 (19 September 1922)

Legislation

WTO Agreements

- Agreement Establishing the World Trade Organization (15 April 1994) 1867 U.N.T.S. 154
- Agreement on Import Licensing Procedures (15 April 1994) 33 I.L.M. 1154
- Agreement on Textiles and Clothing, 1868 U.N.T.S. 14
- Agreement on Trade in Civil Aircraft (15 April 1994)
- Agreement on Trade-Related Investment Measures (15 April 1994) 1868 U.N.T.S. 186
- Annex on Telecommunications (15 April 1994) 33 I.L.M. 1192 (1994)
- General Agreement on Tariffs and Trade (15 April 1994) 55 U.N.T.S. 194
- General Agreement on Trade in Services (15 April 1994) 1869 U.N.T.S. 183
- Protocol of Provisional Application of the General Agreement on Tariffs and Trade (30 October 1947), 55 UNTS 308 A-814
- Reference Paper on Basic Telecommunications Services (24 April 1996) 36 I.L.M. 367 (1997)
- Understanding on Rules and Procedures Governing the Settlement of Disputes (15 April 1994) contained in Annex 2 to the Marrakesh Agreement Establishing the WTO, 1869 U.N.T.S. 401, 33 I.L.M. 1226

Bilateral and Regional Trade Agreements

- Association Agreement between the European Union and the European Atomic Energy Community and their Member States, of the one part, and Georgia, of the other part (27 June 2014) OJ 2014/L 261/4
- Canada – United States Free Trade Agreement (02 January 1988)
- Canada-United States-Mexico Agreement (30 November 2018)
- Comprehensive Economic and Trade Agreement between the European Union and Canada – Consolidated text (2016)
- Comprehensive Agreement for the Trans-Pacific Partnership (8 March 2018)
- Free Trade Agreement between the EFTA States and Singapore (26 June 2002)
- Free Trade Agreement between the European Union and South Korea (16 September 2010)

- Free Trade Agreement between Japan and the United Mexican States for the Strengthening of the Economic Partnership (17 September 2004)
- Free Trade Agreement between the European Union and the Socialist Republic of Vietnam (12 June 2020) OJ 2020/L 186/3
- Energy Charter Treaty (17 December 1994) 2080 U.N.T.S. 95
- Enhanced Partnership and Cooperation Agreement between the European Union and its Member States, of the one part, and the Republic of Kazakhstan, of the other part (21 December 2015) OJ 2016/L 29/3
- Korea – Singapore Free Trade Agreement (4 August 2005).
- North American Free Trade Agreement (17 December 1992) 32 I.L.M. 289 (1993)
- US – Singapore Free Trade Agreement (06 May 2003)
- Treaty Establishing the Energy Community (signed on 25 October 2005) OJ 2006/L 198/18

Other International Agreements

- Convention Relating to the Transmission in Transit of Electric Power, 9 December 1923, 58 LNTS 315
- ECOWAS Energy Protocol, signed 31 January 2003, entered into force (provisionally) 31 January 2003
- Revised Treaty of the Economic Community of West African States (ECOWAS), signed 24 July 1993, entered into force 23 August 1995
- Tratado Marco y Protocolo del Mercado Eléctrico de América Central (Framework Treaty) signed 30 December 1996
- United Nations Framework Convention on Climate Change, Paris Agreement (2015) FCCC/CP/2015/L.9/Rev1
- Vienna Convention on the Law of Treaties (23 May 1969) 1155 U.N.T.S. 331

WTO Documents

- WTO, Communication from the European Union, China, Canada, India, Norway, New Zealand, Switzerland, Australia, Republic of Korea, Iceland, Singapore and Mexico (26 November 2018) WT/GC/W/752
- WTO, Communication from Cuba. Negotiating Proposal on Energy Services, S/CSS/W/144 (March 2002)
- WTO, 'Communication from Japan to the Council on Trade in Services: Negotiating Proposal on Energy Services' (4 October 2001) S/CSS/W/42/Suppl.3
- WTO, Communication from Chile. The Negotiations on Trade in Services, S/CSS/VV/88 (May 2001).

- WTO, Communication from The European Communities and their Member States on GATS 2000: Energy Services' (23 March 2001), EU S/CSS/W/60
- WTO, Communication from the European Communities and Their Member States. GATS 2000: Energy Services, S/CSS/W/60 (March 2001).
- WTO, Communication from Venezuela. Negotiating Proposal on Energy Services, S/CSS/W/69 (March 2001).
- WTO, Communication from Norway. The Negotiations on Trade in Services, S/CSS/W/59 (March 2001).
- WTO, Communication from the United States. Classification or Energy Services, S/CSC/W/27 (May 2000).
- WTO, Working Party on State Trading Enterprises, New and Full Notification Pursuant to Article XVII:4(a) of the GATT 1994 and Paragraph 1 of the Understanding on the Interpretation of Article XVII – United States (10 April 2017) G/STR/N/16/USA
- WTO, Report of the Working Party on the Accession of Ukraine, WT/ACC/UKR/152 (25 January 2008)
- WTO, Report of the Working Party on the Accession of the Kingdom of Saudi Arabia, WT/ACC/SAU/61 (1 November 2005)
- WTO, Report of the Working Party on the Accession of the Sultanate of Oman, WT/ACC/OMN/26 (28 September 2000)
- WTO, Report of the Working Party on the Accession of Mexico (4 July 1986) GATT Document L/6010
- WTO, Council for Trade in Services, Energy Services – Background Note by the Secretariat (12 January 2010) S/C/W/311
- WTO, Council for Trade in Services, Energy Services – Background Note by the Secretariat (09 September 1998) S/C/W/52
- GATT Doc. MTN.GNS/W/120, Services Sectoral Classification List: Note by the Secretariat (10 July 1991)
- WTO, Understanding on the Interpretation of Article XVII of the General Agreement on Tariffs and Trade 1994
- WTO Secretariat, 'Negotiating Group on Trade Facilitation – Draft consolidated negotiating text' (7 October 2011) TN/TF/W/165/Rev.11

Documents of International Organisations

- ECOWAS Energy Protocol, signed 31 January 2003 (not yet entered into force)
- International Law Commission (ILC), Draft Articles on Responsibility of States for Internationally Wrongful Acts, with commentaries (2001) YBILC 2001/II(2).
- OECD, 'Implementing the Paris Agreement: Remaining Challenges and the Role of the OECD' (OECD 2018) 10 <http://www.oecd.org/mcm-2018/documents/C-MIN-2018-12-EN.pdf>
- Protocol on Energy in the Southern African Development Community (SADC) Region (signed 24 August 1998)

- SAPP Inter-Utility Memorandum of Understanding (7 December 1994)
- United Nations, Sustainable Development Goals, SDG 7 ('Ensure access to affordable, reliable, sustainable and modern energy for all.') <https://sustainabledevelopment.un.org/sdg7>
- United Nations, Report of the Drafting Committee of the Preparatory Committee of the United Nations Conference on Trade and Employment (5 March 1947)
- United Nations, System of National Accounts 2008 (United Nations 2009) available at <https://unstats.un.org/unsd/nationalaccount/docs/SNA2008.pdf>.
- United Nations, Provisional Central Product Classification (1991) ST/ESA/STAT/SER.M/77
- United Nations, Havana Reports, U.N. Doc. ICITO/1/8

EU Legislation

- Treaty on European Union (consolidated version) OJ 2012/C 326/13
- Treaty on the Functioning of the European Union (consolidated version) OJ 2012/C 326/47
- Regulation (EU) No 2019/943 of the European Parliament and of the Council on the Internal Market for Electricity (5 June 2019) OJ 2019/L 158/54
- Regulation (EU) 1316/2013 of the European Parliament and the Council establishing the Connecting Europe Facility, amending Regulation (EU) No 913/2010 and repealing Regulations (EC) No 680/2007 and (EC) No 67/2010 [2013] OJ L 348/129
- Regulation (EU) No 347/2013 of the European Parliament and of the Council of 17 April 2013 on guidelines for trans-European energy infrastructure [2013] OJ L 115/39
- Regulation (EC) No 713/2009 of the European Parliament and of the Council establishing an Agency for the Cooperation of Energy Regulators (13 July 2009) OJ 2009/L 211/1
- Regulation (EC) No 714/2009 of the European Parliament and of the Council on conditions for access to the network for cross-border exchanges in electricity and repealing Regulation (EC) No 1228/2003 (13 July 2009) OJ 2009/L 211/15
- Regulation (EC) No 1228/2003 of the European Parliament and of the Council on conditions for access to the network for cross-border exchanges in electricity (26 June 2003) OJ 2003/L 176/1
- Directive (EU) 2019/944 of the European Parliament and of the Council of 5 June 2019 on common rules for the internal market for electricity and amending Directive 2012/27/EU (5 June 2019) OJ 2019/L 158/125
- Directive 2009/72/EC of the European Parliament and of the Council concerning common rules for the internal market in electricity and repealing Directive 2003/54/EC (13 July 2009) OJ 2009/L 211/55

- Directive 2009/73/EC of the European Parliament and of the Council concerning common rules for the internal market in natural gas and repealing Directive 2003/55/EC (13 July 2009) OJ 2009/L 211/94
- Directive 2003/54/EC of the European Parliament and of the Council concerning common rules for the internal market in electricity and repealing Directive 96/92/EC (26 June 2003) OJ 2003/L 176/37
- Directive 2003/55/EC of the European Parliament and of the Council concerning common rules for the internal market in natural gas and repealing Directive 98/30/EC (26 June 2003) OJ 2003/L 176/57
- Directive 96/92/EC of the European Parliament and of the Council concerning common rules for the internal market in electricity (19 December 1996) OJ 1997/L 27/20
- Directive 98/30/EC of the European Parliament and of the Council concerning common rules for the internal market in natural gas (22 June 1998) OJ 1998/L 204/1
- Commission Regulation (EU) No 2017/2195 establishing a guideline on electricity balancing (23 November 2017)
- Commission Regulation (EU) 2015/1222 establishing a guideline on capacity allocation and congestion management (24 July 2015) OJ 2015/L 197/24
- Commission Regulation (EU) 838/2010 on laying down guidelines relating to the inter-transmission system operator compensation mechanism and a common regulatory approach to transmission charging (23 September 2010) OJ 2010/L 250/5
- Council Directive (EEC) on the transit of electricity through transmission grids [1990] OJ L313/30, 31
- Regulation (EEC) 1191/69 of the Council concerning the obligations inherent in the concept of a public service in transport by rail, road and inland waterway [1969] OJ L156/1

Other EU Documents

- European Commission, Commission Staff Working Paper: Energy infrastructure investment needs and financing requirements, SEC (2011) 755 final
- European Commission, 'Services of General Interest in Europe' (Communication) COM (2000) 580 final
- European Commission, 'Achieving the 10% electricity interconnection target – Making Europe's electricity grid fit for 2020' (Communication) COM (2015) 82 final
- European Commission, 'launching the public consultation process on a new energy market design' (Communication) COM (2015) 340 final
- European Commission, 'Energy Infrastructure: Priorities for 2020 and Beyond – A Blueprint for an Integrated European Energy Network' (Communication), COM (2010) 0677 final

- European Commission, 'Clean Energy for All Europeans: Commission welcomes European Parliament's adoption of new electricity market design proposals' Press Release (26 March 2019)
- European Commission, 'Clean Energy for all Europeans Package Completed: Good for Consumers, Good for Growth and Jobs, and Good for the Planet' Press Release (22 May 2019)
- European Commission, 'The European Green Deal' (Communication) COM (2019) 640
- European Commission, 'Overview of Potentially Trade Restrictive Measures Identified Between 2008 and end 2015', available at <http://trade.ec.europa.eu/doclib/docs/2016/may/tradoc_154568.pdf>.
- European Parliament, Briefing: Understanding Electricity Markets in the EU (November 2016) 7 <http://www.europarl.europa.eu/RegData/etudes/BRIE/2016/593519/EPRS_BRI(2016)593519_EN.pdf>
- European Parliament, Resolution on the Commission's second report to the Council and the European Parliament on the state of liberalisation of the energy markets (adopted 6 July 2000)
- European Council (Rhodes, 2 and 3 December 1988), Presidency Conclusions
- European Council (Barcelona, 15 and 16 March 2002), Presidency Conclusions

National Legislation

- Austrian Civil Code (Allgemeines Bürgerliches Gesetzbuch)
- Electricity Act of Austria (Elektrizitätswirtschafts- und Organisationsgesetz (ElWOG)), BGBl I Nr. 143/1998
- National Energy Board Act of Canada (NEB), R.S.C., 1985, c. N-7 (last amended on 29 March 2019)
- Energy Industry Act of Germany (Energiewirtschaftsgesetz) (1935) RGBl. I S. 1451
- German Securities Trading Act (Wertpapierhandelsgesetz, WpHG) of 9 September 1998, BGBl. I S. 2708
- Irish Sale of Goods and Supply of services Act (1980)
- General Law for Electric Services (Mexico) (Ley General de Servicios Eléctricos) (1982), Ley No.1 de Minería
- Norwegian Energy Act, Act no. 50 of 29 June 1990: Act relating to the generation, conversion, transmission, trading, distribution and use of energy etc
- Electricity Regulation Act, Act 4 of 2006 of the Republic of South Africa
- 1999 Electricity Act of Uganda, available at <https://uegcl.com/about/electricity-act/file.html>
- United States: Federal Power Act, 16 U.S.C. 791, 824
- United States: Uniform Commercial Code of the United States (UCC)

Other Institutional Sources

- ACER, 'Market Monitoring Report 2012' (01 December 2012) 69 <https://www.acer.europa.eu/Official_documents/Acts_of_the_Agency/Publication/ACER%20Market%20Monitoring%20Report%202012.pdf>
- Agora Energiewende, The European Power System in 2030: Flexibility Challenges and Integration Benefits (June 2015)
- Asian Development Bank, Power Interconnection Project to Strengthen Power Trade Between Afghanistan, Turkmenistan, Pakistan (ADB Press Release 28 February 2018) <https://www.adb.org/news/power-interconnection-project-strengthen-power-trade-between-afghanistan-turkmenistan-pakistan>
- Booz & Company, 'Benefits of an Integrated EU Energy Market' (2013) Study prepared for the European Commission 89 <https://ec.europa.eu/energy/sites/ener/files/documents/20130902_energy_integration_benefits.pdf>
- Collin Cain and Jonathan Lesser, 'A Common Sense Guide to Wholesale Electricity Markets' (2007) Bates White Economic Consulting <https://www.bateswhite.com/media/publication/55_media.741.pdf>
- ECOWAS Articles of Agreement of the West African Power Pool Organization and Functions (December 2020) <https://www.ecowapp.org/sites/default/files/eng_wapp_articles_of_agreement.pdf>.
- ECOWAS, 'ECOWAS takes steps towards common Monetary Union' (3 April 2019) <https://www.ecowas.int/ecowas-takes-steps-towards-common-monetary-union/>.
- ECOWAS, Supplementary Act A/SA.2/01/08 creating ERERA (18 January 2008), available at <https://erera.arrec.org/wp-content/uploads/2018/07/Resolution-No-011-ERERA-17_Rules-of-PracticeProcedures_ERERA.pdf>.
- EFTA Surveillance Authority, Reply to the Norwegian Ministry of Petroleum and Energy in Case No 66755 (Foreign Trade License – Section 4-2 of the Norwegian Energy Act) (5 November 2010), copy on file with the author
- Energy Charter Secretariat, 'The Trade Amendment of the Energy Charter Treaty Explained to Decision-Makers of Ratifying Countries' <https://energycharter.org/fileadmin/DocumentsMedia/Thematic/Trade_Amendment_Explanations-EN.pdf> (no date).
- Energy Charter Secretariat, 'Restrictions on export of electricity in the Balkan region – update' (ECT Website News Item, 22 February 2012) available at <https://energycharter.org/media/all-news/>
- ENTSO-E, Annual Work Programme 2019 (January 2019) <https://docstore.entsoe.eu/Documents/Publications/ENTSO-%20general%20publications/AWP_2019.pdf>
- ENTSO-E, Ten-Year Network Development Plan (2018) <https://tyndp.entsoe.eu/tyndp2018/>
- ENTSO-E, 'Statistical Yearbook 2011: Glossary of Statistical Terms', available at <https://eepublicdownloads.entsoe.eu/clean-documents/pre2015/publications/

entsoe/Statistical_Yearbook/SYB_2011/121216_SYB_2011_5_Glossary_of_sta
tistical_terms.pdf>.

- ENTSO-E Objectives <https://www.entsoe.eu/about/inside-entsoe/objectives/
- European Energy Exchange, Market Data <https://www.eex.com/en/market-data#/market-data>
- EUROSTAT, 'Electricity Production, Consumption and Market Overview' (July 2018) <https://ec.europa.eu/eurostat/statistics-explained/index.php/Electricity_production,_consumption_and_market_overview#Electricity_generation>.
- EUROSTAT, Electricity Market Indicators, available at <https://ec.europa.eu/eurostat/statistics-explained/>.
- Government of Canada, 'Canada-United States-Mexico Agreement: Energy Provisions Summary' <https://www.international.gc.ca/trade-commerce/trade-agreements-accords-commerciaux/agr-acc/cusma-aceum/energy-energie.aspx?lang=eng>
- Government of Canada, Letter from the U.S./Letter from Canada on Energy (30 November 2018) <https://www.international.gc.ca/trade-commerce/assets/pdfs/agreements-accords/cusma-aceum/letter-energy.pdf>
- Government of South Africa, *Official Guide to South Africa 2017/18: Energy and Water* (Government Communication and Information System 2018) <https://www.gcis.gov.za/sites/default/files/docs/resourcecentre/pocketguide/09-Energy%20and%20Water-1718.pdf>
- Renewable Energy Policy Network for the 21st Century (REN 21) *SADC Renewable Energy and Energy Efficiency Status Report 2015* (REN 21 Secretariat 2015)
- International Electrotechnical Commission, Whitepaper: Global Energy Interconnection (IEC 2016) 18 <https://www.iec.ch/whitepaper/pdf/iecWP-globalenergyinterconnection.pdf>
- International Energy Agency, SDG7: Data and Projections (November 2019) <https://www.iea.org/reports/sdg7-data-and-projections/access-to-electricity>
- International Energy Agency. IEA, Energy Access Outlook 2017 <https://www.iea.org/energyaccess/database/>
- International Energy Agency, World Energy Investment 2016. IEA 2016.
- International Energy Agency, 'Seamless Power Markets' (2014) 8 <https://www.iea.org>
- Intergovernmental Panel on Climate Change Special Report 'Global Warming of 1.5° C' (2018) available at <https://report.ipcc.ch/sr15/pdf/sr15_spm_final.pdf>
- Inter-American Development Bank, 'Energy Integration in Central America: Full Steam Ahead' (25 June 2013) <https://www.iadb.org/en/news/webstories/2013-06-25/energy-integration-in-central-america,10494.html>
- International Renewable Energy Agency (IRENA), Renewables Readiness Assessment Panama (IRENA 2018)
- KU Leuven, 'Cross-border electricity trading: Towards flow-based market coupling' (KU Leuven EI-Fact-Sheet 2015-02) 1, available at <https://set.kuleuven.be/ei/factsheets>
- Max-Planck-Gesellschaft, Electron on a Scale (26 February 2014) <https://www.mpg.de/7961020/electron-mass>

- Natural Resources Canada, Energy Fact Book 2015-2016 (2015) 5 <https://www.nrcan.gc.ca/sites/www.nrcan.gc.ca/files/energy/files/pdf/EnergyFactBook2015-Eng_Web.pdf>
- OECD, Fossil Fuel Support Country Note Norway (April 2019), available at <http://stats.oecd.org/>
- Statement of the Norwegian Ministry of Petroleum and Energy to the EFTA Surveillance Authority (3 February 2010) on Foreign Trade License – Section 4-2 of the Norwegian Energy Act (copy on file with the author)
- The Climate Group, RE 100 Progress and Insights – Annual Report (November 2018) 9 <http://media.virbcdn.com/files/fd/868ace70d5d2f590-RE100ProgressandInsightsAnnualReportNovember2018.pdf>
- UNCTAD, 'WTO Core Principles and Prohibition: Obligations Relating to Private Practices, National Competition Laws and Implications for a Competition Policy Framework' (United Nations 2003) [6], available at <https://unctad.org/en/Docs/ditcclp20032_en.pdf>.
- UNCTAD, Energy and Environmental Services: Negotiating Objectives and Development Priorities (UN 2003) 52, available at <https://unctad.org/system/files/official-document/ditctncd20033_en.pdf>.
- World Bank, 'Regional Power Sector Integration' (Briefing Note 004/10, June 2010) 31
- U.S. Department of Energy, 'Quadrennial Energy Review: Energy Transmission, Storage and Distribution Infrastructure' (April 2015) 6-3 <https://www.energy.gov/policy/downloads/quadrennial-energy-review-first-installment>
- U.S. Energy Information Administration, 'U.S.-Canada electricity trade increases' (9 July 2015) <http://www.eia.gov/todayinenergy/detail.php?id=21992>
- U.S. Energy Information Administration, 'Mexico Week: U.S. – Mexico electricity trade is small, with tight regional focus' (17 May 2013) <https://www.eia.gov/todayinenergy/detail.cfm?id=11311>
- Western Electricity Coordinating Council, '2016 State of Interconnection' <https://www.wecc.biz/Reliability/2016%20SOTI%20Final.pdf>
- Wissenschaftlicher Beirat der Bundesregierung Global Umweltveränderungen (German Advisory Council on Global Change), World in Transition. Towards Sustainable Energy Systems (2004)
- World Economic Forum, 'These are the world's most traded goods' (23 February 2018) <https://www.weforum.org/agenda/2018/02/the-top-importers-and-exporters-of-the-world-s-18-most-traded-goods>
- Xi Jinping, Remarks at the UN Sustainable Development Summit (26 September 2015), <https://sustainabledevelopment.un.org/content/documents/20548china.pdf>

News Articles

- Kirkland & Ellis, Blogpost: USMCA Energy & Environmental Takeaways <https://www.kirkland.com/publications/blog-post/2020/09/usmca-energy-and-environmental-takeaways>.
- The New York Times, 'Tiny Costa Rica has a Green New Deal, too. It Matters for the Whole Planet' (12 March 2019) <https://www.nytimes.com/2019/03/12/climate/costa-rica-climate-change.html>
- David Meyer, 'How a Mysterious Case of "Missing Energy" Caused Europe's Clocks to Run 6 Minutes Slow' Fortune (8 March 2018) available at <https://fortune.com/2018/03/08/kosovo-serbia-energy-grid-frequency/>.
- Zeke Turner, 'In Central Europe, Germany's Renewable Revolution Causes Friction' The Wall Street Journal (16 February 2017) available at <https://www.wsj.com/articles/in-central-europe-germanys-renewable-revolution-causes-friction-1487241180>.
- Kamila Aliyeva, 'Uzbekistan, Turkmenistan Agreed on Electricity Transit' Azernews (23 May 2017) available at <https://www.azernews.az/region/113666.html>
- Mark Del Franco, 'Meet the Wind Project that Knows no Borders' North American Wind Power (Southbury, CT, February 2016) <https://nawindpower.com>.
- 'Power under the Sea: Could a Power Cable from Iceland solve Britain's Energy Problem?' The Economist (20 January 2014) available at <https://www.economist.com/schumpeter/2014/01/20/power-under-the-sea>.
- Ankit Panda, 'Pakistan Will Import Electricity From India' The Diplomat (22 March 2014) available at <https://thediplomat.com/2014/03/pakistan-will-import-electricity-from-india/>.

References

Abbott F (2014) Transfer of technology and a global clean energy grid. Paper Prepared for the World Trade Forum, World Trade Institute

Abu-Akeel A (1999) Definition of trade in services under the GATS: legal implications. Geo Wash J Int Law Econ 32:189

Adebayo A, Adeniji S (2018) Integrated power market in West Africa: an overview. J Public Policy Admin 2:20

Adhekpukoli E The democratization of electricity in Nigeria. Electricity J 2018, 31:1

Adlung R (2006) Public services and the GATS. J Int Economic Law 9:455

Adlung R, Mamdouh H (2017) Plurilateral trade agreements: an escape route for the WTO? WTO Working Paper ERSD-2017-03

Adlung R, Zhang W (2012) Trade disciplines with a trapdoor: contract manufacturing. WTO Staff Working Paper ERSD-2012-11

Agora Energiewende (2015) The European Power System in 2030: flexibility challenges and integration benefits. https://www.agora-energiewende.de/fileadmin/Projekte/2014/Ein-flexibler-Strommarkt-2030/Agora_European_Flexibility_Challenges_Integration_Benefits_WEB_Rev1.pdf

Albath L (2005) Handel und Investitionen in Strom und Gas: Die internationalen Regeln. C. H. Beck, Munich

Amundsen E, Bergman L, Andersson B (1998) Competition and prices on the emerging nordic electricity market. Stockholm School of Economics Working Paper Series in Economics and Finance, Working Paper No. 217. Stockholm School of Economics

Andoni M (2019) Blockchain technology in the energy sector: a systematic review of challenges and opportunities. Renewable Sustain Energy Rev 100:143

Azaria D (2009) Energy transit under the Energy Charter Treaty and the General Agreement on Tariffs and Trade. J Energy Nat Resour Law 27:559

Azaria D (2015) Treaties on transit of energy via pipelines and countermeasures. Oxford University Press, Oxford

Backhaus K, Gausling P, Hildebrand L (2015) Comparing the incomparable: lessons to be learned from models evaluating the feasibility of Desertec. Energy 82:905

Bacon R, Besant-Jones J (2001) Global electric power reform, privatization, and liberalization of the electric power industry. Ann Rev Energy Environ 26:331

Batlle C, Ocaña C (2013) Electricity regulation: principles and institutions. In: Pérez-Arriaga IJ (ed) Regulation of the power sector. Springer, Berlin

Belyi A (2012) The Energy Charter process and energy security. In: Delvaux B, Hunt M, Talus K (eds) EU energy law and policy issues. Intersentia, Cambridge

Besant-Jones J (2006) Reforming power markets in developing countries: what have we learned? Energy and Mining Sector Board Discussion Paper No. 19. https://documents1.worldbank.org/curated/en/483161468313819882/pdf/380170REPLACEMENT0Energy19.pdf

Bhagwati J (2008) Termites in the trading system: how preferential agreements undermine free trade. Oxford University Press, Oxford

Bhala R (2005) Modern GATT law: a treatise on the general agreement on tariffs and trade. Sweet & Maxwell, London

Bielecki J (2004) Electricity trade: overview of current flows and infrastructure. In: Bielecki J, Desta M (eds) Electricity trade in Europe: review of the economic and regulatory challenges. Kluwer Law International, Alphen aan den Rijn

Bielecki J, Desta M (eds) (2004) Electricity trade in Europe: review of the economic and regulatory challenges. Kluwer Law International, Alphen aan den Rijn

Bielecki J, Ervik L (2003) Environment-related restrictions to electricity trade. J Energy Nat Resour Law 21:413

Bigdeli S, Rechsteiner S (2008) Article VIII GATS. In: Wolfrum R, Stoll P, Feinäugle C (eds) Max Planck Commentaries on World Trade Law, vol 6. Martinus Nijhoff Publishers, Leiden

Blouin C (2000) The WTO agreement on basic telecommunications: a reevaluation. Telecommunications Policy 24:135

Booz & Company (2013) Benefits of an integrated European Energy Market. Final report prepared for the directorate-general energy of the European Commission. https://ec.europa.eu/energy/sites/ener/files/documents/20130902_energy_integration_benefits.pdf

Botchway F (2001) International trade regime and energy trade. Syracuse J Int Law Com 1:1

Bouckert S, Goodson T (2019) The mysterious case of disappearing electricity demand. IEA Commentary, 14 February 2019. https://www.iea.org/newsroom/news/2019/february/the-mysterious-case-of-disappearing-electricity-demand.html

Boulle M (2019) Global experience of unbundling national power utilities. University of Cape Town Research Paper. https://www.gsb.uct.ac.za/files/Global_experiences_of_unbundling_national_utilities_MBoulle.pdf

Boute A (2016) Energy trade and investment law: international limits to EU energy law and policy. In: Roggenkamp M et al (eds) Energy law in Europe - National, EU and International Regulation, 3rd edn. Oxford University Press, Oxford

Bowen BH, Sparrow FT, Yu Z (1999) Modelling electricity trade policy for the twelve nations of the Southern African Power Pool (SAPP). Utilities Policy 8:183

Brown L, Trumble W, Stevenson A (eds) (2002) Shorter Oxford english dictionary volume 1: A-M, 5th edn. Oxford University Press, Oxford

Brown M, Sedano R (2004) Electricity transmission: a primer. National Council on Electricity Policy

Brunekreeft G (2005) Regulatory issues in merchant transmission investment. Utilities Policy 13: 175

Buchmüller C (2013) Strom aus erneuerbaren Energien im WTO-Recht. Nomos, Baden-Baden

Cabrera-Colorado O (2018) Increasing U.S.-Mexico cross-border trade in electricity by NAFTA's renegotiation. Energy Law Journal 39:79

Cain C, Lesser J (2007) A common sense guide to wholesale electricity markets. Bates White Economic Consulting. https://www.bateswhite.com/media/publication/55_media.741.pdf

Campbell R (2019) The power marketing administrations: background and current issues. congressional research service. https://sgp.fas.org/crs/misc/R45548.pdf

Casazza J, Delea F (2010) Understanding electric power systems: an overview of technology, the marketplace and government regulation. Wiley, Hoboken

Castalia Strategic Advisors (2009) International experience with cross-border power trading: Report to the Regional Electricity Regulators' Association (RERA) and the World Bank.

https://documents1.worldbank.org/curated/en/843261468006254751/pdf/703710WP0P11140 Border0Power0Trading.pdf

Chatzivasileiadis S, Ernst D, Andersson G (2013) The global grid. Renewable Energy 57:372

Clark E, Lesourd J, Thiéblemont R (2001) International commodity trading: physical and derivative markets. Wiley, New York

Cohen M (2003) B.C. Hydro's Deep Integration with the U.S. through RTO West. BC Citizens for Public Power. http://www.sfu.ca/~mcohen/publications/Electric/hightens.pdf

Coop G, Seif I (2019) Modernization of the ECT: an institutional perspective. Transnational Dispute Management

Correljé A, De Vries L (2008) Hybrid electricity markets: the problem of explaining different patterns of restructuring. In: Sioshansi FP (ed) Competitive Electricity Markets: Design, Implementation, Performance. Elsevier, Amsterdam

Cossy M (2008) The liberalization of energy services: are PTAs more energetic than the GATS? In: Marchetti JA, Roy M (eds) Opening markets for trade in services: countries and sectors in bilateral and WTO negotiations. Cambridge University Press, Cambridge

Cossy M (2009) The liberalization of energy services: are PTAs more energetic than the GATS? In: Marchetti JA, Roy M (eds) Opening markets for trade in services: countries and sectors in bilateral and WTO negotiations. Cambridge University Press, Cambridge

Cossy M (2012a) Energy services under the General Agreement on trade in services. In: Selivanova Y (ed) Regulation of energy in International Trade Law: WTO, NAFTA and Energy Charter, Kluwer Law International, Alphen aan den Rijn

Cossy M (2012b) Energy Trade and WTO Rules: reflexions on sovereignty over natural resources, export restrictions and freedom of transit. In: Hermann C, Terhechte J (eds) European Yearbook of International Economic Law. Springer, Berlin

Cottier T, Espa I (eds) (2017) International Trade in sustainable electricity: regulatory challenges in international economic law. Cambridge University Press, Cambridge

Cottier T, Malumfashi G, Matteotti-Berkutova S, Nartova O, De Sepibus J, Bigdeli SZ (2011) Energy in WTO law and policy. In: Cottier T, Delimatsis P (eds) The prospects of international trade regulation: from fragmentation to coherence. Cambridge University Press, Cambridge

Crastan V (2009) Elektrische Energieversorgung. Springer, Berlin

Crosby D (2012) Energy discrimination and international rules in hard times: what's new this time around, and what can be done. J World Energy Law Bus 5:325

Das Neves M (2014) Electricity interconnection and trade between Norway and Russia. Arctic Rev Law Politics 5:177

De Hautecloque A, Talus K (2012) Capacity to compete: recent trends in access regimes in electricity and natural gas networks. In: Delvaux B, Hunt M, Talus K (eds) EU energy law and policy issues, vol 3. Intersentia, Cambridge

De Montravel G (2004) European Interconnection: State of the Art 2003. In: Bielecki J, Desta MG (eds) Electricity Trade in Europe: review of the economic and regulatory challenges. Kluwer Law International, Alphen aan den Rijn

Dee P, Findlay C (2008a) Trade in infrastructure services: a conceptual framework. a handbook of International Trade in services. Oxford University Press, Oxford

Dee P, Findlay C (2008b) Trade in infrastructure services: a conceptual framework. a handbook of International Trade in services. Oxford University Press, Oxford

Defilla S (2003) Energy Trade under the ECT and accession to the WTO. J Energy Nat Resour Law 21:428

Del Barrio AD, Komatsuzaki S, Horii H (2017) Regional power sector integration: critical success factors in the Central American electricity market. OIDA J Sustain Dev 7:119

Delimatsis P (2015) Services of general interest and the external dimension of the EU Energy Policy. In: Krajewski M (ed) Services of general interest beyond the single market. Springer, Berlin

Deruytter T (2011) Public service obligations in the electricity and gas markets. In: Delvaux B, Hunt M, Talus K (eds) EU energy law and policy issues, vol 3. Intersentia, Cambridge

Desta M (2003) The GATT/WTO system and International Trade in petroleum: an overview. J Energy Nat Resour Law 21:385

Diebold N (2011) Standards of non-discrimination in International Economic Law. Int Comp Law Q 60:831

Dörr O, Schmalenbach K (2018) Vienna Convention on the Law of Treaties: a commentary, 2nd edn. Springer, Berlin

Drake W, Noam E (1998) Assessing the WTO agreement on basic telecommunications. In: Unfinished business: telecommunications after the Uruguay Round. Institute for International Economics, Münster

Dralle T (2018) Ownership unbundling and related measures in the EU Energy Sector: foundations, the impact of WTO law and investment protection. Springer, Berlin

Dralle T, Frey C (2018) Der WTO-Panel-Bericht zum Dritten Energiebinnenmarktpaket. EnWZ 7: 445

Eberhard A, Shkarathan M (2012) Powering Africa: Meeting the Financing and Reform Challenges. Energy Policy 42:9

Economic Consulting Associates (2010) Regional power sector integration: lessons from global case studies and a literature review. ESMAP Briefing Note 004/10. https://www.eca-uk.com/wp-content/uploads/2016/10/Regional-Power-Sector-Integration-Lessons-report.pdf

Ehring L, Selivanova Y (2011) Energy transit. In: Regulation of Energy in International Trade Law: WTO, NAFTA and Energy Charter. Kluwer Law International, Alphen aan den Rijn, p 60

Elektrizitätswerk Heilbronn (ed) (1991) Moderne Energie für eine neue Zeit: Die Drehstromübertragung Lauffen a. N. ZEAG, Zementwerk Lauffen - Elektrizitätswerk Heilbronn AG

El-Hawary M (2008) Introduction to electrical power systems. Wiley, New York

Energy Charter Secretariat (2001) Trade in energy – WTO rules applying under the Energy Charter Treaty. ECT Secretariat

Energy Charter Secretariat (2003) Regional electricity markets in the ECT area. https://www.energycharter.org/fileadmin/DocumentsMedia/Thematic/Regional_Electricity_Markets_2003_en.pdf

Energy Charter Secretariat (2015) The Role of the ECT in fostering regional electricity market integration: lessons learnt from the EU and implications for Northeast Asia. https://www.energycharter.org/fileadmin/DocumentsMedia/Thematic/Northeast_Asia_Study_EN.pdf

Espa I (2015) Export restrictions on critical minerals and metals. Cambridge University Press, Cambridge

Espa I (2017) The treatment of restrictions and financial charges on imports and exports of electricity under EU and International Law. In: Cottier T, Espa I (eds) International trade in sustainable electricity: regulatory challenges in International Economic Law. Cambridge University Press, Cambridge

Farah P, Cima E (2013) Energy trade and the WTO: implications for renewable energy and the OPEC cartel. J Int Econ Law 16:707

Fasihi M, Bogdanov D, Breyer C (2016) Techno-economic assessment of Power-to-Liquids (PtL) fuels production and global trading based on hybrid PV-wind power plants. Energy Procedia 99: 243

Fatouros A (2008) The Energy Charter Treaty: a possible pattern of international cooperation? In: Hague Academy of International Law (ed) Collected courses of the Hague Academy of International Law, vol 332. Brill, Leiden

Feichtner I (2008) The administration of the vocabulary of International Trade: the adaptation of WTO schedules to changes in the harmonized system. German Law J 9:1481

Ferrero M (2012) The Andean electricity market: a competition law analysis. Wm Mary Environ Law 36:769

Ferrey S (2004) Inverting choice of law in the wired universe: thermodynamics, mass and energy. Wm Mary Law Rev 45:1839

Fickling M, Schott J (2011) NAFTA and climate change. Peterson Institute for International Economics, Washington

Gamberale C (2001) Energy services. In: WTO Secretariat (ed) Guide to the GATS: An overview of issues for further liberalization of trade in services. Kluwer Law International, Alphen aan den Rijn

Gatzen C (2007) The economics of power storage: theory and empirical analysis for Central Europe. Oldenbourg Industrieverlag, Munich

Geraets D (2018) Accession to the World Trade Organization: a legal analysis. Edward Elgar, Cheltenham

Gerbaulet C, Weber A (2014) Is there still a case for merchant interconnectors? Insights from an analysis of welfare and distributional aspects of options for network expansion in the Baltic Sea Region. DIW Discussion Paper 1404.

Glachant J, Ruester S (2014) The EU internal electricity market: done forever? Utilities Policy 31: 221

Gnansounou E, Bayem H, Bednyagin D, Dong J (2007) Strategies for regional integration of electricity supply in West Africa. Energy Policy 35:4142

Gottschal E (2009) The role of an energy agency in regulating an Internal Energy Market: cross-border regulation across the line? In: Roggenkamp M, Hammer U (eds) European Energy Law Report VI. Intersentia, Cambridge

Graf R (1999) Modern dictionary of electronics, 7th edn. Newnes, Oxford

Green R (2005) Electricity and markets. Oxford Rev Econ Policy 21:67

Griller S, Obwexer W, Vranes E (eds) (2017) Mega-regional trade agreements: CETA, TTIP, and TiSA – new orientations for EU external economic relations. Oxford University Press, Oxford

Gudas K (2018) The law and policy of International Trade in electricity. Europa Law Publishing, Zutphen

Gundel J (2004) Regionales Wirtschaftsvölkerrecht in der Entwicklung: Das Beispiel des Energiecharta-Vertrages. Archiv des Völkerrechts 42:157

Hammons T, Falcon J, Meisen P (1994) Remote renewable energy resources made Possible by International Electrical Interconnections – a Priority for all Continents' (1994) Power Generation. Technology. http://www.geni.org/globalenergy/library/geni/PowerGeneration/remote-renewable-energy%2D%2Dinternational-electrical-interconnections%2D%2Da-priority-for-all-continents/index.shtml

Held C, Wiesner C (2015) Energierecht und Energiewirklichkeit. Energie & Management

Hill T (1977) On goods and services. Rev Income Wealth 23:315

Hobér K (2010) Investment arbitration and the Energy Charter Treaty. J Int Dispute Settlement 1: 153

Hogan W (2002) Electricity market restructuring: reforms of reforms. J Regulatory Econ 21:103

Hooper E, Medvedev A (2009) Electrifying integration: electricity production and the South East Europe Regional Energy Market. Utilities Policy 17:24

Huarte Melgar B (2015) The transit of goods in public International Law. Brill, Leiden

Hufbauer G, Schott J (2005) NAFTA revisited: achievements and challenges. Columbia University Press, New York

Hughes T (1983) Networks of power: electrification in Western Society 1880-1930. The Johns Hopkins University Press, Baltimore

Hunt S (2002) Making competition work in electricity. Wiley, New York

International Energy Agency (2020) Electricity market report December 2020. https://www.iea.org/reports/electricity-market-report-december-2020

Ikeonu I (2017) Perspectives on regulating a regional electricity market: the ECOWAS experience. https://erranet.org/wp-content/uploads/2017/09/Winner-2-Ikeonu_ECOWAS_ERRA-Award-2017-4.pdf

International Electrotechnical Commission (2016). Whitepaper: global energy interconnection. https://webstore.iec.ch/publication/26002

International Energy Agency (2005) Lessons from liberalized electricity markets. https://www.iea. org/reports/lessons-from-liberalised-electricity-markets

International Energy Agency (2014) Seamless power markets. https://www.iea.org/reports/ seamless-power-markets

International Energy Agency (2019) SDG7: data and projections https://www.iea.org/reports/sdg7-data-and-projections/access-to-electricity

Irwin D, Weiler J (2008) Measures affecting the cross-border supply of gambling and betting services. World Trade Rev 7:71

Jackson J (1969) World Trade and the Law of GATT. Bobbs-Merrill Co., Indianapolis

Jackson J (1991) The World Trading System: law and policy of International Economic Relations. MIT Press, Massachusetts

Jinping X (2015) Remarks at the UN sustainable development summit on 26 September 2015, https://sustainabledevelopment.un.org/content/documents/20548china.pdf

Joskow P (2008) Lessons learned from electricity market liberalization. The Energy Journal, Special Issue – The Future of Electricity: Papers in Honor of David Newbery 11

Joskow P, Tirole J (2005) Merchant transmission investment. J Indus Econ 53:233

Kaplan S (2009) Electric power transmission: background and policy issues. Congressional Research Service Report for Congress

Karapinar B (2012) Defining the legal boundaries of export restrictions: a case law analysis. J Int Econ Law 15:443

Karova R (2011) Regional electricity markets in Europe: focus on the energy community. Utilities Policy 19:80

Keay M (2013) The EU "Target Model" for electricity markets – fit for purpose? Oxford Energy Comment. https://www.oxfordenergy.org/publications/the-eu-target-model-for-electricity-mar kets-fit-for-purpose

Konoplyanik A, Wälde T (2006) Energy Charter Treaty and its role in International Energy. J Energy Nat Resour Law 24:523

Korinek J, Bartos J (2012) Multilateralising Regionalism: disciplines on export restrictions in regional trade agreements. OECD Trade Policy Papers, No 139. https://www.oecd-ilibrary.org

Krajewski M (2003a) Public service and trade liberalization: mapping the legal framework. J Int Econ Law 6:341

Krajewski M (2003b) National Regulation and Trade liberalization in services: the legal impact of the General Agreement on Trade in Services (GATS) on National Regulatory Autonomy. Kluwer Law International, Alphen aan den Rijn, p 87

Krajewski M (2005) Playing by the rules of the game? Specific commitments after US – gambling and betting and the current GATS negotiations. Legal Issues Econ Integr 32:417

Kunz F (2018) Quo Vadis? (Un)scheduled electricity flows under market splitting and network extension in Central Europe. Energy Policy 116:198

Kustova I (2016) A Treaty a la Carte? Some reflections on the modernization of the energy charter process. J World Energy Law Bus 9:357

L'Abbate A, Migliavacca G, Calisti R, Martínez-Anido CB, Chaouachi A, Fulli G (2014) Electricity exchanges with North Africa at 2030. In: Cambini C, Rubino A (eds) Regional energy initiatives: medreg and the energy community. Routledge, Abingdon

Lagendijk V (2008) Electrifying Europe: the power of Europe in the construction of electricity networks. Amsterdam University Press, Amsterdam

Lajous A (2014) Mexican energy reform. Columbia Center on Global Energy Policy. https://www. energypolicy.columbia.edu/research/reports-and-working-papers/mexican-energy-reform

Lakatos A (2004) Overview of the regulatory environment for trade in electricity. In: Bielecki J, Desta MG (eds) Electricity Trade in Europe: review of the economic and regulatory challenges. Kluwer Law International, Alphen aan den Rijn

Laloux D, Rivier M (2013) Technology and operation of electric power systems. In: Pérez-Arriaga IJ (ed) Regulation of the power sector. Springer, Berlin

Lamy P (2013) The Geneva Consensus – making trade work for all. Cambridge University Press, Cambridge

Leal-Arcas R, Filis A, Abu Gosh E (eds) (2014) International Energy Governance. Edward Elgar, Cheltenham

Liliestam J, Ellenbeck S (2011) Energy security and renewable electricity trade — will desertec make Europe vulnerable to the "Energy Weapon"? Energy Policy 39:3380

Lipsky A, Sidak G (1999) Essential facilities. Stan. L. Rev 51:1187

Liu Z (2015) Global energy interconnection. Elsevier, Amsterdam

Long W, Nilsson S (2007) HVDC transmission: yesterday and today. IEEE Power & Energy Magazine 23

Mann C, Liu X (2008) The information technology agreement: Sui Generis or model stepping stone? In: Baldwin R, Low P (eds) Multilateralizing regionalism: challenges for the global trading system. Cambridge University Press, Cambridge

Mäntysaari P (2015) EU electricity trade law: the legal tools of electricity producers in the Internal Electricity Market. Springer, Berlin

Marceau G (2010) The WTO in the emerging energy governance debate. In: Pauwelyn J (ed) Global challenges at the intersection of trade, energy and the environment. Center for Economic and Policy Research, Washington

Marhold A (2015) Fragmentation and the nexus between the WTO and the ECT in global energy governance – a legal-institutional analysis twenty years later. J World Invest Trade 16:389

Marhold A (2021) Energy in International Trade Law. Cambridge University Press, Cambridge

Marhold A, Weiss F (2019) Energy and fossil fuels as a topic of WTO accession protocols. In: Bungenberg M, Krajewski M, Tams C, Terhechte J, Ziegler A (eds) European Yearbook of International Economic Law. Springer, Berlin

Martin J (2010) Central America electric integration and the SIEPAC project: from a fragmented market toward a new reality? CIGRE Energy Cooperation and Security in the Hemisphere Task Force

Massachusetts Institute of Technology (2011) The future of the electric grid: an interdisciplinary MIT Study

Mathur S, Mann P (2014) GATT/WTO accessions and energy security. In: Mathur S, Mann P (eds) Trade, the WTO and Energy Security. Springer, Berlin

Matsushita M, Schoenbaum TJ, Mavroidis PC, Hahn M (2015) The World Trade Organization: law, practice and policy. Oxford University Press, Oxford

Mattoo A (1998) Dealing with monopolies and state enterprises: WTO rules for goods and services. In: Cottier T, Mavroidis PC (eds) State trading in the twenty-first century. University of Michigan Press, Ann Arbor

Mavroidis P (2012) Trade in goods. Oxford University Press, Oxford

Mavroidis P (2016) The regulation of International Trade (Volume I: GATT). Massachusetts Institute of Technology Press, Massachusetts

McDermott K (2012) Cost of service regulation in the investor-owned electric utility industry. Edison Electric Institute, Washington. https://www.ourenergypolicy.org/wp-content/uploads/2012/09/COSR_history_final.pdf

McRae D (2004) What is the future of WTO dispute settlement? J Intl Econ L 7:3

Meeus L, Purchala K, Belmans R (2005) Development of the Internal electricity market in Europe. Electricity J 18:25

Meyer G, Thomas N (2021) Hydrogen: the future of electricity storage? Financial Times Online. https://www.ft.com/content/c3526a2e-cdc5-444f-940c-0b3376f38069

Meyer T (2017) Explaining energy disputes at the World Trade Organization. Int Environ Agreements Politics Law Econ 17:391

Meza C, Amado N, Sauer I (2017) Transforming the Nicaraguan Energy mix towards 100% renewable. Energy Procedia 138:494

Milthorp P, Christy D (2012) Energy issues in selected WTO accessions. In: Selivanova Y (ed) Regulation of energy in International Trade Law: WTO, NAFTA and Energy Charter, Wolters Kluwer, Alphen aan den Rijn

Mitchell A, Heaton D, Henckels C (2016) Non-discrimination and the role of regulatory purpose in International Trade and Investment Law. Edward Elgar, Cheltenham

Müller L (2001) Handbuch der Elektrizitätswirtschaft: Technische, wirtschaftliche und rechtliche Grundlagen, 2nd edn. Springer, Berlin

Nakagawa J (2016) Free trade agreements and natural resources. In: Matsushita M, Schoenbaum TJ (eds) Emerging issues issues in sustainable development: international trade law and policy relating to natural resources, energy, and the environment. Springer, Berlin

Nedumpura J (2014) Energy security and the WTO agreements. In: Mathur S (ed) Trade, the WTO and energy security: mapping the linkages for India. Springer, Berlin

Nicholls D (2019) Op-Ed: what caused the current ESKOM crisis? ESI Africa. https://www.esi-africa.com/industry-sectors/generation/op-ed-what-caused-the-current-eskom-crisis/

Ochoa C, Dyner I, Franco C (2013) Simulating power integration in latin america to assess challenges, opportunities, and threats. Energy Policy 61:267

OECD (2018) Implementing the Paris agreement: remaining challenges and the role of the OECD. OECD, Paris. http://www.oecd.org/mcm-2018/documents/C-MIN-2018-12-EN.pdf

Ortino F (2006) Treaty interpretation and the WTO appellate body report in US – Gambling: a critique. Journal of International Economic Law 9:117

Padilla V (2016) The electricity industry in Mexico: tension between the state and the market. Problemas del Desarollo – Revista Latinoamericana de Economía 47:33–55

Palmeter D, Mavroidis P (1998) The WTO legal system: sources of law. Am J Int Law 92:398

Passer H (1953) Electrical manufacturers 1875-1900: a study in competition, entrepreneurship, technical change and economic growth. Harvard University Press, Cambridge

Pauwelyn J (2005) Rien Ne Va Plus? Distinguishing domestic regulation from market access in GATT and GATS. World Trade Rev 4:131

Petersmann E (1998) GATT law on state trading enterprises: critical evaluation of Article XVII and proposals for reform. In: Cottier T, Mavroidis PC (eds) State trading in the twenty-first century. University of Michigan Press, Michigan

Pierce R, Trebilcock M, Thomas E (2017) Regional electricity market integration: a comparative perspective. Compet Reg Network Indus 8:215

Pierros P, Nüesch S (2000) Trade in electricity: spot on. Journal of World Trade 34:95

Pineau P, Hira A, Froschauer K (2004) Measuring international electricity integration: a comparative study of the power systems under the Nordic Council, MERCOSUR, and NAFTA. Energy Policy 32:1457

Pineau P (2004) Electricity services in the GATS and the FTAA. Energy Studies Rev 12:258

Pineau P (2008) Electricity sector integration in West Africa. Energy Policy 36:210

Plourde A (1990) Canada's international obligations in energy and the free-trade agreement with the United States. J World Trade 24, 5:35

Pogoretskyy V (2013) Freedom of transit and the principles of effective right and economic cooperation: can systemic interpretation of GATT Article V promote energy security and the development of an international gas market? J Int Econ Law 16:313

Pollitt M, McKenna M (2014) Power pools: how cross-border trade in electricity can help meet development goals. World Bank Blog Post. https://beta-blogs.worldbank.org/trade

Poretti P, Rios-Herran R (2006) A reference paper on energy services: the best way forward? Manch J Int Econ Law 3:2

Prada J, Bowman D (2004) The regional electricity market of Central America. Paper presented at the CIGRE 2004 Session, Paris, France, September 2004

Rakhmanin V (2010) Transportation and transit of energy and multilateral trade rules: WTO and Energy Charter. In: Pauwelyn J (ed) Global challenges at the intersection of trade, energy and the environment. Center for Economic and Policy Research, Washington

Rensmann T (ed) (2017) Mega-regional trade agreements. Springer, Berlin

Rios-Herrán R, Poretti P (2012) Energy trade and investment under the North American Free Trade Agreement. In: Selivanova Y (ed) Regulation of energy in International Trade Law. WTO, NAFTA and Energy Charter, Kluwer Law International, Alphen aan den Rijn

Rivier M, Pérez-Arriaga I, Olmos L (2013) Electricity transmission. In: Pérez-Arriaga I (ed) Regulation of the power sector. Springer, Berlin

Roggenkamp M (1994) Implications of GATT and EEC on networkbound energy trade in Europe. J Energy Nat Resour Law 12:59

Roggenkamp M (1995) Transit of networkbound energy: a new phenomenon? World Competition 19:119

Roggenkamp M, Boisseleau F (2005) The liberalisation of the EU electricity market and the role of power exchanges. In: Roggenkamp M, Boisseleau F (eds) The regulation of power exchanges in Europe. Intersentia, Cambridge

Rudenko Y, Yershevich V (1991) Is it possible and expedient to create a global energy network? Int J Global Energy Iss 3:159

Sakmar S (2008) Bringing energy Trade into the WTO: the historical context, current status, and potential implications for the Middle East Region. Ind Int Comp Law Rev 18:89

Sánchez Miranda M (2015) Market access in international electricity trade: is the light on? Graduate Institute of International and Development Studies Research Paper

Sánchez Miranda M (2018) Liberalization at the speed of light: International Trade in electricity and interconnected networks. J Int Econ Law 21:1

Schuler R (2010) The smart grid. The Bridge 40:43

Schwab A (2015) Elektroenergiesysteme: Erzeugung, Transport, Übertragung und Verteilung elektrischer Energie. Springer Vieweg, Berlin

Selivanova Y (ed) (2012) Regulation of energy in International Trade Law. WTO, NAFTA and Energy Charter, Kluwer Law International, Alphen aan den Rijn

Selivanova Y (2014) The WTO agreements and energy. In: Selivanova (ed) Research handbook on International Energy Law. Edward Elgar, Cheltenham

Selivanova Y (2015) Clean energy and access to infrastructure: implications for the global trade system. E15 Expert group on clean energy technologies and the trade system think piece

Sempértegui L (2017) The legal framework for electricity transmission across boundaries in the Andean Region. J Energy Nat Resour Law 35:433

Singh A, Frei T, Chokani N, Abhari R (2016) Impact of Unplanned Power Flows in Interconnected Transmission Systems – Case Study of the Central Eastern European Region. Energy Policy 91: 287

Sioshansi F, Pfaffenberger W (2006) Why restructure electricity markets? In: Sioshansi, Pfaffenberger (eds) Electricity market reform. Elsevier, Amsterdam

Spalding-Fecher R, Senatla M, Yamba F, Lukwesa B, Himunzowa G, Heaps C, Chapman A, Mahumane G, Tembo B, Nyambe I (2017) Electricity supply and demand scenarios for the Southern African Power Pool. Energy Policy 101:403

Talus K (2011) Just what is the scope of the essential facilities doctrine in the energy sector? Third party access-friendly interpretation in the EU v. contractual freedom in the US'. Common Market Law Rev 48:1571

Talus K, Wüstenberg M (2018) WTO panel report in the EU – energy package dispute and the European Commission proposal to amend the 2009 Gas Market Directive. J Energy Nat Resour Law 73:327

Thema Consulting Group (Report prepared for the European Commission October 2013) 'Loop Flows – Final Advice' available at https://ec.europa.eu/energy/sites/ener/files/docu ments/201310_loop-flows_study.pdf

U.S. Department of Energy (2015) Quadrennial energy review: energy transmission, storage and distribution infrastructure. https://www.energy.gov/sites/prod/files/2015/04/f22/QER-ALL%20 FINAL_0.pdf

U.S. Energy Information Administration (2015) Today in energy: U.S.-Canada electricity trade increases. https://www.eia.gov/todayinenergy/detail.php?id=21992

United Nations (2021a) Sustainable development goals https://www.un.org/sustainabledevelopment/energy/

United Nations (2021b) Sustainable development goals, SDG 7. https://sustainabledevelopment.un.org/sdg7

UNCTAD (2000) Trade agreements, petroleum and energy policies

Van Damme I (2009) Treaty interpretation by the WTO appellate body. Oxford University Press, Oxford

Van Damme I (2010) Treaty interpretation by the WTO appellate body. EJIL 21:605

Verneyre F (2004) Regional electricity cooperation and integration. In: Bielecki J, Desta MG (eds) Electricity Trade in Europe: review of the economic and regulatory challenges. Kluwer Law International, Alphen aan den Rijn

Villiger M (2009) Commentary on the 1969 Vienna Convention on the Law of Treaties. Martinus Nijhoff, Leiden

Vittal V (2010) The impact of renewable resources on the performance and reliability of the electricity grid. The Bridge 40:5–12

Von Danwitz T (2006) Regulation and liberalization of the European electricity market – a German view. Energy Law Journal 27:423

Wälde T (1996) Editors preface. In: Wälde TW (ed) The energy charter treaty: an east-west gateway for investment and trade. Kluwer Law International, Alphen aan den Rijn

Wälde T, Gunst A (2004) International energy trade and access to networks. In: Bielecki J, Desta MG (eds) Electricity trade in Europe: review of the economic and regulatory challenges. Kluwer Law International, Alphen aan den Rijn

Wälde T, Gunst A (2006) International energy trade and access to energy networks. Oil, Gas & Energy Law 36(2):191–218

Weekes J, Pearson D, Smith L, Kim M (2019) NAFTA 2.0: drilling down – the impact of CUSMA/USMCA on Canadian Energy Stakeholders. Energy Regulation Quarterly 7(1)

Willemyns I (2016) Disciplines on state-owned enterprises in International Economic Law: are we moving in the right direction? J Int Econ Law 19:657

Wolfrum R (2011) Article XI GATT. In: Wolfrum R, Stoll P, Hestermeyer H (eds) WTO – trade in goods. Max Planck Commentaries on World Trade Law, vol 5. Martinus Nijhoff Publishers, Leiden

World Bank (2010) Regional power sector integration: lessons from global case studies and a literature review. Energy Sector Management Assistance Program (ESMAP), Briefing Note 004/10. https://openknowledge.worldbank.org/handle/10986/17507

World Energy Council Germany (2018) International aspects of a power-to-X-roadmap. Report prepared by Frontier Economics. https://www.weltenergierat.de/wp-content/uploads/2018/10/20181018_WEC_Germany_PTXroadmap_Full-study-englisch.pdf

WTO Secretariat (2010) World Trade Report 2010. World Trade Organization, Geneva

Yanovich A (2012) WTO rules and the energy sector. In: Selivanova Y (ed) Regulation of energy in International Trade Law: WTO, NAFTA and Energy Charter. Kluwer Law International, Alphen aan den Rijn

Yi-Chong X (2017) Sinews of power: the politics of the state grid corporation of China. Oxford University Press, Oxford

Zacharias D (2008) Article I GATS. In: Max Planck Commentaries on World Trade Law, vol 6. Martinus Nijhoff Publishers, Leiden

Zarrilli S (2004) Multilateral rules and trade in energy goods and services: the case of electricity. In: Bielecki J, Desta MG (eds) Electricity Trade in Europe: review of the economic and regulatory challenges. Kluwer Law International, Alphen aan den Rijn

Zedalis R (2007) When do the activities of private parties trigger WTO rules? J Int Econ Law 10:2

Zhang R (2005) Covered or not covered: that is the question. WTO Working Paper, ERSD-2015-11.

Printed by Printforce, the Netherlands